The Emerging Spatial Mind

THE EMERGING SPATIAL MIND

Edited by
JODIE M. PLUMERT
AND
JOHN P. SPENCER

OXFORD
UNIVERSITY PRESS

2007

OXFORD
UNIVERSITY PRESS

Oxford University Press, Inc., publishes works that further
Oxford University's objective of excellence
in research, scholarship, and education.

Oxford   New York
Auckland   Cape Town   Dar es Salaam   Hong Kong   Karachi
Kuala Lumpur   Madrid   Melbourne   Mexico City   Nairobi
New Delhi   Shanghai   Taipei   Toronto

With offices in
Argentina   Austria   Brazil   Chile   Czech Republic   France   Greece
Guatemala   Hungary   Italy   Japan   Poland   Portugal   Singapore
South Korea   Switzerland   Thailand   Turkey   Ukraine   Vietnam

Published by Oxford University Press, Inc.
198 Madison Avenue, New York, New York 10016

www.oup.com

Oxford is a registered trademark of Oxford University Press

Library of Congress Cataloging-in-Publication Data

Plumert, Jodie M.
The emerging spatial mind / Jodie M. Plumert and John P. Spencer.
p. cm.
Includes bibliographical references and index.
ISBN: 978-0-19-518922-3
1. Space perception.   2. Spatial behavior.   3. Spatial ability.   4. Cognition.
5. Cognitive psychology.   6. Developmental psychology.   I. Spencer, John P.   II. Title.
BF469.P59 2007
153.7'52—dc22   2006029130

1 3 5 7 9 8 6 4 2
Printed in the United States of America
on acid-free paper.

DEDICATION

For Tim, Grace, and Will
J.P.

For Larissa, Alekzandr, and Katya
J.S.

CONTENTS

CONTRIBUTORS

EDWARD AWH
Department of Psychology
University of Oregon

LAURA CARLSON
Department of Psychology
University of Notre Dame

SOONJA CHOI
Department of Linguistics and Oriental Languages
San Diego State University

CLARE DAVIES
Ordnance Survey
Great Britain

SHOHEI HIDAKA
Department of Informatics
Kyoto University

JAMES E. HOFFMAN
Department of Psychology
University of Delaware

ALYCIA M. HUND
Department of Psychology
Illinois State University

JANELLEN HUTTENLOCHER
Department of Psychology
University of Chicago

BARBARA LANDAU
Department of Cognitive Science
Johns Hopkins University

LYNN S. LIBEN
Department of Psychology
Pennsylvania State University

STELLA F. LOURENCO
Department of Psychology
Emory University

JOSITA MAOUENE
Department of Psychological and Brain Sciences
Indiana University

LARAINE MCDONOUGH
Department of Psychology
Brooklyn College and City University of
New York Graduate School

TIMOTHY MCNAMARA
Department of Psychology
Vanderbilt University

TERESA V. MITCHELL
Shriver Center
University of Massachusetts

LAUREN J. MYERS
Department of Psychology
Pennsylvania State University

NORA S. NEWCOMBE
Department of Psychology
Temple University

HERBERT L. PICK, JR.
Institute of Child Development
University of Minnesota

JODIE M. PLUMERT
Department of Psychology
University of Iowa

PAUL C. QUINN
Department of Psychology
University of Delaware

KRISTIN R. RATLIFF
Department of Psychology
Temple University

KARA M. RECKER
Department of Psychology
University of Iowa

JOHN J. RIESER
Department of Psychology and Human Development
Vanderbilt University

GREGOR SCHÖNER
Institut für Neuroinformatik
Ruhr-University, Bochum

ANNE R. SCHUTTE
Department of Psychology
University of Nebraska–Lincoln

VANESSA R. SIMMERING
Department of Psychology
University of Iowa

LINDA B. SMITH
Department of Psychological and Brain Sciences
Indiana University

JOHN P. SPENCER
Department of Psychology
University of Iowa

COURTNEY STEVENS
Department of Psychology
University of Oregon

DAVID H. UTTAL
Department of Psychology
Northwestern University

INTRODUCTION

Jodie M. Plumert & John P. Spencer

Human activity and thought are embedded within and richly structured by the space around us. We reach for coffee cups in space. We remember where our keys are in space. We drive our cars to work in space. We talk to one another about space. We draw maps and diagrams of space. We invent devices to help us find our way in space. We think about spaces we can never visit (inside the atom). We think about spaces that are very hard to get to (the moon). Virtually all overt human behavior is spatially grounded and spatially organized. Thus, it is not hyperbole to say that the human mind is spatial.

This volume examines the development of the spatial mind from its humble origins in infancy to its mature, flexible, and (often) skilled adult form. The diversity of research findings and theoretical perspectives in these chapters reflects the upsurge of interest in the development of spatial cognition over the last decade or so. Numerous journal articles have appeared on topics including infants' ability to form spatial categories (Quinn, Cummins, Kase, Martin, & Weissman, 1996; Casasola, Cohen, & Chiarello, 2003), biases in children's memory for location (Huttenlocher, Hedges, & Duncan 1991; Huttenlocher, Newcombe, & Sandberg, 1994; Newcombe, Huttenlocher, Drummey, & Wiley, 1998; Plumert & Hund, 2001; Spencer & Hund, 2003), early language-specific conceptualizations of spatial relations (McDonough, Choi, & Mandler, 2003), and the neural plasticity of spatial abilities (Passarotti et al., 2003; Landau & Zukowski, 2003). An influential authored book on the development of spatial representation and reasoning has also appeared (Newcombe & Huttenlocher, 2000). Despite the

plethora of high-quality work on the topic of spatial cognitive development, there have been relatively few attempts to bring this state-of-the-art
research together into sharp focus. The last edited volumes on children's
spatial cognitive development appeared in the 1980s (Cohen, 1985; Liben,
Patterson, & Newcombe, 1981; Potegal, 1982; Stiles-Davis & Kritchevsky,
1988; Wellman, 1985). Thus, the time is right to bring together the exciting recent theoretical and empirical work on children's spatial development
into a single, edited volume.

Importantly, however, our goal was not mere aggregation of cutting-
edge research. Rather, the rich literature on the emerging spatial mind that
has accumulated over the last 30 years sets the stage for considering a central developmental question: *How* do these changes occur? The book tackles
this question directly by bringing together the top researchers in the field of
spatial cognitive development to provide an in-depth look at candidate processes of change in spatial understanding. Each chapter presents state-of-
the-art research and theory organized around two questions: (1) What
changes in spatial cognition occur over development? (2) How do these
changes come about? More specifically, the authors both describe the developmental changes uncovered in their research and speculate on the processes or mechanisms that lead to these changes. With respect to this latter
issue, the authors provide conceptual and formal theoretical accounts of
developmental processes at multiple levels of analysis (e.g., genes, neurons,
behaviors, social interactions). This strong focus on developmental process
makes the book of interest not only to researchers interested in spatial development but also to researchers interested in understanding cognitive
change more generally.

The core chapters are organized into three parts: Remembering Where
Things Are (part I), Thinking and Talking about Spatial Relations (part II),
and Mapping the Neuropsychological Bases of Spatial Development (part
III). We selected these three themes because they represent "hot" areas
within the field of spatial cognition, areas within which researchers are
making serious progress on the question of how spatial skills develop. The
four chapters in part I address the issues of how children and adults use
metric and nonmetric spatial information to remember previously seen locations (chapters 1 and 2) and to orient themselves with respect to the environment so they can find objects (chapter 3) and navigate effectively (chapter 4). The chapters in part II address fundamental issues of how infants
and young children form spatial categories both before and after the onset
of language (chapters 6 and 7), how language and thought are intimately
linked to the body acting in space (chapters 8 and 9), and how using symbolic representations such as maps constrain (chapter 10) and are constrained by (chapter 9) the development of spatial cognition. The chapters
in part III focus on how the absence of a sensory system (chapter 12) or
the absence of a set of genes (chapter 13) affects the development of spatial skills and how process modeling of the moment-by-moment dynamics
of spatial cognition provides insights into change over longer time scales

(chapter 14). Across the entire volume, the authors draw from a rich array of theoretical perspectives to understand developmental change. In so doing, they address fundamental developmental questions regarding relations between qualitative and quantitative change, learning over short and long time scales, and the emergence of function through organism–environment interaction. We highlight and expand on these themes in our concluding chapter.

In addition to the core chapters, each part of the book ends with a commentary written by a researcher outside of the field of cognitive development, but whose research on spatial cognition is closely tied to the focus of the section. To make progress in understanding the nature of cognition, advances must be made in understanding both how cognitive processes operate in mature organisms and how those processes come to be in the first place. One way to achieve this is relatively common: developmental scientists include a group of adult participants in their research to assess the "mature" cognitive system simultaneously with the developing one. This is evident in the many core chapters in this volume that include adult participants in research, from studies of spatial language to studies of spatial memory and navigation. Less common is direct dialogue between developmental scientists and researchers who specialize in adult spatial cognition. The three commentaries are a first step toward such dialogue. The commentators certainly rose to the occasion, effectively relating the research reported in the chapters to contemporary issues in the adult spatial cognition literature, including the problems of selecting frames of reference (chapter 5), bridging internal and external representations (chapter 11), and the mechanisms that underlie spatial cognition across diverse populations (chapter 15). These commentaries identify points of convergence between adult and child research and identify places where developmental research can further inform our understanding of the basic cognitive processes underlying spatial cognition.

We are tremendously excited about the chapters in this volume—the scope and depth of the ideas and research reported here illustrate how far the field of spatial cognitive development has come over the last 30 years. The authors have also tackled difficult developmental questions (and have been willing to stretch themselves a bit), making this volume a rich source of contemporary thinking about developmental process. We are indebted to the authors for their willingness to contribute to the volume and for their patience with the ensuing review process. We are also grateful to the graduate students (both current and former) in the spatial cognition group at the University of Iowa who argued convincingly that an edited volume on spatial cognitive development was sorely needed, as well as to our current and former graduate students for providing additional reviews of the chapters. Our goal in soliciting these reviews was to ensure that the chapters would be accessible both to beginning and to advanced researchers. These reviews were uniformly excellent. In addition, we thank Valerie Vorderstrasse for her invaluable help in putting the book manuscript together.

Finally, we thank our spouses (Tim Barrett and Larissa Samuelson) for their encouragement and support during the many (many, many) hours we spent putting together this volume.

We conclude our introductory comments by asking in what sense the spatial mind can be said to "emerge"; that is, why *The Emerging Spatial Mind*? The concept of emergence reflects the emphasis in this volume on developmental process—that spatial cognitive development is profoundly shaped by children's step-by-step experiences in context. Thus, the structure and content of the spatial mind are not prescribed. Rather, they arise in time via the complex interplay of influences at multiple levels from genes to neurons to behaviors to the behaviors of social groups. The elegant research programs described herein highlight both this complexity and the deep sense in which spatial abilities can be said to "emerge."

The title also captures our sense that the field of spatial cognition is beginning to cohere around an emerging view of the spatial mind. This view integrates not only insights from the field of spatial cognitive development but also insights from research on adult spatial cognition, the neural bases of spatial cognition, the evolution of spatial thinking, and many more. We hope our efforts have contributed to this broader, emerging vision.

REFERENCES

Casasola, M., Cohen, L. B, & Chiarello, E. (2003). Six-month-old infants' categorization of containment spatial relations. *Child Development, 74,* 679–693.

Cohen, R. (1985). *The development of spatial cognition.* Hillsdale, NJ: Lawrence Erlbaum Associates, Publishers.

Huttenlocher, J., Hedges, L. V., & Duncan, S. (1991). Categories and particulars: Prototype effects in estimating spatial location. *Psychological Review, 98,* 352–376.

Huttenlocher, J., Newcombe, N., & Sandberg, E. H. (1994). The coding of spatial location in young children. *Cognitive Psychology, 27,* 115–147.

Landau, B., & Zukowski, A. (2003). Objects, motions, and paths: Spatial language in children with Williams syndrome. *Developmental Neuropsychology, 23,* 105–137.

Liben, L., Patterson, A. H., & Newcombe, N. (1981). *Spatial representation and behavior across the life span: Theory and application.* New York: Academic Press.

McDonough, L., Choi, S., & Mandler, J. M. (2003). Understanding spatial relations: Flexible infants, lexical adults. *Cognitive Psychology, 46,* 229–259.

Newcombe, N. S., & Huttenlocher, J. (2000). *Making space: The development of spatial representation and reasoning.* Cambridge, MA: The MIT Press.

Newcombe, N., Huttenlocher, J., Drummey, A. B., & Wiley, J. G. (1998). The development of spatial location coding: Place learning and dead reckoning in the second and third years. *Cognitive Development, 13,* 185–200.

Passarotti, A. M, Paul, B. M, Bussiere, J, R, Buxton, R. B, Wong, E. C, & Stiles, J. (2003). The development of face and location processing: An fMRI study. *Developmental Science, 6,* 100–117.

Plumert, J. M., & Hund, A. M. (2001). The development of memory for location: What role do spatial prototypes play? *Child Development, 72,* 370–384.

Potegal, M. (1982). *Spatial abilities: Development and physiological foundations*. New York: Academic Press.

Quinn, P. C., Cummins, M., Kase, J., Martin, E., & Weissman, S. (1996). Development of categorical representations for above and below spatial relations in 3- to 7-month-old infants. *Developmental Psychology, 32*, 942–950.

Spencer, J. P., & Hund, A. M. (2003). Developmental continuity in the processes that underlie spatial recall. *Cognitive Psychology, 47*, 432–480.

Stiles-Davis, J., Kritchevsky, M., & Bellugi, U. (1988). *Spatial cognition: Brain bases and development*. Hillsdale, NJ: Lawrence Erlbaum Associates.

Wellman, H. M. (1985). *Children's searching: The development of search skill and spatial representation*. Hillsdale, NJ: Lawrence Erlbaum Associates, Publishers.

I

REMEMBERING WHERE THINGS ARE

1

USING SPATIAL CATEGORIES TO REASON ABOUT LOCATION

JANELLEN HUTTENLOCHER & STELLA F. LOURENCO

This volume is concerned with spatial development, an adaptively important aspect of cognitive function. Coding the locations of objects and places (food supplies, one's home base, etc.) and being able to use this information to find important locations are critical for humans and other animals. This chapter addresses an important characteristic of location coding, namely, that it is hierarchically organized. At one level, location is specified in terms of distance and direction from stable landmarks (fine-grained coding). At a more general level, location is specified in terms of a region or area (spatial category). The focus of the present chapter is on the role of spatial categories (consisting of regions) in estimating locations that are only inexactly remembered. We also discuss the emergence of spatial categories and their use in estimating location during childhood.

Spatial categories that consist of regions or areas involve two types of information. One type specifies features that are common to instances that are members (see discussion of categories in Smith & Medin, 1981). For example, if a region has a certain climate, and a particular location is in that region, one can infer that the location exhibits that climate. If the region is a desert, all the locations in it will have little rain, influencing the flora found there, and so on. The second type of information in spatial categories specifies the distribution of particular locations in the region. For example, locations might be uniformly distributed over the region, or most locations might be in the northwest quadrant. Information about the distribution may be derived inductively by accumulating data over instances. When locations are clustered in an area and are less dense in surrounding regions, the accumulated information may be used to form a spatial category with boundaries at the edges of the cluster, a central value, and a dispersion around that central value. The notion that categories can be thought of as statistical distributions has been suggested by various investigators (e.g., Anderson, 1991; Ashby & Lee, 1991; Fried & Holyoak, 1984; Homa, 1984). It should be noted, however, that spatial categories need not be inductively based. For example, categories may involve subdivisions of a space separated at axes of symmetry. Such categories may have a presumed distribution; for instance, people may assume they involve uniform distributions of locations.

This chapter focuses on the use of spatial categories to estimate particular locations. Regardless of whether categories are based on inductive or geometric principles, combining category-level information with an inexact fine-grained value can result in more accurate estimation than the use of fine-grained information alone. Accuracy may be increased by using both levels because information in the category indicates where locations are most likely to be. The process of combining information across levels can be modeled as a Bayesian procedure in which prior information is used to improve the average accuracy of estimation. We begin our discussion of this Bayesian procedure by focusing on fine-grained spatial coding. Then we turn to the development of spatial categories and of the hierarchical combination of information at fine-grained and category levels. We also consider the combination of information that is not hierarchically organized, and its role in improving the accuracy of estimation, as well as the origins of information combination in young children and nonhuman animals.

1.1 SPATIAL CODING

Accurate fine-grained coding of the locations of important objects and places is critical to adaptive behavior. It is essential to encode and store target locations in memory sufficiently accurately that the targets can be retrieved later. The coding of spatial locations must enable us to find objects after movement to new locations, even in cases where we are unable to trace our change in position in relation to the target during movement. This problem requires the use of stable landmarks for coding.

1.1.1 Coding in Relation to Landmarks

Coding location in relation to an adjacent landmark simply involves an association between the target and landmark and is not affected by whether there has been movement to a new position. However, when targets and landmarks are not adjacent, location coding involves establishing distance and direction relative to landmarks. Representation in memory of fine-grained information about distance is often inexact. Various factors may contribute to inexactness. One factor is the extent of the distance between a target and a landmark. Coding by eye becomes less accurate as distance increases, as described by Weber's law. Also, location information becomes less exact when visual interference occurs and when time elapses (Huttenlocher, Hedges, & Duncan, 1991). The fine-grained representation of distance may be unbiased even if it is inexact. That is, across a range of accuracy levels, the mean of retrieved values may lie at the true stimulus value, with a normal distribution of uncertainty around this value.

The accuracy of location coding has been shown to improve with increasing age. This increase in accuracy may be due to either or both of two factors: (1) the categories used by older children are more optimal than those used by younger children, as described below (e.g., Huttenlocher, Newcombe, & Sandberg, 1994); and (2) the precision of fine-grained coding itself may increase with age (see chapters 2 and 14).

1.1.2 Self as Landmark

While various types of objects and places may serve as landmarks, viewers themselves are also salient landmarks. An item may be coded as being a certain distance and direction from the self. If the viewer remains stationary, such coding is sufficient for knowing how to find the object. It should be noted that when an object is coded in relation to an outside landmark, it remains critical to know its relation to the self even after movement since this relation is necessary for obtaining the object from one's current location (see Lourenco & Huttenlocher, in press; see also chapter 4).

As noted above, coding an object directly relative to the self is sufficient for finding that object when the viewer remains stationary. It has been claimed that location coding in early childhood is exclusively "ego-centered", such that children relate targets only directly to the self (Piaget & Inhelder, 1948/1967). For example, Bremner and Bryant (1977) presented infants with two identical cloths on a table; an object was hidden under the cloth on one side (e.g., to the infant's right). Then infants were moved around the array by 180°. They continued to search to the right, even when cues marking the correct choice were available (i.e., when one side of the table was painted black and the other side white). These findings showed that infants had coded the target directly in relation to themselves, not in relation to the outside environment. (Note, though, that other work suggests that infants can use the outside environment in coding location [e.g., Acredolo & Evans, 1980; Presson & Ihrig, 1982].)

The relation of a target to the self also can be coded directly, even when movement occurs, if the changing relation to the target is tracked. For example, as a viewer moves relative to an object, the object may go from being in front, to being at the side, to being behind the viewer. However, if a movement has occurred that either could not be or was not tracked, there are two aspects to establishing one's relation to a target: coding that object in relation to stable features of the environment, and coding one's own relation to those stable features. Then the relation between the object and the self can be inferred (e.g., Lourenco, Huttenlocher, & Vasilyeva, 2005).

In many cases, information about a target location is stored in long-term memory. Such information is more likely to involve an association of a target to a particular landmark than an association of a target to a particular viewer position. For example, a frequent location of one's keys may be on the chest of drawers near the door. However, the viewer probably does not have a habitual location relative to the chest, so obtaining the keys involves knowing the position of the keys relative to the chest as well as one's own position relative to that chest. Of course, in some cases, a person does have a habitual position relative to a landmark in a certain spatial context and that position is directly associated with the target object. For example, in a kitchen, the chef may have a habitual location relative to the stove, and the condiments may be in a specific location relative to that stove. In this context, ego-centered coding will be sufficient, and an inference about the relation of the condiments to the self via the stove will not be necessary.

The ability to code a target relative to the self, mediated by the relation of the target to the environment, is seen both in humans and in nonhuman animals. Consider an example from the animal literature. Cheng (1988, 1989) provided evidence that pigeons who learn to find a hidden target (e.g., grain buried in sand) code two kinds of information: the target's relation to nearby landmarks (i.e., landmark-to-target vectors) and their own relation to the landmarks (i.e., self-to-landmark vectors). By coding both the target's relation to landmarks and their own relation to those landmarks, they can (implicitly) compute the distance and direction they must move to retrieve the target (i.e., self-to-target vectors).

1.1.3 The Relation of the Self to Spatial Regions

Spatial coding may also involve locating a target in a particular region. There has been considerable recent work on young children's coding of the location of a target object in an enclosed space that also includes the viewer. The conditions in this work are such that the relation of the target object to the self is not available (e.g., Hermer & Spelke, 1994, 1996; Huttenlocher & Vasilyeva, 2003). A toddler watches a target being hidden in a corner of an enclosure such as a rectangular room. Then the toddler is turned around several times, with eyes covered, to prevent tracking of the relation to the target. Toddlers were found to code the geometric characteristics of a corner (e.g., the longer wall is to the left and the shorter wall is to the right, or vice versa) where the target is located. The geometry of a rectangular room makes it possible to eliminate two of the corners as potential hiding locations, but not to distinguish between the hiding corner and its geometric equivalent. To make this distinction, further information would be required.

In addition to findings showing that a target is coded in relation to space, there is evidence that the viewer's position in relation to the space also is coded: the task is more difficult when the viewer is positioned outside rather than inside the space during the task (Huttenlocher & Vasilyeva, 2003; Lourenco et al., 2005). This finding is clearly inconsistent with the notion that coding is exclusively "environment centered." Cues that relate a target to the outside world do not depend on the viewer's position (cf. Gallistel, 1990). If the position of the self were not involved, the task would not differ in difficulty depending on whether the viewer is inside or outside.

1.2 HIERARCHICAL ORGANIZATION: SPATIAL CATEGORIES

Here we consider spatial categories that specify regions of a space and their function for accuracy in determining the locations of objects. Spatial categories, like categories in general, have boundaries that separate members from nonmembers and also may be characterized by a "prototypic" location that is usually central to the category. In this chapter we consider the role of categories in estimating the locations of particular objects, and here we consider how category information—boundaries and prototypes—may be combined with inexactly represented fine-grained locations in estimation. Combining such information can increase the average accuracy of estimates, as noted above.

1.2.1 Boundaries

In the "classic view," categories are defined by their boundaries; the boundaries specify the necessary and sufficient (defining) conditions for being a member, and all stimuli that fall within the boundaries are equally good members (see Smith & Medin, 1981). It has become widely recognized that there are difficulties with this view since many categories lack clear-cut boundaries. Yet even when boundaries are inexact, they provide the basis for judging whether or not a stimulus is a category member. In philosophical terms, categories are "projectible" (Quinton, 1957). That is, they permit decisions about membership for new stimuli that were never previously encountered. When boundaries are inexact, category judgments are not certain. That is, while it is possible to make decisions about the category membership of new stimuli in these cases, the decisions will be probabilistic.

Boundaries that specify a region that covers a range of locations may have various origins, and differences in origins may be associated with variation in the exactness of boundaries. For spatial categories that are based on distributions of instances (i.e., inductive categories), determining boundaries involves using a set of instances to establish the extreme values of the distribution. Since the boundaries of such categories involve statistical estimation, they will be imprecise to some degree. For spatial categories that are based on geometric principles, such as subdivisions of a larger region along axes of symmetry, the boundaries may be more precisely defined. For example, geometric categories may have boundaries imposed at vertical and horizontal axes of a geometric figure. In addition, spatial categories may be established by convention, such as countries, states, or cities, where the boundaries are exactly specified by legal agreements.

1.2.2 Central Values (Prototypes)

In some cases, categories are appropriately characterized not by boundaries but rather by a "best" or prototypic value. In these cases, categories may have a graded structure; that is, instances may be judged as better or worse depending on their relation to the prototype (e.g., Posner & Keele, 1968). For geometric categories, defined in terms of region shape, the prototype may be the centroid or balance point of the region. For spatial categories defined in terms of a distribution of locations within a region, the prototype is generally the mean or median (i.e., a statistical center). However, it has been noted that best or prototypic category values are not necessarily the central values or means in the category (Barsalou, 1985). For example, an amusement park is a spatial region or category in which the prototypic location that typifies the park may be at the Ferris wheel, even if the Ferris wheel is near the edge of the park.

1.2.3 Using Categories to Estimate Location

As noted above, spatial categories have extent, and targets may be coded as having locations within them, specified by distance from corners or edges, and so on. It is well known that categories can affect the judgment of stimuli. When stimuli are remembered only inexactly, people tend to make biased judgments, reporting stimuli as more similar to a central value than they really are. We have proposed a model that explains category bias in estimating inexactly remembered stimuli (e.g., Huttenlocher et al., 1991). The idea of this model is that category information is used to construct an estimate that best reflects the true stimulus value. As in Bayesian statistics, prior (category) information is incorporated in forming estimates of stimuli that are inexactly remembered. While this process of integrating hierarchically organized information introduces bias in individual estimates by moving them toward category centers, it improves average accuracy by reducing the variability of the estimates. The inexactness of memory for particular locations determines the extent of the adjustment that will most increase the accuracy of estimates.

The intuitive logic behind the use of categories in estimation is that if one is unsure about the value of a particular stimulus, it is advantageous to use prior information about the distribution of stimuli in the category in making an estimate. The weight that should be given to prior information versus a fine-grained value depends on their relative variability. The less certain the information about a fine-grained value, the more important the category. When there is no information about the fine-grained value, and one is forced to guess, one should opt for the category mean. When the instances in a category are more dispersed, the category is less important. Indeed, when the category instances are maximally variable, the category may not contribute noticeably to accuracy, so it may be just as well to use fine-grained information alone.

The weight that should be given to category information to maximally increase accuracy depends on the relative uncertainty of fine-grained and category information at the time an estimate is made. The logic is that the degree of uncertainty of the fine-grained value at this time point is what determines how best to weight category information to maximize accuracy. If there were no uncertainty at the time of estimation, there would be no gain from category information. In general, the importance of category information is greater when less is known about the location of a particular stimulus at the time of estimation.

Here we describe the processes by which fine-grained and category information can be combined and the effect on the accuracy of location estimates. These processes operate on inexact stimulus representations; they include truncation due to category boundaries and weighting with a central value. These processes have been treated in detail in several articles (e.g., Engebretson & Huttenlocher, 1996; Huttenlocher, Hedges, Corrigan, & Crawford, 2004; Huttenlocher, Hedges, Lourenco, Crawford & Corrigan, in press; Huttenlocher et al., 1991; Huttenlocher, Hedges, & Prohaska, 1988; Huttenlocher, Hedges, & Vevea, 2000) and are discussed below.

1.2.3.1 TRUNCATION   The precision of boundaries is important for the accuracy of estimates. If category boundaries are exact, it is possible to prevent misclassifications of inexactly remembered stimuli near those boundaries by truncating values that lie outside the boundaries. Suppose, for example, that one has encountered a set of stimuli covering a range of locations. In recalling an inexactly represented location that is known to be in a particular region, one may nevertheless retrieve a value that is outside the boundary of that region. That value may be rejected as wrong and another value sampled. The rejection process will result in bias in individual estimates because truncation will eliminate part of the distribution of inexactness. However, if the categorization is correct, average accuracy will be increased by eliminating errors.

With precise boundaries, truncation leads to a distinct pattern of bias. Figure 1.1 shows a location near a boundary, together with information as to what happens to the distribution for that location after truncation (based on values inside the boundary). The estimated location will be farther from the boundary than the true value because of rejection of values recalled as outside that boundary. Bias will be greater for a location nearer the boundary because the portion of the distribution of inexactness that overlaps the boundary, and hence is eliminated, will be larger. The top panel in figure 1 shows a stimulus near the boundary, with overlap and bias in reported values. The bottom panel in figure 1 shows the pattern of bias for different stimulus values in the region of that boundary resulting from truncation. It shows the shape of the curve resulting from rejection of values lying at various locations outside that boundary; bias is greatest near the boundary

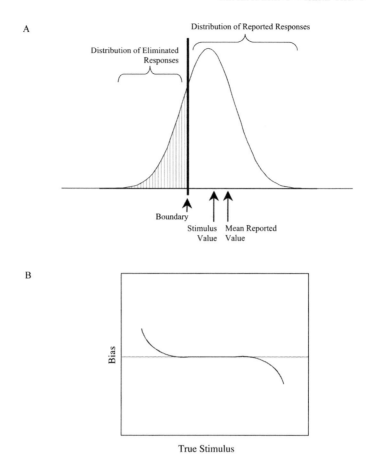

Figure 1.1 How truncation leads to bias in estimation for a particular stimulus value (*top panel*), and the bias it produces (*bottom panel*).

and decreases rapidly with increases in distance from a boundary. Truncation effects at a particular location will be larger when the uncertainty of that location is greater. Truncation can occur when boundaries are somewhat inexact, but the effect will be less marked than with exact boundaries.

1.2.3.2 WEIGHTING WITH A CENTRAL VALUE   Average accuracy also can be increased by combining an inexact fine-grained value with a prototypic central value. That is, if a particular location is remembered only inexactly, weighting it with a central location in the region can improve average accuracy. Weighting an inexact stimulus with a prototype leads to a distinctive pattern of bias. That bias will be linear across the category if stimuli are equally inexact. However, if the representation of stimuli in the category is differentially inexact, the bias will be greater for those stimuli that are represented less exactly.

In a geometric form such as a circle, people tend to divide the overall shape into regions. In particular, there is evidence that they impose vertical and horizontal boundaries, forming quadrants. In a circle, they code particular locations using polar coordinates (i.e., angle and distance from the center of the circle). The evidence comes from Huttenlocher et al. (1991). In this study, people were shown a display with a dot in a circle, and the display was then removed; the distribution of instances presented was uniform across the circle. The participants then reproduced the location of the dot shortly after the original stimulus disappeared. Dots were systematically misplaced toward the central value within each quadrant (i.e., the centroid), as shown in figure 1.2. This pattern of data would be understandable if people imposed vertical and horizontal boundaries on the circle and treated the centroids of the quadrants as prototypes, weighting this category information with an inexact fine-grained value in estimating location.

Inexactness of stimuli affects how category information should be weighted relative to particular values to maximize accuracy. Category information should be weighted more heavily when the fine-grained stimulus value is less exact and also when that category information is more exact (i.e., when the boundaries are more precise or when the dispersion of instances around the prototype is less). The greater the weight of the prototype relative to the inexactness of fine-grained information, the more a stimulus should be moved to the center. Huttenlocher et al. (1991) tested this claim by varying the degree of uncertainty of particular locations. People reproduced the location of a dot either immediately following the removal of the original display or after completing a visual interference task. Responses were more biased toward the center of the categories for the interference condition than for the noninterference condition. That is, with greater uncertainty about location, category information was weighted more heavily relative to memory for specific locations.

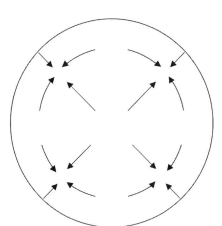

Figure 1.2 The pattern of bias found when people were asked to reproduce the location of dots from memory.

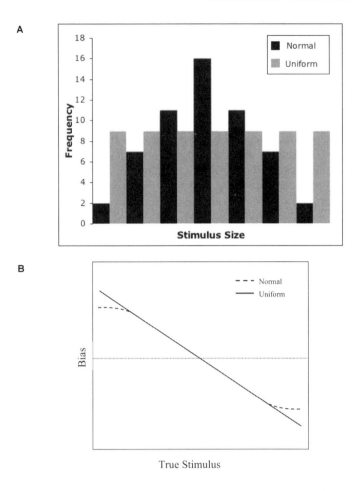

Figure 1.3 (*Top panel*) Uniform versus normal distribution of stimuli. (*Bottom panel*) Mean response bias in the uniform and normal conditions; positive values (*above bias line*) represent overestimation of stimuli, and negative values (*below bias line*) represent underestimation.

Dispersion of instances in the category (prototype uncertainty) also should affect the weighting of category information. While we have used uniform distributions in our research with circular spaces, it would be possible to use uneven distributions. This might affect estimation because, other things being equal, the more concentrated instances are near a category center, the more an inexact value should be adjusted toward that center. Huttenlocher et al. (2000) examined judgments of length and found that when people were presented with stimuli from categories with different distributions, normal versus uniform, bias was affected. The bias curve was steeper in the central region of the category for the normal distribution where the lengths of items were clustered than for the uniform distribution where the lengths were evenly spaced. From the standpoint of rational behavior, this is because the likelihood that the uncertain value is near the center is greater for normal distributions. Further, there was less bias near the edges in the normal than in the uniform condition. Presumably, this is because there are fewer stimuli near the edges for the category in the normal distribution, so the boundaries induced from the observed stimuli will be more uncertain, and not all instances will be classified as members of the category. Adjustment to the category center occurs only for instances that have been classified as members (see, e.g., figure 1.3).

1.2.3.3 TRUNCATION AND PROTOTYPE WEIGHTING TOGETHER Both boundary and prototype effects on a single task were reported by Engebretson and Huttenlocher (1996). They presented people with a display that showed a line in a particular orientation in a frame that was in the shape of either a V or an L. People then were asked to reproduce a line's orientation in a blank frame. They did so either immediately following the removal of the display frame or after an interference task. People tend to impose a boundary in such cases, subdividing a space into equal subregions (vertical boundary for the V frame and diagonal boundary for the L frame). Comparison of lines in the different frames showed that people made fewer category errors with the V than with the L frame. One finding was that people in the interference condition showed more bias toward an angular prototype in the center of each category, indicating that the weighting of categorical information increased as fine-grained certainty decreased (see also Huttenlocher et al., 1991; Spencer & Hund, 2002). For the V frame, the imposed boundary is at the vertical, which is more precise than a diagonal boundary (e.g., Wenderoth, 1994). Another finding was that, with the V frame, but not with the L frame, there was truncation at the axis separating two categories, in addition to weighting with a prototype. Truncation would be expected with a V frame since the axis of separation was at the vertical, which is the most exact boundary.

1.2.3.4 CATEGORY ADJUSTMENT AND DISTANCE JUDGMENT Thus far, we have focused on category effects on estimation of the location of a single stimulus. The model also has implications for bias in the estimation of distances between stimuli. Two inexactly represented stimuli from the same category both will be adjusted toward the center, so the distance between them will be underestimated. When two stimuli are from adjoining categories, they will be adjusted toward the centers of their respective categories, with the nature of the bias depending on the locations of stimuli. That is, if the stimuli lie near the boundary of separation between the categories, the distance will be overestimated because both stimuli are adjusted toward the centers of the categories they are in. However, if the stimuli lie near distal boundaries, adjustment toward the centers of the respective categories will lead to underestimation of the distance between the two stimuli.

Categories also give rise to asymmetries in estimates of the distance between a pair of stimuli depending on the direction in which they are compared. Such asymmetries arise because the extent to which stimuli are adjusted depends on their locations in a category (e.g., McNamara & Diwadkar, 1997; Newcombe, Huttenlocher, Sandberg, Lie, & Johnson, 1999; A. Tversky, 1977). Bias is greater when a stimulus is farther from the center and nearer to the boundary. Consider the estimated distance between two items in a category when one item is near the center and the other is near a boundary. The task involves indicating the location of one item (the target) relative to a fixed item, thus implicitly estimating distance between the two. When the center item is fixed, distance will be underestimated because a target near the boundary will be moved to the center of the category by prototype weighting, and in some cases, by truncation as well. In contrast, when the item near the boundary is fixed at its true location and the one near the center item must be placed, there will not be a corresponding underestimation of distance because there will not be much adjustment for an item near the center. Thus, categories may result in judging the distance between two locations as different depending on the direction of comparison. While such asymmetries of judgments may sound irrational, in the context of our model, they are part of a general mechanism for estimation that *is* irrational, increasing the overall accuracy of estimates.

1.2.4 The Choice of Which Categories to Use

Thus far, we have discussed the use of spatial categories in estimating location without considering why people might use one way of organizing a space into a particular set of categories rather than some other set of categories. Nor have we discussed whether differences in the particular category scheme used may affect accuracy. We have noted that spatial categories can be based on a priori geometric information (e.g., the quadrants of a circle) or induced from a set of exemplars. We have shown that with uniform presentation of instances in a circle, people tend to form geometric categories. However, one could present uneven distributions of instances instead. Then one might expect that people would form inductive categories with boundaries in low-density regions and prototypes in high-density regions. For example, one could make the density of instances greatest at the vertical and horizontal axes of a circle, with few instances at the diagonal axes. Other things being equal, it would be advantageous in this case to form categories with the vertical and horizontal axes as prototypes and the diagonal axes as boundaries. Huttenlocher et al. (2004) attempted to induce categories with prototypes at the vertical and horizontal axes (see figure 1.4). Participants did not alter their geometric categories; rather, responses in all conditions remained biased toward the centers of quadrants defined by vertical and horizontal axes (see figure 1.4, bottom right). In other cases, however, people do alter their categories when the distribution of instances is varied (see, e.g., Spencer & Hund, 2002).

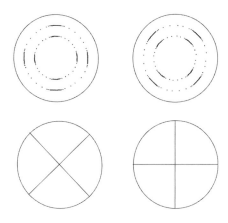

Figure 1.4 The *top row* shows the distribution of dots, and the *bottom row* shows the categories. The *left column* represents the case with clusters at the vertical and horizontal axes. The *right column* represents the case with clusters at diagonal axes.

Let us consider why people in our study might use geometric categories rather than inductive categories centered at the regions of high density. The question might be raised of whether, in these cases, people are using nonoptimal types of estimation. We argue that, actually, the greatest accuracy of estimates may be achieved by the use of geometric categories in which the distribution of stimuli is ignored. The reason is that accuracy of estimates is increased by assigning stimuli to the correct category. Assignment to the wrong category leads to large errors because adjustments will be made in the wrong direction. As noted above, Engebretson and Huttenlocher (1996) showed that people make more errors in category assignment for a boundary at the diagonal axis than for a boundary at the vertical axis. The larger proportion of category errors when boundaries are at the diagonals may outweigh the greater accuracy involved in using density information. Hence, a possible reason why a priori categories would be favored over inductive categories in circular regions with uneven distributions is that they maximize average accuracy because of the greater precision of boundaries. This finding suggests that the potential effects of boundary locations on accuracy of estimation may be incorporated into decisions about what categories to use.

1.2.5 Hierarchical Coding in Animals and Children

It has been shown that rhesus monkeys, like adult humans, use multiple information sources involving hierarchical coding of location (Merchant, Fortes, & Georgopoulos, 2004). With a modified version of the Huttenlocher et al. (1991) paradigm, Merchant and colleagues found that monkeys use fine-grained and categorical information to estimate location, with categorical prototypes being given more weight at longer delays. Recall that Huttenlocher et al. (1991) found that adults divide circles into categories consisting of quadrants, using two dimensions—angle and radius. However, Merchant et al. (2004) found that rhesus monkeys used categorical prototypes involving mostly the radius. That is, if a circle is categorized based

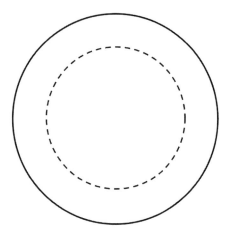

Figure 1.5 An example of radial
categories.

on radial information, the prototypic locations toward which uncertain locations are adjusted would lie on a circular line that divides the circle into
two regions of equal area (see figure 1.5).

Hierarchical coding involving a single dimension also occurs in young
children, as shown in several studies (e.g., Huttenlocher et al., 1994; Sandberg, Huttenlocher, & Newcombe, 1996). The development of hierarchical spatial coding was first investigated by Huttenlocher et al. (1994) using
a task in which children searched for a toy hidden in a long narrow sandbox. At least by 16 months, children were shown to have coded both fine-
grained and category information. Their mean responses for each true location were biased toward the center of the sandbox; the children treated the
sandbox as a single category with boundaries at the perimeter and the prototype at the center. Older children subcategorized the space, dividing the
box into two halves with prototypes at the center of each. Division of a
space along a single dimension into multiple categories was shown to emerge
at different ages for spaces of different sizes. Specifically, 4-year-olds subdivided a small rectangle on a sheet of paper into two categories, but treated
the large sandbox as a single category.

Sandberg et al. (1996) subsequently investigated the estimation of location in the circle task used by Huttenlocher et al. (1991). They showed
that 5- to 7-year-olds, like the rhesus monkey tested by Merchant et al.
(2004), used only one of the dimensions: radial distance. The adult pattern, where both angle and radius were coded hierarchically, was observed
only at 9 years of age.

1.3 NONHIERARCHICAL ORGANIZATION: OTHER CASES
OF INFORMATION COMBINATION

The research we have presented shows how the combination of multiple
sources of information—fine-grained and categorical—increases accuracy

in estimating location. In this and the following section, we show other combinations of multiple information sources that increase accuracy of estimation, even when those sources are not hierarchically organized. For example, as indicated below, the width of an object can be estimated using either visual or haptic (i.e., touch) sources of information, or these two information sources (visual and haptic) can be combined in constructing an estimate of object width. Combining the information from two sources also may increase average accuracy of estimation. In a problem where each source of information is uncertain (i.e., there is variability), combining information from the different sources can reduce variability, leading to greater accuracy of estimation.

It is possible to use multiple location cues that are not hierarchically organized. For example, we have indicated that coding of a target location may be based on the target's position relative to the self or its relation to outside landmarks. It is possible to combine such information sources in estimating location. There is emerging evidence that combining information about an object's relation to outside landmarks and to the self may occur in both children and animals. It also should be noted that with outside landmarks, there is more than one possible source of information; for example, a target could be coded in relation to both proximal and distal landmarks (e.g., Kelly & Spetch, 2001).

If the information from different sources in memory were exact, use of more than one source could not improve accuracy. However, the information in memory is rarely exact. With inexact coding, combining information from different sources can result in a more accurate estimate. In such combinations, more precise information should be weighted more heavily than information that is less precise. There is evidence that humans combine visual and haptic information in a nearly optimal fashion (e.g., Ernst & Banks, 2002; Gepshtein & Banks, 2003). Ernst and Banks (2002) had subjects judge the width of stimuli that were presented visually, haptically, or bimodally. The variance of judgments based on unimodal stimulus information was greater than the variance of judgments based on combined bimodal information (visual and haptic). To best increase accuracy, the weight given to the information that is less variable should be greater than the weight give to the information that is more variable. Vision is often more reliable than haptic information, and in these cases it is weighted more heavily. However, Banks and colleagues found that when visual information is less reliable, people place greater weight on the haptic information. Note that different sources of information may come from the same modality and may be combined to improve accuracy; for example, stereo and texture cues in the visual modality can be combined to increase accuracy (Knill & Saunders, 2003).

There are contexts in which combining different information sources does not necessarily improve the accuracy of estimates. If one or more cues are highly variable, their use may fail to increase accuracy of estimation. Indeed, using multiple cues may constitute an "overfitting" of the available information, in which case the use of multiple information sources may actually reduce accuracy (Gigerenzer, 2000). In this case, it would be best to ignore one of the cues. That is, even when multiple sources are available, it is possible that the optimal strategy could be the "take the best" strategy of using what is most reliable and ignoring other information. Indeed, there are cases where people and animals use only one cue and ignore others.

In the discussion of spatial coding above, we described similarities in location coding across a broad age period as well as across a broad range of species. Let us consider what is known about the similarities across age and species in combining information from multiple sources. Since combining information from different sources can increase the accuracy of estimates, it is of interest to determine whether such a process occurs across age and species.

There are several examples where multiple cues that are not hierarchically related are used by nonhuman animals for estimating location (rats: Whishaw & Tomie, 1997; pigeons: Cheng, 1988; ants: Wehner & Srinivasan, 2003). For example, small mammals combine information about landmarks with information about distance and direction of path (i.e., dead reckoning). Normally, when landmark and path information are not very discrepant, precedence is given to the landmark. However, when landmarks are moved so that landmark and path information are highly discrepant, rats place more weight on the path information, using path information to determine the target's location (Whishaw & Tomie, 1997).

In other cases, animals may use only one information source, ignoring others altogether. As indicated above, cues may be ignored because they are highly variable or biased. This strategy for estimating location has recently been shown experimentally with rats. Shettleworth and Sutton (2005) trained rats to forage in a large arena with their home cage placed at the edge of the arena. The home cage was marked by a prominent beacon that hung over the entrance. In cases when the beacon was shifted by 45° from its usual position, rats continued to rely on the beacon for homing. However, with more substantial shifts of 90°, the beacon was ignored and the rats relied instead on path integration. In neither case did the animals use a combination of cues. Instead, they chose one form of location coding over the other.

Another situation where a single cue is used to the exclusion of other information concerns the disorientation task discussed above, in which children have been shown to code the geometry of an enclosed space (e.g., Hermer & Spelke, 1996). The task was originally developed by Cheng (1986) for use with rats. Cheng showed that, when prevented from keeping track of their movements, rats used the geometry of a rectangular enclosure to locate a target hidden in one of the corners. That is, after disorientation, rats divided their search between the two geometrically appropriate corners (i.e., the correct corner and the corner diagonally opposite to it). When nongeometric landmark information was available to distinguish between the geometrically equivalent corners, rats ignored it, continuing to search solely on the basis of geometry.

While it has been found that young children rely exclusively on geometric information to determine the location of an object hidden in a small enclosure (Hermer & Spelke, 1994, 1996), exclusive use of geometry does not occur in larger spaces (see chapter 3). Although, in a small room, children failed to incorporate information about nongeometric features (i.e., a blue wall), they used both types of information in a larger room (Learmonth, Nadel, & Newcombe, 2002; Learmonth, Newcombe, & Huttenlocher, 2001). These findings suggest that geometric and nongeometric information may be combined in a weighted fashion. Geometry may be privileged because it is more stable across time than is nongeometric information (see Gallistel, 1990). Whether or not nongeometric landmark information is combined with geometry may depend on the ecological validity of nongeometric features; for example, larger features may be more stable and hence more reliable (Cheng & Newcombe, 2005). Further, a variety of mobile animals give more weight to nearer than to farther landmarks in estimation (bees: Cheng, Collett, Pickard, & Wehner, 1987; humans: Spetch, 1995), consistent with Weber's law in which smaller distances would be coded more accurately than larger distances (Cheng, 1992).

1.4 SOURCES OF DEVELOPMENTAL CHANGE IN CATEGORY USE

In this chapter, we have discussed the use of multiple sources of information in estimating particular locations. We have focused on category information, discussing how spatial categories are used in conjunction with inexact fine-grained stimulus values in the estimation of location. Spatial categories in this context can be specified in terms of statistical information concerning the distribution of instances across some region of space. (The distribution can be either inductive, based on a set of instances, or noninductive, based on a presumed distribution of instances.) The notion of adjusting fine-grained values using category information to increase the accuracy of estimation can be likened to Bayesian procedures in statistics. Use of Bayesian procedures involves complex processes. That is, people must form categories that specify boundaries, prototypes, and dispersion of instances around those prototypes. Then they must use these categorical structures in conjunction with fine-grained values to construct stimulus estimates. However, people are unaware of coding different levels of information and combining them to form estimates. They believe that they simply recall stimuli, even though their behavior indicates that they have used Bayesian-like adjustment processes.

There are two different interpretations of why adjustment processes might be automatic and unconscious in adults. The first is that these adjustment processes emerge from earlier explicit reasoning strategies based on statistical principles; processes that combine information across levels may then become automatic because they are used so frequently. However, there is reason to favor an alternative, which holds that the tendency to form categories and combine the category information with fine-grained values constitutes a basic cognitive framework for estimation that is available early in life. The evidence arises in studies that show that, although using categories in estimation involves complex processes, these processes are seen in children as young as 16 months and in nonhuman animals. Given the adaptive importance of accuracy in estimation, it would seem reasonable to suppose that Bayesian-like procedures would have arisen in the course of evolution.

To posit that Bayesian procedures predate experience is quite different from positing innate availability of notions about states of affairs in the world, as in recent claims in the literature. The notion that certain assumptions about the world predate experience and are available from the start of life has been referred to as "core knowledge" (Spelke, Breinlinger, Macomber, & Jacobson, 1992). An example of core knowledge is the notion that objects only remain suspended when supported. Even though the word "knowledge" generally refers to beliefs that are true—that correspond to actual states of affairs in the world—claims such as this one about support might or might not correspond to the world (i.e., they could be either true or false). Clearly, the notion of support is a contingent one that could be either true or false, since one can imagine a world in which objects might remain suspended without support.

Thus, there are important differences between positing Bayesian-like principles, which are not beliefs, as innately available versus positing core knowledge, which concerns content, as innately available. Bayesian procedures are reasoning processes that improve average accuracy and are applicable across domains in cases where instances can be accumulated and used in estimation of inexactly remembered stimuli. Since accuracy of estimation is adaptively important, it is reasonable that such processes might be part of the inherited endowment of both human and nonhuman animals.

Regardless of the origins of estimation procedures, there clearly are important developmental changes in categories and their uses over age. The use of imposed boundaries to subdivide a space emerges only gradually. The experiments we have described show age-related changes in whether and how geometric forms are subdivided. For circles, younger children's categories involve just one dimension (radius), whereas the categories of older children and adults may involve two dimensions (radius and angle). For single-dimensional categories, toddlers do not divide the space, but rather form a single category with a prototype in the center; in contrast, older children subdivide the space into more than one category, with prototypes at the center of each category. These developmental changes would seem to reflect an increasing ability to impose complex categorical structure on a space.

Finally, certain spatial categories can only be formed by creatures that possess the ability to interpret symbols such as maps and spatial language, and the processes used in reasoning about these categories may be complex. For example, constructing spatial categories such as "peninsula" or "island" requires symbolic skills. The ability to subdivide such categories may involve different skills than the subdivision of geometric forms. Generally speaking, such categories will not be symmetric or simple, like circles or rectangles. There is evidence to suggest that irregular shapes based on maps may be schematized in terms of simple geometric figures, and the spatial relations among such categories may be schematized in terms of simple spatial relations such as "above" or "next to" (e.g., Stevens & Coupe, 1978; B. Tversky, 1981). Such schemata can aid accurate judgments of direction among instances but can also lead to bias. For example, in judging the spatial relation between two cities in different states, a simple east–west relation will generally support correct inferences, such as that Las Vegas is east of San Diego. However, the simplification of the category structure will lead to error, such as that Reno also is east of San Diego (Stevens & Coupe, 1978; B. Tversky, 1981). Let us conclude by noting that the study of such categories and reasoning processes, while beyond the scope of this chapter, also are topics that concern the use of spatial categories in reasoning about location.

REFERENCES

Acredolo, L. P., & Evans, D. (1980). Developmental changes in the effects of landmarks on infant spatial behavior. *Developmental Psychology, 16*, 312–318.

Anderson, J. R. (1991). *The adaptive character of thought*. Hillsdale, NJ: Erlbaum.

Ashby, F. G., & Lee, W. L. (1991). Predicting similarity and categorization from identification. *Journal of Experimental Psychology: General, 120*, 150–172.

Barsalou, L. W. (1985). Ideals, central tendency, and frequency of instantiation as determinants of graded structure in categories. *Journal of Experimental Psychology: Learning, Memory, & Cognition, 11*, 629–654.

Bremner, J. G., & Bryant, P. E. (1977). Place versus response as the basis of spatial errors made by young infants. *Journal of Experimental Child Psychology, 23*, 162–171.

Cheng, K. (1986). A purely geometric module in the rat's spatial representation. *Cognition, 23*, 149–178.

Cheng, K. (1988). Some psychophysics of the pigeon's use of landmarks. *Journal of Comparative Physiology. A: Neuroethology, Sensory, Neural, and Behavioral Physiology, 162*, 815–826.

Cheng, K. (1989). The vector sum model of pigeon landmark use. *Journal of Experimental Psychology: Animal Behavior Processes, 15*, 366–375.

Cheng, K. (1992). Three psychophysical principles in the processing of spatial and temporal information. In W. K. Honig & J. G. Fetterman (Eds.), *Cognitive aspects of stimulus control* (pp. 69–88). Hillsdale, NJ: Erlbaum.

Cheng, K., Collett, T. S., Pickard, A., & Wehner, R. (1987). The use of visual landmarks by honeybees: Bees weight landmarks according to their distance from the goal. *Journal of Comparative Physiology. A: Sensory, Neural, and Behavioral Physiology*, *161*, 469–475.

Cheng, K., & Newcombe, N. S. (2005). Is there a geometric module for spatial orientation? Squaring theory and evidence. *Psychonomic Bulletin & Review*, *12*, 1–23.

Engebretson, P. H., & Huttenlocher, J. (1996). Bias in spatial location due to categorization: Comment on Tversky and Schiano. *Journal of Experimental Psychology: General*, *125*, 96–108.

Ernst, M. O., & Banks, M. S. (2002). Humans integrate visual and haptic information in a statistically optimal fashion. *Nature*, *415*, 429–433.

Fried, L. S., & Holyoak, K. J. (1984). Induction of category distributions: A framework for classification learning. *Journal of Experimental Psychology: Learning, Memory, & Cognition*, *10*, 234–257.

Gallistel, C. R. (1990). *The organization of learning*. Cambridge, MA: MIT Press.

Gepshtein, S., & Banks, M. S. (2003). Viewing geometry determines how vision and haptics combine in size perception. *Current Biology*, *13*, 483–488.

Gigerenzer, G. (2000). *Adaptive thinking: Rationality in the real world*. New York: Oxford University Press.

Hermer, L., & Spelke, E. (1994). A geometric process for spatial reorientation in young children. *Nature*, *370*, 57–59.

Hermer, L., & Spelke, E. (1996). Modularity and development: The case of spatial reorientation. *Cognition*, *61*, 195–232.

Homa, D. (1984). On the nature of categories. In G. H. Bower (Ed.), *The psychology of learning and motivation* (Vol. 18, pp. 50–94). San Diego, CA: Academic Press.

Huttenlocher, J., Hedges, L. V., Corrigan, B., & Crawford, L. E. (2004). Spatial categories and the estimation of location. *Cognition*, *93*, 75–97.

Huttenlocher, J., Hedges, L. V., Lourenco, S. F., Crawford, L. E., & Corrigan, B. (in press). Estimating stimuli in contrasting categories: Truncation due to boundaries. *Journal of Experimental Psychology: General*.

Huttenlocher, J., Hedges, L., & Duncan, S. (1991). Categories and particulars: Prototype effects in estimating spatial location. *Psychological Review*, *98*, 352–376.

Huttenlocher, J., Hedges, L. V., & Prohaska, V. (1988). Hierarchical organization in ordered domains: Estimating the dates of events. *Psychological Review*, *95*, 471–484.

Huttenlocher, J., Hedges, L. V., & Vevea, J. L. (2000). Why do categories affect stimulus judgment? *Journal of Experimental Psychology: General*, *129*, 220–241.

Huttenlocher, J., Newcombe, N., & Sandberg, E. H. (1994). The coding of spatial location in young children. *Cognitive Psychology*, *27*, 115–147.

Huttenlocher, J., & Vasilyeva, M. (2003). How toddlers represent enclosed spaces. *Cognitive Science*, *27*, 749–766.

Kelly, D. M., & Spetch, M. L. (2001). Pigeons encode relative geometry. *Journal of Experimental Psychology: Animal Behavior Processes*, *27*, 417–422.

Knill, D. C., & Saunders, J. A. (2003). Do humans optimally integrate stereo and texture information for judgments of surface slant? *Vision Research*, *43*, 2539–2558.

Learmonth, A. E., Nadel, L., & Newcombe, N. S. (2002). Children's use of landmarks: Implications for modularity theory. *Psychological Science*, *13*, 337–341.

Learmonth, A. E., Newcombe, N., & Huttenlocher, J. (2001). Toddlers' use of metric information and landmarks to reorient. *Journal of Experimental Child Psychology*, *80*, 225–244.

Lourenco, S. F., & Huttenlocher, J. (in press). Using geometry to specify location: Implications for human children and nonhuman animals. *Psychological Research*.

Lourenco, S. F., Huttenlocher, J., & Vasilyeva, M. (2005). Toddlers' representations of space: The role of viewer perspective. *Psychological Science*, *16*, 255–259.

McNamara, T. P., & Diwadkar, V. A. (1997). Symmetry and asymmetry of human spatial memory. *Cognitive Psychology*, *34*, 160–190.

Merchant, H., Fortes, A. F., & Georgopoulos, A. P. (2004). Short-term memory effects on the representation of two-dimensional space in the rhesus monkey. *Animal Cognition*, *7*, 133–143.

Newcombe, N., Huttenlocher, J., Sandberg, E., Lie, E., & Johnson, S. (1999). What do misestimations and asymmetries in spatial judgment indicate about spatial representation? *Journal of Experimental Psychology: Learning, Memory, & Cognition*, *23*, 986–996.

Piaget, J., & Inhelder, B. (1967). *The child's conception of space*. New York: Norton. (Originally published 1948).

Posner, M. I., & Keele, S. W. (1968). On the genesis of abstract ideas. *Journal of Experimental Psychology*, *77*, 353–363.

Presson, C. C., & Ihrig, L. H. (1982). Using mother as a spatial landmark: Evidence against egocentric coding in infancy. *Developmental Psychology*, *18*, 699–703.

Quinton, A. (1957). Properties and classes. *Proceedings of the Aristotelian Society*, *48*, 33–58.

Sandberg, E. H., Huttenlocher, J., & Newcombe, N. (1996). The development of hierarchical representation of two-dimensional space. *Child Development*, *67*, 721–739.

Shettleworth, S. J., & Sutton, J. E. (2005). Multiple systems for spatial learning: Dead reckoning and beacon homing in rats. *Journal of Experimental Psychology: Animal Behavior Processes*, *31*, 125–141.

Smith E. E., & Medin, D. L. (1981). *Categories and concepts*. Cambridge, MA: Harvard University Press.

Spelke, E. S., Breinlinger, K., Macomber, J., & Jacobson, K. (1992). Origins of knowledge. *Psychological Review*, *99*, 605–632.

Spencer, J. P., & Hund, A. M. (2002). Prototypes and particulars: Spatial categories are formed using geometric and experience-dependent information. *Journal of Experimental Psychology: General*, *131*, 16–37.

Spetch, M. L. (1995). Overshadowing in landmark learning: Touch-screen studies with pigeons and humans. *Journal of Experimental Psychology: Animal Behavior Processes*, *21*, 166–181.

Stevens, A., & Coupe, P. (1978). Distortions in judged spatial relations. *Cognitive Psychology*, *10*, 422–437.

Tversky, A. (1977). Features of similarity. *Psychological Review*, *84*, 327–352.

Tversky, B. (1981). Distortions in memory for maps. *Cognitive Psychology*, *13*, 407–433.

Wehner, R., & Srinivasan, M. V. (2003). Path integration in insects. In K. J. Jeffery (Ed.), *The neurobiology of spatial behaviour* (pp. 9–30). Oxford: Oxford University Press.

Wenderoth, P. (1994). The salience of vertical symmetry. *Perception*, *23*, 221–236.

Whishaw, I. Q., & Tomie, J. A. (1997). Perseveration on place reversals in spatial swimming pool tasks: Further evidence for place learning in hippocampal rats. *Hippocampus*, *7*, 361–370.

2

ORGANISM–ENVIRONMENT INTERACTION IN SPATIAL DEVELOPMENT
Explaining Categorical Bias in Memory for Location

Jodie M. Plumert, Alycia M. Hund,
& Kara M. Recker

In his book *The Ecological Approach to Visual Perception*, James Gibson introduced the notion of an affordance:

> The affordances of the environment are what it *offers* the animal, what it *provides* or *furnishes*, either for good or for ill. The verb *to afford* is found in the dictionary, but the noun *affordance* is not. I have made it up. I mean by it something that refers to both the environment and the animal in a way that no existing term does. It implies the complementarity of the animal and the environment. (J. J. Gibson, 1979, p. 127)

A critical concept here is the complementarity of the organism and environment. In other words, possibilities for action depend on *both* the characteristics of the organism and the structure of the environment (e.g., water offers a surface of support for a water bug but not for a human). Within the ecological perspective, this concept of the mutuality between the organism and the environment has mainly been applied to understanding perception and action (e.g., Adolph, 2000; E. J. Gibson & Pick, 2000; Lockman, 2000; Plumert, Kearney, & Cremer, 2004; Rieser, Pick, Ashmead, & Garing, 1995; Warren, 1984). Thus, changes in the environment and changes in the organism (or both) lead to changes in possibilities for action. For example, Karen Adolph and her colleagues (Adolph, 1997, 2000; Adolph, Eppler, & Gibson, 1993; Eppler, Adolph, & Weiner, 1996) have shown that toddlers' decisions about whether to descend a slope depend both on walking skill (a characteristic of the organism) and on the steepness of the slope (a property of the environment). Changes in walking skill and changes in the steepness of the slope fundamentally alter the interaction between the perceiver and the environment, leading to changes in possibilities for action. In this chapter, we expand this view of perception/action to the domain of cognition: perceiving, acting, and *thinking* emerge out of the interaction of the characteristics of the organism and the characteristics of the environment. Moreover, we argue that this view of organism–environment interaction provides a particularly good framework for conceptualizing how spatial thinking emerges over time.

The chapter is divided into three sections. First, we outline our general theoretical approach and its implications for understanding spatial development. We then provide examples from our own work to illustrate how bias in memory for location emerges out of the interaction of the structure available in the task and the characteristics of the cognitive system. We conclude with thoughts about why we need the concept of organism–environment interaction to understand change over both short and long time scales.

2.1 THE THEORETICAL FRAMEWORK

What does it mean to say that spatial thinking (or any kind of thinking) is a joint function of the characteristics of the organism and the structure of the environment? Put simply, thinking emerges out of interactions between the organism and the environment that take place in the context of solving problems. Thus, to fully understand any behavior both in the moment and over development, we cannot simply examine the characteristics of the organism or what the environment offers the organism. Rather, we must understand how the two *interact* at any given point in time and how these organism–environment interactions change over time. This view necessarily implies that thinking (like perceiving and acting) is a dynamic process in which changes in the organism or the environment (or both) alter the nature of the interaction, resulting in changes in thinking. From this perspective, cognition is not something that sits in the head of the organism. Rather, thinking is an emergent product of a system that includes both the organism and the environment.

An important consequence of this view is that neither the organism nor the environment has causal priority for explaining behavior either in the moment or over development. Organisms cannot perceive, move, or think independent of environmental structure, and environmental structure has no meaning independent of the characteristics of the organism. In ecological terms, organisms use the available information in the environment to guide thinking, but what is "available" is constrained by the characteristics of the organism. Thus, the functional value of environmental structure is constrained by the cognitive system (e.g., information-processing skills and background knowledge). Likewise, information-processing skills and background knowledge can only function in the context of environmental structure. In a nutshell, thinking can only happen as the organism and the environment work together as a unified system. Like possibilities for action, possibilities for thought (e.g., solutions to problems) are created in the moment based on what the cognitive system and the environment bring to the table. This necessarily means that we need to understand both the characteristics of the cognitive system (an endeavor traditionally left to the field of information processing) and the structure available in the environment (both physical and social) for guiding thinking.

What are the implications of this view for understanding changes in spatial thinking over developmental time scales? From an ecological perspective, the key to understanding developmental change is to specify how experience leads to changes in the organism–environment interaction (E. J. Gibson, 1988; E. J. Gibson & Pick, 2000). Like Piaget's concepts of assimilation and accommodation or Vygotsky's ideas about scaffolding and the zone of proximal development, this view suggests that there is a cyclical quality to organism–environment interaction over both shorter and longer time scales. That is, changes in the organism lead to changes in the information that is available, thereby allowing the organism to experience the environment in a new way. In turn, these new experiences lead to further changes in the organism at both neural and behavioral levels. Thus, interaction with environmental structure is necessary to produce changes in the organism, but the structure that is "available" (i.e., can be experienced) is constrained by the characteristics of the organism. In the past, research from an ecological perspective has focused on how changes in the action capabilities of the organism lead to changes in the amount or type of perceptual information that is "available," and how experiences with using new perceptual information to guide action lead to further changes in the organism (Adolph, 1997; J. J. Gibson & Gibson, 1955). We argue that this developmental framework is also relevant for thinking about how cognitive change occurs. In particular, changes in cognitive skills (e.g., attention, memory, or strategy use) lead to changes in the amount or type of information that is available for solving specific problems. Experience using new information to solve specific problems leads to further changes in cognitive skills. For example, experience using salient environmental structure (e.g., physical barriers that separate locations into regions) to organize searches for objects may lead to improvements in children's spatial clustering strategies. In turn, these improvements in spatial clustering strategies might allow children to exploit more subtle environmental structure (e.g., perceptual boundaries that separate locations into regions) to organize their searches for objects. As this example illustrates, the developmental changes we see in children's spatial thinking come about through recurrent organism–environment interactions that alter how the cognitive system interacts with environmental structure to solve everyday problems.

We now turn to considering empirical examples of organism–environment interaction drawn from our own work on the development of spatial memory. The goal here is to provide examples of how one must simultaneously consider both what the child (or adult) brings to the situation and what the environment provides in order to construct a coherent account of the processes underlying thinking in the moment and changes in thinking over time. Although the ecological approach emphasizes the importance of studying how organisms solve problems in everyday environments, we focus on problem solving in small-scale laboratory tasks designed to capture important aspects of the real world such as perceptually salient boundaries and spatially organized experience. Note that we draw both from concepts about the characteristics of the cognitive system from mainstream information-processing approaches and from ideas about the structure of the environment from a traditional ecological approach. We believe that this admittedly unconventional wedding of the two approaches leads to a much richer picture of spatial thinking and development than does either one alone.

2.2 EMPIRICAL EXAMPLES OF ORGANISM–ENVIRONMENT INTERACTION: CATEGORICAL BIAS IN MEMORY FOR LOCATION

Imagine you are a child who has "borrowed" your sister's toys to play with while she is away visiting a friend. Now, your task is to put those toys back exactly where they were before so that she will never notice that they have been touched. How do you accomplish this? From a traditional information-processing perspective on spatial memory, the accuracy and bias of your placements depend solely on how the cognitive system codes, maintains, and retrieves spatial information. We argue that this perspective reflects only half of the story (i.e., the part about what is in the head of the organism). To provide a complete description of how people reproduce locations, we need to consider how the processes of coding, maintaining, and retrieving spatial information are intimately linked to environmental structure. In the pages that follow, we illustrate the importance of organism–environment interaction for understanding the development of spatial thinking using our program of research on how children and adults reproduce sets of previously learned locations. These studies clearly show that it is impossible to predict bias in placements by referring to age or task structure alone. Rather, variations in how the same age group responds to different task structures and how different age groups respond to the same task structure suggest that biases in location estimation emerge out of the interaction of the cognitive system and environmental structure.

Our basic task involves a learning phase and a test phase. Participants first learn the locations of 20 miniature objects marked by dots on the floor of an open, square box (approximately 3 ft long × 3 ft wide × 12 inches high) placed on the floor of a laboratory room (see figure 2.1). We typically provide structure during learning (e.g., boundaries subdividing the box into quadrants) so that the locations are organized into four groups of five locations. Participants first watch while the experimenter names the objects and places them one at a time on the dots until all 20 objects have been placed. The experimenter then gives the objects to the participants one at a time and asks them to try to place them on the correct dots. The test phase begins after participants reach a learning criterion of placing all the objects correctly in a single trial. During test, participants attempt to place the objects in the correct locations *without* the aid of the dots marking the locations and other structure organizing the locations (e.g., boundaries). It is important to note that participants are given no foreknowledge of the test prior to this point in the session. We record the *x* and *y* coordinates of each object to obtain a precise measure of where participants placed the objects. Our primary measures are mean and variable error (computed based on the absolute distance from the correct locations) and center displacement (the degree to which people place the objects belonging to the same spatial group closer together than they actually are). In this chapter, we focus primarily on the analyses of center displacement. We refer the reader to the published articles for a complete description of all results.

The focus of this work is on understanding how "decisions" about where to place the objects emerge out of the interaction of available task structure and the cognitive processes involved in coding, maintaining, and retrieving spatial information. We are especially interested in the tendency

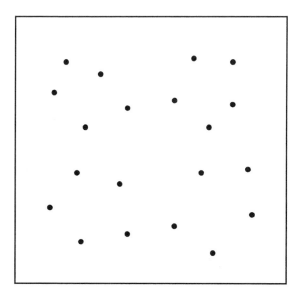

Figure 2.1   Layout of locations on the floor of the box.

to place objects belonging to the same spatial group closer together than they really are (i.e., categorical bias). Systematic bias in placements is thought to be a signature of the underlying processes that govern decisions about placements (Huttenlocher, Hedges, & Duncan, 1991; Spencer & Hund, 2002). As in the Category-Adjustment model proposed by Huttenlocher et al. (1991), we assume that children and adults code both fine-grained, metric information about the precise location of each object and coarse-grained, categorical information about the group or region to which each location belongs. Remembering the precise location of each object is necessary for distinguishing nearby locations from each other. Likewise, remembering the group to which each location belongs is useful for reducing the demands of remembering 20 individual locations. We assume that categorical bias reflects the "push" and "pull" of memory for both the individual locations and the spatial groups. When memory for the spatial groups (i.e., associations among locations in the spatial groups) is strong relative to memory for the individual locations, people place the objects closer together than they really are. Conversely, when memory for the individual locations is strong relative to memory for the spatial groups, people exhibit little or no categorical bias in their placements.

A major question underlying these notions about categorical bias is what governs the strength of memory for fine-grained and categorical information? From a traditional perspective, patterns of bias depend solely on how the cognitive system codes, maintains, and retrieves fine-grained and categorical information. At most, the environment plays a supporting role in providing cues for encoding and retrieving information. From an ecological perspective, however, environmental structure and the cognitive system are inextricably linked as part of a complete system. That is, patterns of bias emerge out of the *interaction* of structure available in the task and the characteristics of the cognitive system. Hence, both differences in the cognitive system and differences in the available perceptual structure can alter the interaction, leading to changes in the pattern of categorical bias. For example, we might expect to see more categorical bias when multiple cues are available to code the spatial groups during learning. Likewise, we might expect to see less categorical bias as people become more certain of the individual locations (e.g., through age-related changes in the precision of fine-grained coding). Experimental manipulations of either environmental structure (e.g., imposing boundaries that divide locations into groups) or the cognitive system (e.g., strengthening fine-grained memory through repeated opportunities for learning) can reveal the nature of these underlying interactions that govern object placements.

Across multiple experiments, our goal was to examine how bias in placements varies in response to manipulations of environmental structure while children and adults are coding and reproducing sets of locations. We have examined how categorical bias emerges out of interactions of task structure and coding processes by providing cues for organizing the locations into groups during learning. In particular, we have examined how children and adults use visible boundaries subdividing the space, experience with visiting nearby locations close together in time, and categorical relatedness between objects occupying the same region to organize the locations into groups, leading to systematic variations in categorical bias at test (Hund & Plumert, 2003, 2005; Hund, Plumert, & Benney, 2002; Plumert & Hund, 2001). Likewise, we have examined how categorical bias varies in response to interactions of task structure and retrieval processes by varying the available perceptual structure at test (Plumert & Hund, 2001). Again, note that our focus is on using experimental manipulations of task structure to understand how interactions between the cognitive system and task structure produce systematic changes in decisions about where to place objects (i.e., categorical bias). This contrasts with a more traditional focus on using experimental manipulations of task structure to understand aspects of the cognitive system itself (e.g., using precues to understand how attention operates).

We have chosen to study 7-, 9-, and 11-year-old children and adults because we hypothesize that important developmental changes are occurring in the cognitive system during late childhood and early adulthood. These developmental changes fundamentally alter the interaction between the cognitive system and the task structure because they lead to differences in the amount and kind of information that is "available" for use. First, we hypothesize that the precision of fine-grained, metric coding is improving between the ages of 7 and 11 years (and possibly between 11 years and adulthood). In virtually every study that we have conducted to date, there is a linear decrease in mean and variable error across these ages (see also Hund & Spencer, 2003; Spencer & Hund, 2003). The hypothesized increase in the precision of fine-grained coding likely depends on recurrent organism–environment interactions that occur as children repeatedly face the problem of localizing objects, thereby leading to increasing sensitivity to distance and direction from landmarks (for related ideas, see Schutte & Spencer, 2002; Schutte, Spencer, & Schöner, 2003; Spencer & Hund, 2002, 2003). Second, we hypothesize that strategic coding of spatial information also may be increasing across this age range. When a cue for forming spatial groups (e.g., visible boundaries) is present during the learning phase, the group to which each object belongs is readily apparent. Adults may incorporate this information into an explicit spatial clustering strategy designed to reduce the demands of remembering all 20 object–location pairings (see also Plumert, 1994). Children notice the groups of locations but may be less likely to use this information strategically. As a result, adults form much stronger associations among the locations within each group than do children. These stronger associations increase the "pull" from the spatial groups, increasing the likelihood of bias in placements. In the next sections, we review specific evidence regarding the ways in which children and adults code and reproduce locations in the context of our location memory task.

2.2.1 Coding Locations: How Do Cues for Forming Spatial Groups Influence Categorical Bias?

We have carried out several studies examining how the availability of cues for forming spatial groups during learning affects categorical bias at test (Hund & Plumert, 2003, 2005; Hund et al., 2002; Plumert & Hund, 2001). We are especially interested in how the structure available for organizing the locations into groups (e.g., visible boundaries, spatiotemporal experience) interacts with characteristics of the cognitive system (i.e., age-related changes in the coding of fine-grained and categorical information) to produce particular patterns of categorical bias. Thus far, we have looked at three types of cues for forming spatial groups: visible boundaries subdividing the space, experience with visiting nearby locations close together in time, and categorical relations between objects occupying the same region. We have also examined how flexibly children and adults can shift between one organization of the locations and another as a function of the structure supporting each organization.

2.2.1.1 VISIBLE BOUNDARIES Visible boundaries that divide locations into groups are perhaps the most obvious source of perceptual structure for forming spatial groups (Allen, 1981; Kosslyn, Pick, & Fariello, 1974; McNamara, 1986; Newcombe & Liben, 1982). Our first study in this program of research examined how boundary salience during learning influenced categorical bias at test (Plumert & Hund, 2001). Seven-, 9-, and 11-year-old children and adults learned the locations of 20 unrelated objects in a random order. In the *walls* condition, interior walls the same height as the exterior walls divided the box into four quadrants. In the *lines* condition, lines on the floor divided the box into four quadrants. In the *no boundaries* condition, no visible boundaries were present. After participants reached the learning criterion, the test phase began. The experimenter removed the dots marking the locations and any boundaries subdividing the space. Participants then attempted to place the objects in the correct locations.

The primary question of interest was whether children and adults in each boundary condition placed the objects belonging to each group closer together than they actually were. As expected, participants exhibited greater categorical bias when boundaries were present during learning than when they were not present. In addition, they exhibited more categorical bias when more salient boundaries were present during learning than when less salient boundaries were present. One-sample *t*-tests comparing center displacement scores to the expected score of 0 revealed that both adults and 11-year-olds in the walls condition and adults in the lines condition placed the objects significantly closer together than they really were (see figure 2.2). In the no boundaries condition, however, children and adults showed very little categorical bias. In fact, 7-, 9-, and 11-year-olds placed the objects significantly farther from the category centers than they really were. Thus,

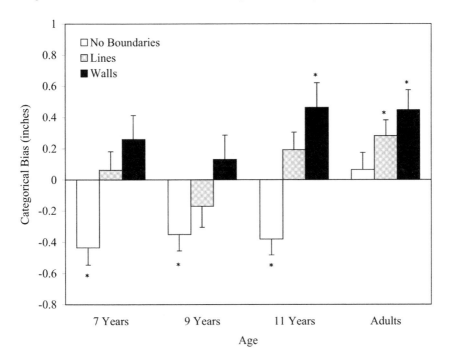

Figure 2.2 Categorical bias exhibited by each age group when boundaries were present or absent during learning. Positive scores reflect bias toward the category centers; negative scores reflect bias away from category centers. *Significant results ($p < .05$) of one-sample t-tests (df = 11) comparing the displacement score to the expected score with no displacement (i.e., 0 inches).

when no cues were available to organize the locations into groups, children and adults had difficulty forming strong associations among the locations within each quadrant of the box.

What do these results tell us about organism–environment interaction? As figure 2.2 shows, all age groups responded to boundary salience. Categorical bias was always highest in the walls condition, intermediate in the lines condition, and lowest in the no boundaries condition. This clearly shows that the salience of perceptual structure during learning affected categorical bias at test. More salient boundaries helped children and adults create stronger associations among the locations in the spatial groups as they were learning the locations. Stronger associations led to greater "pull" from the spatial groups when participants placed the objects at test. Note, however, that the magnitude of categorical bias in the three boundary conditions differed across the four age groups. This indicates that there were developmental differences in how the cognitive system interacted with the structure in the task. Unlike adults, children (with the exception of the 11-year-olds in the walls condition) did not place the objects in the spatial groups significantly closer together than they really were. Subsequent studies have also revealed that children often do not show significant levels of categorical bias when only lines or walls divide the locations into groups (Hund & Plumert, 2002, 2003; Hund et al., 2002). Apparently, boundaries alone often are not sufficiently salient to help children form strong connections among the locations within the spatial groups. Without strong connections, children do not place objects closer together than they really are at test. These differences between children and adults underscore the idea that the extent to which children and adults make use of environmental structure is constrained by the characteristics of the organism. Even though children and adults were provided with the same perceptual structure during learning, adults were more able to make use of the organization than were children. Together, these findings highlight that understanding how the cognitive system and task structure interact is necessary to fully explain behavior.

2.2.1.2 EXPERIENCE WITH VISITING NEARBY LOCATIONS CLOSE TOGETHER IN TIME Another cue that people can use to form spatial groups is spatiotemporal experience (Clayton & Habibi, 1991; Curiel & Radvansky, 1998; McNamara, Halpin, & Hardy, 1992; Sherman & Lim, 1991). Specifically, experience with visiting several locations close together in time may lead people to form associations among those locations. For example, suppose a child and her parent spend Saturday morning shopping at several downtown stores and stop for lunch at a nearby restaurant. This spatiotemporally contiguous experience (and similar experiences on other days) may strengthen the relations among this particular restaurant and set of stores. As a result, the child and parent may think that this restaurant and set of stores are closer together than they really are. In many cases, temporal contiguity may be influenced by visible boundaries: physical barriers or perceptual boundaries may guide locomotion (or decisions about locomotion) such that people usually visit sites on one side of a boundary before visiting sites on the opposite side. These examples again illustrate the cyclical quality of organism–environment interactions over time. That is, structure in the environment constrains how people experience the environment. In turn, these experiences shape how the cognitive system organizes knowledge of the environment (see Mou & McNamara, 2002, for a discussion of "conceptual north"). Once in place, such knowledge constrains how people experience (i.e., interact with) the environment.

In the study described below, we examined how children and adults use spatiotemporal experience and visible boundaries to remember locations (Hund et al., 2002). Seven-, 9-, 11-year-old children and adults learned 20 locations with lines subdividing the box into four quadrants. In the *random learning* condition, participants learned the locations in a random order (i.e., our standard learning procedure). In the *contiguous learning* condition, participants experienced the locations belonging to each quadrant together in time during learning. Participants first watched while the experimenter placed all five objects in one quadrant, then placed five objects in another quadrant, and so on. During the subsequent learning trials, the experimenter handed participants the objects from one quadrant before moving on to another quadrant. Thus, participants placed the objects quadrant by quadrant during the learning phase of the experiment. The order of quadrants and the order of locations within quadrants were randomized for each learning trial. For both conditions, the experimenter removed the dots marking the locations and the boundaries subdividing the box prior to test.

The primary question of interest was whether children and adults in each learning condition placed the objects belonging to each group closer together than they actually were. As shown in figure 2.3, adults placed objects belonging to the same spatial group significantly closer together than they really were in both the random and contiguous learning conditions. In contrast, none of the child age groups placed the objects significantly closer together than they actually were following random experience with the locations during learning. In the contiguous learning condition, however, 9- and 11-year-olds placed objects belonging to the same spatial group significantly closer together than they really were. Seven-year-olds showed a very similar pattern, but their center displacement scores in the contiguous learning condition did not differ significantly from 0 due to high variability in their placements.

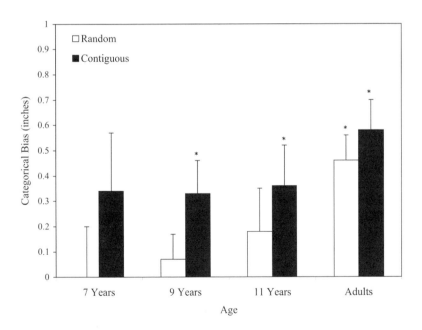

Figure 2.3 Categorical bias exhibited by each age group in the random and contiguous learning conditions. Positive scores reflect bias toward the category centers. *Significant results ($p < .05$) of one-sample t-tests (df $= 11$) comparing the displacement score to the expected score with no displacement (i.e., 0 inches).

The finding that adults exhibited categorical bias in both learning conditions whereas children only exhibited categorical bias in the contiguous learning condition again supports the idea that categorical bias emerges out of the interaction of task structure (e.g., spatiotemporal experience and visible boundaries) and the cognitive system. Adults easily formed strong associations among the locations within each group even when only a single cue (visible boundaries) organized the locations into groups. In contrast, children formed strong associations among the locations within each group only when two cues (visible boundaries and spatiotemporal contiguity) organized the locations into groups. Thus, age differences in the coding of fine-grained and categorical information interacted with the structure provided in the task to produce different patterns of categorical bias.

2.2.1.3 CATEGORICAL RELATIONS AMONG OBJECTS OCCUPYING NEARBY LOCATIONS Another type of environmental structure that people might use to form spatial groups is categorical relations among objects occupying nearby locations. In everyday environments, thematically or categorically related objects often are found together. For example, fruits, vegetables, dairy products, and meats are typically located in different areas of the grocery store. Quite likely, this kind of structure helps people organize locations into groups. In the experiments described below, we asked whether children and adults use categorical relations among objects to organize locations into groups (Hund & Plumert, 2003). Our goal was to examine how manipulations of environmental structure (i.e., categorical relations among objects occupying nearby locations) interact with age differences in the coding of fine-grained and categorical information to produce differences in patterns of categorical bias.

In Experiment 1, children and adults learned the locations of 20 objects belonging to four categories: animals, vehicles, food, and clothing. In the *related* condition, objects belonging to the same object category were located in the same quadrant of the box. In the *unrelated* condition, the same objects and locations were used, but they were randomly paired. In both conditions, the experimenter gave the objects to participants in a random order on each learning trial. After participants reached the learning criterion, they attempted to place the objects in the correct locations without the aid of the dots marking the locations. Of particular interest was whether participants in the related condition would place the objects belonging to the same group closer together than would participants in the unrelated condition, suggesting that children and adults use information about objects to organize memory for locations.

Overall, participants in the related condition placed the objects significantly closer to the centers of the spatial groups than did participants in the unrelated condition. As shown in figure 2.4, however, categorical bias in the related condition followed a U-shaped developmental pattern. Seven- and 9-year-olds and adults in the related condition placed the objects belonging to the same spatial group significantly closer together than they

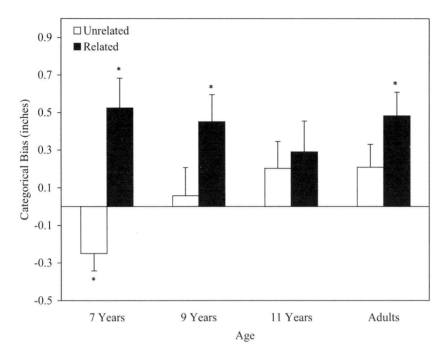

Figure 2.4 Categorical bias exhibited by each age group when categorically related or unrelated objects occupied the four quadrants of the box. Positive scores reflect bias toward the category centers; negative scores reflect bias away from category centers. *Significant results ($p < .05$) of one-sample *t*-tests (df = 11) comparing the displacement score to the expected score with no displacement (i.e., 0 inches).

actually were. In contrast, 11-year-olds in the related condition did not place the objects significantly closer together than they actually were. In the unrelated condition, both children and adults showed very little categorical bias. In fact, 7-year-olds placed the objects significantly *farther* from the category centers than they actually were and showed bias toward the corners of the box. Again, this shows that children and adults have trouble forming strong spatial groups in our task when no obvious cues are available to organize the locations into groups.

Why did the 11-year-olds in the related condition show only minimal categorical bias? One possibility is that their strong memory for the individual locations effectively counteracted the "pull" from their memory for the spatial groups. To test this possibility, we conducted a second experiment in which two categorical cues were present (i.e., object relatedness and visible boundaries), thereby increasing the strength of the spatial groups. All aspects of Experiment 2 were the same as in Experiment 1 except that visible boundaries divided the box into four quadrants during learning. We expected that 11-year-olds in the related condition would place objects belonging to the same group closer together than would their counterparts in the unrelated condition, suggesting that coincident cues (i.e., visible boundaries and object relatedness) lead to stronger associations among the locations in the spatial groups.

As shown in figure 2.5, the pattern of categorical bias in the unrelated condition followed a U-shaped pattern. Thus, when unrelated groups of objects were separated by boundaries, the magnitude of categorical bias followed a U-shaped developmental pattern similar to that seen when related objects were not separated by visible boundaries. In contrast, the pattern of categorical bias in the related condition no longer followed a U-shaped pattern. Instead, all age groups placed the objects belonging to the same spatial groups significantly closer together than they really were. The finding that providing two coincident cues for coding the spatial groups (i.e., visible boundaries and object relatedness) erased the U-shaped pattern in categorical bias supports the claim that boosting the associations among the locations in the spatial groups changed the dynamics of the interaction. That is, strengthening the associations increased the "pull" of memory for spatial groups relative to memory for the individual locations, leading to increased categorical bias in 11-year-olds' placements.

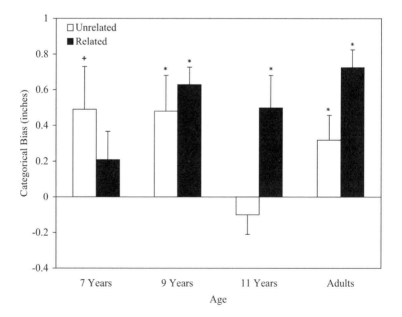

Figure 2.5 Categorical bias exhibited by each age group when categorically related or unrelated objects were divided by boundaries. Positive scores reflect bias toward the category centers; negative scores reflect bias away from category centers. *Significant results ($p < .05$) of one-sample t-tests (df $= 11$) comparing the displacement score to the expected score with no displacement (i.e., 0 inches).

The U-shaped developmental patterns of categorical bias seen in these experiments provide particularly compelling examples of organism–environment interaction because they illustrate how differences in the cognitive system and differences in the task structure alter the interaction between the cognitive system and the task structure, leading to changes in the pattern of categorical bias. On the side of the cognitive system, there are age-related changes both in the coding of fine-grained, metric information and in the coding of coarse-grained, categorical information. In all of our studies, adults exhibit significantly less mean and variable error than do the younger children. By 11 years of age, coding of fine-grained, metric information is nearly as good as that of adults. In contrast, strategic coding of the spatial groups appears to be undergoing change between 11 years of age and adulthood. Unlike children, adults form very strong associations among the locations in the spatial groups because they rely heavily on spatial clustering strategies to learn the locations. We hypothesize that adults exhibit strong categorical bias in their placements because their memory for the individual locations (though very good) cannot counteract the strong "pull" of the spatial groups. Eleven-year-olds often do not exhibit categorical bias in their placements because their strong memory for the individual locations effectively counteracts the weaker "pull" of the spatial groups. In contrast, 7- and 9-year-olds exhibit categorical bias in their placements because their relatively weak memory for the individual locations cannot counteract the "pull" from the spatial groups. Thus, the younger age groups exhibit categorical bias because their coding of the individual locations is relatively weak, whereas the adults exhibit categorical bias because their coding of the spatial groups is relatively strong. Together, these findings illustrate how characteristics of the cognitive system (e.g., age-related differences in the coding of fine-grained and categorical information) and structure available in the task (e.g., types of cues available for coding the spatial groups) jointly determine patterns of categorical bias.

2.2.1.4 STABILITY AND FLEXIBILITY IN ORGANIZING LOCATIONS INTO GROUPS　Our interest in understanding how categorical bias emerges from organism–environment interactions has led us to examine the stability and flexibility with which children and adults organize locations into groups. By its very nature, flexibility implies an interaction between the characteristics of the cognitive system and structure available in the environment. For example, the ability to shift between two organizations of the same set of locations means that both the environmental structure specifying the different organizations and the cognitive processes necessary for picking up those organizations must be in place. Variations in either environmental structure or cognitive processes (or both) will alter the flexibility with which children and adults can shift between alternative organizations of the same set of locations.

　　We investigated how environmental structure and the cognitive system interact to produce flexibility in organizing locations in a series of four experiments (Hund & Plumert, 2005). We will focus on the third and fourth experiments here. The basic design involved giving children and adults spatiotemporal experience specifying one organization of the locations at one point in time and then giving them spatiotemporal experience specifying another organization of the same locations at a later point in time. Of particular interest was how the perceptual structure in the task and the spatiotemporal experience with the locations interacted to produce different patterns of flexibility at different ages.

As in previous studies, the box contained 20 locations marked by dots. These locations were arranged so that they could be organized in two specific ways—each forming four groups of five locations. In one case, groups were located along each side of the box (i.e., the *side-defined* groups; see figure 2.6A), and in the other case, groups were located in each quadrant of the box (i.e., the *quadrant-defined* groups; see figure 2.6B). Displacement directions of eight target locations differentiated between the two patterns of organization. As shown in figure 2.6, the target locations were included in different groups depending on whether the side-defined or quadrant-defined groups were highlighted during learning. We used the eight target locations to calculate two displacement scores: a side displacement score and a quadrant displacement score. The side displacement score reflected the degree to which participants systematically placed the eight target objects closer to the corners corresponding to the side-defined groups than they actually were.

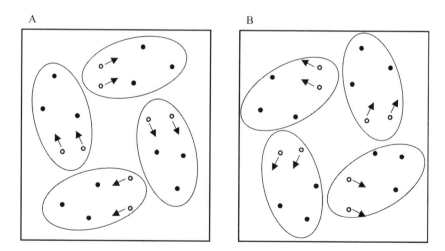

Figure 2.6 Diagram of the experimental apparatus and locations. Circles mark the 20 locations, and open circles mark the eight target locations. Ovals show the two different ways the 20 locations were experienced during learning in the side-defined and quadrant-defined conditions. Arrows show the predicted pattern of displacement for the target locations in each condition at test. (*A*) Locations experienced together in the side-defined condition. (*B*) Locations experienced together in the quadrant-defined condition. The arrows and ovals are for illustration only.

Conversely, the quadrant displacement score reflected the degree to which participants systematically placed the eight target objects closer to the corners corresponding to the quadrant-defined group than they actually were.

The experimental design included two testing sessions separated by approximately 5 days. During the first session, 7-, 9-, and 11-year-olds and adults experienced either the locations belonging to the quadrant-defined groups together in time during learning (Experiment 3) or the locations belonging to the side-defined groups together in time during learning (Experiment 4). After learning, participants attempted to replace the objects without the aid of the dots marking the locations. At the beginning of the second session, participants were asked to replace the original objects in the correct locations without the aid of the dots. This repeated assessment following a long delay provided an index of the stability of categories based on spatiotemporal cues. After this initial test, participants learned the locations of a new set of objects using a new spatiotemporal organization. The locations were identical to those learned at the first session; however, the objects and spatiotemporal organization differed across sessions. In Experiment 3, participants experienced locations belonging to the side-defined groups together in time, whereas in Experiment 4, participants experienced the locations belonging to the quadrant-defined groups together in time. In both experiments, comparison across sessions provided an index of flexibility in category formation.

This design allowed us to examine how spatiotemporal experience and perceptual structure interact to produce particular patterns of flexibility in spatial categorization. Note that in Experiment 3, the initial organization (during Session 1) was relatively strong because it was consistent with participants' spatiotemporal experience with the locations and with the perceptual structure of the task space (i.e., the axes of symmetry in the box). The subsequent organization (during Session 2) was not as strong because it was consistent with participants' spatiotemporal experience with the locations, but it was inconsistent with the perceptual structure of the task space. In contrast, in Experiment 4, the initial organization (during Session 1) was consistent with participants' spatiotemporal experience of the locations and inconsistent with the perceptual structure of the task space, whereas the subsequent organization (during Session 2) was consistent both with people's experience with the locations and with the perceptual structure of the task space.

Analysis of displacement scores revealed that adults demonstrated clear organization at Session 1, maintained this organization over a long delay, and flexibly shifted to a new organization at Session 2. For the children, the pattern of initial organization and stability was similar across the two experiments. All three age groups demonstrated clear organization during the test phase of Session 1 and remarkable stability of this organization over a long delay. In contrast, the pattern of flexibility differed across experiments. When children experienced the quadrant-defined groups together in time at Session 1 and the side-defined groups together in time at

Session 2, none of the age groups demonstrated a shift in organization following the change in spatiotemporal experience. When children experienced
the side-defined groups together in time at Session 1 and the (stronger)
quadrant-defined groups together in time at Session 2, 7- and 11-year-olds
showed a clear shift in organization following the change in spatiotemporal experience.

   These results again underscore the idea that the processes that give rise to
categorical bias are dynamic, involving the interaction of the cognitive system
(e.g., coding and maintenance of spatial information) and available perceptual structure over time. At Session 1, both children and adults organized the
locations in ways consistent with the initial spatiotemporal organization they
experienced. At Session 2, adults were able to shift to a new organization
based on their subsequent experience with either the side-defined or the
quadrant-defined groups of locations. In contrast, children (i.e., 7- and 11-
year-olds) showed a shift in organization at Session 2 only when they experienced the quadrant-defined groups of locations together in time during the
second session. That is, they demonstrated flexibility when the initial spatiotemporal organization conflicted with perceptual cues (e.g., when the side-
defined groups were experienced together in time during the first session)
and the new spatiotemporal organization was consistent with perceptual cues
(e.g., when the quadrant-defined groups were experienced together in time
during the second session). Children did not show a shift in organization
when the initial spatiotemporal organization was consistent with perceptual
cues and the new spatiotemporal organization conflicted with perceptual
cues. Together, these results nicely illustrate how organism–environment interactions at one point in time (i.e., Session 1) affect organism–environment
interactions at a later point in time (i.e., Session 2).

2.2.2 Reproducing Locations: How Does the Available Perceptual Structure at Test Influence Categorical Bias?

Thus far, we have discussed experimental manipulations designed to alter
the interaction of the cognitive system and the task structure during learning. These findings leave open the question of how the cognitive system
and the task structure interact when children and adults are in the process
of replacing the objects during the test phase. We addressed this question
by examining whether changing the available perceptual structure during
the test phase influences categorical bias (Plumert & Hund, 2001). (Note
that some of these data were presented above in our discussion of how the
salience of boundaries during learning influences categorical bias.) In particular, do children and adults exhibit more categorical bias when boundaries are present during learning but not during test than when boundaries
are present during both learning and test? We reasoned that taking away
perceptual structure at test that was available at learning would be more dis-
ruptive to memory for fine-grained, metric information than to memory
for coarse-grained, categorical information. Specifically, people likely rely

on boundaries and other landmarks to retrieve precise information about individual locations at test, whereas people may not need boundaries to retrieve memory for the spatial groups at test. Greater uncertainty about the individual locations (i.e., in the absence of boundaries) should lead to greater "pull" from the spatial groups. Hence, children and adults should exhibit more categorical bias when boundaries are absent than when present during test. Participants learned 20 locations with either walls or lines subdividing the box into four quadrants. During the test phase, boundaries were either present or absent while participants attempted to replace the objects without the aid of the dots.

As expected, participants exhibited more categorical bias, when no boundaries were present at test than when boundaries were present at test. One-sample *t*-tests comparing center displacement scores to 0 revealed that when boundaries were present during test, not even the adults showed significant categorical bias. In fact, 7- and 9-year-olds placed the objects significantly farther from the category centers than they really were (see figure 2.7). In contrast, when the boundaries were *not* present during test, 11-year-olds and adults in the walls condition and adults in the lines condition placed the objects closer together than they really were, exhibiting significant categorical bias.

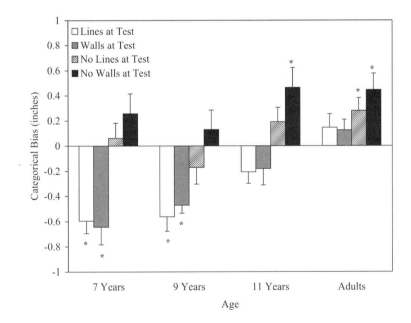

Figure 2.7 Categorical bias exhibited by each age group when there were boundaries or no boundaries during test. Positive scores reflect bias toward the category centers; negative scores reflect bias away from category centers. *Significant results ($p < .05$) of one-sample *t*-tests (df = 11) comparing the displacement score to the expected score with no displacement (i.e., 0 inches).

Given that all aspects of the procedure were the same up to the moment participants began placing the objects at test, these results demonstrate that decisions about where to place the objects during the test phase emerged out of the interaction of memory for the locations and perceptual structure available in the task at the time of test. In particular, we propose that during learning, adults coded the distance and direction of the locations relative to the boundaries and formed strong connections among the locations within each group. When the boundaries were present at test, adults could rely on their memory for the precise locations of the objects relative to the boundaries. When perceptual structure was absent at test, however, adults could not readily use their memory for the precise locations of the objects relative to the boundaries. (This idea is supported by better placement accuracy when boundaries were present than absent during test.) In the absence of boundaries during test, adults relied more heavily on their memory for the spatial groups, leading to greater categorical bias. Children also exhibited greater bias when boundaries were absent than when they were present at test, but with the exception of the 11-year-olds in the more salient boundary condition, the level of categorical bias was not significantly greater than 0. In fact, children exhibited significant pull toward the *corners* of the box, resulting in center displacement scores that were significantly less than 0. These findings suggest that children formed weaker connections among the locations within each group than did the adults. As a consequence, the "pull" from the spatial groups was not strong enough to offset their memory for the individual locations even when there was less perceptual support during test. Together, these results provide an intriguing example of how decisions about where to place the objects are not solely about what is in the head. Rather, placements emerge out of the interaction of the memory representation and the available perceptual structure.

2.3 CONCLUSIONS

The program of research presented here illustrates why we need the concept of organism–environment interaction to understand changes in spatial thinking over both short and long time scales. The experiments showing that U-shaped developmental patterns of categorical bias can be created or destroyed depending on the presence of single versus multiple cues for forming spatial groups (Hund & Plumert, 2003) provide particularly compelling examples of organism–environment interaction because they illustrate how categorical bias depends both on the characteristics of the cognitive system (e.g., age-related changes in coding and maintaining fine-grained and categorical information) and on the structure available in the task (e.g., single vs. multiple cues). In short, differences in the cognitive system and differences in the task structure alter the interaction between the cognitive system and the task structure, leading to systematic changes in the pattern of categorical bias.

From this way of thinking, neither the cognitive system nor environmental structure has causal priority in explaining behavior. We cannot explain patterns of categorical bias by referring only to task structure (e.g., presence or absence of boundaries) or by referring only to developmental differences in the cognitive system (e.g., strategic encoding of spatial groups). Our studies have repeatedly shown that all age groups exhibit categorical bias under some task conditions but not under others. For example, adults always show significant categorical bias when at least one cue is available during learning, but they do not show bias when no cues are available during learning. Thus, it is impossible to predict categorical bias by referring to age alone. Likewise, our studies have repeatedly shown that the four age groups frequently differ in how they respond to the same task structure. For example, children and adults often differ in how they respond to cues for organizing the locations into groups, such as visible boundaries, spatiotemporal experience, or object relations. Clearly, children and adults extract different things from their experience with these tasks even though the task structure is identical for all participants. These variations in how the same age group responds to different task structure and how different age groups respond to the same task structure support the idea that categorical bias emerges out of the interaction of the cognitive system and the task structure.

2.3.1 Understanding Change Over Short Time Scales

A key question raised by our results is *how* do interactions between the cognitive system and the task structure give rise to particular patterns of categorical bias? First, interactions that occur when people are coding locations determine the strength of memory for the individual locations and the spatial groups. (Note that the strength of these representations can change if delays are imposed between learning and reproducing locations; see Hund & Plumert [2002].) As discussed throughout this chapter, we assume that strong coding of the individual locations preserves precise metric information about distance and direction, whereas strong coding of the spatial groups (i.e., associations between the locations belonging to the same spatial group) pulls locations toward each other in memory. Task structure that highlights the spatial groups (e.g., multiple cues for forming spatial groups) should lead to stronger associations between locations belonging to the same spatial group. Likewise, task structure that makes it easier to code the individual locations (e.g., repeated opportunities to learn the locations) should lead to stronger memory for the individual locations (see Recker, Plumert, & Hund, 2006).

Second, we propose that these memory representations interact with the perceptual structure available at test to produce "decisions" about where to place the objects. How might this work? We assume that when children and adults are replacing the objects, they are trying to recreate an array that "matches" the remembered array (i.e., an array that "looks right" to them).

Their ability to recreate the remembered array depends both on the similarity of perceptual structure between learning and test and on the state of their memory for the individual locations. When perceptual structure at test is dissimilar to that available during learning (e.g., boundaries are present at learning but not at test) or when memory for the precise locations becomes fuzzy (e.g., due to delays between learning and test or restricted opportunities to learn the locations), people have difficulty creating a visual array that matches the remembered array (see Hund & Plumert, 2002; Recker et al., 2006). In sum, when there is a weak coupling between what people remember and what they see, placements can become ungrounded. This then opens the door for systematic bias such as compression of distances between objects in the same spatial group (or drift away from a midline axis; see Spencer & Hund, 2003).

2.3.2 Understanding Change Over Developmental Time Scales

Thus far, we have focused on how organism–environment interactions lead to changes in thinking that emerge in the moment or over brief time scales (i.e., the course of the experiment). But how do organism–environment interactions lead to changes in thinking over the longer term? Of particular interest is how changes come about in the fine-grained coding of individual locations and the coarse-grained coding of spatial groups. We start with the assumption that long-term developmental change emerges out of recurrent organism–environment interactions (see also Newcombe & Huttenlocher, 2000). That is, changes in the cognitive system lead to increased sensitivity to environmental structure for coding location. In turn, increased sensitivity to environmental structure leads to change in the cognitive system (e.g., more precise coding of individual locations or more strategic coding of spatial groups). From this perspective, interaction with environmental structure for coding location is necessary to produce changes in the organism, but the amount and type of structure that are "available" (i.e., can be used) at any point in development are constrained by the characteristics of the cognitive system. In the paragraphs that follow, we focus on ideas about how the ability to form spatial groups might emerge. (For ideas about how changes in the coding of fine-grained detail might come about, see chapter 14.)

We propose that developmental change in the ability to organize locations into groups emerges out of experience with noticing salient cues that highlight connections among nearby locations and with using spatial clustering strategies in supportive tasks. Although research directly comparing cues for forming spatial groups is scarce, a handful of studies have shown that the salience of cues influences how easily children organize locations into groups (Hund & Plumert, 2005; Kosslyn et al., 1974, Newcombe & Liben, 1982; Nichols-Whitehead & Plumert, 2001; Plumert & Hund, 2001). For example, Nichols-Whitehead and Plumert (2001) found that 3- and 4-year-olds' object retrieval was more organized when a tall opaque or short opaque boundary divided a small dollhouse in half than when a tall transparent boundary divided the dollhouse in half. Thus, it appears that children respond to more visually salient boundaries before they respond to less visually salient boundaries. More recently, we found that 7- to 11-year-old children used spatiotemporal contiguity to form spatial groups when they experienced *all* of the locations in one group together before moving on to the next group, but not when they experienced only 75% of the locations in one group together before moving on to another group (Hund & Plumert, 2005). In contrast, adults used spatiotemporal contiguity to form spatial groups in both conditions. Again, this suggests that sensitivity to structure for forming spatial groups undergoes change during development. Over the long term, we assume that children's experiences with more salient structure heighten their sensitivity to less salient structure for forming spatial groups. At this point, however, we know of no empirical demonstrations that this is the case (even within the course of an experiment). Clearly, this is an issue that requires further investigation, perhaps within the context of a microgenetic study.

Experience with using spatial clustering in highly supportive tasks may also produce developmental change in children's sensitivity to spatial groups. Spatial clustering refers to the tendency to order locations based on proximity or membership in a spatial region or group, such as visiting nearby locations together in time when searching for a hidden object. A number of studies have shown that older children use spatial clustering in a broader range of tasks than do younger children (e.g., Cornell & Heth, 1986; Plumert, 1994; Plumert, Pick, Marks, Kintsch, & Wegesin, 1994; Wellman, Somerville, Revelle, Haake, & Sophian, 1984). For instance, one of the first ways in which children use spatial clustering is in searching for objects. Thus, 4-year-olds retrieve the objects from one cluster of locations before retrieving those in another cluster (Wellman et al., 1984). Somewhat later, children begin to use their spatial clustering skills in verbal tasks such as giving directions for finding missing objects (Plumert et al., 1994). By 12 years of age, children also use spatial clustering to structure their free recall of object locations. Thus, when asked to recall the locations of a set of objects, 12-year-olds recall the locations by spatial region (Plumert, 1994, Experiment 2). Finally, at around 16 years of age, adolescents apply spatial clustering to structure their recall of object names. When recalling the furniture from their home, for example, 16-year-olds, but not younger children, group furniture items by room (Plumert, 1994, Experiment 1).

We hypothesize that children first use strategies in tasks that make the relevant features of the problem more salient (Folds, Footo, Guttentag, & Ornstein, 1990; Gauvain, 1993; Miller, 1990). To use a spatial clustering strategy, children must focus on the spatial connections among the locations. Tasks such as searching for objects, giving directions for finding objects, and recalling the names of objects differ in how explicitly they draw attention to the spatial connections among the object locations. For example, a task such as giving directions to someone for finding a set of objects may readily draw younger children's attention to the spatial connections among objects by making the listener's movement through space more salient. Specifically, imagining the listener in the space may prime them to think about locations nearby the listener (Morrow, Greenspan, & Bower, 1987). When faced with an unstructured task such as free recall, however, younger children may have difficulty focusing on the spatial connections among the objects because the explicitly stated goal of the task is to remember what the objects are, not where they are located. In fact, in situations in which both categorical and spatial organization are available (e.g., recalling the furniture from one's home), younger children attend more to the categorical than to the spatial relations among the items (Plumert, 1994).

Children's experiences with repeatedly using spatial clustering in highly supportive task contexts may guide their attention to the spatial connections among objects. Once cued about these spatial connections, children may be able to use their spatial clustering skills in less supportive task contexts, leading to the emergence of spatial clustering in tasks that provide less spatial support. In fact, there is evidence showing that experience with using spatial clustering in a more supportive task facilitates children's ability to use spatial clustering in a less supportive task. Plumert et al. (1994) found that when 6-year-olds gave directions for finding a set of objects and then went to search for those objects, they exhibited low levels of spatial clustering in their directions but high levels of spatial clustering in their searches. However, when they were allowed to search for the objects before giving directions for finding them, they exhibited high levels of spatial clustering in their subsequent directions. These results suggest that although children apply their spatial clustering skills to searching before they apply those same skills to giving directions, experience with using spatial clustering during searching facilitates 6-year-olds' ability to apply their spatial clustering skills to the more difficult task of direction giving.

Likewise, Plumert and Strahan (1997) found that 10-year-olds could be induced to use spatial clustering in a free recall task if given experience with using spatial clustering in a tour-planning task first. In contrast, 8-year-olds exhibited relatively low levels of spatial clustering in their subsequent free recall regardless of whether they performed the tour-planning task or the free recall task first. These results suggest that experience with the more supportive tour-planning task cued 10-year-olds about the spatial connections among the objects. Once cued, 10-year-olds could apply a spatial clustering strategy to the less supportive free recall task. Thus far, these empirical demonstrations of transfer are limited to situations in which the child transfers a spatial clustering strategy from a simpler to a more complex task, but with the same objects and locations. Further work is needed to determine whether children can transfer spatial clustering strategies from simpler to more complex tasks when the objects and locations change as well.

Do noticing salient cues for forming spatial groups and using spatial clustering strategies in supportive tasks act as mechanisms for change in everyday life? In the laboratory, we can carefully control the order in which children experience cues or tasks. Children's everyday experiences with cues for forming spatial groups and tasks calling for spatial clustering strategies are likely to be considerably less orderly. For example, children may be exposed to less salient cues for forming spatial groups before they are exposed to highly salient cues. Likewise, they may encounter more difficult tasks before they encounter less difficult ones. However, the sensitivity of the cognitive system to environmental structure may provide a built-in mechanism for ensuring that children's everyday experiences are more orderly than they may seem at first glance. With an immature cognitive system, young children's "experiences" may well be limited to noticing only salient cues for forming spatial groups and using spatial clustering in highly supportive tasks. Thus, young children do not experience a bewildering array of inputs simply because they are not sensitive to these inputs. This constraint on experience imposed by the cognitive system may be critical for ensuring that the child's experience of environmental structure proceeds in an orderly fashion. (See Newport [1990] for similar ideas about how immature cognitive abilities might constrain young children's experiences with linguistic input.)

2.3.3 CONCLUDING THOUGHTS   Although the idea of the complementarity between the organism and environment may not seem like a particularly radical (or even novel) idea, much of the work in cognitive development implicitly rejects the idea that thinking is a joint function of the characteristics of the organism and the structure of the environment (for similar assessments, see Elman et al., 1996; Thelen & Smith, 1994). For example, some researchers interested in uncovering innate concepts or core knowledge have argued for a separation of cognitive competence and task performance (Baillargeon, 2001; Spelke, 2000). This has led to a never-ending search for the "right" task to tap some underlying core competence. Likewise, researchers interested in showing how learning experiences or task conditions influence thinking are often most interested in studying the cognitive system per se rather than in understanding how thinking emerges out the interaction of the task and the cognitive system (Cohen, 2004; Rovee-Collier, 1999). Although describing the information available in the environment and describing the characteristics of the cognitive system are necessary and important endeavors, they are only beginning steps to understanding how cognition happens in the moment and changes over time. We argue that researchers must ultimately focus on the interactions of the cognitive system and environmental structure over time to fully understand how thinking emerges over short and long time scales.

ACKNOWLEDGMENTS   This work was supported by grants from the National Institutes of Health (R03-HD36761) and the National Science Foundation (BCS-0343034) awarded to J.M.P. and from the National Institutes of Health (F31-MH12985) awarded to A.M.H. We gratefully acknowledge the many undergraduate research assistants who helped with data collection and coding. We also thank the children and parents who participated in these studies.

REFERENCES

Adolph, K. E. (1997). Learning in the development of infant locomotion. *Monographs of the Society for Research in Child Development*, *62*, 1–164.

Adolph, K. E. (2000). Specificity of learning: Why infants fall over a veritable cliff. *Psychological Science*, *11*, 290–295.

Adolph, K. E., Eppler, M. A., & Gibson, E. J. (1993). Crawling versus walking infants' perception of affordances for locomotion over sloping surfaces. *Child Development*, *64*, 1158–1174.

Allen, G. L. (1981). A developmental perspective on the effects of "subdividing" macrospatial experience. *Journal of Experimental Psychology: Human Learning and Memory*, *7*, 120–132.

Baillargeon, R. (2001). Infants' physical knowledge: Of acquired expectations and core principles. In E. Dupoux (Ed.), *Language, brain, and cognitive development: Essays in honor of Jacques Mehler* (pp. 341–361). Cambridge, MA: MIT Press.

Clayton, K., & Habibi, A. (1991). Contribution of temporal contiguity to the spatial priming effect. *Journal of Experimental Psychology: Learning, Memory, and Cognition*, *17*, 263–271.

Cohen, L. B. (2004). Modeling the development of infant categorization. *Infancy*, *5*, 127–130.

Cornell, E. H., & Heth, C. D. (1986). The spatial organization of hiding and recovering of objects by children. *Child Development*, *57*, 603–615.

Curiel, J. M., & Radvansky, G. A. (1998). Mental organization of maps. *Journal of Experimental Psychology: Learning, Memory, and Cognition*, *24*, 202–214.

Elman, J. L., Bates, E. A., Johnson, M. H., Karmiloff-Smith, A., Parisi, D., & Plunkett, K. (1996). *Rethinking innateness: A connectionist perspective on development*. Cambridge, MA: MIT Press.

Eppler, M. A, Adolph, K. E., & Weiner, T. (1996). The developmental relationship between infant's exploration and action on slanted surfaces. *Infant Behavior & Development*, *19*(2), 259–264.

Folds, T. H., Footo, M. M., Guttentag, R. E., & Ornstein, P. A. (1990). When children mean to remember: Issues of context specificity, strategy effectiveness, and intentionality in the development of memory. In D. F. Bjorklund (Ed.), *Children's strategies: Contemporary views of cognitive development*. Hillsdale, NJ: Lawrence Erlbaum.

Gauvain, M. (1993). The development of spatial thinking in everyday activity. *Developmental Review*, *13*, 92–121.

Gibson, E. J. (1988). Exploratory behavior in the development of perceiving, acting, and the acquiring of knowledge. *Annual Review of Psychology*, *39*, 1–41.

Gibson, E. J., & Pick, A. D. (2000). *An ecological approach to perceptual learning and development*. New York: Oxford University Press.

Gibson, J. J. (1979). *The ecological approach to visual perception*. Hillsdale, NJ: Lawrence Erlbaum.

Gibson, J. J., & Gibson, E. J. (1955). Perceptual learning: Differentiation or enrichment? *Psychological Review*, *62*, 32–41.

Hund, A. M., & Plumert, J. M. (2002). Delay-induced bias in children's memory for location. *Child Development*, *73*, 829–840.

Hund, A. M., & Plumert, J. M. (2003). Does information about what things are influence children's memory for where things are? *Developmental Psychology*, *39*, 939–938.

Hund, A. M., & Plumert, J. M. (2005). The stability and flexibility of spatial categories. *Cognitive Psychology*, *50*, 1–44.

Hund, A. M., Plumert, J. M., & Benney, C. J. (2002). Experiencing nearby locations together in time: The role of spatiotemporal contiguity in children's memory for location. *Journal of Experimental Child Psychology*, *82*, 200–225.

Hund, A. M., & Spencer, J. P. (2003). Developmental changes in the relative weighting of geometric and experience-dependent location cues. *Journal of Cognition & Development*, *4*, 3–38.

Huttenlocher, J., Hedges, L. V., & Duncan, S. (1991). Categories and particulars: Prototype effects in estimating spatial location. *Psychological Review*, *98*, 352–376.

Kosslyn, S. M., Pick, H. L., Jr., & Fariello, G. R. (1974). Cognitive maps in children and men. *Child Development*, *45*, 707–716.

Lockman, J. J. (2000). A perception-action perspective on tool use development. *Child Development*, *71*, 137–144.

McNamara, T. P. (1986). Mental representation of spatial relations. *Cognitive Psychology*, *18*, 87–121.

McNamara, T. P., Halpin, J. A., & Hardy, J. K. (1992). The representation and integration in memory of spatial and nonspatial information. *Memory & Cognition*, *20*, 519–532.

Miller, P. H. (1990). The development of strategies of selective attention. In D. F. Bjorklund (Ed.), *Children's strategies: Contemporary views of cognitive development*. Hillsdale, NJ: Lawrence Erlbaum.

Morrow, D. G., Greenspan, S. L., & Bower, G. H. (1987). Accessibility and situation models in narrative comprehension. *Journal of Memory and Language*, *26*, 165–187.

Mou, W., & McNamara, T. P. (2002). Intrinsic frames of reference in spatial memory. *Journal of Experimental Psychology: Learning, Memory, and Cognition*, *28*, 162–170.

Newcombe, N. S., & Huttenlocher, J. (2000). *Making space: The development of spatial representation and reasoning*. Cambridge, MA: MIT Press.

Newcombe, N., & Liben, L. S. (1982). Barrier effects in the cognitive maps of children and adults. *Journal of Experimental Child Psychology*, *34*, 46–58.

Newport, E. L. (1990). Maturational constraints on language learning. *Cognitive Science*, *14*, 11–28.

Nichols-Whitehead, P., & Plumert, J. M. (2001). The influence of boundaries on young children's searching and gathering. *Journal of Cognition and Development*, *2*, 367–388.

Plumert, J. M. (1994). Flexibility in children's use of spatial and categorical organizational strategies in recall. *Developmental Psychology*, *30*, 738–747.

Plumert, J. M., & Hund, A. M. (2001). The development of memory for object location: What role do spatial prototypes play? *Child Development*, *72*(2), 370–384.

Plumert, J. M., Kearney, J. K., & Cremer, J. F. (2004). Children's perception of gap affordances: Bicycling across traffic-filled intersections in an immersive virtual environment. *Child Development*, *75*, 1243–1253.

Plumert, J. M., Pick, H. L., Jr., Marks, R. A., Kintsch, A. S., & Wegesin, D. (1994). Locating objects and communicating about locations: Organizational differences in children's searching and direction-giving. *Developmental Psychology*, *30*, 443–453.

Plumert, J. M., & Strahan, D. (1997). Relations between task structure and developmental changes in children's use of spatial clustering strategies. *British Journal of Developmental Psychology, 15*, 495–514.

Recker, K. M., Plumert, J. M., & Hund, A. M. (2006). *How do biases in memory for location change over learning?* Unpublished Manuscript.

Rieser, J. J., Pick, H. L., Ashmead, D. H., & Garing, A. E. (1995). Calibration of human locomotion and models of perceptual-motor organization. *Journal of Experimental Psychology: Human Perception and Performance, 21*, 480–497.

Rovee-Collier, C. (1999). The development of infant memory. *Current Directions in Psychological Science, 8*, 80–85.

Schutte, A. R., & Spencer, J. P. (2002). Generalizing the dynamic field theory of the A-not-B error beyond infancy: Three-year-olds' delay- and experience-dependent location memory biases. *Child Development, 73*, 377–404.

Schutte, A. R., Spencer, J. P., & Schöner, G. (2003). Testing the dynamic field theory: Working memory for locations becomes more spatially precise over development. *Child Development, 74*, 1393–1417.

Sherman, R. C., & Lim, K. M. (1991). Determinants of spatial priming in environmental memory. *Memory & Cognition, 19*(3), 283–292.

Spelke, E. S. (2000). Core knowledge. *American Psychologist, 55*, 1233–1243.

Spencer, J. P., & Hund, A. M. (2002). Prototypes and particulars: Geometric and experience-dependent spatial categories. *Journal of Experimental Psychology: General, 131*, 16–37.

Spencer, J. P., & Hund, A. M. (2003). Developmental continuity in the processes that underlie spatial recall. *Cognitive Psychology, 47*, 432–480.

Thelen, E., & Smith, L. B. (1994). *A dynamic systems approach to the development of cognition and action.* Cambridge, MA: MIT Press.

Warren, W. H. (1984). Perceiving affordances: Visual guidance of stair climbing. *Journal of Experimental Psychology: Human Perception and Performance, 10*, 683–703.

Wellman, H. M., Somerville, S. C., Revelle, G. L., Haake, R. J., & Sophian, C. (1984). The development of comprehensive search skills. *Child Development, 55*, 472–481.

3

EXPLAINING THE DEVELOPMENT OF SPATIAL REORIENTATION
Modularity-Plus-Language versus the Emergence of Adaptive Combination

Nora S. Newcombe & Kristin R. Ratliff

All mobile organisms occasionally face the important adaptive problem of determining where they are when they have been disoriented by rapid movement (e.g., tumbling down a hill) or by passive movement without visual landmarks (e.g., traveling by subway). It has recently been proposed that a wide array of nonhuman animal species, as well as human children, solve this problem using a geometric module that only accepts information about the shape of enclosing spaces (Cheng, 1986; Gallistel, 1990; Hermer & Spelke, 1994, 1996; see Cheng & Newcombe, 2005, for an overview). In a modular view, various sources of spatial information are processed independently in separable cognitive processing units (e.g., Wang & Spelke, 2002). However, investigators have argued that, starting at 6 years of age in humans, productive control of spatial language, specifically the terms "right" and "left," allows the operation of this geometric module to be supplemented by the use of featural information, such as the color of surfaces in the environment (e.g., Hermer-Vazquez, Moffett, & Munkholm, 2001; Hermer-Vazquez, Spelke, & Katsnelson, 1999).

Modularity is typically associated with nativist views (although this relation is by no means forced by logic; Fodor, 2001). However, there is a problem for innatist modularity claims: how to explain developmental change. In the case of the geometric module, Spelke and associates have solved the problem of why features as well as geometry start to be used to reorient by postulating what is essentially a grafting process. In such a process, use of features as well as geometry occurs when the language faculty (which itself can be argued to be a largely innate module) matures sufficiently to supplement the output of its sister module. In this formulation, Vygotsky supplements Chomsky and Fodor to explain development.[1] This "modularity-plus-language" view has only two explanatory mechanisms: innate endowment and linguistic mediation.

There are alternatives, however, to the modularity-plus-language position and its simple explanation of developmental change. There is a good deal of evidence, in a variety of domains, that information sources are frequently combined to determine judgments and behavior, using weighting mechanisms. For example, judgments of an object's size can be based on information from either vision or touch; when both kinds of information are available, people combine the two sources in a fashion weighted by the variance associated with each source (Banks, 2005; Ernst & Banks, 2002). This integration rule is an application of Bayes's rule and leads to judgments that approach statistical optimality. In the spatial domain, Huttenlocher, Hedges, and Duncan (1991; see also chapter 1) have proposed a hierarchical combination model in which estimates of an object's location are based on a combination of fine-grained and categorical information. These sources of information are combined according to Bayesian rules in a fashion that depends on the certainty with which each kind of information has been coded (with greater uncertainty associated with greater variance). Also in the spatial domain, Hartley, Trinkler, and Burgess (2004) have developed a *boundary proximity model* of human memory for location within enclosed spaces that uses a mixture of absolute and relative distance information. Encoding of absolute distance from a wall is more accurate and less variable when the distance is short, while encoding of relative distances (ratios of distances from various walls) is less dependent on how close a location is to a wall. Hence, absolute information is weighted more heavily when encoding locations close to walls while relative information is weighted more heavily when walls are distant (i.e., when a location is in the middle of the enclosure).

The overall family of such approaches to understanding estimation and judgment tasks can be called the adaptive combination view (Newcombe & Huttenlocher, 2006). The three specific models we have mentioned so far concentrate on uncertainty and variability in encoding of various kinds of information, all of which are clearly relevant to the task at hand. However, there may be additional influences on weighting. Notably, the salience of various kinds of information would clearly be expected to affect probability of use. Even more important for development, an organism's history of using particular kinds of information (i.e., learning) would naturally affect the weighting placed on that information source (as is envisioned in connectionist models of development). In terms of the task of reestablishing spatial orientation, an adaptive combination view suggests the possibility that geometric and featural information are utilized in varying degrees at varying points in development, in a fashion that reflects the certainty and variance with which the two kinds of information are encoded, along with their salience and perceived usefulness.

The adaptive combination viewpoint is a general one, which could potentially be applied to many lines of cognitive development, not just the spatial domain. This viewpoint has elements in common with several current approaches to cognitive development, including connectionism, dynamic systems, and Siegler's overlapping waves theory (see discussion in Newcombe & Huttenlocher, 2006). It has an empiricist flavor, because it seems natural to suppose that the weightings in an integrative process are affected by experience. However, there are potentially nativist elements, as well. Initial weightings might be, at least in part, innately specified, and what kinds of information are treated as relevant to what kinds of actions may well need to be set at an appropriate starting point. It is also possible that a Bayesian learning process is itself a basic rather than acquired attribute of the organism (see Elman et al., 1996).

The purpose of this chapter is to discuss these two views—modularity-plus-language and adaptive combination—concentrating particularly on the issue that most clearly demarcates them: modularity. First, we discuss what is meant by the term "module." It is a term in very widespread use, but different people mean quite different things by it. Second, we describe in greater detail the evidence favoring the geometric module hypothesis and the further hypothesis that it can be augmented by spatial language (for a more extended review, see Cheng & Newcombe, 2005). Third, we present reasons to doubt the modularity-plus-language view. Fourth, we consider how an adaptive combination approach would describe the known phenomena, what predictions it would make, and how it would address potential criticisms.

3.1 WHAT DO WE MEAN WHEN WE SAY MODULARITY?

Modularity has been an extremely attractive concept in cognitive science recently and has even received wide attention in the popular scientific press. For example, one science journalist has written with authority that "your brain is not a general-purpose computer with one unified central processor. It is an assemblage of competing subsystems—sometimes called 'modules'—specialized for particular tasks" (Johnson, 2004, p. 26). In fact, it has become increasingly common to hear the claim that the mind/brain is *massively* modular, that is, that it consists of an assemblage of modules (e.g., Pinker, 1997; Sperber, 1994; but for doubts, see Fodor, 2001; Buller, 2005). This trend is correlated with several other trends in cognitive and developmental science: interest in the evolutionary bases of cognition; a frequent focus on separate cognitive domains, such as spatial competence, as well as (or sometimes to the exclusion of) domain-general faculties, such as attention; neuroscience findings concerning the specific cortical areas that support cognitive functions; and widespread acceptance of the idea that many cognitive capabilities have strong innate bases. Painting with a broad brush, many investigators have embraced the view that evolution has selected for particular cognitive skills that are present at least in skeletal form at birth and that are supported by discrete areas of the brain. However, these various lines of thought are not as tightly and inevitably woven together as they first appear, and the term "modularity" means different things to different people. In this section, we analyze how best to use the term with precision.

A useful place to begin is with Fodor's (1983) *Modularity of Mind*. This book is, arguably, the historical starting point for discussion of modularity in cognitive science. There are three interesting aspects of Fodor's (1983) treatment of the term "modularity." First, he strongly emphasized the functional isolation of cognitive modules, an element of modularity that has often been ignored in subsequent research. For instance, he wrote that, "What I take to be perhaps the most important aspect of modularity [is] something that I shall call 'informational encapsulation'" (p. 37). Encapsulation is illustrated by the example of the Müller-Lyer illusion (see figure 3.1). No matter how certain a person is that the horizontal lines in such a figure are in fact equal in length, it is not possible to see them as equal—the line with the outward-facing arrows always looks longer. Thus, the visual system is encapsulated (or, to use a synonym, impenetrable) with respect to conscious knowledge.

A second interesting aspect of Fodor's (1983) book is that he argued that only input systems are likely to be modular: "Central systems are, in important respects, *un*encapsulated, and . . . it is primarily for this reason that they are not plausibly viewed as modular" (p. 103). This position differs markedly from subsequent usage by many cognitive scientists, who have freely postulated such central modules as a theory of mind module or a cheater detection module (e.g., Cosmides & Tooby, 1992; Scholl & Leslie, 1999; but see also Buller, 2005). Fodor argued that central systems such as thinking, reasoning, and decision making could not be modular because "the representations that input systems deliver have to interface somewhere" (pp. 101–102).

A third important aspect of Fodor's (1983) treatment of modularity is that he emphasized the linkage between modularity and the concepts that

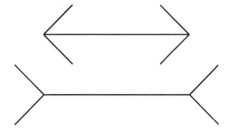

Figure 3.1 The Müller-Lyer illusion. The horizontal lines are equal in length, but they appear unequal.

are now virtually synonymous with it in the minds of many cognitive scientists: domain specificity, nativism, and neural specialization. He wrote quite specifically that "modular cognitive systems are domain specific, innately specified, hard wired, autonomous, and not assembled" (p. 37). While he did not explicitly mention adaptive value and natural selection (and, in his 2001 book, doubted the extent of the connection between modularity and these concepts), the idea that modular cognitive systems are created by evolutionary forces seems very attractive to many other theorists (e.g., Pinker, 1997). Today, these various terms are often used virtually interchangeably. For example, in a recent article on working memory, domain specificity and modularity were regarded as equivalent: "One model, developed by Goldman-Rakic and colleagues, postulates a modular organization of working memory based on the type of information processing (the domain specificity hypothesis)" (Romanski, 2004, p. 421). Similarly, again choosing a convenient recent example, Akhtar (2004) equates nativism and modularity: "The main goal of nativists . . . is to verify a specific theory of linguistic competence that suggests that linguistic knowledge is innate and modular" (p. 459).

Modularity should not, however, be casually regarded as synonymous with nativism, domain specificity, neural specialization, or abilities shaped by evolution. Each of these concepts is historically correlated with modularity, but each of them could be true without modularity being true, and their validity needs to be considered independently. Let us begin with the relation of modularity and nativism, for which reflection reveals that neither concept strictly entails the other. On the one hand, modularity could be emergent and hence *not* nativist (e.g., Karmiloff-Smith, 1992). On the other hand, there could conceivably be strong innate determination of cognitive capacities and representations without a modular organization of mind. Indeed, revising his 1983 views, Fodor (2001) now says, "The argument between nativists and empiricists that Chomsky revived is orthogonal to the argument over whether, and to what extent, mental processes are encapsulated" (pp. 57–58). Nevertheless, the relation between modularity and nativism is a tricky one, both because the two ideas are strongly correlated in the minds of many cognitive developmentalists, and because the question of what evidence counts for and against a nativist position is actually fairly unclear (Newcombe, 2002).

Modularity and nativism are independent, but the case is different for the other three concepts correlated with modularity (i.e., domain specificity, neural specialization, and abilities shaped by evolution). For these concepts, there are entailments, but the entailments are asymmetric, at least as long as modularity is taken to include encapsulation. That is, modularity implies the other concepts, but the other concepts do not imply modularity. Although it is hard to imagine how an encapsulated module could be domain general, domain specificity does not require encapsulation. That is, domain-specific aspects of the cognitive system, such as spatial working memory, need not be isolated from other cognitive functions.[2] In fact, for most specialized systems like this, isolation might destroy their usefulness. Similarly, while any encapsulated module would seem to require support from a specialized neural area,[3] neural specialization does not entail modularity. If specialized brain areas "talk to" one another to support a function, as they almost always do, there is no encapsulation.

Finally, while modularity would not be likely to exist without evolutionary pressure, adaptive problems can be solved without modularity. Evolutionary psychology has been strongly identified with the Swiss Army knife metaphor of mental life, in which the mind/brain is analogically mapped to a bundle of tools, each well designed for solving a different problem—scissors for cutting paper in the case of the Swiss army knife; foraging for food, avoiding predators, and navigating a landscape in the case of the mind/brain. However, even if one accepts this analogy, encapsulated modules are not necessarily implied. One of the originators of evolutionary cognitive psychology, Leda Cosmides, has in fact said in an online interview that "I have discovered that some people misunderstand the Swiss Army knife metaphor—they think the claim is that these programs do not share information or work together. All these functionally specialized, domain-specific programs are designed to work together to produce behavior. They share information, pass it back and forth, and so on," (Fischer & Araya, 2001, question 7).

Where does this leave the matter of what we should mean when we say "modularity"? Investigators clearly have many correlated attributes in mind when they use the term, yet these vary across theorists, and not all of the attributes are necessary and sufficient parts of a rigorous definition of the term. In fact, if the encapsulation criterion is not met, it is not clear that the term "module" is helpful at all (see Fodor, 2001; Seok, 2006). It would likely be better to be specific, to say "domain specificity" if that is what is meant, or "dependent on a specific cortical area" if that is what is meant, and so on. Investigators are, of course, free to use a term like modularity without requiring encapsulation if they like, but little is gained and much may be lost by doing so, because readers are left with a false sense of functional separation where there may be none intended. As Lewis Carroll wrote in a different context: " 'The question is,' said Alice, 'whether you can make words mean so many different things.' "

Given this background, we can now turn back to the tale of the geometric module itself. The geometric module is an interesting test case for the utility of the modularity concept, precisely because bold claims have been made for its encapsulation. Other "modules" may simply be cases of developmentally emergent functions with domain-specific properties supported by specialized brain areas that have adaptive functions. An important reason to be interested in the geometric module is that it is one of the few modules of the many that have been proposed that seems to meet Fodor's encapsulation criterion. When investigators discuss other hypothesized modules, such as a theory of mind module or a cheater detection module, they rarely make such bold claims about encapsulation. Thus, the existence or nonexistence of an encapsulated geometric module is a matter of considerable interest, because demonstrating the phenomenon securely would show that there could be a cognitively interesting module that corresponds to Fodor's (1983) conceptualization. In fact, a modular spatial reorientation system might be an example of what Fodor thought unlikely, namely, a modular central system.

3.2 EVIDENCE FAVORING THE MODULARITY-PLUS-LANGUAGE VIEW

When we emerge from a subway station, we look around for clues as to which way we are facing and how to relate what we see to our knowledge of the spatial relations in the current environment. Similarly, animals that have just been engaged in rough-and-tumble play with other animals might, once the engagement is complete, search for information about how they are now placed in the environment. Cheng (1986) made the fascinating discovery that, after disorientation of this kind, animals reorient using the metric information given by the lengths and angles that form the shape of the surrounding environment. Specifically, he trained rats to find food hidden in one corner of a rectangular cage with unmarked walls, for example, in one of the two corners where a long wall is to the left of a short wall. As long as the rats remained oriented, they could distinguish between the two corners having the same geometric characteristics. However, once they were disoriented, the rats searched for the reward equally often at the geometrically identical corners.

A further aspect of Cheng's experiments showed that the animals did not simply use geometric information—they also relied on it to the exclusion of nongeometric information that would augment it and make it possible to search correctly. When the rectangular cage had additional landmarks, such as wall markings or smells, that removed the ambiguity between the congruent corners, the rats did not use the landmark information. Rather, they continued to divide search evenly between the correct and reverse corners. Thus, Cheng showed that the rats encoded the geometric properties of the space (i.e., the length of the walls and their relation at the corners) but did not incorporate the nongeometric features in their representation of the room to guide their reorientation. Gallistel (1990) cited these data prominently in his extended arguments for the existence of a geometric module.

Human children at 18–24 months of age have shown similar search patterns for a hidden toy within a symmetric rectangular environment (Hermer & Spelke, 1994, 1996). In a rectangular room with all white walls, young children used geometric information to reorient within the room, dividing their searches for the hidden toy evenly between the correct and reverse corners. When a colored wall was added, although children should have enough information to distinguish the correct corner and to successfully complete the task, children's search rates remained identical to those in the all-white room. Hermer and Spelke proposed that children's failure to conjoin the geometric and nongeometric information was based on their use of an encapsulated and task-specific mechanism: the geometric module.

Although rats and children both show evidence of a dominant geometric representation that guides reorientation to the neglect of nongeometric information, human adults easily combine geometric and nongeometric spatial information to reorient in a symmetric environment. Hermer-Vazquez et al. (1999) found that, after disorientation in a rectangular room with all white walls and one blue wall, human adults showed no encapsulation, successfully reorienting to find the correct corner of the room as expected. However, when adults were simultaneously engaged in a verbal shadowing task of repeating words to produce continuous speech, they were no longer able to flexibly combine the two kinds of information and were limited to using only the geometric information to reorient. Adults who performed a nonverbal control task were easily able to combine geometric and nongeometric information to reorient. These data suggest that the joint use of featural and geometric information requires linguistic support. Hermer-Vazquez et al. (1999) concluded that adults are able to overcome the encapsulation found among young children by acquiring spatial language and engaging linguistic processing to utilize nongeometric features in conjunction with geometric information. Specifically, Hermer-Vazquez et al. (1999) claimed that the language faculty serves as a system of representation that connects to other systems of representation, allowing the arbitrary combination of information from distinct sources.

Children develop the ability to appropriately use the spatial terms "left" and "right" around the age of 6 years. This age is also the one at which they successfully complete the reorientation task using features. Hermer-Vazquez et al. (2001) investigated this coincidence of ages further. They gave a variety of cognitive tests, including nonverbal intelligence, digit span, visuospatial span, production of spatial terms (above–below, in front–behind, left–right), and comprehension of these same spatial terms to a group of children around this age, as well as testing them in the reorientation task. The only variable that predicted children's ability to reorient using features as well as geometry was their production of the terms "left" and "right." Based on these data, Hermer-Vazquez et al. (2001) argued that control of such linguistic terms was essential in allowing for rapid and flexible use of features in reorientation.

3.3 EVIDENCE AGAINST THE MODULARITY-PLUS-LANGUAGE VIEW

Taken together, the data from rats, human children, and human adults seem to make a powerful and elegant case for an encapsulated geometric module that is present in early development, and perhaps innate, but that is eventually supplemented (one might even say "breached" or "pierced") by the use of language. However, there is also contradictory evidence. The data that cast doubt on the notion of an encapsulated geometric module come first from nonhuman animals. In the absence of language, it would seem unlikely that they would ever use features to reorient, yet many studies have shown that they do. We review some illustrative work here (for a more complete discussion, see Cheng & Newcombe, 2005). Although the work with nonhuman animals might seem decisive, the data from humans used to support the modularity-plus-language view uses a different paradigm that involves much less training, and thus the story of human development requires separate consideration. We review evidence that very young children do sometimes use features as well as geometry to reorient. We also examine further the claim that human adults can use features as well as geometry to reorient only when their linguistic capacity is not otherwise engaged through verbal shadowing.

3.3.1 No Encapsulation in Nonhuman Animals

In experiments using chickens, Vallortigara, Zanforlin, and Pasti (1990) found that the birds utilized direct features in their reorientation within a rectangular enclosure. As seen previously with rats, when no distinguishing features were present in the space, the chickens relied on geometric encoding to guide their searches for food at the geometrically identical corners (correct and opposite). Unlike rats, however, once four distinctive panels were placed on each corner, the chickens were able to use the direct featural information to disambiguate the space and search the correct corner.

Kelly, Spetch, and Heth (1998) found similar results using pigeons, in that the birds used both direct and indirect nongeometric information in conjunction with the geometry of the room shape to guide their search for food after disorientation in a rectangular enclosure. Some pigeons were trained with featural information available in the corners throughout the entirety of the experiments, whereas other pigeons initially only had an ambiguous symmetric enclosure. All pigeons used the room shape to guide their reorientation, and once features were added for all environments, the pigeons successfully used both geometric and nongeometric information. When the nongeometric features were in conflict with the geometry of the room (achieved through rotating the feature panels), the history of the pigeon's exposure to the featural cues affected their reliance on them. The pigeons trained with featural information available from the first trial showed a reliance on nongeometric information, whereas the pigeons trained initially only with geometry showed a mixture of using features and geometry.

Monkeys also show no encapsulation, using both geometric and nongeometric knowledge to locate a reward (Gouteux, Thinus-Blanc, & Vauclair, 2001). In a rectangular room, monkeys successfully reoriented using a colored wall to find a specific corner. Interestingly, although the monkeys used large featural cues (i.e., a colored wall) to distinguish between the correct and incorrect corner, they did not use small featural cues. This coincides with the idea of cue validity, in that small objects are more likely to move and thus provide less stable landmarks than do big objects that are more of-ten helpful in providing a stable distant landmark.

Sovrano, Bisazza, and Vallortigara (2003) provided perhaps the most striking evidence against a geometric module with experiments using fish, specifically *Xenotoca eiseni*. In a small rectangular fish tank, the fish encoded landmarks of either featured panels in each corner or a colored wall. Using the available nongeometric information in conjunction with the geometry, the fish successfully located an exit from the smaller tank to a larger, more desirable fish tank with vegetation and other fish. Interestingly, however, Sovrano et al. (2003) also found that the fish spontaneously encoded the geometric information of the space even when the nongeometric informa-tion was all that was necessary to distinguish the correct corner, perhaps in-dicating the importance of relying on geometric information in addition to nongeometric information.

3.3.2 No Encapsulation in Very Young Children

Evidence from nonhuman animals does not support the encapsulation of a geometric module and suggests that language is *not* crucial to combining geometric and nongeometric information. Despite this strong evidence, doubts have been raised about whether animal results are sufficient to dis-prove the modularity-plus-language view. Hermer-Vazquez et al. (2001) argue that the nonhuman animal data are linked to extensive training, and only human adults flexibly and easily use landmarks together with geomet-ric information in order to reorient. However, evidence against modularity has emerged with human research as well, specifically with children where minimal training has been used.

Learmonth, Newcombe, and Huttenlocher (2001) examined Hermer and Spelke's (1994, 1996) claims in experiments that differed in a few re-spects from the original study: (1) the room in which the experiment was conducted was four times larger than the very small room used in the orig-inal experiments (8×12 feet rather than 4×6 feet), and (2) the presence or absence of features was manipulated between groups rather than varied for a single child. Learmonth et al. (2001) confirmed the finding that disori-ented children use geometric information to find a toy, indicating their ability not only to code metric extent (see also Huttenlocher, Newcombe, & Sandberg, 1994) but also to relate one distance to another (i.e., "the long wall to the left of the short wall"). However, when various nongeometric landmarks were added in the context of the larger room (including a col-ored wall in one experiment, and in other studies a door and/or a bookcase flush with the wall that could mark a toy's location either directly or indi-rectly), children between 18 and 24 months *did* use the nongeometric cues as well as the geometry of the space.

What accounts for this very different pattern of findings? Learmonth, Nadel, and Newcombe (2002) focused on whether the size of the sur-rounding space was at least one of the controlling factors, and in fact con-firmed that the encapsulation result appears for the small room but that nongeometric information is used in the larger room. This finding is important because it can be argued that the larger space is a more ecologically valid setting in which to examine orientation, which after all does occur in an environment that typically extends for large distances around an active agent. That is, the Learmonth et al. (2001) studies should not be seen as a small caveat on the result of Hermer and Spelke (1994, 1996) or as simply showing that, in an easier task, geometry may not take precedence (Bertenthal, 2005). Rather, the results of Hermer and Spelke should be seen as a special case that may not occur very often in nature. Data from such a situation are interesting in the same way that a visual illusion is: they may tell us something about the mind (as illusions can tell us about the visual system), but they require great care in interpretation because they do not represent a frequently occurring pattern of functioning.

Examining the various studies of children's reorientation broken down by age groups, Cheng and Newcombe (2005) combined data across studies to create a graph of the age trends in above-chance use of geometry (i.e., choice of one of the geometrically correct corners) and use of features (i.e., choice of the unique corner identified by the feature) in the two room sizes (see figure 3.2). At all ages studied—from toddlers to adults—participants showed above-chance use of features in the larger room. By contrast, only

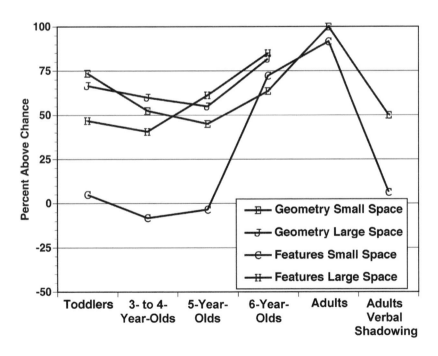

Figure 3.2 Developmental changes in use of geometric and featural cues. Values below zero reflect participants performing below chance. From Cheng and Newcombe (2005).

participants 6 or more years of age used features in the small room. Additionally, it is always more difficult to find the correct corner in the smaller room, even for the older age groups. Interestingly, although very young children do use the nongeometric information available in the large room, there is also age-related improvement in search accuracy. Specifically, using the colored wall as a landmark to distinguish between the geometrically identical corners in the large room increases both between 4 and 5 years of age and between 5 and 6 years. The idea that language is vital to use of features cannot explain the above-chance performance by toddlers in the larger room, improvement in use of features prior to acquisition of the terms "left" and "right," or the room size effect itself.

Newcombe (2005) proposed two ways to explain the effect of room size on use of features. One possibility was that spatial orientation mechanisms may not be fully engaged in cases where it is difficult to move around in an active and exploratory way. A second explanation focused on the fact that landmarks are typically more likely to be used in spatial tasks when they are distant from, rather than close to, an observer (see also Hupbach & Nadel, 2005; Nadel & Hupbach, 2006). In a series of studies (Learmonth, Newcombe, Hansell, & Jones, 2005), we have explored the impact of these factors, using a paradigm in which children stay within a small, centrally located rectangular area the same size as the room in Hermer and Spelke (1994, 1996) that is located within a larger rectangular room the same size as used in the Learmonth et al. (2001) experiments. One wall of the larger room was colored. We also varied the location of the hidden toy. In our first study, it was located within the small enclosure and, thus, distant from the walls of the larger room and the feature, whereas in our studies 2 and 3 it was located in a corner of the larger room adjacent to the walls. The basic results are summarized in table 3.1, which also lists the results of Hermer and Spelke (1994, 1996) and Learmonth et al. (2001).

There are several interesting inferences that can be made from table 3.1. First, the possibility of easy physical action seems to be important. When it is restricted, we see that success in using features to find the hidden

Table 3.1 How Task Variations Affect the Age at Which Colored Walls as Well as Geometry Are Used to Reorient

	Colored Wall Distant?	Action Possible?	Target Adjacent to Space with Colored Wall?	Age at First Feature Use
Hermer and Spelke (1994, 1996)	No	No	Yes	6 years
Learmonth et al. (2001)	Yes	Yes	Yes	18 months
Study 1	Yes	No	No	6 years
Studies 2 and 3	Yes	No	Yes	4 years

toy occurs at a later age. Specifically, the contrast between the work of Learmonth et al. (2001, 2002) and studies 2 and 3 is instructive. The only element of these paradigms that varies is whether or not action is restricted, and as a function of this fact, the age at which use of features is first evident varies from 18 months when action is possible to 4 years when it is not. Second, whether the colored wall is distal or proximal also makes a difference. The age of successful use of features was 6 years in the studies of Hermer and Spelke (1994, 1996) but only 4 years in studies 2 and 3; these studies differ only in how far away the colored wall is from the child. Third, another factor that makes a difference is whether or not the target is adjacent to the space in which there is one colored wall. The age at which use of features was first observed was reduced from 6 years in study 1, when the target was hidden in a corner of the unfeatured central enclosure, to 4 years in studies 2 and 3, when targets were proximal to the space in which one wall was colored. In short, both of the factors that we hypothesized might account for the room size effect have an influence, and a third factor has been identified that has an effect, as well. In addition, we note that there is nothing privileged about the 5- to 6-year transition seen in the studies of Hermer and Spelke (1994, 1996). The bottom line of table 3.1 shows that a sudden transition to use of features occurred between the ages of 3 and 4 years. Along similar lines, Hupbach and Nadel (2005) found a transition at this age to use of both features and geometry in a rhombus-shaped enclosure. Such earlier transitions, before the acquisition of the terms "left" and "right," further weakens the case for the unique importance of the acquisition of spatial language. In addition, the fact that transitions vary depending on contextual factors suggests the overall inadequacy of a modular view.

3.3.3 No Unique Effect of Verbal Interference in Human Adults

Given the strong evidence against a modularity-plus-language view that we have reviewed so far, why do adults *not* use nongeometric landmarks when they are engaged in a verbal interference task? We suggest that there are two possible ways to explain these results. First, in the Hermer-Vazquez et al. (1999) study, adults were simply informed prior to the disorientation procedure that "you will see something happening that you should try to notice" and that they would be asked about what they saw. After these vague instructions, and with no practice trials, participants engaged in the search task with concurrent shadowing in a rectangular room with a blue wall, followed by search without shadowing in that room and by search in an all-white room. Order was not counterbalanced. It is possible that, if given a clearer idea of the demands of the reorientation task, adult participants would search the correct corner at greater than chance levels *even while* engaged in verbal shadowing. Second, the verbal shadowing task used by Hermer-Vazquez et al. (1999) might disrupt the ability to use featural landmarks for reasons other than (or in addition to) interference with a linguistic encoding process. Another possibility is that a concurrent task reduces the ability to integrate various kinds of spatial information. Hermer-Vazquez et al. (1999) had used a nonverbal rhythm-clapping task to argue against this possibility, but this control might be inadequate because it would be expected to engage different processing mechanisms than those involved in combining types of spatial information (Newcombe, 2005).

To examine these possibilities, Ratliff and Newcombe (2005) conducted several studies using Hermer-Vazquez et al.'s (1999) dual-task paradigm, with and without modifications. With regard to the issue of understanding task demands, we found that adults who received explicit instructions as to the nature of the search task successfully integrated the nongeometric and geometric information in a rectangular white room with one blue wall, even while engaged in a verbal interference task. By contrast, adults who received the Hermer-Vazquez et al. (1999) task exactly as they gave it found the correct corner significantly less often. The elimination of the shadowing effect with modest additional information concerning the task undermines the idea that language is absolutely necessary to the use of features to reorient.

A second issue is whether a nonverbal *spatial* interference task would impair the use of features for reorientation. Ratliff and Newcombe (2005) asked adults to perform the reorientation task while simultaneously engaging in a visual-imagery task based on a design by Brooks (1968). The spatial visualizing task significantly reduced adults' ability to use the blue wall. If language were necessary to the use of features, this task should have had no effect.

3.3.4 Interim Summary

Overall, these results provide substantial evidence that human and nonhuman animals use both geometric and nongeometric information to reestablish orientation to the environment. There is little evidence for an encapsulation of geometric information and perhaps even weaker evidence for the role of language in overcoming "encapsulation." Nevertheless, there are still some significant puzzles regarding the interrelations between geometric and featural information. First, is it the case that geometric information is primary? As we have seen, features fail to be used in some situations, such as the case of young children in a very small room, but geometry seems to always be a part of the picture. Does this mean that geometric information is always more important than nongeometric information, with the latter added as a luxury or as a second step? Similarly, errors in the studies we have examined are overwhelmingly directed to the geometrically congruent corner, not to a featurally specified corner (i.e., the corner made by a colored and a white wall coming together with the opposite relation of short and long from the correct corner). Why do geometric errors predominate? Does their predominance indicate the greater importance of geometric information and its possible primary nature? Second, the findings we have reviewed undermine the modularity-plus-language view, but they do not themselves directly answer the question of what framework should supplant that view or how to account for the development we see. We turn now to an adaptive combination perspective, which we think can provide a way to think about both issues.

3.4 ADAPTIVE COMBINATION OF SPATIAL INFORMATION

As described above, adaptive combination models suggest that the certainty and variability of the encoding of various sources of information regarding location (or anything else) determines the weight placed on the different kinds of information. Information that is less variable and more certain is more likely to be used. In addition, we noted that salience and learning history are likely also important determinants of weighting. We now turn to examining whether thinking in these terms is helpful in understanding the relatively greater reliance apparently placed on geometric than on featural information in many situations. We argue that many of the paradigms used in studies considered so far have presented geometric information that is easily encoded with great certainty and minimum variability, and that is highly salient. These situations have, in addition, often used featural information that would be expected to be encoded with more variability or that is low in salience. Thus, we have been assessing situations in which geometric information could be expected to predominate. We go on to consider how an adaptive combination perspective helps us answer the question of mapping developmental change in spatial reorientation performance.

3.4.1 Why Does Geometric Information Seem to Predominate?

A fully enclosed and regular shape can be encoded with great certainty and little if any variability. After all, the full enclosure completely and unambiguously specifies the shape, and no other shapes are possible that are consistent with the perceptually available information. But such spaces are extremely uncommon in the natural environment. Typically, although clearly there is variation across ecologies, geometric information will occur in the form of separated aspects of the surround. For example, there might be a cliff face in the distance, a stream closer by, and a rock or a tree trunk in the immediate vicinity. Thus, a key question regarding geometric sensitivity is whether it is exhibited in cases where shape is partial and fragmentary—suggested rather than completely displayed. In this case, one may argue that geometric information is uncertain and variable, because there is always more than one geometric form that is consistent with the available evidence when there are gaps in the surrounding space.

The evidence on the use of geometric information when there is not complete enclosure suggests that geometry is less powerful in this case. For example, although Benhamou and Poucet (1998) found that rats could use the geometry of three distinct landmarks arranged in an isosceles triangle to swim to a hidden platform, rats took longer to learn in this situation than in a typical swimming pool task in which cues surrounding the pool are available (Poucet, Lenck-Santini, & Save, 2003). Similarly, in studies with children where shape has been defined by objects placed at the vertices of a triangle or rectangle, it has been difficult to find evidence for early use of geometry in reorientation work (Gouteux & Spelke, 2001; but see Garrad-Cole, Lew, Bremner, & Whitaker, 2001). In mapping studies, use of geometry is greatly reduced when figures are specified by dashes rather than complete lines, and even more when the figures are indicated only by their vertices (Vasilyeva, 2005). In studies where participants look at a space from the outside rather than being enclosed by it, use of geometry is also reduced (Gouteux, Vauclair, & Thinus-Blanc, 2001; Hupbach & Nadel, 2005; Huttenlocher & Vasilyeva, 2003).[4] One reason for this reduction may be that geometric information is more distinctive when viewed from inside a space, as shown in figure 3.3.

Although we have some evidence of the effect of incomplete enclosure on use of geometry, there are additional ways in which geometry may not be as powerful as hitherto estimated. First, geometry is importantly concerned with angles as well as with length. Acquisition of the ability to use angular information to reorient appears several years after the ability to use relative length (Hupbach & Nadel, 2005), suggesting that geometric information is not always used by very young children. Second, the salience of geometric information from relative length might be expected to vary with the ratio of long and short walls, or with the number of walls, two variables that have never been systematically manipulated.

In contrast to the use of a very strong kind of geometric information, many experiments have used features that could be predicted to be encoded

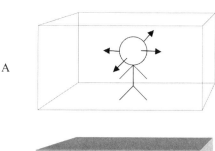

A

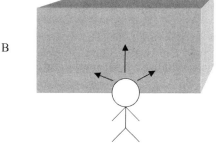

B

Figure 3.3 When an observer is inside a space (as in A) as opposed to viewing an enclosure from outside (as in B), the geometry of the space is more distinct, as defined by angles of observation. Adapted from Huttenlocher and Vasilyeva (2003).

variably. One of the most notable examples concerns whether the features are distal or proximal. The location of a distal feature can be encoded with more certainty than the location of a proximal feature, because movement around a local area creates only small variations in the location of the distal feature but very large variations in the location of a local feature. We have already seen the importance of the distal versus proximal variable in the room-in-room studies, and there is further evidence of its importance from recent work with nonhuman animals. Fish make relatively more geometric errors when trained in a small tank and more feature errors when trained in a large tank (Sovrano, Bisazza, & Vallortigara, 2005). Similarly, chicks faced with conflicting geometric and featural cues relied on geometry to reorient in a small enclosure but used features to a greater extent in a larger environment (Sovrano & Vallortigara, 2006; Vallortigara, Feruglio, & Sovrano, 2005).

Additional variables affect the likelihood of using features. When their location is variable, features can be expected to be less relied on, and the presence of features has sometimes been varied within a single session for a single participant (e.g., Hermer & Spelke, 1996), thereby introducing a lack of certainty in encoding. In addition, experimenters have occasionally used small objects as features, which creates uncertainty because such objects frequently move with respect to target locations and hence will have a variable history of usefulness. Confirming the importance of size, Gouteux, Thinus-Blanc, and Vauclair (2001) in fact found that monkeys were more likely to use larger than smaller features to reorient. It may be argued that a colored wall, if present throughout a session, presents powerful featural information—yet consider the fact that the affordance of the wall is to prevent movement or the possibility of seeing the external world, and that the color is irrelevant to that affordance. That is, the affordance of the surface may dominate its color in encoding.

In short, research so far has mainly examined the relative use of geometry and features in situations in which geometry is instantiated in a very powerful fashion and features are less powerfully instantiated. The adaptive combination point of view would predict that reliance on geometric information will be proportionately reduced as gaps are introduced, as complexity of the shape is increased, as regularity of the shape is reduced, and as enclosure is eliminated. The adaptive combination view also predicts that reliance on featural information will increase as features are more distant, larger, and invariantly present.

This perspective also helps to understand some otherwise puzzling results concerning overshadowing (and the lack thereof) in spatial reorientation studies. Beacons (i.e., landmarks right at the target location) typically overshadow other landmarks in spatial learning; that is, the spatial relations of the other landmarks to a target are not learned if a beacon suffices to find the target. This result has been obtained in a wide variety of species (Biegler & Morris, 1999; Diez-Chamizo, Sterio, & Mackintosh, 1985; Roberts & Pearce, 1999; Rodrigo, Chamizo, McLaren, & Mackintosh, 1997; Spetch,

1995). However, beacons do *not* seem to overshadow learning of geometry, again in a wide variety of species (Hayward, McGregor, Good, & Pearce, 2003; Kelly et al., 1998; Pearce, Ward-Robinson, Good, Fussell, & Aydin, 2001; Sovrano et al., 2003; Tommasi & Vallortigara, 2000; Wall, Botly, Black, & Shettleworth, 2004). This obligatory processing of geometry has sometimes been seen as evidence for some form of modularity. However, there is another interpretation. We know that biologically salient stimuli are not subject to cue competition in some forms of learning (e.g., classical conditioning), although less salient stimuli are (Denniston, Miller, & Matute, 1996; Miller & Matute, 1996). Similarly, geometric information may be immune from overshadowing in situations in which it is very salient, that is, instantiated with maximum power and minimum uncertainty.

3.4.2 Explaining the Development of Reorientation

Development of spatial reorientation capabilities may be conceptualized as the acquisition of the ability to encode relevant aspects of the environment with precision, and the learning of an optimal mix of weights to attach to these kinds of environmental information based on their past usefulness. By 18 months, the youngest age so far studied in the reorientation studies, children clearly have the ability to encode both geometric and featural information (Newcombe & Huttenlocher, 2000). But their acquisition of an optimal mix of information clearly consumes some time during development. In figure 3.2, the basic pattern appears to be the increased use of features, with geometry present from the start. (The developmental function looks different in large versus small rooms, both in timing of when features begin to be used and in the abruptness of age-related change, and yet features do seem less powerful in both contexts.) But this pattern of developmental change may not be inevitable; it may depend instead on the environments in which human children are currently raised.

We may imagine that human infants seek to orient and reorient themselves repeatedly, using whatever information is available. Some pieces of information might prove completely irrelevant. Other kinds of information may be very difficult to use due to the lack of specificity with which they can be encoded. For example, odors are difficult to localize, at least for our species. Over time, repeated experiences of this kind establish weightings of the likelihood of use and/or the extent of reliance on different kinds of information based on their certainty and their history of usefulness (or cue validity). In this view, geometry predominates early in human development because it has been experienced repeatedly in almost every environment that babies are in—parks and forests are infrequent experiences in modern society compared to cars and cribs and rooms. Features of the most useful kind—distant ones—are less frequently available in these enclosed environments. Further, when children are outside, they may not be allowed to roam as freely as would be necessary to engage their orientation skills and afford them the experiences of locating targets using distant features.

The most powerful evidence for this idea so far comes from a recent report showing that features overshadow geometry learning for wild-caught mountain chickadees that have spent very little time in enclosed rectilinear environments (Gray, Bloomfield, Ferrey, Spetch, & Sturdy, 2005). The chickadees *can* use geometry when it is the only information available, but they rely on it to a reduced extent than do other (domesticated) organisms studied so far. Additional suggestive support for this idea comes from the fact that training history has been shown to affect reliance on features versus geometry (pigeons: Kelly et al., 1998; but see also Kelly & Spetch, 2004; humans: Kelly & Bischof, 2005) and that, as we have seen, size of the surrounding environment affects the relative power of geometry and features.

3.5 CONCLUSION

The modularity-plus-language position presents a view in which an innate module remains unchanged in development, supplemented at some point by language. We have argued that this position cannot account for the available data and have proposed an adaptive combination framework as an alternative. This framework is actually a general one that could be applied to many lines of development, both in the spatial domain and in other domains. The adaptive combination approach provides an account of why some sources of information are weighted more heavily than others in many lines of cognitive development, including the task of determining orientation, and suggests an account of development that stresses the acquisition of a dynamically changing mix of use of various information sources. Changes in this mix are likely to be importantly affected by children's history of spatial action, to be conditioned by their motor development and their socially supported opportunities for exploration, and to be affected by the characteristics of the environment with which they interact. Future research can explore specific hypotheses generated by this framework. In this chapter, we have identified some important themes, including systematic variation of the certainty and variability of different kinds of information, as well as their perceptual salience and their cue validity (or learning history). Cue validity can be investigated through within-experiment manipulation or, excitingly, through altering rearing history (in research with nonhuman animals, e.g., the mountain chickadee). Investigations along these lines have the promise of yielding detailed insights into the fine-grained process of developmental change.

NOTES

1. Interestingly, proponents of culturally centered views of human development have often cited Spelke's arguments on this topic with approval while simultaneously arguing vociferously against nativism—a paradoxical juxtaposition (e.g., Levinson, 2003; see Newcombe, 2005).

2. Fodor (1983) agreed that a system could be domain specific but unencapsulated. But he also argued that a domain-general system could, at least in theory, be

encapsulated, noting that a system of this kind might "give some answer to any question; but it gives its answers off the top of its head—for instance, by reference to less than all the relevant information" (p. 104). However, he considered this possibility unlikely—as indeed it would seem to be!

3. To quote Fodor (1983) again, "If input analysis is modular . . . you might expect a kind of brain in which there is stable neural architecture associated with perception-and-language" (p. 118). With respect to the geometric module hypothesis, some neuroimaging work has in fact suggested that an area of the brain that has been termed the parahippocampal place area preferentially processes information about the shape of surrounding spaces (Epstein, DeYoe, Press, Rosen, & Kanwisher, 2001; Epstein, Graham, & Downing, 2003; Epstein & Kanwisher, 1998). However, other investigators disagree about this specialization (Maguire, Burgess, et al., 1998; Maguire, Frith, Burgess, Donnett, & O'Keefe, 1998).

4. While one possible objection to the data on use of geometry when viewed from outside a space is that the geometric module only operates when one is within the space (Wang & Spelke, 2002), the fact that geometry is used at all in this situation suggests that what is happening is not the engagement versus lack of engagement of a module but rather a weakened reliance on, or probability of use of, an information source.

REFERENCES

Akhtar, N. (2004). Nativist versus constructivist goals in studying child language. *Journal of Child Language*, *31*, 459–462.

Banks, M. S. (2005). The benefits and costs of combining information between and within senses. In J. J. Rieser, J. J. Lockman, & C. A. Nelson (Eds.), *Minnesota symposia on child psychology: Vol. 33. Action as an organizer of learning and development* (pp. 161–198). Mahwah, NJ: Lawrence Erlbaum.

Benhamou, S., & Poucet, B. (1998). Landmark use by navigating rats (*Rattus norvegicus*) contrasting geometric and featural information. *Journal of Comparative Psychology*, *112*, 317–322.

Bertenthal, B. I. (2005). Theory, methods, and models: A discussion of the chapters by Newcombe and Thelen & Whitmyer. In J. J. Rieser, J. J. Lockman, & C. A. Nelson (Eds.), *Minnesota symposia on child psychology: Vol. 33. Action as an organizer of learning and development* (pp. 281–298). Mahwah, NJ: Lawrence Erlbaum.

Biegler, R., & Morris, R. G. (1999). Blocking in the spatial domain with arrays of discrete landmarks. *Journal of Experimental Psychology: Animal Behavior Processes*, *25*, 334–351.

Brooks, L. (1968). Spatial and verbal components of the act of recall. *Canadian Journal of Psychology*, *22*, 349–368.

Buller, D. J. (2005). *Adapting minds*. Cambridge, MA: MIT Press.

Cheng, K. (1986). A purely geometric model in rat's spatial representation. *Cognition*, *23*, 149–178.

Cheng, K., & Newcombe, N. (2005). Is there a geometric module for spatial orientation? Squaring theory and evidence. *Psychonomic Bulletin & Review*, *12*, 1–23.

Cosmides, L., & Tooby, J. (1992). Cognitive adaptations for social exchange. In J. H. Barkow et al. (Eds.), *The adapted mind: Evolutionary psychology and the generation of culture* (pp. 163–228). New York: Oxford University Press.

Denniston, J. C., Miller, R. R., & Matute, H. (1996). Biological significance as a determinant of cue competition. *Psychological Science*, *7*, 325–331.

Diez-Chamizo, V., Sterio, D., & Mackintosh, N. J. (1985). Blocking and overshadowing between intramaze and extra-maze cues: a test of the independence of locale and guidance learning. *Quarterly Journal of Experimental Psychology. B, Comparative & Physiological Psychology, 37*, 235–253.

Elman, J. L., Bates, E. A., Johnson, M. H., Karmiloff-Smith, A., Parisi, D., & Plunkett, K. (1996). *Rethinking innateness: A connectionist perspective on development*. Cambridge, MA: MIT Press.

Epstein, R., DeYoe, E. A., Press, D. Z., Rosen, A. C., & Kanwisher, N. (2001). Neuropsychological evidence for a topographical learning mechanism in parahippocampal cortex. *Cognitive Neuropsychology, 18*, 481–508.

Epstein, R., Graham, K. S., & Downing, P. E. (2003). Viewpoint-specific scene representations in human parahippocampal cortex. *Neuron, 37*, 865–876.

Epstein, R., & Kanwisher, N. (1998). A cortical representation of the local visual environment. *Nature, 392*, 598–601.

Ernst, M., & Banks, M. (2002). Humans integrate visual and haptic information in a statistically optimal way. *Nature, 415*, 429–433.

Fischer, A. & Araya, R. (2001, October 28). Interview with Leda Cosmides. Retrieved October 25, 2006, from http://www.psych.ucsb.edu/research/cep/ledainterview.htm.

Fodor, J. A. (1983). *Modularity of mind: An essay on faculty psychology*. Cambridge, MA: MIT Press.

Fodor, J. A. (2001). *The mind doesn't work that way: The scope and limits of computational psychology*. Cambridge, MA: MIT Press.

Gallistel, C. (1990). *The organization of learning*. Cambridge, MA: MIT Press.

Garrad-Cole, F., Lew, A. R., Bremner, J. G., & Whitaker, C. J. (2001). Use of cue configuration geometry for spatial orientation in human infants (*Homo sapiens*). *Journal of Comparative Psychology, 115*, 317–320.

Gouteux, S., & Spelke, E. S. (2001). Children's use of geometry and landmarks to reorient in an open space. *Cognition, 81*, 119–148.

Gouteux, S., Thinus-Blanc, C., & Vauclair, J. (2001). Rhesus monkeys use geometric and nongeometric information during a reorientation task. *Experimental Psychology: General, 130*, 505–519.

Gouteux, S., Vauclair, J., & Thinus-Blanc, C. (2001). Reorientation in a small-scale environment by 3-, 4-, and 5-year-old children. *Cognitive Development, 16*, 853–869.

Gray, E. R., Bloomfield, L. L., Ferrey, A., Spetch, M. L., & Sturdy, C. B. (2005). Spatial encoding in mountain chickadees: Features overshadow geometry. *Biology Letters, 1*, 314–317.

Hartley, T., Trinkler, I., & Burgess, N. (2004). Geometric determinants of human spatial memory. *Cognition, 94*, 39–75.

Hayward, A., McGregor, A., Good, M. A., & Pearce, J. M. (2003). Absence of overshadowing and blocking between landmarks and the geometric cues provided by the shape of a test arena. *Quarterly Journal of Experimental Psychology. B, Comparative & Physiological Psychology, 56*, 114–126.

Hermer, L., & Spelke, E. (1994). A geometric process for spatial reorientation in young children. *Nature, 370*, 57–59.

Hermer, L., & Spelke, E. (1996). Modularity and development: The case of spatial reorientation. *Cognition, 61*, 195–232.

Hermer-Vazquez, L., Moffet, A., & Munkholm, P. (2001). Language, space, and the development of cognitive flexibility in humans: The case of two spatial memory tasks. *Cognition, 79*, 263–299.

Hermer-Vazquez, L., Spelke, E., & Katsnelson, A. (1999). Sources of flexibility in human cognition: Dual task studies of space and language. *Cognitive Psychology*, *39*, 3–36.

Hupbach, A., & Nadel, L. (2005). Reorientation in a rhombic environment: No evidence for an encapsulated geometric module. *Cognitive Development*, *20*, 279–302.

Huttenlocher, J., Hedges, L. V., & Duncan, S. (1991). Categories and particulars: Prototype effects in estimating spatial location. *Psychological Review*, *98*, 352–376.

Huttenlocher, J., Newcombe, N. S., & Sandberg, E. H. (1994). The coding of spatial location in young children. *Cognitive Psychology*, *27*, 115–148.

Huttenlocher, J., & Vasilyeva, M. (2003). How toddlers represent enclosed spaces. *Cognitive Science*, *27*, 749–766.

Johnson, S. (2004). *Mind wide open: Your brain and the neuroscience of everyday life*. New York: Scribner.

Karmiloff-Smith, A. (1992). *Beyond modularity: A developmental perspective on cognitive science*. Cambridge, MA: MIT Press.

Kelly, D., & Bischof, W. (2005). Reorienting in images of a 3-D rectangular environment. *Journal of Experimental Psychology: Human Perception & Performance*, *31*, 1391–1403.

Kelly, D., & Spetch, M. (2004). Reorientation in a two-dimensional environment: II. Do pigeons (*Columba livia*) encode the featural and geometric properties of a two-dimensional schematic of a room? *Journal of Comparative Psychology*, *118*, 384–395.

Kelly, D., Spetch, M., & Heth, C. (1998). Pigeons' encoding of geometric and featural properties of a spatial environment. *Journal of Comparative Psychology*, *112*, 259–269.

Learmonth, A., Nadel, L., & Newcombe, N. S. (2002). Children's use of landmarks: Implications for modularity theory. *Psychological Science*, *13*, 337–341.

Learmonth, A., Newcombe, N. S., Hansell, N., & Jones, M. (2005, October). *Action and reorientation ability: The role of restricted movement at 3 and 5 years*. Paper presented at the meeting of the Cognitive Development Society, San Diego, CA.

Learmonth, A., Newcombe, N. S., & Huttenlocher, J. (2001). Toddler's use of metric information and landmarks to reorient. *Journal of Experimental Child Psychology*, *80*, 225–244.

Levinson, S. C. (2003). *Space in language and cognition: Explorations in cognitive diversity*. Cambridge: Cambridge University Press.

Maguire, E., Burgess, N., Donnett, J., Frackowiak, R., Frith, C., & O'Keefe, J. (1998). Knowing where and getting there: A human navigation network. *Science*, *280*, 921–924.

Maguire, E. A., Frith, C. D., Burgess, N., Donnett, J. G., & O'Keefe, J. (1998). Knowing where things are: Parahippocampal involvement in encoding object locations in virtual large-scale space. *Journal of CognitiveNeuroscience*, *10*, 61–76.

Miller, R. R., & Matute, H. (1996). Biological significance in forward and backward blocking: Resolution of a discrepancy between animal conditioning and human causal judgment. *Journal of Experimental Psychology: General*, *125*, 370–386.

Nadel, L., & Hupbach, A. (2006). Cross-species comparisons in development: The case of the spatial "module." In M. H. Johnson & Y. Munakata (Eds.), *Attention and performance XXI*. Oxford: Oxford University Press.

Newcombe, N. S. (2002). The nativist-empiricist controversy in the context of recent research on spatial and quantitative development. *Psychological Science, 13,* 395–401.

Newcombe, N. S. (2005). Evidence for and against a geometric module: The roles of language and action. In J. J. Rieser, J. J. Lockman, & C. A. Nelson (Eds.), *Minnesota symposia on child psychology: Vol. 33. Action as an organizer of learning and development* (pp. 221–241). Mahwah, NJ: Lawrence Erlbaum.

Newcombe, N. S. (2005). Language as destiny? Or not. (Essay review of S. C. Levinson, *Space in language and cognition: Explorations in cognitive diversity*). *Human Development, 48,* 309–314.

Newcombe, N. S., & Huttenlocher, J. (2000). *Making space: The development of spatial representation and reasoning.* Cambridge, MA: MIT Press.

Newcombe, N. S., & Huttenlocher, J. (2006). Development of spatial cognition. In W. Damon & R. Lerner (Series Eds.) and D. Kuhn & R. Siegler (Vol. Eds.), *Handbook of child psychology: Vol. 2. Cognition, perception and language* (6th ed., pp. 734–776). Hoboken, NJ: John Wiley & Sons.

Pearce, J. M., Ward-Robinson, J., Good, M. A., Fussell, C., & Aydin, A. (2001). Influence of a beacon on spatial learning based on the shape of the test environment. *Journal of Experimental Psychology: Animal Behavior Processes, 27,* 329–344.

Pinker, S. (1997). *How the mind works.* New York: Norton.

Poucet, B., Lenck-Santini, P. P., & Save, E. (2003). Drawing parallels between the behavioral and neural properties of navigation. In K. J. Jeffery (Ed.), *The neurobiology of spatial behaviour* (pp. 187–198). Oxford: Oxford University Press.

Ratliff, K., & Newcombe, N. (2005). Human spatial reorientation using dual task paradigms. *Proceedings of the Annual Cognitive Science Society, 27,* 1809–1814.

Roberts, A. D. L., & Pearce, J. M. (1999). Blocking in the Morris swimming pool. *Journal of Experimental Psychology: Animal Behavior Processes, 25,* 225–235.

Rodrigo, T., Chamizo, V. D., McLaren, I. P. L., & Mackintosh, N. J. (1997). Blocking in the spatial domain. *Journal of Experimental Psychology: Animal Behavior Processes, 23,* 110–118.

Romanski, L. M. (2004). Domain specificity in the primate prefrontal cortex. *Cognitive, Affective, & Behavioral Neuroscience, 4,* 421–429.

Scholl, B. J., & Leslie, A. M. (1999). Modularity, development and "theory of mind." *Mind & Language, 14,* 131–153.

Seok, B. (2006). Diversity and unity of modularity. *Cognitive Science, 30,* 347–380.

Sovrano, V., Bisazza, A., & Vallortigara, G. (2005). Modularity as a fish (*Xenotoca eiseni*) views it: Conjoining geometric and nongeometric information for spatial reorientation. *Journal of Experimental Psychology: Animal Behavior Processes, 29,* 199–210.

Sovrano, V., Bisazza, A., & Vallortigara, G. (2005). Animals' use of landmarks and metric information to reorient: effects of the size of the experimental space. *Cognition, 97,* 122–133.

Sovrano, V. & Vallortigara, G. (2006). Dissecting the geometric module: A sense-linkage for metric and landmark information in animals' spatial reorientation. *Psychological Science.*

Sperber, D. (1994). The modularity of thought and the epidemiology of representations. In L. A. Hirschfeld & S. A. Gelman (Eds.), *Mapping the mind: Domain specificity in cognition and culture* (pp. 39–67). New York: Cambridge University Press.

Spetch, M. L. (1995). Overshadowing in landmark learning: Touch-screen studies with pigeons and humans. *Journal of Experimental Psychology: Animal Behavior Processes*, *21*, 166–181.

Tommasi, L., & Vallortigara, G. (2000). Searching for the center: Spatial cognition in the domestic chick (*Gallus gallus*). *Journal of Experimental Psychology: Animal Behavior*, *26*, 477–486.

Vallortigara, G., Feruglio, M., & Sovrano, V. (2005). Reorientation by geometric and landmark information in environments of different size. *Developmental Science*, *8*, 393–401.

Vallortigara, G., Zanforlin, M., & Pasti, G. (1990). Geometric modules in animal spatial representations: a test with chicks (*Gallus gallus*). *Journal of Comparative Psychology*, *104*, 248–254.

Vasilyeva, M. (2005, April). *Early ability to use geometric information on mapping tasks*. Paper presented at the meeting of the Society for Research in Child Development, Atlanta, GA.

Wall, P. L., Botly, L. C. P., Black, C. K., & Shettleworth, S. J. (2004). The geometric module in the rat: Independence of shape and feature learning in a food finding task. *Learning & Behavior*, *32*, 289–298.

Wang, R., & Spelke, E. (2002). Human spatial representation: Insights from animals. *Trends in Cognitive Sciences*, *6*, 376–382.

4

USING LOCOMOTION TO UPDATE SPATIAL ORIENTATION
What Changes with Learning and Development?

JOHN J. RIESER & HERBERT L. PICK, JR.

Spatial orientation is dynamic. When mobile organisms locomote, their perspectives rotate and translate such that their self-to-object distances and directions change in ways tightly coupled with their locomotion. The need to keep up-to-date on such changes is ubiquitous across widely ranging situations. When people walk in lighted places with portions of their surroundings in view, locomotion is visually guided and dynamic changes in spatial orientation are at least partially visible. However, even when locomotion is visually guided, the changes in spatial orientation are never totally visible, since people cannot see things that have passed out of their field of view or have become occluded by walls or other barriers. In addition, people often locomote "blind" because they cannot see or they walk with eyes closed or in the dark. When people walk "blind," they typically keep up-to-date on dynamic changes in their spatial orientation by using information associated with their locomotion.

This chapter focuses on human spatial orientation and how it changes with learning and development. We take a central problem to be how people keep up-to-date on their dynamically changing spatial orientation when they locomote actively, by crawling, walking, running, or biking, or when they locomote more passively, by being carried in someone's arms or by traveling as a pilot or passenger on a sailboat, plane, train, or automobile. Many of the same principles apply whenever one is actively or passively exploring the surroundings with eyes open or eyes closed, when one is recalling surroundings from earlier experiences, when one is fantasizing surroundings constructed from stories or imagination, or when one is watching simulated virtual surroundings.

The chapter begins with a brief historical overview of techniques and devices that people have used over the centuries for navigation, which serves to distinguish the major problems involved in maintaining spatial orientation during self-movement. We then develop our thesis in four parts. In section 2, we present definitions and concepts that create the framework of our theory that action, perception, and representation are coupled together as a functionally organized system. In section 3, we spell out our theory and sketch some of the empirical reasons why we think it is a good way to characterize and explain how adults use movement to update spatial orientation. Section 4 illustrates the application of our model to the development of using movement information to update position. The section begins with a description of the normative development of updating during the early years of life. We suggest that the perception–action–representation system does not emerge as an integrated whole, but instead emerges in pieces that originate in action-specific forms of learning. Section 4 ends by considering the development of this system without a life history of visual experience or with impaired vision. We conclude in section 5 by discussing some of the more general implications of our views, for action, perception, and representation across a wide range of activities, and describe two different ways the functional organization of the system might emerge during learning and development.

4.1 HISTORICAL INTRODUCTION
OF NAVIGATIONAL SKILLS

Maintaining spatial orientation during self-movement is an ancient problem. Archeological evidence indicates that our ancestors roamed across the plains, among the mountains, and through the jungles. They could find their way to sources of food and water and back again to home. Clearly, they must have kept track of where they were. There are no records of how they did this, but logically their methods must have included strategies for estimating or sensing changes in distance and in direction.

It was not until much later and in connection with sea travel that there are records about how such spatial orientation was accomplished. The problem remains the same, determining direction and distance traveled. With sea travel, the problem of determining distance and direction can be subdivided, since in some situations environmental cues are present and in others they are absent. For example, environmental cues are available when traveling along a coast, so in good weather the direction of points of interest is visually available, as is the progression of landmarks or distance traveled. Staying oriented by such information is referred to in modern parlance as piloting. Even when out of sight of land, environmental information can still be available, at least for direction, from relatively far distance. This is the case in using the direction of stars as in celestial navigation. The navigational systems of different traditional cultures exploit stars for directional information. A beautiful example is that of traditional Micronesian navigators sailing their outrigger canoes on long journeys in the South Pacific. They take advantage of the fact that particular stars always rise in the same direction on the horizon. As any particular star rises, it is followed by another star appearing on the horizon in about the same direction, resulting in a series of stars moving successively across the sky in an arc. The sky path of such a sequence of stars is called a linear constellation. Such a linear constellation can always provide information about one's direction of travel (for more complete discussions, see Gladwin, 1970; Hutchins, 1995).

Stars are not always visible (e.g., in the daytime or when it is cloudy), and then direction must be determined by different means. The magnetic compass served well for this purpose beginning about the twelfth century. When out of sight of land, distance traversed is not quite as easily solved, and travelers must use different means than progression based on landmarks. Of course, sailors have an intuitive sense of speed based on their experience with the strength of wind and how their ship progresses when landmarks are in sight. However, their intuitive sense is only approximately correct. A somewhat more definitive method came into practice by the sixteenth century. This was known as the chip log method. A chip of a log was tied to a rope and dropped over the stern of the ship. The rope was paid out as the ship moved on, away from the log chip, which remained essentially stationary in the water. The time taken for a specific length of rope to be paid out provided a means for estimating the ship's speed. (The length of paid-out rope was indicated by knots tied in the rope, which is the origin of use of the term "knot" for specifying nautical speeds.) Once the ship's speed was measured, distance of travel was determined by how long one sailed at that speed.

By keeping track of distances sailed in various directions, it was possible to estimate the distance and direction of one's home port or other known locations even though they were out of sight. This process of integrating direction and distance of movement over time came to be called dead reckoning, a variation of the term "deduced reckoning." Keeping track of this information for extended periods of time became a problem in itself. One technique that worked for a period of a few hours involved a device called a *toleta* or traverse board. This was essentially a round pegboard on which pegs could be inserted at various angles around the center indicating direction of travel, with distance from the center indicating distance traveled in that direction. Distances beyond that shown on the traverse board needed to be transcribed into a logbook. It is interesting to note that Columbus' logbook strongly suggests that he used such dead reckoning to navigate in his voyages to America (Cohen, 1992).

Another way to keep track of travel information is to use maps or navigational charts. To the extent that the chart is accurate, this is a useful way to represent where one is. Map making has a very long history. One early and persistent problem was how to represent the spherical surface of the earth on a two-dimensional planar surface. One solution is the Mercator projection, developed in the sixteenth century. (This is a method of map making in which earth's surface is represented as rectangular; the meridians are drawn equidistant and parallel to each other. The distance between parallels increases with distance from equator.) The Mercator projection has the disadvantage of distorting sizes and shapes of land masses and sea areas, but for navigational purposes it has the advantage that straight lines between two points on the chart would yield a constant angle or course that could be steered on the ocean to go from one location to another. The general idea of representing spatial layouts by means of two-dimensional maps became extremely common. It became so common that when psychologists and others began to think about how spatial information was mentally represented, they coined the term "cognitive map" (Tolman, 1948). However, there may be a cost to this analogy because it tends to reify the mental representation in a way that can be misleading.

4.2 BASIC CONCEPTS AND DEFINITIONS

The same fundamental problems of navigation and spatial orientation exist for more ordinary, day-to-day activities, ranging from reaching across a table to attain an object, to finding one's way from building to building or across a city or region. In this section, we elaborate this assertion in the context of specifying our basic definitions and concepts, using the example of the activity of locomotion.

4.2.1 Locomotion

It is useful to conceive of locomotion as both an action (it serves to change position and facing direction), and as an event that is perceived in terms of its speed, direction, and distance (or in other words, a change in spatial orientation). The action and perceptual event of locomotion occur in different situations and time frames (Rieser & Pick, 2002). For example, it involves short-range guidance to steer around obstacles in one's immediate surroundings and longer range guidance to find one's way to faraway destinations. As with both of these types of guidance, most goals of locomotion are embedded in the surrounding environment, and it makes sense that the perceptual representation of locomotion is generally embedded in the near-by or farther-flung surrounding environment and that people perceive their location relative to one or more features of the surrounding environment as a frame of reference. We assume that the perception of location includes the viewer's distances and/or directions relative to one or more of the environmental features.

What information is available for guiding locomotion? People move from place to place in many ways. Some movements are active, in the sense that people move actively under their own steam (whether by bipedal locomotion when walking on foot or skating or biking, or quadripedal locomotion when crawling), and other movements are passive, such as when a person is a passenger aboard a train, plane, or car. Of course, there are intermediate forms of locomotion, such as when one drives a car or pilots a ship. Active and passive forms of locomotion alike result in afferent information that specifies one's movement, but only active forms involve *efference*, which directs the movements, and *efference-copy*, which enables the comparison of the actual feedback with the expected feedback based on the action plan (von Holst & Mittelstaedt 1950).

Afferent information originates from different sense modalities—for example, input from joint, muscle, and vestibular senses likely specifies movement in body-centered terms, which can in turn be integrated in environmental terms. Quite likely, the availability of different sources of information changes with development. Younger infants can look around but cannot locomote in order to reach distal goals. Thus, like the early navigators, they can register direction of objects in view, but unlike the navigators, they cannot guide locomotion. What is it, we wonder, that prelocomotor infants know about their dynamic spatial orientation when they are carried passively from place to place?

Thinking along these lines, we distinguish rotational locomotion (Pick, Rieser, Wagner, & Garing, 1999) and translational locomotion (Rieser, Pick, Ashmead, & Garing, 1995). By *rotational locomotion*, we mean turning in place. Here the informational result is a rotation in perspective, such that the self-to-object distances do not change at all and the directions of all objects change at the same rate. By *translational locomotion*, we mean moving along any straight line to reach a new location. The informational result is a translation in perspective, such that the self-to-object distances and directions all change at different rates, depending on their distance and direction relative to the person's direction of locomotion. Rotations in perspective can be accomplished by looking around visually, and young infants have some capability of controlling rotations in their perspective. Translations in perspective primarily depend on achieving the capability to crawl, scoot, roll, or walk. Ordinarily, locomotion often consists of a combination of rotation and translation, for example, when walking a curved path.

It is important to note that theoretically locomotion, like any action, can be described in *kinematic* terms (i.e., in terms of the limb trajectories and velocities of different limbs in space and time), in *dynamic* terms (i.e., in terms of the spatiotemporal patterns of forces exerted to move the limbs along their trajectories), and in *environmental* terms (i.e., in terms of changes in the person's distance and directions relative to things in the perceived or remembered surrounding environment). In this chapter, we focus on describing locomotion in environmental terms.

4.2.2 Position and Frames of Reference

When locomoting, whether for purposes of steering or for wayfinding, the position of an obstacle or goal needs to be registered. Abstractly (and practically), position is defined in relation to a frame of reference. Two different frames of reference seem generally useful: a body-centered frame and an environment-centered frame (Pick, Yonas, & Rieser, 1979). By a *body-centered* frame of reference, we mean one that encodes the position of body parts relative to other body parts or encodes the position of the whole body relative to its own prior position(s). During locomotion, one can notice the position of the whole body and the distances and directions of locomotor movements relative to a series of earlier positions without reference to the environment. For rotational locomotion, for example, one can turn in the left or right direction, and distances can be encoded in terms of number and size of steps taken. For translational locomotion, one can move forward or backward, and distances can be encoded in anatomical units such as stride lengths or eye heights. For complex paths, one can encode the distance of the path as well as its intrinsic shape. In each of these cases, body positions and locomotor movements can be perceived and encoded in body-centered terms, and environmental position does not enter into the immediate perception. (While the relative position of two or more body parts may not be relevant to locomotion of the whole body through the environment, it is surely relevant to a broad range of human activity, e.g., whenever one slaps a mosquito, or when classical ballerinas move into first position with feet or arms. It is broadly useful in producing body gestures, facial expressions, and sign language. It is also relevant to the accomplishment of the locomotor motor act, e.g., cyclic positioning of the legs in walking.) It is important to note that limb position relative to the body as a frame of reference can be specified in multiple ways, resulting from inputs originating from vision, proprioceptive cues (i.e., sensory input via receptors) from joints, muscles, and the vestibular system (which is sensitive to acceleration in various directions), and movement cues that specify change from one body position to another position.

Locomotor movement using a body-centered frame of reference is analogous to the navigational dead reckoning referred to in the introduction. However, in both cases, the navigators' goal is that their dead reckoning has a correspondence to particular places in the environment. Consider two major goals of guiding human locomotion: steering around obstacles and potentially dangerous hazards in one's path of travel, and wayfinding to reach destinations that are not perceptually present. In both cases, it is useful to keep up-to-date on one's position relative to the immediate features of the surroundings (for steering) and relative to the farther away features of the environment (for wayfinding). By *environment-centered* frame of reference, we refer to the position of a body part or the position of the whole body in relation to some feature or features of the environment. Many actions—whether performed by eye, hand, or foot—are organized relative to objects in the surrounding environment. And they need to be up-dated to take into account the actor's locomotor movements, whether it is shifting one's gaze while on the run on a basketball court to stay focused on the goal, or shifting one's reach to answer the telephone while turning to greet a friend entering the office.

4.2.3 Perspective, Position, and Self-to-Object Distances and Directions

The terms "position" and "perspective" are used with different meanings across widely differing fields of the cognitive and social sciences. Following Gibson (1979), we reserve use of *perspective* to refer to the network of self-to-object distances and directions that is available at a given point of obser-vation. Gibson's definition of "perspective structure" contrasts with his definition of "invariant structure," that is, the object-to-object distances and directions, which do not vary with the changes in a person's perspective associated with moving from place to place.

From our point of view, most tasks of daily life are embedded in the surrounding environment and need to be coordinated with one's current self-to-object distances and directions, or to anticipate one's future perspec-tives. Mature spatial behavior in real time depends on coordinating one's ac-tions with a perspective that is updated in conjunction with locomotion and planning one's actions depending on anticipated changes in perspective.

4.2.4 Local and Global Frames of Reference for Perceiving and Knowing About Self-Movement

How is this perspective updated in conjunction with locomotion? Vision and hearing can specify self-movement relative to the body as a frame of reference and relative to the environment as a frame of reference. Body-centered visual and auditory flow information for self-movement naturally occur in many situations, for example, when walking in a snowstorm or in a dense forest. Here, only local optical and auditory flow cues would be available to specify instantaneous changes in speed and acceleration. The self-movement information is disembedded in the sense that it is not directly tied to places as defined by a global frame of reference. And indeed, in studies of sensitivity to optical flow specifying rotational and translational locomotion (Berthoz, 2000, Berthoz, Pavard, & Young, 1975; Warren, 1995), subjects were able to judge body-centered features of self-movement such as the direction and/or the speed of rotation and translation. Global geometrical cues provided, for example, by the walls of a room, the shape of the city road, or ridgelines in the forest would not be available. The optical and non-optical forms of environmental flow infor-mation relative to a very local frame of reference could not specify changes in "place" per se, but instead they could be integrated over space and time with a global frame of reference. (This is analogous to the use of dead reck-oning by navigators.) On the other hand, where a global frame of reference is available, obviously, one can see and hear directly how one is moving as in navigational piloting.

4.2.5 Updating, Spatial Knowledge, Representation, and Cognitive Maps

Whether adjusting posture to balance or locomoting to reach a target, it is important keep up-to-date on changes in position that result from moving part or all of the body. Updating likely occurs in different ways in different situations, depending on the information available in a given situation and depending on the capabilities of the person. Sometimes one can simply see (or hear) the target location and use visual (or auditory) feedback to reach it. Often, however, one cannot see the target directly—for example, when one has turned away or moved so that vision is occluded by obstacles. In situations such as these, one cannot use vision or other forms of sensory input alone to navigate to the goal, and instead, one needs to have knowledge of the goal's distance and direction relative to one's position, and coordinate one's locomotion with that knowledge. This knowledge is often referred to as a cognitive map. This chapter emphasizes situations where continuous visual or auditory information specifying one's position relative to the target is not directly available, and instead, locomotor actions need to be coordinated with knowledge of the goal's location.

People usually know a lot about the spatial properties of their immediate surroundings, and about their far-reaching surroundings, as well. In any given physical situation, some of what is known is specified by the various forms of sensory stimulation. However, even when in the physical situation, people sometimes are shut off from direct sensory input, so some of what they know reflects storage in a memory system. The temporal duration of this storage can vary widely, ranging, for example, from the instant of an eye blink, to walking to the bathroom in the dark of night, to wintertime's musings about summer's sailing, and to autobiographic memories of a lifetime with or without vision. This leads to the concept of representation of spatial information.

The term "representation" comes with numerous and more specific meanings than the term "knowledge," since at least the time of Piaget and Inhelder (1956) for the field of child development, and Mountcastle and Henneman (1952) and Hubel and Wiesel (1965) in the field of brain science. Consider three examples. First, in understanding vision, one issue is how the geometrical relations in the physical space are mapped onto the two-dimensional retina, and then, in turn, how they are perceived, understood, and remembered (e.g., Hubel & Wiesel, 1965). How well does vision preserve the Euclidean relations, that is, metric values for distances and directions connecting the observer to features of the surroundings and/or different features of the surroundings to each other?

Second, what are the types of knowledge that adults acquire when learning about a new place? Siegel and White (1975) hypothesized a learning sequence in which adults initially reconnoiter a place and notice the identities of various salient landmarks and features. Next, they notice and encode the particular sequence of landmarks they encounter during particular routes. Finally, they coordinate their knowledge derived from walked routes in order to notice and encode the Euclidean relations, that is, the object-to-object metric distances and directions in the spatial layout of landmarks and traveled routes, and the self-to-object distances and directions that span the duration of a complex route or various routes in a neighborhood.

Third, what kinds of developmental changes occur in children's understanding of space? Piaget and Inhelder (1956) and their followers (e.g., Laurendeau, 1970) theorized an age-related sequence. According to their theory, children first notice the relations defined by topological geometry (these include the names and sequential order along the exploratory walk). Next, they notice the relations defined by projective geometry (these include the number of sides of objects or turns in the route walked). Finally, they register the relations defined by Euclidean geometry (these includes the metric distances of angle and extent). For example, within topology, location can be specified in terms of landmarks (e.g., between landmarks A and B); in terms of projective geometry, location can be specified as along the straight line connecting two landmarks; and within Euclidean geometry, it can be specified as the distance and/or direction from two or more landmarks. However, we are concerned mainly with Euclidean relations, that is, how children keep up-to-date on their metric distance and direction relative to things in the surrounding environment.

4.2.6 Unified and Fragmented Instances of Spatial Knowledge

The term "cognitive map" typically refers to knowledge of landmarks, routes, distances, and directions that is spatially unified, tied together by the spatial frame of the map. But spatial knowledge of a given locale often results from the spatiotemporal integration of different types of information and comes in paths explored during episodes that are fragmented in space and time. For steering locomotion, people integrate dynamic optical flow cues with motor cues in order to steer around obstacles (Warren, Kay, Zosh, Duchon, & Sahue, 2001), and at least in some situations, the integration seems to involve an optimal weighting of the various cues (see Cheng, Shettleworth, Huttenlocher, & Rieser, 2006). An example of episodes that are fragmented in space and in time is exploration of different regions of the same neighborhood from one day to the next. Initially, it might be that knowledge of the different regions would stand alone, independent of knowledge of nearby regions, as suggested by Siegel and White (1975), but eventually for those who frequently find their way, the different regions become integrated into a unified whole. Montello and Pick (1993) demonstrated such integration across a short time span. We have little to say about processes that are extended like this across relatively long durations of time and large regions of space except to observe that probably complexity, and temporal or spatial duration per se are likely to make a difference (for a discussion of related issues, see chapter 10).

4.2.7 Learning and Development

With respect to locomotion, our point of view is that development consists of learning that is sometimes constrained differently at different ages. Different ages bring changes in endogenous characteristics such as limb size, visual acuity, and brain maturation; they bring changes in functional capabilities, for example, whether one can sit up or crawl or walk; and they bring changes in the goals that come with endogenous and functional changes. In this chapter, we emphasize age-related changes in motor capabilities and how these changes reasonably constrain a developing person's goals. Consider that young infants can reach for things and may remember very local spatial layout. Although infants undergo a lot of passive locomotion when they are carried from place to place, they cannot actively locomote to reach remembered targets; because of this, there seems to be little incentive to notice or remember the locations of things. That is, capabilities constrain goals.

4.3 PERCEPTION–ACTION–REPRESENTATION AS A FUNCTIONALLY ORGANIZED SYSTEM

Our view is that perception, action, and representation are coupled together as a functionally organized system with respect to perceiving space, acting in space, and learning and remembering space. Specific forms of action transform the structure of the actor's perspective of a visual scene in predictable ways, and transform the scene's *representation*, as well (Rieser, 1999). Consider, for example, how one's representation of a room changes when turning 90° with eyes closed versus walking forward with eyes closed. In this section, we provide a summary of the main features of our perception–action–representation model, spell out some of its main predictions for adult performance, and then consider how such a functional organization might emerge during learning and development.

4.3.1 Perception–Action Coupling

Action and perception are coupled together in the sense that they function to inform each other. People perceive in order to act (i.e., to know when, where, and how to direct their actions), and they act in order to perceive (i.e., to explore the properties of the objects, environments, or events that interest them). Importantly, motor actions cause predictable environmental consequences. A main feature of our model is that people are sensitive to and learn the perception–action correlations (through perceiving efferent and afferent features of their own actions and the perceptible environmental consequences of their actions) when they occur in the service of significant goals. Qualitatively different categories of perceptual event are correlated with functionally different forms of action. For example, postural control and body sway go with cyclical forward–backward or left–right optical flow, whereas turning in place goes with rotational flow, and going from place to place goes with translational flow (radial expansion if one is looking in the direction of locomotion). Throwing and kicking an object through space go with the object moving through a parabolic trajectory. And so forth. There is a fundamental issue as to the form of the perceptual events. Are they environmental consequences or correlated higher order perceptual properties, for instance, optical flow patterns? This question is addressed in the concluding section.

4.3.2 Representation–Action Coupling

Like action and perception, action and representation are coupled together, as well, which can be demonstrated whenever people coordinate the force and direction of their action with their knowledge of the locations of things in their surroundings. Our earliest demonstrations of this occurred when we studied how blind people and blindfolded sighted people managed to find their way when walking without access to perceptual information about the changing locations of things in the surrounding environment (Rieser, Guth, & Hill, 1986). Coordinating actions with memory representations of things is ubiquitous in daily life, occurring, for example, whenever you turn away from your conversational partner and boost the gain of your speaking, when you reach to answer the phone while turning to greet someone entering your office, and when you throw a pass to a running receiver, anticipating the receiver's future location.

For this chapter, the case of locomotion is especially relevant. When people look at their surroundings and then close their eyes and walk, they keep up-to-date on dynamic changes in their spatial orientation. This is true in ordinary situations in which the environmental context was recently seen (e.g., when children play pin the tail on the donkey), or not recently seen (e.g., when walking to find the bathroom at night), or never seen because one is blind. It is true even when knowledge of the environmental context was gained days, weeks, or months (and we assume years) earlier (Rieser, Garing, & Young, 1994). It is true for knowledge of imaginary places that were visually experienced via computer-generated virtual environments (Plumert, Kearney, & Cremer, 2004; Thompson et al., 2005; Williams, Narasimham, Westerman, Rieser, & Bodenheimer, 2006) or described in stories read aloud to children and adults (Franklin & Tversky, 1990 Franklin, Tversky, & Coon, V. 1992; Ray, 2003).

4.3.3 Empirical Evidence for Perception–Action– Representation Coupling

We conducted a series of experiments showing that learning the coupling of perception and action accounts for the coupling of representation and action (Rieser et al., 1995). The task was a simple one of looking at a target located straight ahead, putting on a blindfold and sound system to make it impossible to see or hear the direction or distance of environmental sounds, and then attempting to walk to the remembered target without environmental feedback. Adults perform this task remarkably well (e.g., Rieser, Ashmead, Talor, & Younquist, 1991). How is it, we wondered, that they know the calibration of their locomotion relative to their visual perception, that is, the scale of their locomotor activity in relation to the scale of the visually perceived and subsequently remembered target distance? In many situations, efferent and afferent information associated with locomotion is correlated with environmental information specifying rates of translation and rotation relative to objects that can be seen, heard, or touched while walking. We hypothesize that learning the perception–action coupling in such situations accounts for being able to act on the representation–action coupling. In other words, we hypothesize that when locomoting with normal feedback (usually visual, but also auditory and tactual), people notice the correlation between their motor action and its perceptual consequence. This correlation can then be acted upon when the environment cannot be perceived but is represented mentally.

We put the hypothesis to a test by experimentally manipulating the perception–action relation. Walking without vision was pretested and posttested by asking subjects to look at targets that ranged from 8 to 12 meters straight ahead and then to attempt to walk to these targets while equipped with blindfold and sound system. During the intervening learning phase, people walked on a motor-driven treadmill (the treadmill controlled their biomechanical rate of forward walking) while being towed behind a tractor (the tractor controlled their rate of movement through the environment). In the biomechanically faster condition, subjects walked on the treadmill at a rate of about 6 mph while they were towed at a rate of 3 mph. In the biomechanically slower condition, subjects walked on the treadmill at about 3 mph while being towed about 6 mph.

We predicted that people who experienced the biomechanically faster condition would tend to walk too far during the posttests. We hypothesized that they would learn that their locomotor activity resulted in a slower than usual rate of movement through the visible environment, and then act on this new learned relation when walking without vision to the remembered target. Conversely, we predicted that people who experienced the biomechanically slower condition would walk too short a distance during the posttests. The results in both conditions fit closely with our predictions. These data support our model that perception, action, and representation function as a system and show that learning the perception–action coupling accounts for the representation–action coupling. Pick et al. (1999) reported analogous experiments demonstrating the people readily recalibrate their rotational locomotion, as well.

4.3.4 The Perception–Action–Knowledge System Is Functionally Organized

A main feature of our point of view is that the perception, action, and representation system is functionally organized. James Gibson emphasized that, for perception, any given event is perceptually specified through multiple modalities of information. For the purposes of motor control, it is the same event, independent of the particular modality specifying it, and needs to be responded to as such (Gibson, 1966, 1979). This is the case when the event consists of looking or touching to learn the spatial layout of features of a person's face, or looking, listening, or walking to learn the spatial layout of features of the immediate surroundings. Actions need to be coordinated with any and all sources of information, and it makes sense to suppose that they are integrated and unified into a single knowledge representation (Avraamides, Loomis, Klatzky, & Golledge, 2004; Cheng et al., 2006; Loomis, DaSilva, Philbeck, & Fukusima, 1996). A result of such a functional organization is that multiple perceptual inputs would specify the same event, and as such, the same functionally adaptive motor response would follow a wide range of perceptual inputs.

Our thesis is that the perception of dynamic changes in spatial orientation, however they are specified, should lead to equivalent motor adjustments. Thus, learning in the context of one type of information for changes in spatial orientation should transfer to situations where other types are available.

Both Bernstein (1967) and Reed (1982) made a similar case for action as well as action systems. Just as the concept of functionally organized perceptual systems depends on defining functionally equivalent classes of perceptual information, so too the concept of an action system depends on defining functionally equivalent classes of action. More than others, Bernstein identified the defining issue of motor control theory as "there are many ways to skin a cat." By this, he meant that a given action goal could be accomplished via a plenitude of specific actions as defined in terms of the kinematics and/or dynamics of the action. This is easy to see if one thinks of the multiple trajectories that can be used to reach for and grasp a cup, catch a fly ball, or walk from one place to another. Mussa-Ivaldi and colleagues have studied the motor learning involved in moving a joystick along a path and the learning, anticipating, and taking into account predictable forces that are imposed during the movement (Bizzi & Mussa-Ivaldi, 2001; Conditt, Gandolfo, & Mussa-Ivaldi, 1997). Their studies show that when the initial practice and learning are highly constrained, there is a very narrow range of transfer, even to highly similar movements made with the same limb, but when the practice and learning are highly variable, then there is much broader transfer. Thus, the functional equivalence implied in Bernstein's and Reed's action system concept may depend on the nature of the movement in question.

We have conducted tests with skilled adults on the functional organization of various classes of action. Consider these two related to locomotion. First, Rieser et al. (1995) recalibrated the forward walking of adults in the biomechanically faster condition described above and then tested whether the learning transferred to a form of translational locomotion that differed in overall speed, cadence, muscular coordination, and stride length. The transfer form of locomotion was sidestepping during which people moved their lead foot to the left or right, followed by the lag foot, and so on, until they perceived themselves to have reached the remembered target location. The results indicated complete transfer—that is, during the posttests, adults overshot the remembered targets by the same amount when sidestepping as when forward walking. Second, Berry (2000) conducted an analogous test of transfer for the recalibration of locomotion. In her study, subjects stepped on a circular treadmill in a biomechanically faster condition in which their biomechanical stepping rate was about 6 rpm whereas they were turning at a slower 3-rpm rate relative to the surrounding environment. After a 10-minute recalibration learning phase, subjects consistently turned too far when trying to step in place for a full turn. Berry wanted to know whether this recalibration of turning on foot would transfer to turning that was implemented by hand. To test this, she asked subjects to stand on a swivel that was surrounded by a circular railing and push themselves along the railing by hand. As predicted, people consistently turned themselves too far when trying to complete a full turn to face the remembered target. In this case, however, transfer from foot to hand was incomplete, and the magnitude of change when turning by hand during the posttests averaged about half the magnitude when turning by foot.

These demonstrations of transfer of learned recalibration fit squarely with the hypothesis that the perception–action–representation system is functionally organized. However, both translational locomotion and rotational locomotion are highly practiced adult skills, so the studies do not provide any information about whether a functional organization is characteristic for novel skills or for young children. Transfer and generalization of learning from one action to another are especially relevant for proximal–distal patterns of action in development, given that younger children are able to explore the properties of their surroundings first by looking at or touching them and only later by crawling or walking to explore them. To what degree, we ask, does learning to guide visual search for objects transfer to nonvisual search for objects by hand or by foot?

4.4 APPLYING THE PERCEPTION–REPRESENTATION– ACTION SYSTEM THEORY TO THE CASE OF DEVELOPING SKILL IN UPDATING DYNAMIC SPATIAL ORIENTATION DURING MOVEMENT

In this section, we apply the functionally organized model of action, perception, and representation to two cases of human development. The first case focuses on normal development. It emphasizes the implications of the model for what skills children should learn, when they might learn these skills in terms of the prerequisite forms of motor ability and experience, and what learned skills should transfer to and speed up learning other skills. We posit that the system is functionally organized by adulthood but that the functional organization has a developmental history and emerges by fits and starts during earlier years of life. The second case focuses on how experience facilitates the development of dynamic spatial orientation when walking without vision. It applies the model to help understand why people who are blind sometimes experience difficulty at maintaining their orientation relative to things in the known surroundings.

4.4.1 Motion and Updating in Relation to Normative Development

In this section, we illustrate the implications of a perception–action system perspective for the early development of updating. The illustration characterizes a sequence during which infants use different types of information to accomplish several tasks. First is information to update needed changes in balance when sitting and then standing and to keep up-to-date on variations in the slope of the ground and use that information to crawl safely and then walk safely. Then there is information to update changes in the open path to reach a desirable object and using that information to guide reaching around barriers and then locomotion around barriers. There is subsequently information to update changes in spatial orientation that result from locomoting or being carried and using the information to guide their anticipatory looking, reaching, crawling, or walking. We describe this sequence because we hypothesize that it reflects principles at work as an increasingly unified perception–action–representation system develops.

Infants are sensitive to motion for guiding action at a very young age. For example, von Hofsten and Lindhagen (1979) have shown that a moving object is a salient elicitor of reaches in the first weeks of life. Moving targets will elicit pursuit eye movements by 2–3 months of age (Aslin, 1993; von Hofsten, Vishton, Spelke, Feng, & Rosander, 1998; Rosander & von Hofsten, 2004). Wentworth and Haith (1998) showed that infants as young as 1 month of age can watch light targets appear in a consistent spatiotemporal pattern and anticipate the target's future location by looking there before it arrives. And von Hofsten (2003) showed that when a smoothly moving objects go behind an occluding barrier, that infants anticipate the time and location where the object will reemerge. The latter two situations capture some of the complexity of moving targets.

These studies of visual looking behavior show that infants can update or visually anticipate the future times and places of objects that move along predictable trajectories. But when and how can they update their own spatial orientation, and anticipate the changing self-to-object distances and directions that result from their own movement?

We assume that updating depends on learning the correlation between action and environmental flow in relation to a frame of reference. The types of opportunity for such learning change with age, in terms of both the type of locomotion and the flow. Opportunities to learn this relation vary developmentally from being passively carried by an adult to quadripedal crawling to bipedal walking. In terms of biomechanical information, being passively carried results in afference (sensory input) from the vestibular and somatosensory (deep pressure) systems, but not joint or muscle afferents and not any efference. Visual-environmental information varies: when one is passively carried, that information is from an adult standing eye height, but when one is crawling, the eye height is close to the ground.

Functional goals and capabilities also vary with age. Such changes have important consequences for spatial orientation because the relevance of attending to the correlation of movement and position information depends on these goals and capabilities. For example, when people actively steer their locomotion, it makes sense for them to attend to the correlation of their motor activities and changing position, whereas when babies are carried in arms, attending to this correlation seems less useful.

On a comparative level, the difference between active and passive movement is illustrated by the classic studies of Hein, Held, and others suggesting that the efference associated with active, self-produced locomotion is critical to learning the relation of locomotion and environmental flow. They found that kittens that actively moved through a small circular environment learned how to visually guide their actions, whereas kittens that were passively carried through the same surroundings did not learn how to visually guide their actions (Held & Hein, 1963). Two alternative interpretations of this work make sense. One interpretation is that developing sensitivity depends on efference; that is, learning to visually guide actions depends on learning the correlation of efference with optical-environmental flow afference (referred to as reafference). The other interpretation is about affordances (i.e., what the environment provides in the way of functional relevance of movements); that is, the kittens that are passively carried do not care about the correlation of passive locomotion with environmental flow, because it is not relevant to anything they can do. In follow-up experiments, kittens were given active visual experience with one eye open and received only passive visual experience with the other eye open. These kittens could visually guide their actions when tested with the active eye but not when tested with the passive eye (Hein & Diamond, 1971). These latter results seem to argue against the functional alternative.

With respect to human locomotion, how early do children perceptually guide their spatial orientation? We begin with a consideration of balance. Infants 7 and 9 months of age have been shown to use optical flow to maintain sitting posture. For example, Bertenthal and Bai (1989) manipulated optical flow using a moving room situation in which a room with textured walls and ceiling was rolled across a stationary floor on which a stationary observer was centered. Slight movement of the room in the direction of one's gaze provides optical information as if one were swaying backward. A natural reaction is to lean forward (and, conversely, backward for a slight room movement opposite to one's direction of gaze). Infants sitting in the center of the room leaned in the direction of its oscillating forward and backward motion. The leaning of the 7-month-olds was driven primarily by movement of the whole room, whereas the sway of the 9-month-olds was influenced by the whole room or the sidewalls alone (and, to a lesser extent, the front wall alone). Balance and posture are critical as infants begin to stand up and walk. Importantly, other studies have shown that optical flow also controls the posture of newly standing infants (Bertenthal and Bai, 1989; Lee & Lishman, 1975). It would appear that the use of optical flow to maintain balance in sitting transfers to the new action of standing.

Locomoting up and down inclined slopes is a task that combines both maintenance of balance and translational movements. How well do infants negotiate such slopes? To investigate this, Adolph (1997) presented crawling babies with down slopes that varied in steepness. She found that babies with little experience crawling and no experience with such slopes were poor at deciding which slopes they could safely crawl down, but with crawling experience they became skilled and reliably crawled down slopes they could manage and avoided slopes that were too steep. In a series of short-term longitudinal studies, she then assessed the same babies when they began to walk. Her results showed that although the individual babies could discriminate very well which slopes they could not safely *crawl* down, they would indiscriminately attempt to *walk* down slopes of any steepness. Their perception–action learning was specific to crawling and had to be reacquired for walking.

Consider what kinds of transfer might be expected from crawling to walking. Here are a few of the many possibilities. (1) Infants who had mastered the task for crawling might apply the same perception–action mapping to walking down the slopes. In this case, their walking choices should not have been indiscriminate. They should have avoided the same slopes in walking as they had in crawling. (2) Mastery of the task for crawling might have meant that optical flow information for balance in combination with information for steepness could signal danger. In this case, they might have been generally cautious in approaching the slopes for walking. (3) The task of walking down the slope was regarded by the infants as a completely new one that bore no relation to the earlier crawling task. In this case, there should be no transfer from crawling to walking. (4) The infants had learned to pay attention to optical flow for balance in crawling down slopes; however, because walking (unlike standing balance discussed above) was such a new skill, they had no idea how to use it on the slopes in relation to the optical flow. Only the third and fourth possibilities would be congruent with the lack of transfer found by Adolph.

The possibility of not recognizing the similarity between formally analogous tasks arises again in a perception–action task even closer to the dynamic spatial orientation emphasis of our discussion. This is an example of steering around barriers investigated by Lockman (1984). He presented babies with a situation where they were motivated to reach around or locomote around a barrier to retrieve a toy. In a series of short longitudinal studies, Lockman found that babies who could reach, but not yet crawl or walk, learned to reach around the barrier to retrieve the toy. But when these same babies started to crawl, they did not immediately locomote around the barrier. They seemed to need to discover anew this detour requirement, as if it needs to be learned in the context of the specific action. One possibility for why this might be the case is that the visual perspective would have varied, from babies sitting in front of a barrier to babies looking at a barrier from crawling or walking position. This hypothesis is simply that they did not visually recognize that the "barrier" problem posed for locomotion was the same as one they had already mastered for reaching.

What is known about infants' spatial orientation when moved around spaces without barriers, when they are still carried in arms (or slings or backpacks)? There is mixed evidence about whether infants during the first 6 months of life use the shape of the room to find a hidden target. It is clear that in some conditions they can find a hidden target when all they need to do is search in the vicinity of one salient distinctive landmark, and it is equally clear that they cannot find a hidden target if they need to limit their search to particular locations specified relative to the landmark (e.g., left or right, or in front or behind) or if they need to organize their search locations relative to more than one landmark (Bushnell, McKenzie, Lawrence, & Connell, 1995; Lew, Bremner, & Lefkovitch, 2000).

But can infants use information from their self-movement to relocate a hidden target? They can, if they are able to use their body as a frame of reference. For example, if infants look at a hidden target and then look away, they can look again and relocate its hidden position, by turning their eyes and/or head and/or trunk in the same egocentric direction. But if infants' physical position is changed by carrying them to a new location such that they can no longer use the body as a frame of reference, infants fail to relocate the hidden object (see Acredolo, 1978; Lew et al., 2000; Rieser, 1979). For instance, Acredolo (1978) placed 6-month-old infants at one end of a rectangular room facing the center. The infants were auditorily conditioned to look at one side of the room by turning their head to the right (or left). They were then moved to the other end of the room, turned to again face the center, and presented with the auditory signal. The infants predominantly turned to the right rather than to the original side of the room. By contrast, 16-month-olds in the same procedure predominantly turned to the original side of the room. Thus, infants in this situation shifted from using a body frame of reference to an environmental frame between 6 and 16 months of age. This is consistent with the earlier suggestion that prelocomotor children do not pay attention to environmental flow.

Do children who are starting to engage in self-controlled locomotion begin to pay attention to the changing distance and direction of objects and update their spatial orientation as they move? Relevant evidence has been summarized by Campos et al. (2000). They found that children who have engaged in self-produced locomotion learn to respond to the environmental position of objects rather than the egocentric position of objects. It makes no difference whether the self-produced movement is accomplished by crawling or by experience in walkers by precrawling infants. In addition, Campos and colleagues report evidence that infants with locomotor experience are more attentive to distant objects in their environment than are infants without such experience. In sum, it seems that going from passive movement through the environment to active self-produced locomotion is correlated with a shift from egocentric to exocentric frames of reference.

4.4.2 Spatial Learning and Cognitive Maps That Result from Exploring Places

Heretofore, the spaces under discussion have been simple, more or less apprehendable from one observation point at one glance. However, consider a case in which an observer must look around to perceive the whole space. To apprehend the whole space in the sense of knowing the spatial relations among all the objects/locations in the space, knowledge must be integrated from a series of typically partially overlapping perceptions. In most natural environments, the spatial layout is even more complex and is not visible from a single station point, even with multiple looks—one needs to locomote through the layout. The problem of integrating the sequence of perceptions is greater because the sequence contains views that often are nonoverlapping and can involve greater or lesser intervals of time. These requirements lead naturally to such labels as "mental representations of spatial layout" or "cognitive maps." If a unified representation of the layout is constructed from this perceptual sequence, an observer should be able to stand at any location and point directly toward any other location. Such a test could be carried out with eyes open or closed since many target locations would be out of sight of the pointing location. Such representations could also permit observers to make Euclidean distance judgments of target locations even though the targets might be out of sight. Indeed, such pointing performance and distance estimations have been considered an operational definition of a survey or configural type of cognitive map.

Spatial knowledge does not always have the form of configural cognitive maps, and much has been written about the form of representation of spatial knowledge. Recall the previous discussion of the types of knowledge that adults acquire when learning about a new place: Siegel and White (1975) hypothesized a learning sequence in which adults first notice the identities of various salient landmarks and features; next they notice and encode the particular sequence of landmarks they encounter during particular routes, and finally they notice and encode the Euclidean relations, that is, the metric distances and directions in the spatial layout of landmarks and traveled routes. Moreover, recall the discussion of Piaget and Inhelder's (1956) view of spatial development: an age-related sequence from noticing topological relations, to projective geometrical relations, to Euclidean geometrical relations. It is important to note that the dynamic spatial orientation when walking without vision under test conditions like those described above is possible only if people are able to integrate the metric distances of the turns and translations in their route with knowledge of remembered target locations. At the level of action, perception, and representation, sensitivity to metric relations starts earlier in life than Siegel and White and

Piaget and Inhelder had supposed. But whereas it is clear that young children are sensitive to the metric properties of their own walks relative to their immediate surroundings, it is similarly clear that even older children and adults sometimes fail to integrate the landmarks they have encountered across farther-ranging explorations into a unified spatial representation (e.g., see Allen, Kirasic, Siegel, & Herman, 1979).

4.4.3 The Role of Visual Experience in Nonvisual Spatial Orientation

Besides the relevance of movement in the acquisition of spatial knowledge, how do you know where you are as you move around a space? This seems to be a silly question if you are moving around a cluttered space with vision—you can see where you are. But it is not so silly if your destination is out of sight or if everything is out of sight, such as when you are trying to find your way in the dark. You have to update your position so that you can move appropriate distances and change directions appropriately. Children have some skill at this, as evidenced by casual observation of their pin-the-tail-on-the-donkey games and as supported by experimental evidence, as well. By 2 years of age, for example, toddlers can use self-movement information, when they walk along U-shaped routes in the dark, to keep track of their starting position. Rider and Rieser (1988) had children in the dark leave their parent in one room and move through a short hallway and into an adjacent room. The children were able to point directly to their parent. Subsequent research indicated that 4-year-olds were able to keep up-to-date on changes in perspective across longer and more complicated patterns of self-movement, patterns involving as many as three turns in both left and right directions (Rieser & Rider, 1991).

In thinking about exploring a space with vision, one can overlook the fact that biomechanical and vestibular information are also present. Vision provides layout information about all the distal objects in the field of view. However, when exploring spatial layouts without vision (or audition and olfaction), such as when navigating in the dark, one can acquire almost immediately the egocentric distance and direction from a starting location (A) to an object one encounters (B). The proprioceptive and vestibular sense modalities provide information about how far the body has moved in what direction. What is lacking is other interobject information. So it is relatively easy to build up a *routelike* cognitive map going from A to B to C. If one goes from A to B and from A to C, it is also possible to infer the direction and distance between A and C and hence to begin to build up a survey-type cognitive map out of route elements. Rieser et al. (1986) taught a group of blindfolded subjects to move from a home base to a location A and from the home base to a location B, to location C, and so on, but never directly from one location to another. Nevertheless, after walking to any one location, the subjects were able to point relatively easily and accurately directly to any other location.

These investigators also trained a group of congenitally blind persons in the same manner. The congenitally blind observers had much more difficulty than the blindfolded sighted participants in making the spatial inference between the various locations. Apparently, having years of visual experience facilitates making spatial inferences when operating without vision. But what is it about the past visual experience of sighted subjects that enables them to make such inferences when moving without vision? The blind subjects and blindfolded sighted subjects could point easily and accurately to all locations from home base. Unlike the blind subjects, the blindfolded sighted subjects updated where they were in their environment after they had moved away from home base to a new location. How could past visual experience help them do this? Consider the following possibility: with vision, any time one moves, there is massive and consistent optical stimulation specifying how the distance and direction of objects in the environment change. This information helps to calibrate biomechanical stimulation so that when one can depend on a calibrated biomechanical system when deprived of vision (for some experimental support for this line of reasoning, see Pick et al., 1999; Rieser et al., 1995).

A life history of visual experience is correlated with skillful dynamic spatial orientation. The data are clear, but they are not universally consistent. For example, several studies have reported statistically significant deficits in spatial learning or spatial orientation of persons with early-onset blindness compared with sighted persons who make the judgments without vision (e.g., Rieser, Lockman, & Pick, 1980; Worchel, 1951). This difference makes sense if one hypothesizes that visual experience plays an important role in the development of nonvisual spatial orientation (e.g., the ability to remain oriented in the dark). But without hypothesizing this, it seems unexpected because people who lack vision early in life have much more motivation to acquire skillful orientation when walking without vision and have much more practice trying to do it than do sighted persons equipped with blindfolds.

Although it is clear that visual experience strongly facilitates nonvisual spatial orientation, it is similarly clear that visual experience is not necessary. The evidence for this is that some people who are born without vision or who have early visual loss can compete with anyone in terms of spatial orientation. A study by Rieser, Hill, Talor, Bradfield, and Rosen (1992) showed that it is broad-field vision, not highly acute vision, that plays the critical role. Their methods assessed learning the spatial layout of very familiar neighborhoods. They showed that those with early-onset small visual fields and those with congenital blindness were sharply more deficient in performance than any of the other participant groups.

Although the empirical evidence for a deficit related to early-onset small-field vision or blindness seems clear, the underlying processes are uncertain. As we have suggested, the deficit might reflect lack of access to visual environmental flow information, which is necessary for calibration of locomotion. If this is the case, one might wonder why people with such visual impairment do not substitute acoustical flow for optical flow. It may be that the differentiated acoustic environment is not as rich as the optical environment. Moreover, acoustic flow may not provide as valid information for self-movement. Sound-emitting objects, which would form one basis for acoustic flow, are often themselves moving objects. Thus, the component of acoustic flow due to self-movement would need to be separated from that due to object movement. This difficulty could discourage blind persons from developing capacity to use acoustical flow. A possible way to overcome such discouragement would be to place stationary sound sources (auditory "beacons") in the environment of visually impaired persons, especially developing children.

It is also possible that vision provides a necessary input for the development of the parts of the brain that mediate spatial updating. It is clear that visual experience is necessary for the development of the occipital cortex. And it is clear that, in the absence of visual experience, the occipital cortex is recruited by audition and by touch (for a discussion of related issues, see chapter 12). What are not so clear are the functional (cognitive and behavioral) implications. One possible explanation is that the recruitment of the occipital cortex by touch and/or hearing leads to increased sensitivity in touch and/or hearing for persons with congenital blindness. It is clear that blind persons have more sensitivity to some types of higher order information—for example, for hearing, they are more skillful at echolocating, and for touch, they are more skillful at reading Braille. This might be attributable to their greater practice and motivation to learn than others, or it may reflect a learning advantage due to greater capacity in relevant areas of cortex.

Of course, there are other possible explanations for the deficit of performance of those with early-onset small visual fields or congenital blindness. The deficit might reflect lack of access to global geometrical information readily available to vision distal objects. Or it might reflect insufficient experience for discovering a strategy to use global information when it is available.

4.5 CONCLUSIONS AND ADDITIONAL IMPLICATIONS OF THE FUNCTIONALLY ORGANIZED SYSTEM FOR SKILL LEARNING AND HUMAN DEVELOPMENT

Spatial orientation is dynamic whenever one moves. Keeping up-to-date on such changes in self-to-object distances and directions is essential for a wide range of functional activities. This is the case for vocal communication, since people need to adjust the loudness of their speaking to take into account the distance and direction of their listener (Rieser, Hill, Talor, Bradfield, & Rosen, 1992). This is the case for facial expressions, gestures, and other forms of social behavior to make sure that their expressions and gestures do not violate culturally defined rules governing intimacy and distances and to make sure they are visible at a distance. And it is the case for the many activities of daily living that involve finding one's way back to places learned about during earlier explorations.

Given its ubiquity across so many of the tasks of daily living, it makes sense that dynamic spatial orientation is mediated by a flexible array of environmental information, ranging from the types of global geometrical information that are often provided by the walls of a room, the streets in a town, or the ridgelines of a forest to the presence of beacons provided by the sun or sounds of the ocean. In this chapter, we have focused on how people use the efferent and afferent motor information correlated with their own locomotion to keep up-to-date on the changes in their perspective that result from their locomotion. To help understand how adults do this, we described our model of a functionally organized system coupling together action, perception, and representation and applied the model to explain some of the feats of adult spatial orientation, including transfer of the recalibration of locomotion from one form of translational locomotion to other forms. In addition, we applied the model to help understand the early development of dynamic spatial orientation.

The model of a functionally organized perception–action–representation system fits the facts for the highly practiced activities of dynamic spatial orientation of adults. Some of the facts of child development seem to fit the model, but others do not fit. And we do not know whether unskilled adult action shows the same functional organization. We assume that this indicates that the functional organization of the system emerges gradually during the course of child development and adult learning.

Concerning the facts of child development discussed above, Adolph (1997, 2000) showed that infants learn to judge what slopes are safe to crawl, but they do not transfer that knowledge when they start to walk. Lockman (1984) showed that infants learn to reach around a barrier to retrieve a hidden object, but they do not transfer that knowledge when they start to locomote. Facts such as these lead us to hypothesize that the functional organization of the system, where there is transfer of learning across functionally equivalent actions, is not an innate or intrinsic property of the system. Rather, we suppose that it might be self-organizing such that a functional organization results from learning and development.

If this is the case, what might the organizational process be like? We suggest two alternatives hypotheses. One is a top-down process, driven by the goals of actions. According to this hypothesis, different actions that can be used to accomplish the same goal would become equivalent within the system as a result of there being interchangeable ways to accomplish the same goal. The idea is that functional organization would result from the intention to accomplish a particular category of goal—translating position to go and get an object, rotating facing direction to reach and grasp an object, or throwing or kicking an object to move it through space. Functional organization would emerge from noticing common goals across varying actions. According to this view, one might suppose that when new actions first emerge during development, they are practiced in order to master new coordinations, and they are not instrumental in the service of particular goals. As the muscular coordinations per se improve, the organization would emerge as new actions are practiced more and more often in the service of particular instrumental goals.

The other organizational process is bottom-up, driven by the perceptual consequences of actions. The idea is that actions result in qualitatively different types of perceptual consequences. For example, translational locomotion results in translation in perspective, rotational locomotion results in rotation in perspective, and hurling objects results in trajectories that are separated in space and time from the agent of the action. Functional organization would emerge from noticing that sometimes very different motor movements co-occur with the same category of perceptual consequence. That is, unvarying classes of perceptual events are associated in space and time with widely varying forms of action. One might suppose that when new actions first emerge during development, they are not precisely controlled and result in poorly defined categories of perceptual events; as the actions become more precisely controlled, the unvarying classes of resulting perceptual events become easier to detect.

In fact, it could be that both processes are involved at different stages of development or of mastery of a skill. Perhaps early on a bottom-up process is dominant but then functional organization emerges. Think of a coach or a dance or music instructor who has a pupil endlessly practice exercises to master coordination before their functional significance is realized in the goal activity. Once such functional significance is realized, the pupil can look for other ways to accomplish the same goal (i.e., begin to engage in goal-directed exploratory behavior). Thus, bottom-up processes may provide a foundation for the emergence of functional organization, but top-down processes may be necessary for the development of a perception–action–representation system organized around instrumental goals.

REFERENCES

Acredolo, L. P. (1978). Development of spatial orientation in infancy. *Developmental Psychology*, *14*, 224–234.

Adolph, K. E. (1997). Learning in the development of infant locomotion. *Monographs of the Society for Research in Child Development*, *62*, 1–140.

Adolph, K. E. (2000). Specificity of learning: Why infants fall over a veritable cliff. *Psychological Science*, *11*, 290–95.

Allen, G. L., Kirasic, K. C., Siegel, A. W., & Herman, J. F. (1979). Developmental issues in cognitive mapping: The selection and utilization of environmental landmarks. *Child Development*, *50*, 1062–1070.

Aslin, R. N. (1993). Perception of visual direction in human infants. In C. E. Granrud (Ed.), *Twenty-third Carnegie-Mellon symposia on cognition: Visual perception and cognition in infancy* (pp. 91–119). Hillsdale, NJ: Erlbaum.

Avraamides, M., Loomis, J., Klatzky, R., & Golledge, R. (2004). Functional equivalence of spatial representations derived from vision and language: Evidence form allocentric judgments. *Journal of Experimental Psychology: Learning, Memory & Cognition*, *30*, 801–814.

Bernstein, N. (1967). *The coordination and regulation of movements*. Oxford: Pergamon Press.

Berry, D. (2000). *Does recalibration of turning with the feet transfer to turning with the hands?* Unpublished Masters thesis, Vanderbilt University, Nashville, TN.

Bertenthal, B. I., & Bai, D. L. (1989). Infants' sensitivity to optical flow for controlling posture. *Developmental Psychology, 25,* 936–945.

Berthoz, A. (2000). *The brain's sense of movement.* Cambridge, MA: Harvard University Press.

Berthoz, A., Pavard, B., & Young, L. R. (1975). Perception of linear horizontal self motion induced by peripheral vision (linear vection): Basic characteristics and visual vestibular interactions. *Experimental Brain Research, 23,* 471–489.

Bizzi, E., & Mussa-Ivaldi, F. (2001). The acquisition of motor behavior. In G. Edelman & J.-P. Changeux (Eds.), *The brain* (pp. 217–232). New Brunswick, NJ: Transaction Publishers.

Bushnell, E. W., McKenzie, B. E., Lawrence, D. A., & Connell, S. (1995). The spatial coding strategies of one-year-old infants in a locomotor search task. *Child Development, 66,* 937–958.

Campos, J. J., Anderson, D. I., Barbu-Roth, M. A., Hubbard, E. M., Hertenstein, M. J., & Witherington, D. (2000). Travel broadens the mind. *Infancy, 1,* 149–219.

Cheng, K., Shettleworth, S. J., Huttenlocher, J., & Rieser, J. J. (2006). *Bayesian integration of spatial information.* Manuscript submitted for publication.

Cohen, J. M., C. (1992). *The four voyages of Christopher Columbus.* New York: Penguin.

Conditt, M., Gandolfo, F., & Mussa-Ivaldi, F. (1997). The motor system does not learn the dynamics of the arm by rote memorization of past experience. *Journal of Neurophysiology, 78,* 554–560.

Franklin, N., & Tversky, B. (1990). Searching imagined environments. *Journal of Experimental Psychology: General, 119,* 63–76.

Franklin, N., Tversky, B., & Coon, V. (1992). Switching points of view in spatial mental models. *Memory & Cognition, 20,* 507–518.

Gibson, J. J. (1966). *The senses considered as perceptual systems.* Boston, MA: Houghton Mifflin.

Gibson, J. J. (1979). *The ecological approach to visual perception.* Boston, MA: Houghton Mifflin.

Gladwin, T. (1970). *East is a big bird: Navigation and logic on Puluwat Atoll.* Cambridge, MA: Harvard University Press.

Hein, A., & Diamond, R. M. (1971). Contrasting development of visually triggered and guided movements in kittens with respect to interocular and interlimb equivalence. *Journal of Comparative & Physiological Psychology, 76,* 219–224.

Held, R., & Hein, A. (1963). Movement-produced stimulation in the development of visually guided behavior. *Journal of Comparative & Physiological Psychology, 56,* 872–876.

Hubel, D. N., & Wiesel, T. N. (1965). Receptive fields and functional architecture in two nonstriate visual areas (18 and 19) of the cat. *Journal of Neurophysiology, 28,* 229–289.

Hutchins, E. (1995). *Cognition in the Wild.* Cambridge, MA: MIT Press.

Laurendeau, M. (1970). *The development of the concept of space in the child.* New York: International Universities Press.

Lee, D. N., & Lishman, J. R. (1975). Visual proprioceptive control of stance. *Journal of Human Movement Studies, 1,* 87–95.

Lew, A. R., Bremner, J. G., & Lefkovitch, L. P. (2000). Development of relational landmark use in six- to twelve-month-old infants in a spatial orientation task. *Child Development, 71,* 1179–1190.

Lockman, J. J. (1984). The development of detour ability during infancy. *Child Development*, 55, 482–491.

Loomis, J. M., DaSilva, J., Philbeck, J., & Fukusima, S. (1996). Visual perception of location and distance. *Current Directions in Psychological Science*, 5, 72–77.

Montello, D., & Pick, H. L., Jr. (1993). Integrating knowledge of vertically aligned large-scale spaces. *Environment & Behavior*, 25, 457–484.

Piaget, J., & Inhelder, B. (1956). *The child's conception of space*. New York: Routledge & Kegen Paul.

Pick, H. L., Jr., Rieser, J. J., Wagner, D., & Garing, A. E. (1999). The recalibration of rotational locomotion. *Journal of Experimental Psychology: Human Perception & Performance*, 25, 1179–1188.

Pick, H. L., Jr., Yonas, A., & Rieser, J. J. (1979). Spatial reference systems in perceptual development. In M. Bornstein & W. Kessen (Eds.), *Psychological development from infancy*. (pp. 115–145) Hillsdale, NJ: Erlbaum.

Plumert, J., Kearney, J. K., & Cremer, J. F. (2004). Children's perception of gap affordances: Bicycling across traffic-filled intersections in an immersive virtual environment. *Child Development*, 75, 1243–1253.

Ray, S. D. (2003). *Children's ability to imagine what they are read: Generating visual imagery from verbal descriptions*. Unpublished doctoral dissertation, Vanderbilt University, Nashville, TN.

Reed, E. S. (1982). An outline of a theory of action systems. *Journal of Motor Behavior*, 14, 98–134.

Rider, E. A., & Rieser, J. J. (1988). Pointing at objects in other rooms: Young children's sensitivity to perspective after with and without vision. *Child Development*, 59, 480–494.

Rieser, John J. 1979. Spatial orientation of six-month-old infants. *Child Development*. 50, 1078–1087.

Rieser, J. J. (1999). Dynamic spatial orientation and the coupling of representation and action. In R. Golledge (Ed.), *Cognitive mapping and spatial behavior* (pp. 168–190). Baltimore, MD: Johns Hopkins Press.

Rieser, J. J. and Pick, H. L. Jr. (2002). Perception and representation of human locomotion. In W. Prinz & B. Hommel (Eds.), *Attention and performance XIX: Common mechanisms in perception and action*. (pp. 177–194). Oxford: Oxford University Press.

Rieser, J. J., Ashmead, D. A., Talor, C., & Youngquist, G. (1991). Visual perception and the guidance of locomotion without vision to previously seen targets. *Perception*, 19, 675–689.

Rieser, J. J., Garing, A. E., & Young, M. F. (1994). Imagery, action, and young children's spatial orientation: It's not being there that counts, it's what one has in mind. *Child Development*, 65, 1262–1278.

Rieser, J. J., Guth, D. A., & Hill, E. W. (1986). Sensitivity to perspective structure while walking without vision. *Perception*, 15, 173–188.

Rieser, J. J., Hill, E. W., Talor, C. R., Bradfield, A., & Rosen, S. (1992). Visual experience, visual field size, and the development of nonvisual sensitivity to the spatial structure of outdoor neighborhoods explored by walking. *Journal of Experimental Psychology: General*, 12, 210–221.

Rieser, J. J., Lockman, J. J., & Pick, H. L., Jr. (1980). The role of visual experience in knowledge of spatial layout. *Perception & Psychophysics*, 28, 185–190.

Rieser, J. J., McMillan, A., Pick, H. L., & Berry, D. M. (1998). *Changes in the vocal intensity of whispering without vision as a function of the recalibration of rotational locomotion*. Presentation at a meeting of the Psychonomics Society, Dallas, TX, November, 1998.

Rieser, J. J., Pick, H. L., Jr., Ashmead, D. A., & Garing, A. E. (1995). The calibration of human locomotion and models of perceptual-motor organization. *Journal of Experimental Psychology: Human Perception & Performance, 21*, 480–497.

Rieser, J. J., & Rider, E. A. (1991). Young children's spatial orientation with respect to multiple targets when walking without vision. *Developmental Psychology, 27*, 97–107.

Rosander, K., & von Hofsten, C. (2004). Infants' emerging ability to represent occluded object motion. *Cognition, 91*, 1–22.

Siegel, A. W., & White, S. H. (1975). The development of spatial representations of large-scale environments. *Advances in Child Development & Behavior, 10*, 9–55.

Thompson, W. B., Creem-Regehr, S. H., Mohler, B. J., & Willemsen, P. (2005). Investigations on the interactions between vision and locomotion using a treadmill virtual environment. In Proceedings of the SPIE/IS&T Human Vision & Electronic Imaging Conference, 481–492.

Tolman, E. C. (1948). Cognitive maps in rats and men. *Psychological Review, 55*, 189–208.

von Hofsten, C. (2003). Infants' ability to track and reach for temporarily occluded objects. *Developmental Science, 6*, 86–99.

von Hofsten, C., & Lindhagen, K. (1979). Observations on the development of reaching for moving objects. *Journal of Experimental Child Psychology, 28*, 158–173.

von Hofsten, C., Vishton, P., Spelke, E., Feng, Q., & Rosander, K. (1998). Predictive action in infancy: Tracking and reaching for moving objects. *Cognition, 67*, 255–285.

von Holst, E., & Mittelstaedt, H. (1950). Das Reafferenzprinzip: Wechselwirkungen zwischen Zentralnervensystem und Peripherie. *Naturwissenschaften, 37*, 464–476.

Warren, W. H. (1995) Self-motion: Visual perception and visual control. In *Handbook of perception and cognition: Vol. 5. Perception of space and motion* (pp. 263–325). San Diego: Academic Press.

Warren, W. H., Kay, B. A., Duchon, A. P, Zosh, W., & Sahuc, S. (2001). Optic flow is used to control human walking. *Nature Neuroscience, 4*, 213–216.

Wentworth, N., & Haith, M. M. (1998). Infants' acquisition of spatiotemporal expectations. *Developmental Psychology, 34*, 247–257.

Williams, B., Narasimham, G., Westerman, C., Rieser, J., & Bodenheimer, B. (in press). Functional similarities in spatial orientation in real and virtual environments. *ACM Transactions on Applied Perception*.

Worchel, P. (1951). Space perception and orientation in the blind. *Psychological Monographs, 65*, 1–28.

5

COMMENTARY: THE NATURE AND DEVELOPMENT OF SPATIAL REFERENCE SYSTEMS

Timothy McNamara

The chapters in part I provide excellent overviews of important lines of research on the development of spatial memory and orientation abilities. I see no need to summarize the chapters here, as all of them are well written and readily accessible. Instead, I want to examine a thread that ties them together, namely, the nature of the spatial reference systems used in perception and memory to locate objects, remember the locations of objects, and guide action in space (see also chapter 14).

Spatial reference systems are essential for the specification of location and orientation in space. The location of Murfreesboro, Tennessee, for example, can be specified by describing its position with respect to the boundaries of the state (e.g., Murfreesboro is in the center of Tennessee), by providing coordinates of latitude and longitude on the surface of the earth (e.g., Murfreesboro is located at 35°55' N and 086°22' W), or by describing its position relative to an observer (e.g., Murfreesboro is 31 miles southeast of me as I write this paragraph). Humans store spatial information in memory about many familiar environments, and just as spatial reference systems are required to specify the locations of objects in physical space, so too spatial reference systems must be used by the human memory system to represent the remembered locations of objects in the environment.

A spatial reference system is a relational system consisting of reference objects, located objects, and the spatial relations that exist between them (e.g., Rock, 1992; Talmy, 1983). Note that according to this definition, a reference frame consisting of orthogonal axes is just one of many types of spatial reference systems. Many schemes for classifying spatial reference systems have been proposed (e.g., Levinson, 1996; Pani & Dupree, 1994; Tversky, Lee, & Mainwaring, 1999). For the purposes of understanding how spatial memories are used in navigation, it is useful to distinguish egocentric and environmental reference systems. Egocentric reference systems specify the locations of objects with respect to the observer and include retinal-, head-, and body-based coordinate systems. Environmental reference systems specify the locations of objects with respect to elements of the environment, such as the sun's azimuth, the perceived direction of gravity, or other objects or landmarks. A fundamental problem in spatial cognition research is to determine the types of spatial reference systems used to perceive and remember the spatial structure of the environment.

5.1 REORIENTATION AND ENVIRONMENTAL SHAPE

The research summarized and cited by Newcombe and Ratliff in chapter 3 has shown that reorientation relies heavily on environmental reference systems, especially the shape of the surrounding environment. Although all of the experimental work to date has investigated small-scale, engineered environments, the findings would seem to generalize to large-scale, natural environments, as well. Newcombe and Ratliff argue convincingly that the capabilities required to take advantage of the geometry of extended surfaces do not form a module in Fodor's (1983) sense and that the ability to use nongeometric features to reorient does not depend on the acquisition of language. However, there is still something special about environmental shape and the geometry of extended surfaces. For instance, although there seem to be clear cases in which geometric information but not nongeometric information is used, the converse is not true. It is possible that this pattern of results has emerged because, as argued by Newcombe and Ratliff, experiments conducted so far have used geometries that were salient, easy to encode, constant across trials, and very familiar to participants. By contrast, the nongeometric cues were often less salient (e.g., small), potentially more variable (e.g., proximal vs. distal), and less reliable (e.g., target-feature spatial relation changed within sessions).

Other evidence not subject to these criticisms also indicates that there is something special about environmental shape. In a recent series of experiments (Mou, McNamara, Rump, & Xiao, in press), we investigated the effect of disorientation on the remembered locations of objects (see also Holmes & Sholl, 2005; Waller & Hodgson, 2006). These experiments followed up some intriguing studies by Wang and Spelke (2000), which showed that disorientation disrupted remembered relative locations of objects in a room but not remembered relative locations of the corners of the room. Wang and Spelke explained these findings in the context of a theory in which object location and environmental shape are stored in different processing systems using different reference systems (egocentric vs. environmental, respectively). We hypothesized that the results might be a function of whether participants could readily apprehend the shape of the "environment," not whether the environment consisted of objects or extended surfaces. The results of our experiments showed that disorientation did not disrupt the remembered locations of objects any more than turning in place to a new facing direction if people were able to apprehend the shape of the configuration of objects at the time of learning. Disorientation disrupted remembered locations of objects when the layout of the objects was irregular and participants were unable to view it from a single vantage point.

Although these findings contradict the basis of Wang and Spelke's (2000, 2002) claim that object location and environmental shape are processed and represented in different systems, they also vindicate their conjecture that people reorient with respect to environmental shape. Our findings indicate that the "shape" of an environment may be defined by configurations of objects or landmarks in addition to extended surfaces. A possible point of tension between our findings and those summarized in chapter 3 by Newcombe and Ratliff exists in the different effects of learning from within versus outside a space. Our findings suggest that the shape of a collection of objects is easier to perceive and to represent from an external viewing perspective, from which the layout can be perceived from a single vantage point, than from an internal viewing perspective, from which the layout can be perceived only be integrating multiple views of the environment. By contrast, Newcombe and Ratliff review evidence suggesting that the use of geometry to find a hidden object is reduced when participants view the space from outside rather than from inside. It will be interesting to see how these paradoxical findings are resolved.

Two obvious follow-ups to the line of research reviewed by Newcombe and Ratliff would be to conduct analogous experiments in natural, outdoor environments to determine the developmental time course of the use of geometric and nongeometric features under such conditions, and to conduct experiments on populations of subjects that have limited experience with engineered environments. Both lines of work would be very helpful in assessing the generality of these findings to spatial memory and reorientation in natural settings, although cross-cultural studies are inherently limited in their ability to be informative about the causes of any observed differences between populations of subjects.

5.2 LOCATION AT THE CATEGORICAL AND FINE-GRAINED LEVELS

Chapter 1 by Huttenlocher and Lourenco and chapter 2 by Plumert, Hund, and Recker both examine the nature of spatial categories and memory for locations within spatial categories. For example, a set of car keys might be remembered as being on the coffee table (a spatial category) and as being a particular distance and angular direction from one of the corners of the table (location within the category). A major contribution of Huttenlocher and her colleagues has been to develop a detailed model of how categorical and inexact "fine-grained" information about location are combined to report the remembered location of an object. These two sorts of information correspond to types of nonmetric and metric spatial reference systems, respectively. Returning to the example, the description of the location of the keys as "on the coffee table" does not rely on metrics of distance, direction, and so forth, and therefore is nonmetric, whereas the description in terms of distance and direction from the table's corner uses a metric reference system.

One series of experiments suggests that people use polar-coordinate-like systems to represent, at the fine-grained level, the location of a dot in a circle (e.g., Huttenlocher, Hedges, & Duncan, 1991). It is interesting that research on spatial memory using completely different paradigms suggests that the direction from one object to another also may be represented with respect to a reference direction or axis (e.g., Mou, McNamara, Valiquette, & Rump, 2004). An important aspect of such a representation is that it uses an environmental reference system ("environment centered") and is orientation dependent. The key notions are that the direction from one object to another is defined with respect to a reference direction selected at the time of learning and that in many, if not most, cases, this reference direction corresponds to the person's viewing perspective at the time of learning. Theories based on such representations can predict that performance will be dependent on viewing perspective even though the representation uses an environmental reference system (e.g., Mou et al., 2004).

I have often wondered how a change in viewing perspective would influence the types of spatial coding or the combination of information from multiple levels in the standard paradigm developed by Huttenlocher and her colleagues. It is well documented that long-term spatial memory is orientation dependent (e.g., McNamara, 2003). People can recall and recognize interobject spatial relations more efficiently from some perspectives than from others. These privileged perspectives are usually aligned with (parallel or orthogonal to) experienced points of view (e.g., Shelton & McNamara, 2001) but also may be aligned with salient intrinsic axes of the environment (e.g., Mou & McNamara, 2002). The spatial categories observed by Huttenlocher and her colleagues are aligned with the observer's viewing perspective at the time of study. What would happen if participants viewed the dot within the circle from one perspective (which we will define as 0°) but were asked to recall the location of the dot from a point of view misaligned with the study view (e.g., ±135°)? In the absence of environmental cues (e.g., testing in darkness), participants would almost certainly recall the location relative to axes rotated the same amount as their movement; that is, they would act as though they had not moved. But what if salient environmental cues existed? It seems likely that they would reconcile their new viewpoint with the reference axes in the representation, leading to increased latencies and errors, and perhaps systematic biases. Research along these lines could be very informative about how perceptual experiences, memories of experiences, and the geometry of the environment interact in spatial cognition and performance (e.g., Spencer & Hund, 2002).

In chapter 2, Plumert, Hund, and Recker summarize an important line of research that extends Huttenlocher's work by examining in detail the development of sensitivities to categorical and to fine-grained information in more complex environments. This line of research has revealed several important findings, including that error in remembering the locations of objects decreases approximately linearly with age, suggesting that the ability to represent fine-grained location information improves with age, that young children often do not show categorical bias in object placements unless multiple cues (e.g., perceptual boundaries and spatial-temporal contiguity) define the categories of objects, and that categorical bias sometimes forms a U-shaped pattern across ages, with significant levels of bias for young children (e.g., 7- and 9-year-olds), no bias for 11-year-olds, and significant bias for adults.

Plumert and her colleagues explain their results in the context of a theoretical framework that emphasizes organism–environment interactions in understanding the development of perceptual and cognitive abilities and skills. According to this framework, which has intellectual foundations in Gibson's ecological approach to visual perception, in order to understand human behavior and its development, one must examine how characteristics of the cognitive system (e.g., sensitivity to boundaries in space) interact with information available in the environment (e.g., presence or absence of physical boundaries) and how these interactions change with development. For instance, Plumert and her colleagues explain the U-shaped function as follows: As stated previously, fine-grained coding seems to improve with age, reaching asymptote at about 11 years of age. Categorical coding may be only moderately strong until adulthood. Children 7 and 9 years old may rely more on categorical coding because fine-grained coding is so imprecise, whereas 11-year-old children may rely on fine-grained coding because it is better developed and more precise than categorical coding, and adults may be influenced by categorical coding because it is so strong.

A complementary way to conceptualize the basis of hierarchical coding of spatial information is that it results from the use of spatial reference systems at different scales (e.g., Poucet, 1993). For example, participants in the studies of Plumert and colleagues may represent the locations of the objects with respect to each other using intrinsic reference systems defined within each quadrant (e.g., Mou & McNamara, 2002; Tversky, 1981). The locations of the quadrants may be represented with respect to each other using an intrinsic reference system in which the quadrants are "objects." Such a representation might preserve, among other things, information about the identities of the quadrants and their relative positions. In such small-scale spaces, the intrinsic reference directions within each quadrant are almost certainly aligned, such that conceptual "north" is the same in all regions (e.g., Shelton & McNamara, 2001). But in a large-scale space, which cannot be viewed from a single vantage point, these reference directions may initially be misaligned, and become aligned only through appropriate experiences (e.g., Montello & Pick, 1993).

From this perspective, categorical bias could result from many sources. It is possible that bias is caused by the use of separate intrinsic reference systems for each quadrant, by representing interobject spatial relations with greater density or strength within versus between quadrants, by the quadrant-level spatial reference system, or by some other mechanism. Experiments aimed specifically at testing these explanations would be needed to hone in on the likely causes of categorical bias. Whatever the mechanism or mechanisms may be, an additional process in which different sources of information are weighted differently depending on their fidelity or the task demands will probably be needed to explain some of the more complex findings, such as the nonmonotonic pattern in categorical bias across age. One especially interesting result is the finding that younger children show significant negative categorical bias under certain conditions, such as when boundaries are absent during learning and testing and when boundaries are present during learning and testing. These findings suggest that younger children might be representing locations of the objects with respect to whatever structures are provided during learning (the walls and corners of the box in the no boundary conditions; the walls, corners, and quadrant boundaries in the boundaries conditions) and then using these structures as reference frames for object placement (e.g., McNamara & Diwadkar, 1997; Newcombe, Huttenlocher, Sandberg, Lie, & Johnson, 1999; Sadalla, Burroughs, & Staplin, 1980).

5.3 LOCOMOTION AND SPATIAL UPDATING

Chapter 4 by Rieser and Pick examines the perceptual and cognitive processes that people use to keep track of their position in an environment as they locomote. The authors are especially interested in the relations between perception, action, and representation. They view these processes as tightly coupled in a functionally organized system in the service of perceiving space, acting in space, and learning and remembering space.

A key feature of their model is that people are sensitive to and learn how their actions affect their perceptions and vice versa. These relations are referred to as perception–action correlations. People also use representations to guide actions (e.g., walking to the bathroom at night in the dark) and actions to update representations (e.g., being able to point to your office after a walk to the bookstore across campus). One of their key claims is that learning the coupling between action and perception explains the coupling between action and representation. In a creative and influential series of experiments, Rieser, Pick, and colleagues showed that relatively brief recalibration of the perception–action coupling produces predictable changes in the representation–action coupling. For example, walking on a treadmill at a speed of 6 mph while being towed behind a tractor at speed of 3 mph led people to walk too far on posttests requiring them to walk without vision to a target.

Another fascinating result is that recalibration in one perception–action system (e.g., forward walking) transfers to another system (e.g., side stepping). These findings indicate that transfer is occurring at a high functional level (e.g., getting from point A to point B) and not at sensorimotor levels. These kinds of functional relations must be learned, however, because they do not always exist for infants. For example, experience in crawling does not generalize to walking, and experience in reaching around barriers for prelocomotor infants does not generalize to crawling around barriers (see chapter 4 for references).

When people move from place to place, as when they drive from home to work or walk across a college campus, they must keep track of their location and orientation with respect to objects and landmarks in the environment to avoid getting lost or disoriented. This sort of spatial updating also occurs in imagination. So, for example, when giving directions, we need to know how an imagined turn (e.g., "when you get to Blair, make a left") will change the directions between our bodies and other objects in the environment (e.g., after a left turn, objects that were previously in front will now be on the right). Rieser and Pick assume that spatial updating, which is accomplished in the representation–action system, is efficient and automatic, as illustrated by peoples' abilities to keep track of locations in the surrounding environment when they locomote without vision (e.g., Rieser, 1989; Rieser, Guth, & Hill, 1986).

There is no question that spatial updating is easier when people walk or turn to new positions or points of view than when they only imagine doing so (but see Wraga, 2003). One likely cause of the difficulty of imagined spatial updating is interference resulting from the conflict between the awareness of one's physical position in an environment and the discrepant position one has to adopt in imagination (e.g., May, 2004). Recent studies have also shown that spatial updating may not be as efficient as comparisons between actual and imagined locomotion might lead one to believe. Mou et al. (2004) required participants to learn the locations of objects in a room, walk to the center, and turn to appropriate facing directions before pointing to objects, from either actual or imagined positions. Pointing performance was best when the imagined heading was parallel to the original learning perspective, even when participants were facing in other directions; in other words, turning to a heading that differed from the learning view introduced costs in pointing to objects. An important difference between Mou et al.'s experiments and other investigations of spatial updating is that the layout contained more objects or was spatially more complex. In sum, although spatial updating is certainly more efficient when people physically locomote than when they imagine moving, spatial updating is not automatic, in the sense of being obligatory and cost free.

The findings of Mou et al. (2004) argue strongly that people update their location and orientation with respect to an environmental representation of object-to-object spatial relations. At the same time, walking through apertures (e.g., doorways), staying on paths (e.g., sidewalks), and avoiding obstacles—all examples of steering—would seem to require the computation and representation of self-to-object spatial relations. Recent investigations of the effects of disorientation on spatial memories suggest that the human spatial memory and navigation system does indeed rely on enduring representations of object-to-object spatial relations and transient representations of self-to-object spatial relations (e.g., Mou et al., in press; Waller & Hodgson, 2006).

To my knowledge, comparable investigations have not been conducted with children. When do children acquire the ability to learn the layout of a collection of objects according to a salient intrinsic axis that is different from their viewing perspective? Do the effects of disorientation on spatial memories depend on whether children can readily apprehend the shape of the layout of objects, as they do for adults? When does this dependency develop? Does simply turning to a new facing direction disrupt spatial memory for children in the way it seems to for adults? Studies seeking answers to these questions would be very informative about the development of the cognitive and perceptual processes involved in navigation in familiar environments.

5.4 SUMMARY AND CONCLUSIONS

The chapters in part I provide exceptionally clear overviews of four lines of research on the development of spatial memory, locomotion, and orientation and, in so doing, reveal crucial insights about the spatial reference systems used to locate objects, remember the locations of objects, and guide action in space. Children can reorient with respect to geometric and nongeometric features of the environment, and although the relative importance of these features almost certainly depends on context, task demands, and past experiences of the child, environmental shape nevertheless seems to play an especially important role, even into adulthood. Children acquire at a very young age the ability to represent location using both categorical, nonmetric and fine-grained, metric reference systems. As perceptual and cognitive systems develop, categorical coding becomes more complex, stronger, and less reliant on multiple environmental cues, and fine-grained coding becomes more precise. Humans depend on such representations to guide actions, such as locomotion. The ability to interact effectively with the world using representations of it may develop, in part, from learning correlations between actions and resulting perceptions. Early in development, this learning seems to be limited to specific perception–action couplings, but over the course of development, learning becomes organized around achieving certain ends (e.g., rotating to a new point of view), not the unique changes in perception that result from a particular action. Recent investigations of spatial updating in adults indicate that steering may depend on a transient egocentric system, whereas wayfinding and staying oriented in the environment rely on an enduring environmental system. An especially promising line of research is to examine the development of these capabilities in childhood.

REFERENCES

Fodor, J. A. (1983). *Modularity of mind: An essay on faculty psychology*. Cambridge, MA: MIT Press.

Holmes, M. C., & Sholl, M. J. (2005). Allocentric coding of object-to-object relations in over-learned and novel environments. *Journal of Experimental Psychology: Learning, Memory, and Cognition, 31*, 1069–1087.

Huttenlocher, J., Hedges, L. V., & Duncan, S. (1991). Categories and particulars: Prototype effects in estimating spatial location. *Psychological Review, 98*, 352–376.

Levinson, S. C. (1996). Frames of reference and Molyneux's question: Crosslinguistic evidence. In P. Bloom, M. A. Peterson, L. Nadel, & M. F. Garrett (Eds.), *Language and space* (pp. 109–169). Cambridge, MA: MIT Press.

May, M. (2004). Imaginal perspective switches in remembered environments: Transformation versus interference accounts. *Cognitive Psychology, 48*, 163–206.

McNamara, T. P. (2003). How are the locations of objects in the environment represented in memory? In C. Freksa, W. Brauer, C. Habel, & K. Wender (Eds.), *Spatial cognition III: Routes and navigation, human memory and learning, spatial representation and spatial learning* (pp. 174–191). Lecture Notes in Computer Science 2685. Berlin: Springer.

McNamara, T. P., & Diwadkar, V. A. (1997). Symmetry and asymmetry in human spatial memory. *Cognitive Psychology, 34*, 160–190.

Montello, D. R., & Pick, H. L., Jr. (1993). Integrating knowledge of vertically aligned large-scale spaces. *Environment and Behavior, 25*, 457–484.

Mou, W., & McNamara, T. P. (2002). Intrinsic frames of reference in spatial memory. *Journal of Experimental Psychology: Learning, Memory, & Cognition, 28*, 162–170.

Mou, W., McNamara, T. P., Rump, B., & Xiao, C. (in press). Roles of egocentric and allocentric spatial representations in locomotion and reorientation. *Journal of Experimental Psychology: Learning, Memory, & Cognition*.

Mou, W., McNamara, T. P., Valiquette, C. M., & Rump, B. (2004). Allocentric and egocentric updating of spatial memories. *Journal of Experimental Psychology: Learning Memory & Cognition, 30*, 142–157.

Newcombe, N., Huttenlocher, J., Sandberg, E., Lie, E., & Johnson, S. (1999). What do misestimations and asymmetries in spatial judgement indicate about spatial representation? *Journal of Experimental Psychology: Learning, Memory, & Cognition, 25*, 986–996.

Pani, J. R., Dupree, D. (1994). Spatial reference systems in the comprehension of rotational motion. *Perception, 23*, 929–946.

Poucet, B. (1993). Spatial cognitive maps in animals: New hypotheses on their structure and neural mechanisms. *Psychological Review, 100*, 163–182.

Rieser, J. J. (1989). Access to knowledge of spatial structure at novel points of observation. *Journal of Experimental Psychology: Learning, Memory, & Cognition, 15*, 1157–1165.

Rieser, J. J., Guth, D. A., & Hill, E. W. (1986). Sensitivity to perspective structure while walking without vision. *Perception*, *15*, 173–188.

Rock, I. (1992). Comment on Asch and Witkin's "Studies in Space Orientation II." *Journal of Experimental Psychology: General*, *4*, 404–406.

Sadalla, E. K., Burroughs, W. J., & Staplin, L. J. (1980). Reference points in spatial cognition. *Journal of Experimental Psychology: Human Learning & Memory*, *6*, 516–528.

Shelton, A. L., & McNamara, T. P. (2001). Systems of spatial reference in human memory. *Cognitive Psychology*, *43*, 274–310.

Spencer, J. P., & Hund, A. M. (2002). Prototypes and particulars: Geometric and experience-dependent spatial categories. *Journal of Experimental Psychology: General*, *131*, 16–37.

Talmy, L. (1983). How language structures space. In H. L. Pick, Jr., & L. P. Acredolo (Eds.), *Spatial orientation: Theory, research, and application* (pp. 225–282). New York: Plenum Press.

Tversky, B. (1981). Distortions in memory for maps. *Cognitive Psychology*, *13*, 407–433.

Tversky, B., Lee, P. U., & Mainwaring, S. (1999). Why speakers mix perspectives. *Journal of Spatial Cognition & Computation*, *1*, 399–412.

Waller, D., & Hodgson, E. (2006). Transient and enduring spatial representations under disorientation and self-rotation. *Journal of Experimental Psychology: Learning, Memory, & Cognition*, *32*, 867–882.

Wang, R. F., & Spelke, E. S. (2000). Updating egocentric representations in human navigation. *Cognition*, *77*, 215–250.

Wang, R. F., & Spelke, E. S. (2002). Human spatial representation: Insights from animals. *Trends in Cognitive Sciences*, *6*, 376–382.

Wraga, M. J. (2003). Thinking outside the body: An advantage for spatial updating during imagined versus physical self-rotation. *Journal of Experimental Psychology: Learning, Memory, & Cognition*, *29*, 993–1005.

II

THINKING AND TALKING ABOUT SPATIAL RELATIONS

6

ON THE INFANT'S PRELINGUISTIC CONCEPTION OF SPATIAL RELATIONS

Three Developmental Trends and Their Implications for Spatial Language Learning

PAUL C. QUINN

There has been a long-standing interest in understanding the relative contributions of nonlinguistic perceptual processing and language-specific lexical learning to how young children come to represent the meaning of spatial terms (H. H. Clark, 1973). In the modern literature on space and language, there has been increased recognition that accounting for the acquisition of the semantics of spatial relational concepts is a complex undertaking, with debate centering on whether language plays a selectionist (Mandler, 1996), interactionist (Bowerman & Choi, 2001), combinatorial (Hermer-Vazquez, Spelke, & Katsnelson, 1999), or restructuring (Majid, Bowerman, Kita, Haun, & Levinson, 2004) role in the overall process. One limitation to this literature is that, until recently, only a handful of studies were available on how infants parse space prior to language. As observed by Regier (1996), "There is no account of nonlinguistic spatial conceptual development and the manner in which this might affect the linguistic categorization of space" (p. 158).

In the last several years, new evidence has begun to emerge indicating that prelinguistic infants display considerable flexibility in terms of being

117

able to form concepts for a variety of spatial relations, some of which are not present in their parental language (Casasola & Cohen, 2002; Hespos & Spelke, 2004; McDonough, Choi, & Mandler, 2003). These data are consistent with the view that spatial language learning serves to maintain those conceptual distinctions that are generated by nonlinguistic spatial conceptual processes. The evidence has led Hespos and Spelke (2004) to propose that spatial language learning may thus be analogous to the acquisition of the sound system of one's native language (Werker, 1989) and species-specific development in face processing (Pascalis, de Haan, & Nelson, 2002).

The purpose of this chapter is to review a line of studies suggesting that infants prior to 1 year of age are not completely flexible in terms of the spatial relations that they can represent and that developmental trends occur prelinguistically that may subsequently be reflected in spatial language learning. Thus, while some of the modern literature has emphasized the influence that spatial language learning exerts on nonlinguistic spatial cognition (Casasola, 2005a; Majid et al., 2004), in this chapter I suggest some ways in which nonlinguistic spatial concept formation may have implications for spatial language acquisition. In examining the evidence, I emphasize descriptions of developmental changes that have been observed in spatial cognition during the period prior to language production: from birth to 10 months of age. The focus is on the representation of small-scale, two-dimensional, spatial-relational concepts, including ABOVE, BELOW, LEFT, RIGHT, and BETWEEN.

6.1 CAN PRELINGUISTIC INFANTS CATEGORIZE SPATIAL RELATIONSHIPS? THE CASE OF ABOVE VERSUS BELOW

Spatial-relational terms pick out equivalence classes of spatial arrangements of objects. As a consequence, for prelinguistic development to supply linguistic mechanisms with representations that could support the acquisition of spatial-relational terms, such representations would need to be categorical in nature. It thus becomes important to determine whether preverbal infants can represent spatial relations categorically. For instance, can young infants, based purely on perceptual experience and without the benefit of linguistic labeling or some other form of instruction, represent the spatial relations ABOVE versus BELOW (Quinn, 1994)? ABOVE and BELOW seemed like reasonable candidates for spatial-relational concepts that infants might represent nonlinguistically, given cross-linguistic evidence that UNDER is among the first spatial terms to be acquired by children (Johnston, 1988; Johnston & Slobin, 1979; Meints, Plunkett, Harris, & Dimmock, 2002; Weist, Lyytinen, Wysocka, & Atanassova, 1997).

To test whether young infants could form a representation of ABOVE that excluded examples of BELOW, 3-month-olds were familiarized with stimuli depicting a small movable target stimulus (i.e., a dot) in an

ABOVE relation relative to a larger stationary referent stimulus (i.e., horizontal bar). As shown in figure 6.1A, there were four familiar stimuli, each depicting the dot in a distinct location above the bar. The infants were then given a novel category preference test that paired a stimulus displaying the dot in a novel location above the bar with a stimulus in which the dot appeared below the bar. The rationale behind this test is that if infants can represent the equivalence of the stimuli depicting the dot above the bar, then they should generalize this representation to the novel ABOVE stimulus and display a novel category preference (as measured in looking time) for the BELOW stimulus. Notably, if the infants were representing information about just the dot or the bar, or both but not their relation, then one would not expect a preference for either test stimulus, given that both depict the dot and the bar. Figure 6.1B shows how a comparable sequence of familiarization and test trials was used to test whether infants could form a representation for BELOW that excluded instances of ABOVE. Results showed that infants in both the ABOVE and BELOW familiarization conditions displayed a preference for the test stimulus depicting the novel spatial relation. The findings are consistent with the idea that quite young infants could form category representations for the spatial relations ABOVE and BELOW.

Is it necessary to explain performance in the Quinn (1994) study in terms of infants representing spatial-relational concepts? Might there be a less elaborate account of the observed pattern of looking? For example, is it possible that the infants simply responded on the basis of absolute distance information, preferring the stimulus in which the dot was located farther away from the familiar dot locations? Figure 6.2, which redepicts the design of the experiment to highlight its spatial particulars, illustrates that the

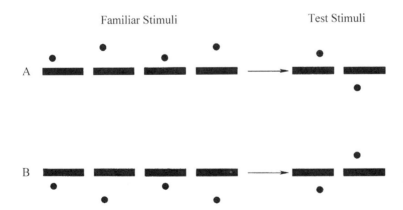

Figure 6.1 Familiarization and test stimuli used to investigate whether infants could represent the spatial relations ABOVE (*A*) and BELOW (*B*) in Quinn (1994).

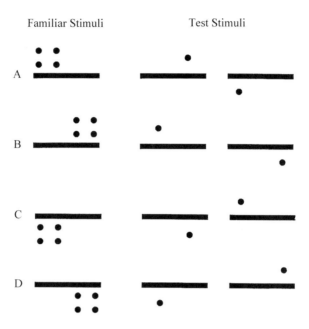

Figure 6.2   Design of the Quinn (1994) categorization experiment reillustrated to highlight the distance relations of the dot in the familiarization and test stimuli. Familiarization stimuli shown to the left represent a composite of the four exemplars.

answer is no. As shown in the left panels, for different groups of infants, during the course of familiarization, the dot appeared in the four corner locations of the top (or bottom) left or top (or bottom) right quadrant of the stimulus. In the novel category preference test, the novel instance of the familiar category depicted the dot in a novel location on the same side of the bar (shifted to the right or left of the familiar dot locations), whereas the novel instance of the novel category depicted the dot on the opposite side of the bar (either below or above the bar). Importantly, the dot in the novel category exemplar was moved the same distance away from the familiar dot locations (either down or up) as the dot in the novel exemplar of the familiar category (which was moved to the right or left). This means that the test trial preferences of the infants could not have been based on absolute distance information relative to the familiarization stimuli.

One might ask another question about the performance of infants in Quinn (1994), namely, whether it is justified to conclude that infants were representing ABOVE and BELOW as spatial-relational *categories*. Given that categorization refers to equivalent responding to a class of discriminably different instances (Bruner, Goodnow, & Austin, 1956), novel category preferences can be interpreted as evidence for categorization only if the individual exemplars of the familiar category are shown to be discriminably different. If the stimuli are not discriminable, the categorization experiment reduces to a test of discrimination between the nondiscriminable members of the familiar category (which become effectively one stimulus) and the novel exemplar from the novel category. To examine this issue, Quinn (1994) tested infants on their ability to discriminate between randomly selected pairs of stimuli depicting the same relation. The results from this control experiment indicated that the infants could discriminate among the various ABOVE stimuli, on the one hand, and the different BELOW stimuli, on the other. This finding implies that the infants were registering the changes in the location of the dot as it appeared above or below the bar and were in fact representing ABOVE and BELOW relations as categories of discriminably different exemplars.

Although the discussion thus far has ruled out distance-based responding and within-category discrimination as accounts of the novel category preferences observed in Quinn (1994), two alternatives remain to be considered before an explanation based on infants' representing ABOVE versus BELOW concepts can be fully embraced. First, as may be observed in figure 6.2, in the changeover from familiarization to test trials, the dot depicted in the novel exemplar of the familiar category moved horizontally (to the right or left of the familiar dot locations) whereas the dot shown in the novel exemplar of the novel category moved vertically (down or up from the familiar dot locations). Thus, infants could merely have responded preferentially to the vertical over horizontal direction of dot displacement. The fact that directional words such as "up" and "down" are among the earliest words to be produced in the child's spatial lexicon is consistent with this possibility (Choi & Bowerman, 1991).

Second, the location of the horizontal bar was coincident with the location of the horizontal midline of the stimulus. If infants spontaneously engaged in a mental bisection of the stimulus into top and bottom halves, they may have encoded the dot locations categorically, but in relation to an internally generated midline rather than the externally available bar. The fact that children as young as 4 years encode the location of a dot on a rectangular piece of paper in relation to an internally generated vertical midline is in accord with this suggestion (Huttenlocher, Newcombe, & Sandberg, 1994).

Both the vertical displacement and mental bisection explanations of the novel category preferences in Quinn (1994) imply that the horizontal bar is unnecessary for producing the observed pattern of performance. Thus, both accounts predict that the same test-trial looking preferences should be observed if the original ABOVE versus BELOW categorization experiment were repeated with stimuli that did not contain the horizontal bar. If infants were encoding the spatial relation between dot and bar, however, then the novel category preferences should drop to chance for stimuli depicting just the dot in its various locations without the bar. Quinn (1994) conducted the no-bar control experiment and null preferences were observed, thereby upholding the original explanation that infants represented the spatial-relational concepts of ABOVE and BELOW.

Subsequent research has shown that these ABOVE versus BELOW results are replicable, even with different stimuli. For example, when the ABOVE versus BELOW categorization experiment was repeated with 3- to 4-month-old infants, but with the dot changed to a diamond and the horizontal bar composed of squares (thereby adding some pattern complexity; see figure 6.3), infants continued to display a preference for the novel spatial relation (Mash, Quinn, Dobson, & Narter, 1998; Quinn, Cummins, Kase, Martin, & Weissman, 1996). Given that the referent object, the bar, must in some sense be constructed by the infants in these studies, one can ask whether there is any evidence that the infants are using the entire bar here versus a subset of the squares or just a single square. Studies show that infants are sensitive to Gestalt grouping principles (Quinn & Bhatt, 2005a, 2005b; Quinn, Brown, & Streppa, 1997; Quinn & Schyns, 2003), and by virtue of good continuation, proximity, and similarity, the squares should group together to form a whole bar. Following the same principles, the diamond target is a different shape, off-line, and farther away from the squares (comprising the referent bar) than the squares are to each other, so the target diamond and the referent bar should have been perceived as spatially distinct entities. These follow-up studies indicate that the categorization of ABOVE and BELOW spatial relations by young infants is a robust finding, replicable with different stimulus sets, and thus likely representative of a general phenomenon.

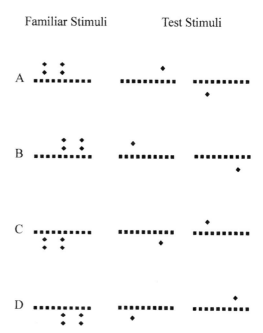

Figure 6.3 Familiarization and test stimuli used to examine whether infants could represent the spatial relations ABOVE (*A, B*) and BELOW (*C, D*) in Quinn et al. (1996).

6.2 IMPLICATIONS FOR LANGUAGE LEARNING AND LOCATION CODING

Data showing that infants as young as 3 months of age can partition space into categories defined by the positional arrangements of objects imply that spatial language is not necessary for the early acquisition of at least some spatial-relational concepts. As suggested by Murphy (2002), language has to have some cognitive structure to work on if it is going to be mapped onto environmental referents in an efficient manner. The studies on the representation of ABOVE and BELOW by preverbal infants suggest that structure comes in the form of perceptual categories, organized by similarity, in which the different instances of ABOVE are registered as similar to each other and being in one grouping, with the various exemplars of BELOW also recognized as similar to one another, but dissimilar from the instances of ABOVE, and hence represented in a different category. If the infants represented the familiar category exemplars depicted in figures 6.1–6.3 as unrelated to each other, then it is hard to envision how such spatial terms as ABOVE and BELOW could be readily comprehended and produced by young children. Also consistent with the idea that language is not required to represent ABOVE versus BELOW are the findings that nonhuman animals (baboons and capuchin monkeys) that lack language can respond to the stimuli used in Quinn (1994) in terms of the ABOVE and BELOW relations of the target object and horizontal referent bar (Depy, Fagot, & Vauclair, 1999; Spinozzi, Lubrano, & Truppa, 2004).

Findings from Mash et al. (1996), Quinn (1994), and Quinn et al. (1996) also suggest that the major cognitive processes corresponding to a contemporary dual-system model of hierarchical spatial coding hypothesized to be operating in children and adults may have their starting points in early infancy. Both behavioral and neural data point to distinct systems for processing both categorical spatial relations between objects (e.g., object above vs. below bar) and finer grained distance relations between objects located within categories (e.g., object in one vs. another location above bar) (Huttenlocher, Hedges, & Duncan, 1991; Koenig, Reiss, & Kosslyn, 1990; Kosslyn et al., 1989; Laeng, 1994; Newcombe & Huttenlocher, 2000; see also chapter 2). The evidence from the infant studies indicates that categorical processing of spatial relations and discrimination of the finer grained changes in object location within the spatial-relational categories are both present by 3 months of age. The data thus suggest that the fundamental components of the "categories and particulars" model of spatial location coding are functional in quite young infants. With this starting point in place, we now consider developmental changes in prelinguistic spatial cognition, with an eye toward instances where such changes appear to foreshadow analogous developments in the acquisition of spatial language.

6.3 DEVELOPMENTAL TREND 1: LANDMARK (POINT) TO FRAMEWORK (REGION) REPRESENTATIONS

Can young infants represent spatial-relational concepts other than ABOVE versus BELOW? Quinn (2004) investigated whether 3- to 4-month-olds could represent LEFT versus RIGHT, using stimuli identical to those employed by Quinn et al. (1996) to investigate ABOVE versus BELOW, except that the bar was vertically instead of horizontally oriented. The experimental design illustrating the familiar and test stimuli is shown in figure 6.4. Infants familiarized with stimuli depicting a diamond in discriminably different locations to the left or right of the bar preferred a stimulus depicting the diamond on the opposite side of the bar over a stimulus displaying the diamond in a new position on the same side of the bar. This finding indicates that young infants can represent the spatial-relational categories of LEFT versus RIGHT.

The spatial-relational category contrasts of ABOVE versus BELOW and LEFT versus RIGHT have the common requirement of encoding the location of a target object in relation to a single referent object. Quinn, Norris, Pasko, Schmader, and Mash (1999) examined whether 3- to 4-month-olds could also represent BETWEEN, a spatial-relational category that requires encoding the location of a target object in relation to two referent objects.

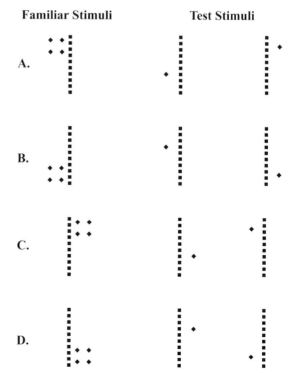

Figure 6.4 Familiarization stimuli (a composite of the four exemplars) and test stimuli used to determine whether infants form category representations for LEFT (*A*, *B*) or RIGHT (*C*, *D*) in Quinn (2004).

The experimental procedure was identical to that used by Quinn (1994, 2004), Quinn et al. (1996), and Mash et al. (1998), and the stimuli are depicted in figure 6.5. Infants were presented with a diamond appearing in different locations between two bars (displayed either as rows or columns) and then shown a test stimulus depicting the diamond in a new location between the bars paired with a test stimulus showing the diamond outside the bars (either above or below the rows or to the left or right of the columns). The infants did not prefer either test stimulus. Moreover, the same null result was obtained in a follow-up experiment in which familiarization time was doubled, indicating that the failure to observe a novel category preference was not simply a reflection of there being more information to encode (i.e., two bars instead of one; but see Casasola, 2005b). Quinn et al. (1999) then tested a group of 6- to 7-month-olds, and the preference for the novel spatial relation was observed, indicating that the older infants had represented BETWEEN. Control experiments upheld this interpretation by

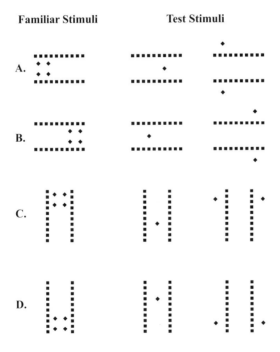

Figure 6.5 (*A, B*) Familiarization stimuli (a composite of the four diamond-between-rows exemplars) and test stimuli used to determine whether infants could form a category representation for BETWEEN. The test stimulus depicted to the right is a composite of the two diamond-outside-rows exemplars. (*C, D*) Familiarization stimuli (a composite of the four diamond-between-columns exemplars) and test stimuli used to determine whether infants could form a category representation for BETWEEN. The test stimulus depicted to the right is a composite of the two diamond-outside-columns exemplars. Adapted from Quinn et al. (1999).

demonstrating that infants did not have a spontaneous preference for stimuli depicting the diamond outside the bars over stimuli depicting the diamond between the bars and were sensitive to the changes in the location of the diamond between the bars.

The fact that younger infants readily formed category representations for ABOVE versus BELOW and LEFT versus RIGHT, whereas only older infants provided evidence of a category representation for BETWEEN, suggests that representations that require encoding the relation between a target and single referent emerge developmentally earlier than representations that require encoding the relation between a target and two referents. It is interesting that infants display success in tasks requiring them to encode a target object located to one or another side of a vertical or horizontal referent line, but respond with a null preference in a task requiring encoding a target object located in the region between two horizontal lines or two vertical lines. The infant data may have a correspondence with a distinction that has been made in the literature on the encoding of spatial location information in children and adults (Huttenlocher & Newcombe, 1984; Newcombe & Huttenlocher, 2000; Talmy, 1983). In particular, Huttenlocher and Newcombe (1984) distinguished between location coding in relation to a single landmark and location coding in relation to multiple landmarks that constitute a local spatial framework. Similarly, Newcombe and Huttenlocher (2000) drew a distinction between point landmarks and "landmarks seen as constituting a region" (p. 15). Likewise, Talmy (1983) differentiated location coding involving "one object's spatial disposition in terms of another" (p. 230) and "more than one referent object" (p. 245). Moreover, the findings reviewed in Huttenlocher and Newcombe (1984) indicate that young children can represent targets in relation to single landmarks before 3 years of age, but that encoding of targets in relation to multiple landmarks that define a local spatial framework does not appear until 5 years of age. These data led Huttenlocher and Newcombe (1984) to propose that children move from landmark to framework coding during development. Together, the infant categorization and child location-encoding data are in accord with a general developmental trend from encoding targets in relation to *point* referents to encoding targets in relation to *region* referents. This trend is of theoretical interest because it runs counter to the claim that children initially begin to encode space in terms of topological concepts such as enclosure and only subsequently represent Euclidean concepts in which objects are represented in relation to horizontal or vertical reference lines (Piaget & Inhelder, 1967).

The point-to-region progression observed in the infant categorization studies is consistent with spatial language acquisition data showing that monoreferential spatial terms (e.g., "under") are comprehended by children between 2 and 3 years of age, whereas bireferential spatial terms (e.g., "between") are not comprehended until children are 3 to 4.5 years of age (Weist et al., 1997). The combination of findings leads to the intriguing suggestion that the order of acquisition of spatial-relational concepts in preverbal infants might predict the order of acquisition of the relevant words in the child's spatial lexicon. Here is an instance where spatial language acquisition appears to recapitulate preverbal spatial conceptual acquisition. At one level, this idea does not make sense: if a preverbal infant represents the concept BETWEEN, even though this acquisition occurs developmentally later than the representation of concepts such as ABOVE and BELOW, then there is no particular reason why toddlers and young children should find the spatial term "between" harder to learn than the spatial terms "above" and "below." However, at another level, the idea harkens back to Piaget's (1954) notion of *decalage*, in which children are hypothesized to solve a problem at the level of perception, but not at the level of verbal expression. That is, what an infant learns at an early age at the level of perception may have to be relearned later at the level of verbal thought. This way of thinking would be consistent with the argument that there is some level of independence between prelinguistic conceptual organization, on the one hand, and language-labeling practices, on the other (Papafragou, Massey, & Gleitman, 2002), although the fact that the same progressions are occurring in each suggests that both may be governed by the same general principles of learning and development, a point addressed in the concluding section.

What may also play a role in producing this correspondence is the interaction between the cognitive system and the task structure. In particular, one might expect to see the same relative ordering of spatial relations across visual and verbal tasks because the task structure specifying BETWEEN relations is more complex than that specifying ABOVE/BELOW or LEFT/RIGHT relations (though verbal tasks are more difficult overall than visual tasks). As noted, framework representations may be more complex than landmark representations. A related possibility is that BETWEEN requires infants to represent an object as being ABOVE (or to the right of) one referent at the same time that the object is also being represented as BELOW (or to the left of) another referent. While infants may be able to represent one object as ABOVE (or to the right of) or BELOW (or to the left of) another, they may have difficulty in terms of representing both relations simultaneously in the computation of BETWEEN. An additional possibility is that BETWEEN is more constrained in terms of distance separating the referent objects. That is, ABOVE/BELOW and LEFT/RIGHT can be used across a wide range of distances from the referent objects, whereas BETWEEN may be more selectively applied when the two referents are close (see Plumert & Hawkins, 2001).

Consistent with the suggestion that how children grasp spatial terms mirrors their performance on nonlinguistic spatial tasks are the findings that 3- and 4-year-olds use IN and ON to disambiguate identical locations much more readily than BY (e.g., "the mouse is in the bag on the chair" vs. "the mouse is in the bag by the chair"; see Plumert, Ewert, & Spear, 1995; Plumert & Hawkins, 2001). This pattern of emergence parallels the order in which English-speaking children acquire these terms (e.g., Washington & Naremore, 1978).

6.4 DEVELOPMENTAL TREND 2: SIMPLE
TO COMPOUND RELATIONS

There is an unexamined alternative to the idea that infants in Quinn (1994, 2004), Quinn et al. (1996), and Mash et al. (1998) represented the spatial-relational concepts of ABOVE versus BELOW and LEFT versus RIGHT. In particular, it is possible that the infants were simply representing an arbi-trary *crossing* of one object (e.g., a dot or diamond) relative to another (i.e., the bar). That is, in each of the cited investigations, the change from one spatial relation to another (i.e., from left to right or right to left and from above to below or below to above) was confounded with an object crossing from one side to the other side of a reference bar. This aspect of the exper-imental design left open the question of whether the infants might simply have been responding to any crossing of a target object from one side to the other side of a reference bar. To examine this possibility, Quinn (2004) re-peated the spatial categorization experiment that was the basis for the argu-ment that infants could represent ABOVE versus BELOW and LEFT ver-sus RIGHT, except that the bar was oriented at 45°, rather than at 0° (horizontal) or 90° (vertical). The stimuli are shown in figure 6.6. If the in-fants are merely responding to the crossing of a target object (e.g., dia-mond) with respect to a referent object (e.g., bar), then a preference for the novel spatial relation should be maintained. Alternatively, if the infants in the earlier studies were representing spatial relations such as ABOVE, BELOW, LEFT, and RIGHT, then one would not expect a preference for

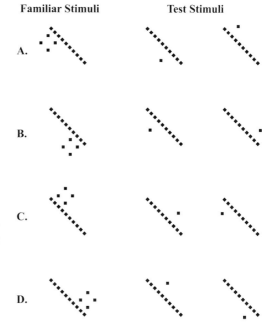

Familiar Stimuli   **Test Stimuli**

A.

B.

C.

D.

Figure 6.6   Familiarization stimuli (a composite of the four exemplars) and test stim-uli used to determine whether infants could form category representations for BELOW-LEFT (*A, B*) and ABOVE-RIGHT (*C, D*) in Quinn (2004).

the novel spatial relation, given that the crossing in this case is more arbitrary and does not map cleanly onto a fundamental spatial relational concept. The infants did not prefer the novel spatial relation, and a follow-up experiment demonstrated that the null preference outcomes were not the result of a failure to process the diagonal orientation of the bar. Infants familiarized with the bar oriented at 45° or 135° counterclockwise from vertical, and then preference tested with both orientations, showed a preference for the novel orientation. Taken together, the findings imply that the previous studies investigating the categorization of spatial relation information by infants were demonstrating that infants can represent ABOVE versus BELOW (Mash et al., 1998; Quinn, 1994; Quinn et al., 1996) and LEFT versus RIGHT (Quinn, 2004), rather than simply responding to a crossing of one element (e.g., diamond) from one to the other side of another element (e.g., bar).

It is of theoretical interest that infants categorically encoded the spatial relation of a target and referent object when the referent object was oriented horizontally (Mash et al., 1998; Quinn, 1994; Quinn et al., 1996) or vertically (Quinn, 2004), but not diagonally (Quinn, 2004). The results obtained with infants seem to foreshadow the finding that adults remember the location of points in a two-dimensional space in terms of categories marked by the horizontal and vertical axes of the space, rather than the diagonal axes of the space (Huttenlocher et al., 1991). They also bring to mind Rosch's (1975) report that, for adults, horizontal and vertical but not diagonal axes serve as cognitive referents for organizing spatial orientation information. In a stimulus placement task, Rosch (1975) observed that deviations 10° away from horizontal and vertical, but not away from diagonal, were placed closer to true horizontal and vertical than true horizontal and vertical were placed closer to the 10° deviations. The results of the infant categorization studies show that young infants can represent ABOVE and BELOW categories relative to a horizontal axis and LEFT and RIGHT categories relative to a vertical axis, but do not represent ABOVE-LEFT and BELOW-RIGHT categories relative to a diagonal axis. The findings are significant in that they imply that infants are doing something more than simply subdividing a space into two regions based on available referents. Moreover, the horizontal and vertical axes, but not diagonal axes, may provide the spatial domain with initial structure by serving as cognitive referents for the categorical coding of spatial relation information even in early infancy (Quinn, 2000).

The data further suggest that there may be a set of simple spatial-relational concepts that (a) cannot be decomposed into more basic elements (i.e., are not derivable from other spatial-relational concepts), (b) correspond with single words (e.g., ABOVE, BELOW, LEFT, RIGHT), and (c) are learned more readily than compound spatial-relational concepts (e.g., ABOVE-LEFT, BELOW-RIGHT). One is reminded of the domain of color, for which it is believed that a small number of basic color categories are biologically given and cannot be broken down into more elemental

experiences (Quinn, Rosano, & Wooten, 1988; Quinn, Wooten, & Ludman, 1985). Moreover, the basic color terms that correspond with the elemental color categories are acquired developmentally prior to color terms
that correspond to composite color experiences (Berlin & Kay, 1969; Kay
& McDaniel, 1978).

As noted above, some of the recent thinking on the topic of space and
language can be described as neo-Whorfian, characterized by the perspective that language acquisition helps to structure the concepts being formed
(Bowerman & Levinson, 2001). However, the present data are consistent
with the idea that while infants are powerful learners of spatial relation concepts, they do not learn all relations equally well. BELOW-LEFT versus
ABOVE-RIGHT of a diagonal bar is a more difficult spatial category distinction for infants to learn than ABOVE versus BELOW a horizontal bar
and LEFT versus RIGHT of a vertical bar. The nonlinguistic differences
may have a correspondence with later linguistic differences in that children
learning English eventually come to comprehend spatial terms such as
"above," "below," "left," and "right," whereas English does not have any
single-word spatial terms to express direction away from the diagonal.
More generally, just as some aspects of language acquisition may shape
concept formation, some aspects of concept formation may shape language
acquisition. As Landau (2003) has suggested, "The basic spatial terms—
those that are monomorphemic—are few in number, and they appear to
capture a distinctive set of spatial relationships . . . these spatial 'meanings'
might have originated in the way the brain encodes location nonlinguistically." The findings reported here provide support for Landau's (2003)
observation and indicate that the ability to represent some spatial relations
(ABOVE vs. BELOW a horizontal axis or LEFT vs. RIGHT of a vertical
axis) as more fundamental than others (ABOVE-RIGHT vs. BELOW-
LEFT of a diagonal axis) may be derived from the very early settings of our
perceptual-cognitive system. Whether such settings reflect either true initial
starting points, perhaps derived from our recent evolutionary history of
walking upright through a structured world (H. H. Clark, 1973), or the effects of early experience remains an important question to be answered.

6.5 DEVELOPMENTAL TREND 3: CONCRETE
TO ABSTRACT REPRESENTATIONS

To support the linguistic acquisition of spatial terms, representations for
spatial relations would need to be generalizable across variation in objects.
Adults observe many different objects in a variety of spatial relations and
maintain their spatial concepts despite changes in the objects. For example,
adults can be presented with A above B, and then subsequently with C
above D, and recognize the equivalence of the ABOVE relation, despite
variation in the objects depicting the relation. In addition, children from
about the age of 2.5 years can encode the equivalence of spatial relations
across at least some variation among the particular objects depicting the

relations (Deloache, Kolstad, & Anderson, 1991; Uttal, Schreiber, & Deloache, 1995).

To examine the level of abstraction of young infants' representation of spatial relation information, 3- and 4-month-olds were administered an object-variation version of the ABOVE versus BELOW categorization task (Quinn et al., 1996). As shown in figure 6.7, four distinct shapes appeared above or below the bar during familiarization, and in the preference test, a novel shape in the familiar spatial relation was paired with the same shape in a novel spatial relation. The shapes were randomly selected for each infant from among seven shapes shown to be discriminably different in a control experiment (i.e., arrow, diamond, dollar sign, dot, letter E, plus sign, triangle). If the infants form category representations for ABOVE and BELOW despite variation in the objects depicting the relations, then the preference for the novel spatial relation observed in the original ABOVE versus BELOW experiment conducted without object variation should be maintained. Alternatively, if the infants do not form category representations for ABOVE versus BELOW, then one would not expect a preference for either test stimulus, given that each contains a familiar referent bar and the

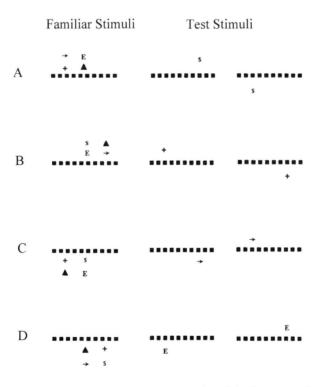

Figure 6.7 Familiarization exemplars (a composite of the four exemplars) and test stimuli used in the object-variation version of the ABOVE versus BELOW categorization task in Quinn et al. (1996).

same novel target shape. Young infants did not differentially attend to either test stimulus, a result that held true even when the infants were provided with additional familiarization time (Quinn, Polly, Furer, Dobson, & Narter, 2002). However, when older infants in the age range between 6 and 7 months were tested, a preference for the novel spatial relation was observed. The findings from the two age groups support the idea that category representations of spatial relations may initially be restricted to the objects depicting the relations but, with development, become more abstract such that various objects can be presented in the same relation and the equivalence of the relation is preserved despite the variation.

Subsequent experimentation has confirmed the concrete-to-abstract hypothesis for the development of spatial-relational concepts in infants. For example, Quinn et al. (2002) questioned whether the failure of the younger infants to represent abstract ABOVE and BELOW concepts in the object-variation version of the spatial categorization task might simply reflect that infants were distracted away from the spatial nature of the task because of either the object variation during familiarization or object novelty during the preference test. However, when the object-variation version of the ABOVE versus BELOW categorization task was repeated, in one case with only a single object presented during familiarization (thereby eliminating object variation during familiarization) or in another case with infants prefamiliarized with the object that would moments later appear on the test trials (thus reducing object novelty during test trials), the 3- to 4-month-olds continued to divide their attention between the test stimuli. In a different modification of the object-variation version of the ABOVE versus BELOW categorization task, however, one in which an object-bar relation shown during test trials matched with an object-bar relation that was presented during familiarization, the younger infants did prefer the novel spatial relation. The design of this latter task is illustrated in figure 6.8.

What does this sequence of failures and single success tell us? It appears that infants are binding specific objects with individual spatial representations as each exemplar is presented. On each trial, when a new pair of objects is presented, a new spatial representation is formed. For example, with the familiarization sequences shown in figures 6.7A and 6.8A, the infants would represent the specific instances ARROW ABOVE BAR, PLUS SIGN ABOVE BAR, E ABOVE BAR, and TRIANGLE ABOVE BAR but not link these instances together in a more general representation of OBJECT ABOVE BAR or ABOVE. This account explains why the infants divide their attention when presented during test trials with a stimulus depicting a dollar sign above the bar paired with a stimulus depicting the dollar sign below the bar (as shown in figure 6.7A). DOLLAR SIGN ABOVE BAR is represented as a novel stimulus, and so is DOLLAR SIGN BELOW BAR. Neither matches an object-bar relation that was presented during familiarization. The account also explains why infants prefer the novel spatial relation when presented during test trials with a stimulus depicting a triangle above the bar paired with a stimulus showing the triangle

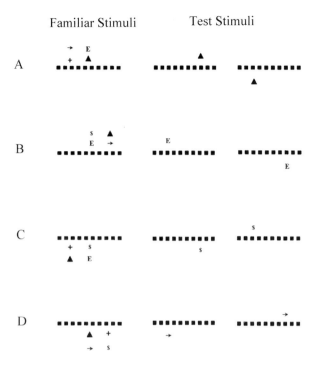

Figure 6.8 Familiarization exemplars (a composite of the four exemplars) and test stimuli used in the modified object-variation ABOVE versus BELOW categorization task in Quinn et al. (2002).

below the bar (as shown in figure 6.8A). The TRIANGLE ABOVE BAR test stimulus matches with the representation of the TRIANGLE ABOVE BAR familiarization stimulus, whereas the TRIANGLE BELOW BAR test stimulus does not match any of the representations formed during familiarization.

Overall, then, young infants seem to encode the spatial relations between specific pairs of objects but not spatial relations abstracted across a number of different pairs of objects. The ability to form a concrete concept for A ABOVE Z appears to have developmental primacy over the ability to form an abstract concept of A, B, C, and D ABOVE Z that can be generalized to E ABOVE Z. Although the encoding of spatial relation information by young infants lacks abstraction, it provides the concreteness necessary to support a spatial memory system that must remember the relative location of specific objects. A question for which we do not currently have an answer is whether older, 6- to 7-month-old infants, who have been shown to represent abstract ABOVE and BELOW concepts, continue to represent the concrete version of the concepts, as well. This question remains open at least in part because of the difficulty of testing for the concrete version of the concept in an age group that has already demonstrated an ability to represent the abstract version of the concept. That is, if the older infants succeeded on a version of the task in which an object-bar relation shown during test trials matched with an object-bar relation that was presented during familiarization (as depicted in figure 6.8), one would not know whether it was the abstract or concrete version of the concept that was mediating performance. This ambiguity aside, it would be adaptive for infants to retain the specifics of the exemplars in order to remember information about a specific object in relation to a particular landmark.

In addition to the concrete-to-abstract developmental shift that characterizes the representation of ABOVE and BELOW, infants' representation of BETWEEN appears to undergo the same shift (Quinn, Adams, Kennedy, Shettler, & Wasnik, 2003). However, the developmental time frame during which the shift occurs is from 6–7 to 9–10 months, rather than from 3–4 to 6–7 months as was observed for the representations of ABOVE and BELOW. This finding is of significance because it indicates that a broadly transferable abstraction ability does not have a rapid onset at 6–7 months, such that all category representations for spatial relations formed by that age could take on an abstract nature (see Mandler, 2000). Rather, the difference in developmental timing for the concrete-to-abstract developmental shift observed for ABOVE and BELOW, on the one hand, and BETWEEN, on the other, suggests that the concrete representations for different spatial relations emerge at different points in developmental time depending on their ease of initial acquisition (e.g., landmark vs. framework representations) and that each representation undergoes its own period of development (approximating several months) from concrete to abstract.

The finding that what infants learn for ABOVE and BELOW by 6–7 months of age does not readily transfer to the representation of BETWEEN is consistent with what Hespos and Baillargeon (2001) have reported for how infants learn categories of dynamic physical events such as occlusion and containment. Infants can represent height as a variable relevant for predicting the outcomes of occlusion events by 4.5 months of age but do not represent height as relevant for guiding expectations about containment events until 7.5 months of age. The decalages that characterize infants' representation of spatial and physical concepts are consistent with the idea that each concept has its own learning trajectory, even though there may be predictable developmental progressions (e.g., from concrete to abstract cognitive structures) occurring within each trajectory.

The concrete-to-abstract developmental trend in the representation of spatial relation information has also been observed in spatial categorization tasks involving realistic objects and dynamic stimulus presentations of containment and support relations in the age range from 10 to 18 months (Casasola, 2005; Casasola & Cohen, 2002). In addition, Cohen and Oakes (1993) have reported a similar developmental trend for infants' representations of causal relations between objects. When 10-month-old infants initially begin to represent the causal relations between pairs of objects during the presentation of dynamic collision events, the representation of causality is facilitated when the objects playing the roles of "agent" and "recipient" are kept constant.

The correspondence between data on the representation of spatial and causal relations in preverbal infants is suggestive of a more general concrete-to-abstract developmental trajectory that may occur in the acquisition of a variety of concepts (Colunga & Smith, 2003). The concrete-to-abstract developmental trend observed in the preverbal period for infants' representation of spatial and causal relations also appears to foreshadow a developmental trend observed in relational language acquisition. According to Tomasello's (1992) "verb island hypothesis," the mapping of novel verbs onto novel action events is conservative and done on a case-by-case basis. Just as preverbal infants do not transfer spatial and causal relations across objects, language-learning toddlers do not transfer structure across verbs that express action relations. Thus, in preverbal learning of spatial and causal relations, and in linguistic learning of verbs that express action relations, children move from concrete item-based constructions to more general and abstract forms. Once more then, a developmental trend observed in preverbal concept acquisition seems to have a language-learning analogue.

6.6 SUMMARY AND CONCLUSIONS

This chapter reviews a line of studies investigating how infants parse space prior to language. Such evidence is critical for understanding the contribution that nonlinguistic spatial cognition makes toward the acquisition of a spatial lexicon. The data indicate that well before infants are producing language, they are forming category representations for spatial relations. These representations are likely to be derived from core processes that allow infants to process space hierarchically (in terms of categorical spatial relations and finer grained location differences between objects within categories) and that serve to structure space in ways that language may then build on to create language-specific semantic categories (E. V. Clark, 2004).

A theoretical approach to object category development by infants has been developed by Quinn and Eimas (1996, 1997, 2000). In this approach, early category development occurs through the application of perceptual processes and learning processes that permit associations and links. One can ask whether such an approach would also be applicable to the domain of space. The position taken here is that while the two forms of categorization operating on object versus spatial inputs may tap different brain processes, that is, what versus where mechanisms (Mishkin, Ungerleider, & Macko, 1983; but see Johnson & Vecera, 1996), the operation of categorization as a core process (e.g., the representation of consistent structure against a backdrop of changing exemplars) remains the same in both cases.

In support of the proposal that categorization is a core cognitive process that provides a starting point for knowledge acquisition independently of the stimulus domain in which it is operative, there is evidence to indicate that some of the same trends that have been observed in object category development may also be observed in spatial category development. For example, both object and spatial categories may vary in their ease of acquisition depending on their structural complexity. In the object domain, global-level categories such as animals and vehicles may be formed early on the basis of single attribute comparisons such as legs versus wheels or curvilinear versus rectilinear contours, whereas basic- and subordinate-level categories such as cats versus dogs and St. Bernards versus beagles may be formed subsequently on the basis of multiple attribute comparisons that rely on distinguishing specific values along a number of shared features (Quinn, 2002). Likewise, in the spatial domain, representations for ABOVE and BELOW may be formed readily by comparing the location of a target object to just one other object (a landmark representation), whereas a representation for BETWEEN may be formed less readily because it requires comparison of a target object to multiple objects that define a local spatial framework (a framework representation).

An additional example of commonality in the development of object and spatial categorization concerns the emergence of unitary, more naturally cohering concepts versus compound, more arbitrary concepts. In the domain of objects, computational learning systems designed to simulate the object categorization behavior of young infants in tasks measuring looking time categorically differentiated mammals (e.g., cats, dogs, elephants, rabbits) from furniture (e.g., beds, chairs, dressers, and tables) more rapidly than between arbitrary categories consisting of both mammals and furniture (e.g., cats, elephants, beds, and chairs vs. dogs, rabbits, dressers, and tables; see Quinn & Johnson, 1997). In the same way, in the domain of space, infants learn basic spatial categories such as ABOVE or RIGHT more efficiently than spatial categories consisting of more arbitrary combinations of these basic categories (e.g., ABOVE-RIGHT).

One further example supporting the idea of categorization as a core process in the development of representations for object and spatial information is the trend toward increasing abstraction in both domains. Specifically, for objects, the category representations of young infants are likely to be based on perceptual features that can be detected from the surfaces of the exemplars. Such representations may then serve as perceptually based placeholders for the accumulation of more abstract knowledge acquired beyond infancy. Similarly, for space, representations for spatial relations appear at first to be tied to the visible features of the objects depicting these relations but become more abstract as the representations become able to incorporate a variety of objects that display the relation. In this way, category representations for objects and spatial relations can be viewed as adaptive mental structures for partitioning experience in ways that provide a starting point for the growth of cognitive organization and content.

Just as there are correspondences between prelingual object and spatial category development, there are also developments in the category representations for spatial relations occurring prelingually that seem to have language-learning counterparts. First, preverbal infants learn landmark representations (e.g., ABOVE, BELOW, LEFT, RIGHT) earlier than framework representations (e.g., BETWEEN). An analogous linguistic trend has been observed when young children acquire monoreferential spatial terms such as "under" before they acquire bireferential spatial terms such as "between." Second, preverbal infants more readily represent simple spatial relations that can be expressed with single words (e.g., ABOVE, BELOW, LEFT, RIGHT) more readily than compound spatial relations that cannot be expressed with monomorphemic spatial terms (e.g., ABOVE-LEFT vs. BELOW-RIGHT). Third, prior to language, category representations for spatial relations undergo a concrete-to-abstract shift. Broad generalizable representations for spatial relations are derived from precursor representations that are tied to the perceptual particulars of the objects depicting the relations. A linguistic phenomenon that resembles the concrete-to-abstract shift can be found in verb learning, which also seems to move from specific items to general forms as children acquire language to express action relations.

As mentioned at the beginning of the chapter, some of the recent work at the interface of space and language has suggested that language-specific lexicalization patterns may restructure (e.g., Majid et al., 2004), select (e.g., Hespos & Spelke, 2004), or combine (e.g., Hermer-Vazquez et al., 1999) nonlinguistic spatial representations to help produce the semantics of spatial terms acquired by children (Bowerman & Levinson, 2001). In these various scenarios, language is affecting cognition. The present discussion has emphasized an influence in the opposite direction, namely, one in which progressions in nonlinguistic spatial cognition foreshadow subsequent trajectories in spatial semantic development. That similar ontogenetic trends can be observed in the acquisition of nonlinguistic spatial categories and language-specific semantic categories suggests that both may be constrained by general principles of perception, learning, and development.

ACKNOWLEDGMENTS   Preparation of this chapter was supported by grants HD-42451 and HD-46526 from the National Institute of Child Health and Human Development. I thank Jodie Plumert and John Spencer for inviting the contribution and providing helpful comments on an earlier draft of the manuscript. Feedback from an anonymous graduate student reviewer was also appreciated.

REFERENCES

Berlin, B., & Kay, P. (1969). *Basic color terms: Their universality and evolution*. Berkeley: University of California Press.

Bowerman, M., & Choi, S. (2001). Shaping meanings for language: Universal and language-specific in the acquisition of spatial semantic categories. In M. Bowerman & S. C. Levinson (Eds.), *Language acquisition and conceptual development* (pp. 475–511). Cambridge: Cambridge University Press.

Bowerman, M., & Levinson, S. C. (Eds.). (2001). *Language acquisition and conceptual development*. Cambridge: Cambridge University Press.

Bruner, J. S., Goodnow, J. J., & Austin, G. A. (1956). *A study of thinking*. New York: Wiley.

Casasola, M. (2005a). Can language do the driving? The effect of linguistic input on infants' categorization of support spatial relations. *Developmental Psychology*, *41*, 183–192.

Casasola, M. (2005b). When less is more: How infants learn to form an abstract categorical representation of support. *Child Development*, *76*, 279–290.

Casasola, M., & Cohen, L. B. (2002). Infant categorization of containment, support, and tight fit spatial relationships. *Developmental Science*, *5*, 247–264.

Choi, S., & Bowerman, M. (1991). Learning to express motion events in English and Korean: The influence of language-specific lexicalization patterns. *Cognition*, *41*, 83–121.

Clark, E. V. (2004). How language acquisition builds on cognitive development. *Trends in Cognitive Sciences*, *8*, 472–478.

Clark, H. H. (1973). Space, time, semantics, and the child. In T. E. Moore (Ed.), *Cognitive development and the acquisition of language* (pp. 27–63). New York: Academic Press.

Cohen, L. B., & Oakes, L. M. (1993). How infants perceive a simple causal event. *Developmental Psychology*, *29*, 421–433.

Colunga, E., & Smith, L. B. (2003). The emergence of abstract ideas: Evidence from networks and babies. *Philosophical Transactions by the Royal Society*, *358*, 1205–1214.

Deloache, J. S., Kolstad, V., & Anderson, K. (1991). Physical similarity and young children's understanding of scale models. *Child Development*, *62*, 111–126.

Depy, D., Fagot, J., & Vauclair, J. (1999). Processing of above/below categorical spatial relations by baboons (*Papio papio*). *Behavioral Processes*, *48*, 1–9.

Hermer-Vazquez, L., Spelke, E. S., & Katsnelson, A. S. (1999). Sources of flexibility in human cognition: Dual task studies of space and language. *Cognitive Psychology*, *39*, 3–36.

Hespos, S. J., & Baillargeon, R. (2005). Infants' knowledge about occlusion and containment events: A surprising discrepancy. *Psychological Science*, *12*, 141–147.

Hespos, S. J., & Spelke, E. S. (2004). Conceptual precursors to language. *Nature*, *430*, 453–456.

Huttenlocher, J., Hedges, L. V., & Duncan, S. (1991). Categories and particulars: Prototype effects in estimating spatial location. *Psychological Review*, *98*, 352–376.

Huttenlocher, J., & Newcombe, N. (1984). The child's representation of information about location. In C. Sophian (Ed.), *Origins of cognitive skills* (pp. 84–111). Hillsdale, NJ: Erlbaum.

Huttenlocher, J., Newcombe, N., & Sandberg, E. H. (1994). The coding of spatial location in young children. *Cognitive Psychology*, *27*, 115–148.

Johnson, M. H., & Vecera, S. P. (1996). Cortical differentiation and neurocognitive development: The parcellation conjecture. *Behavioural Processes*, *36*, 195–212.

Johnston, J. R. (1988). Children's verbal representation of spatial location. In J. Stiles-Davis, M. Kritchevsky, & U. Bellugi (Eds.), *Spatial cognition* (pp. 195–206). Hillsdale, NJ: Erlbaum.

Johnston, J. R., & Slobin, D. (1979). The development of locative expressions in English, Italian, Serbo-Croatian, and Turkish. *Journal of Child Language*, *6*, 529–545.

Kay, P., & McDaniel, C. K. (1978). The linguistic significance of the meanings of basic color terms. *Language, 54*, 610–646.

Koenig, O., Reiss, L. P., & Kosslyn, S. M. (1990). The development of spatial relation representations: Evidence from studies of cerebral lateralization. *Journal of Experimental Child Psychology, 50*, 119–130.

Kosslyn, S. M., Koenig, O., Barrett, A., Cave, C. B., Tang, J., & Gabrieli, J. D. E. (1989). Evidence for two types of spatial representations: Hemispheric specialization for categorical and coordinate relations. *Journal of Experimental Psychology: Human Perception & Performance, 15*, 723–735.

Laeng, B. (1994). Lateralization of categorical and coordinate spatial functions: A study of unilateral stroke patients. *Journal of Cognitive Neuroscience, 6*, 189–203.

Landau, B. (2003). Axes and direction in spatial language and spatial cognition. In E. van der Zee & J. Slack (Eds.), *Representing direction in language and space* (pp. 18–38). Oxford: Oxford University Press.

Majid, A., Bowerman, M., Kita , S., Haun, D. B., & Levinson, S. C. (2004). Can language restructure cognition? The case for space. *Trends in Cognitive Sciences, 8*, 108–114.

Mandler, J. M. (1996). Preverbal representation and language. In P. Bloom, M. A. Peterson, L. Nadel, & M. F. Garrett (Eds.), *Language and space* (pp. 109–169). Cambridge, MA: MIT Press.

Mandler, J. M. (2000). Perceptual and conceptual processes. *Journal of Cognition & Development, 1*, 3–36.

Mash, C., Quinn, P. C., Dobson, V., & Narter, D. B. (1998). Global influences on the development of spatial and object perceptual categorization abilities: Evidence from preterm infants. *Developmental Science, 1*, 85–102.

McDonough, L., Choi, S., & Mandler, J. M. (2003). Understanding spatial relations: Flexible infants, lexical adults. *Cognitive Psychology, 46*, 229–259.

Meints, K., Plunkett, K., Harris, P. L., & Dimmock, D. (2002). What is "on" and "under" for 15-, 18-, and 24-month-old infants? Typicality effects in early comprehension of spatial preopositions. *British Journal of Developmental Psychology, 20*, 113–130.

Mishkin, M., Ungerleider, L. G., & Macko, K. A. (1983). Object vision and spatial vision: two cortical pathways. *Trends in Neuroscience, 6*, 414–417.

Murphy, G. L. (2002). *The big book of concepts*. Cambridge, MA: MIT Press.

Newcombe, N., & Huttenlocher, J. (2000). *Making space: The development of spatial representation and reasoning*. Cambridge, MA: MIT Press.

Papafragou, A., Massey, C., & Gleitman, L. (2002). Shake, rattle, 'n' roll: the representation of motion in language and cognition. *Cognition, 84*, 189–219.

Pascalis, O., de Haan, M., & Nelson, C. A. (2002). Is face-processing species-specific during the first year of life? *Science, 296*, 1321–1323.

Piaget, J. (1954). *The construction of reality in the child*. New York: Basic Books.

Piaget, J., & Inhelder, B. (1967). *The child's conception of space*. New York: Norton.

Plumert, J. M., Ewert, K., & Spear, S. J. (1995). The early development of children's communication about nested spatial relations. *Child Development, 66*, 959–969.

Plumert, J. M., & Hawkins, A. M. (2001). Biases in young children's communication about spatial relations: Containment versus proximity. *Child Development, 72*, 22–36.

Quinn, P. C. (1994). The categorization of above and below spatial relations by young infants. *Child Development, 65*, 58–69.

Quinn, P. C. (2000). Perceptual reference points for form and orientation in young infants: Anchors or magnets? *Perception & Psychophysics*, *62*, 1625–1633.

Quinn, P. C. (2002). Early categorization: A new synthesis. In U. Goswami (Ed.), *Blackwell handbook of childhood cognitive development* (pp. 84–101). Oxford: Blackwell Publishers.

Quinn, P. C. (2004). Spatial representation by young infants: Categorization of spatial relations or sensitivity to a crossing primitive? *Memory & Cognition*, *32*, 852–861.

Quinn, P. C., Adams, A., Kennedy, E., Shettler, L., & Wasnik, A. (2003). Development of an abstract category representation for the spatial relation BETWEEN in 6- to 10-month-old infants. *Developmental Psychology*, *39*, 151–163.

Quinn, P. C., & Bhatt, R. S. (2005a). Good continuation affects discrimination of visual pattern information in young infants. *Perception & Psychophysics*, *67*, 1171–1176.

Quinn, P. C., & Bhatt, R. S. (2005b). Learning perceptual organization in infancy. *Psychological Science*, *16*, 515–519.

Quinn, P. C., Brown, C. R., & Streppa, M. L. (1997). Perceptual organization of complex visual configurations by young infants. *Infant Behavior & Development*, *20*, 35–46.

Quinn, P. C., Cummins, M., Kase, J., Martin, E., & Weissman, S. (1996). Development of categorical representations for above and below spatial relations in 3- to 7-month-old infants. *Developmental Psychology*, *32*, 642–650.

Quinn, P. C., & Eimas, P. D. (1996). Perceptual organization and categorization in young infants. In C. Rovee-Collier & L. P. Lipsitt (Eds.), *Advances in infancy research* (Vol. 10, pp. 1–36). Norwood, NJ: Ablex.

Quinn, P. C., & Eimas, P. D. (1997). A reexamination of the perceptual-to-conceptual shift in mental representations. *Review of General Psychology*, *1*, 271–287.

Quinn, P. C., & Eimas, P. D. (2000). The emergence of category representations during infancy: Are separate perceptual and conceptual processes required? *Journal of Cognition & Development*, *1*, 55–61.

Quinn, P. C., & Johnson, M. H. (1997). The emergence of perceptual category representations in young infants: A connectionist analysis. *Journal of Experimental Child Psychology*, *66*, 236–263.

Quinn, P. C., Norris, C. M., Pasko, R. N., Schmader, T. M., & Mash, C. (1999). Formation of a categorical representation for the spatial relation between by 6- to 7-month-old infants. *Visual Cognition*, *6*, 569–585.

Quinn, P. C., Polly, J. L., Furer, M. J., Dobson, V., & Narter, D. B. (2002). Young infants' performance in the object-variation version of the above-below categorization task: A result of perceptual distraction or conceptual limitation? *Infancy*, *3*, 323–347.

Quinn, P. C., Rosano, J. L., & Wooten, B. R. (1988). Evidence that brown is not an elemental color. *Perception & Psychophysics*, *43*, 156–164.

Quinn, P. C., & Schyns, P. G. (2003). What goes up may come down: Perceptual process and knowledge access in the organization of complex visual patterns by young infants. *Cognitive Science*, *27*, 923–935.

Quinn, P. C., Wooten, B. R., & Ludman, E. J. (1985). Achromatic color categories. *Perception & Psychophysics*, *37*, 198–204.

Regier, T. (1996). *The human semantic potential: Spatial language and constrained connectionism*. Cambridge, MA: MIT Press.

Rosch, E. H. (1975). Cognitive reference points. *Cognitive Psychology*, *7*, 532–547.

Spinozzi, G., Lubrano, G., & Truppa, V. (2004). Categorization of above and below spatial relations by tufted capuchin monkeys (*Cebus apella*). *Journal of Comparative Psychology, 118*, 403–412.

Talmy, L (1983). How language structures space. In H. L. Pick & L. Acredolo (Eds.), *Spatial orientation: Theory, research, and application* (pp. 225–282). New York: Plenum Press.

Tomasello, M. (1992). *First verbs: A case study of early grammatical development.* Cambridge: Cambridge University Press.

Uttal, D. H., Schreiber, J. C., & Deloache, J. S. (1995). Waiting to use a symbol: The effects of delay on children's use of models. *Child Development, 66*, 1875–1889.

Washington, D. S., & Naremore, R. C. (1978). Children's use of spatial prepositions in two- and three-dimensional tasks. *Journal of Speech & Hearing Research*, 21, 151–165.

Weist, R. M., Lyytinen, P., Wysocka, J., & Atanassova, M. (1997). The interaction of language and thought in children's language acquisition: A crosslinguistic study. *Journal of Child Language, 24*, 81–121.

Werker, J. F. (1989). Becoming a native listener. *American Scientist, 77*, 54–59.

7

ADAPTING SPATIAL CONCEPTS FOR DIFFERENT LANGUAGES
From Preverbal Event Schemas to Semantic Categories

SOONJA CHOI & LARAINE MCDONOUGH

Recent studies have shown that children explore spatial relations from early in life, are sensitive to differences between relations (chapter 6 this volume), and form spatial concepts during their first year (McDonough, Choi, & Mandler, 2003). For example, by 5–8 months of age, infants detect the differences between a container and a cylindrical object that functions as a container but does not have the necessary criteria (a bottom) for containment (Aguiar & Baillargeon, 1998; Baillargeon, 1995). By 9 months of age, infants categorize perceptually varied containers and support relations (McDonough et al., 2003). How infants come to understand relations such as containment and begin to categorize objects based on these relations has been quite controversial, and different perspectives have arisen as to how such tasks can be accomplished. Early views suggested that spatial concepts, concepts that require analysis of the relation between one or more objects and generalizing the structure of the relation to other objects, were too difficult for infants. For example, if one believed that infants were limited to only perceiving individual objects or features of objects, then spatial relations would be difficult to extract. But advances in our understanding of infant perceptual and cognitive abilities have taught us that infants are capable of examining scenes and analyzing events such that they can make sense of regularities about the physical and social world around them (Baillargeon & Wang, 2002; Hespos & Spelke, 2004; Mandler, 2004).

A different view of the early development of spatial concepts is that concepts about the world need the guidance of linguistic input and are intimately related to language acquisition (Bowerman, 1996; Bowerman & Choi, 2001). That is, language teaches infants spatial concepts. Yet the challenge to this perspective is that infants need some semblance of conceptual understanding before language can be learned in a meaningful way. In this chapter, we provide an overview of our research showing that there is truth to be found in these different views of spatial concept development; indeed, they are more compatible than previously thought. Some spatial concepts are formed prior to language, yet they are then aligned through the guidance of linguistic input to match the semantic categories specific to the language being acquired. In some cases, the boundaries of preverbal spatial categories match these semantic categories. In other cases, we suggest that either the boundaries will fade or new boundaries will become evident as language is acquired.

We believe that an understanding of early spatial concepts will be found in an examination of both early cognitive abilities and the gentle[1] but influential guidance of language acquisition. We embrace the view that both preverbal concepts and linguistic input are required before infants learn the semantic categories that adult speakers in their culture consider important. To begin, we offer an overview of how languages can differ in the domain of spatial relations.

7.1 CROSS-LINGUISTIC DIFFERENCES IN SPATIAL SEMANTIC CATEGORIES

Languages differ greatly in the way they *semantically* categorize spatial relations. Consider, for example, the containment and support relations that infants explore early on. Although these two relations seem distinct in a straightforward way, it is only so from the perspective of an English speaker (or someone who speaks a language that has similar semantic structure). In fact, languages differ in the way they group and partition various types of containment and support relations (Bowerman, 1996a, 1996b; Bowerman & Choi, 2001; Bowerman & Pederson, 1992; Brown, 1994; Levinson, Meier, & the Language and Cognitive Group, 2003). Bowerman's (1996b) cross-linguistic comparison is illuminating in this regard. In this comparison, Bowerman takes three examples that involve notions of contact, support, and containment (see figure 7.1):

A. A cup on a table
B. A handle on a cupboard door
C. An apple in a bowl

In English, both A and B are routinely called "on," which is used for all types of support, such as support by horizontal surface (A) or by attachment (B).

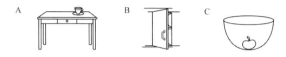

Figure 7.1   Instances of support (*A*), attachment (*B*), and containment (*C*). Adapted from Bowerman (1996b).

The support relation is distinguished from the containment relation, such as C. All types of containment relations are called "in" in English.

In Finnish, situations like B are grouped linguistically with those like C (both are encoded with the same case ending -*ssa*, usually translated as "in"), and for A a different case ending (-*lla*, usually translated as "on") is needed. Bowerman (1996b) suggested that in this system, attachment to an external surface such as B can be seen as similar to prototypical containment C, based on the feature of "incorporation." That is, in B and C, the figure objects (i.e., the apple and the handle) are intimately incorporated into the ground objects (i.e., the bowl and the door). Dutch represents yet a third pattern, in which all three situations are treated as distinct, and different morphemes are assigned to them. The particle *aan* is used for the situation B, because *aan* expresses relations of hanging and other types of attachment. On the other hand, the particle *op* is used for A, and *in* for C. And in a fourth pattern, displayed by Spanish, it is quite unnecessary to differentiate among A, B, and C—a single preposition *en* can be applied to all of them. These cross-linguistic differences suggest that what we have previously considered as universal categories/concepts of containment and support are quite language specific.

Korean presents a fifth pattern in the classification of containment and support. The spatial term *kkita*[2] in Korean is a case in point. The spatial relation denoted by *kkita* is something like "put *x* in a tight-fitting relationship with *y*" regardless of whether or not it involves containment. As shown in figure 7.2, the category of *kkita* crosscuts the categories of "put in" and "put on," and it extends to some situations that are considered neither "putting in" nor "putting on" (e.g., button a button or snap a snap). Thus, this everyday verb in Korean has no English counterpart.[3] In fact, what English speakers treat as a unified category of "containment" is for speakers of Korean semantically diverse: "tight-fitting" containment events such as "putting a book into a matching box-cover" is described with *kkita*, and these events are treated as different from "loose-fitting" containment events such as "putting a Lego piece into a box," which are described with the verb *nehta*, "put *x* loosely into a container." (Actually, the category of *nehta* encompasses not only loose containment events but also loose encirclement events, for instance, putting a *loose* ring *on* a pole; see figure 7.2.) Moreover, as noted in figure 7.2, several of the "put in" events in English are expressed by specific verbs in Korean. For example, having a cigarette in the mouth is referred to by the verb *mwulta*, which specifically refers to holding something partially in the mouth.

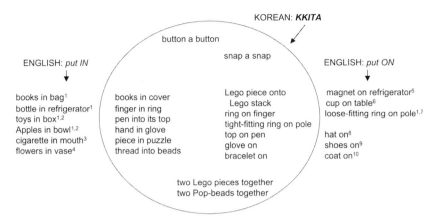

Figure 7.2   Spatial categorization of *in/on* in English and *kkita* in Korean. In Korean, the non-*kkita* events are expressed with different verbs. The gloss here is only approximate:

[1] *nehta*, "put *x* loosely in a container";

[2] *tamta*, "put small objects in downward motion in a container that one can carry";

[3] *mwulta*, "hold *x* partially in mouth between teeth";

[4] *kkocta*, "put an elongated object partially into a container or ground";

[5] *pwuthita*, "attach a flat surface of an object on another object";

[6] *nohta*, "put *x* loosely on surface";

[7] *kelta*, "hook *x* on *y*";

[8] *ssuta*, "put *x* to cover head";

[9] *sinta*, "put *x* on feet";

[10] *ipta*, "put clothing to cover body."

Reprinted from "Preverbal spatial cognition and language-specific input: Categories of containment and support," by Choi, S., in R. Golinkoff & K. Hirsh-Pasek (eds.), *When action meets words: How children learn verbs* (pp. 191–207), with permission from Oxford University Press.

In contrast to English, in which a term is often used across many varied contexts (e.g., "in" or "on"), Korean terms will specify a relationship between specific entities, and as such, more contextual information is considered when describing the relation. This does not mean that English cannot express the same ideas. One can, after all, say that a cigarette is pursed between one's lips or is even dangling from a person's lips. But more often, we would just say that there is a cigarette "in" the person's mouth. We assume the canonical position of the cigarette and would not assume that the cigarette is completely enclosed inside of the mouth unless stated as such. These options—use of paraphrases, verbs with or without particles—are available in English; by contrast, a single Korean term, for instance, *mwulta*, specifies partial support by the mouth. No English word is equivalent to this description.

Just as Korean breaks down the category of "put in," it also breaks down the domain of "put on" in English. Here again, the partitioning is quite extensive: attaching a figure to the exterior surface of a ground object with a complementary three-dimensional shape (e.g., putting a top on a pen or a Lego block on a stack of Legos) falls into the "tight fit" category of *kkita*, while juxtaposing objects with flat surfaces (e.g., magnet on refrigerator) is *pwuthita*. Also, placing an object on a roughly horizontal surface (e.g., cup on table) is *nohta*, and putting a clothing item to cover the head is *ssuta* (distinguished from putting clothing on the trunk [*ipta*], and feet [*sinta*]). (See Bowerman and Choi [2001] for further discussion of spatial semantic categories in English and Korean.) In summary, in Korean, *kkita* cares centrally about the fit between complementary shapes between a figure or a ground but is indifferent to whether this fit is obtained by insertion, covering, surface attachment, or encirclement. In contrast, in English "put in" requires the figure to end up in an interior space or volume of the ground but is indifferent to whether the fit between figure and ground is tight or loose. When the relation does not involve containment, "put on" is used.

7.2 DEVELOPMENT OF SPATIAL CATEGORIES AND SPATIAL SEMANTICS

The magnitude of cross-linguistic differences in spatial semantics suggests significant flexibility in infant cognition that enables them to learn language-specific systems. In fact, recent cross-linguistic studies have shown that, from virtually the beginning of language development, children's semantic organization is shaped by the language-specific system. In particular, Choi and colleagues have studied children learning English and Korean (Bowerman & Choi, 1994; Choi & Bowerman, 1991; Choi, McDonough, Bowerman, & Mandler, 1999). In their cross-linguistic studies examining acquisition of two spatial terms in English and Korean (the prepositions/particles "on" and "in" in English, and the verb *kkita*, "to fit tightly or interlock," in Korean), Choi and colleagues have shown that 2-year-olds learning English and Korean already use spatial terms in a language-specific way (Bowerman & Choi, 1994; Choi & Bowerman, 1991) and that 18- to 23-month-olds understand spatial terms according to the semantic principles of the target language (Choi et al., 1999).

The Choi et al. (1999) study used a preferential looking method to examine when children begin to acquire the language-specific meanings of "in" and *kkita* by English- and Korean-learning children, respectively. In this preferential design, two (dynamic action) scenes are simultaneously shown side by side. Through the speaker located in middle, the child hears the target spatial word (embedded in a sentence, e.g., "Who's putting it *in*"). Only one of the scenes matches the target word. The child's eye gaze is recorded and is coded later (off-line) in terms of direction (left, right, away) of the eye gaze. If the child understands the target word according to the adult grammar, he/she will look longer at the matching scene than at the nonmatching scene. The results showed that English- and Korean-learning children are sensitive to the language-specific meanings from as early as 18 months of age: English learners comprehended *in* to be that of containment regardless of degree of fit, whereas Korean learners comprehended *kkita* to be that of tight fit regardless of containment.

The finding of early acquisition of language-specific semantics triggered our interest in spatial cognition in preverbal infants as well as the role of language on spatial categorization. This led us to address two primary questions in our research: (1) if English- and Korean-learning children acquire language-specific semantics of spatial categories classifying *dynamic* spatial events according to the input language from 18 months, then such spatial categorization presumably begins from the preverbal period; and (2) if preverbal infants conceptualize spatial categories, then which categories are learned preverbally and what are the cognitive consequences of an early acquisition of language-specific semantics? We begin our discussion of these questions with research on the development of spatial categorization from infancy to adulthood. We then present our theory of how such early spatial categorization can take place and how it interacts with the input language.

7.2.1 Categories of Tight and Loose Containment

McDonough et al. (2003) examined two categories of containment in preverbal infants (9-, 11-, and 14-month-olds) raised in English- or Korean-speaking environments. Recall that whereas the Korean language systematically distinguishes between tight- and loose-fit containment relations, English does not. Using a preferential looking method, we first familiarized infants with six pairs of video scenes that all depicted the same type of spatial relation (either a tight–in or loose–in relation, depending on the familiarization condition the child was assigned to; see, e.g., figure 7.3). Then, during the test trials, we presented them with a pair of new scenes (i.e., scenes with new objects not shown during the familiarization period), one depicting the relation that they were familiarized with and the other depicting a novel relation (see figure 7.4). The test pair showed, for example, "putting sponge letters into tight-fitting mats (tight–in)" and "putting sponge letters in large bowls (loose–in)." For those children familiarized with the tight–in relation, the tight–in scenes would be the familiar relation, and for those familiarized with the loose–in relation, the loose–in scenes would be the familiar relation.

In all scenes, a person was shown demonstrating activities with objects that were being placed relative to one another. We also varied the objects in terms of their shapes, textures, and colors as much as possible. Thus, if children show a systematic pattern in their looking behavior during the test trials (e.g., by looking at a familiar relation consistently longer than a novel relation), it is because they have analyzed and abstracted the relation common in these events and not because of any particular preferences for objects. Furthermore, such results would suggest to us that they are able to not only distinguish between the two relations but also categorize the relations

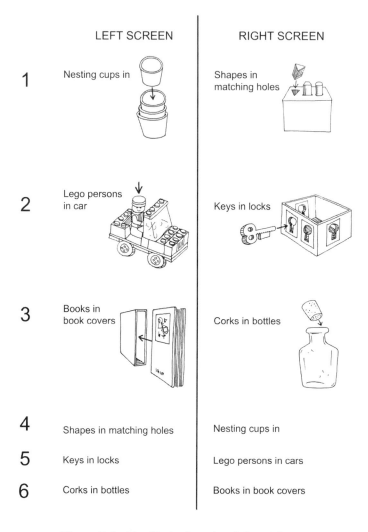

Figure 7.3   Familiarization stimuli for *Tight IN*.

across a large and varied array of objects. Thus, the key measurement is the
duration of eye gaze to familiar versus novel relations during the test trials.

As shown in figure 7.5, infants in both linguistic communities showed
a systematic looking preference for the familiar relation during the test trials. No main effect for age was found for either group. Thus, regardless of
the relation with which they had been familiarized, infants in all three age
groups looked longer at the familiar relation than at the novel relation (i.e.,
familiarity effect); that is, the infants who were familiarized with the
tight–in relation looked longer at the tight–in test scenes, and those familiarized with the loose–in relation looked longer at the loose–in test scenes
(McDonough et al., 2003). Clearly, the children raised in English-speaking

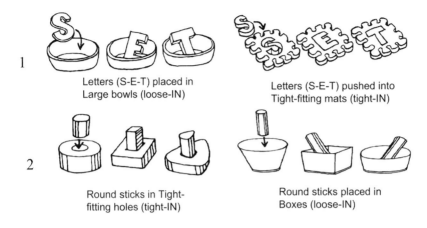

Figure 7.4   Test pairs: *Tight-IN* versus *Loose IN*.

environments and those raised in Korean-speaking environments differentiated the two relations. These findings have been corroborated by Hespos and Spelke (2004) and Casasola, Cohen, and Chiarello (2003).

Our results suggest that 9- to 14-month-old preverbal infants (whether being raised in English or Korean environments) have fine-grained concepts of containment based on the fit feature: they can distinguish categorically between tight-fit containment and loose-fit containment relations. This is despite the fact that this distinction is not grammatically made in English spatial semantics (i.e., the spatial prepositional system in English).

At this point, we should add that in McDonough et al. (2003), we also reported an earlier experiment we had conducted using the same preferential

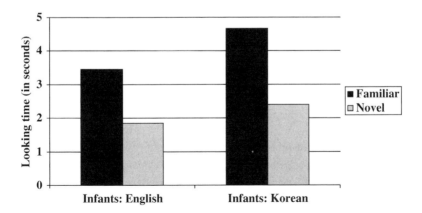

Figure 7.5   *Tight IN* versus *Loose IN* relations in infant data (preverbal 9-, 11-, and 14-month-old infants raised in English-speaking homes and those raised in Korean-speaking homes).

looking design. In that experiment, we tested whether preverbal infants (9–14 months of age) in English environments could differentiate between tight-containment (tight–in) and loose-support (loose–on) events—two categories that English and many other languages distinguish. The results showed that they could. These findings, taken together with the above findings on tight–in versus loose–in events, demonstrate that subcategories of containment are formed during the preverbal stage as well as a category of loose support (loose–on) events. The data thus suggest that infants develop an extended set of concepts prelinguistically, including those not made in the ambient language.

7.2.2 Influence of Language on Nonverbal Categorization Tasks: The Case of Containment Relations

In McDonough et al. (2003), we also tested adult speakers of English and Korean on their sensitivity to the distinction between tight-fit versus loose-fit containment. The purpose of this study was to examine whether language, once mastered, influences nonlinguistic categorization of space. In this experiment, we used both the preferential looking method (the same method as in the experiments with preverbal infants) and an oddity task (in which adults were asked to choose which of four actions was different from the other three). We found that language-specific semantics influenced adult speakers' nonlinguistic sensitivities: English speakers did not spontaneously attend to the difference between tight- versus loose-fit containment (in the looking behavior and in the oddity task), whereas Korean speakers did.[4] This finding, together with the finding on preverbal infants (i.e., infants can distinguish between tight- and loose-containment relations regardless of the semantics of the ambient language), suggests that preverbal infants develop sensitivity to a set of spatial relations larger than is needed to learn the ambient language but that, as they become fluent speakers, the language they have learned selectively channels their attention to linguistically relevant features.

At this point, it is important to note that the cross-linguistic differences we found in the adult speakers of English and Korean were not an all-or-none finding. A few English speakers made reference (albeit indirectly) to the fit of the relations, and a few Korean speakers did not. One of the most important qualities of human cognition is its creative potential and creativity requires flexibility. Views that language constrains thought completely have difficulty accounting for the advent of new terminology and new ways of using the words we already know. Also, it is not clear that people consistently rely on language (consciously or unconsciously, purposefully or spontaneously) to interpret their surroundings. For example, when one's language does not have lexical terms to consistently distinguish one relation from another, such as tight–in versus loose–in, such ideas may not automatically occur to the person in some contexts but may occur in others. However, when a language encodes a particular distinction in a grammatically systematic way such that speakers typically (if not always) use different verbs or particles to distinguish two relations (e.g., tight vs. loose distinction in Korean), such a linguistic (semantic) distinction may tend to permeate nonlinguistic thought, as found by McDonough et al. (2003). The question, then, is when in development this begins to occur.

Choi (2006a) addressed this using the same nonverbal preferential looking method as in the McDonough et al. (2003) study. She examined young learners (2-year-olds) of English and Korean on the distinction between tight–in and loose–in. Results showed a decline in English learners in their sensitivity to the distinction between the two categories from 24 months to 29 months. More specifically, whereas 24-month-old English learners distinguished between the two types of containment, 29-month-olds did so only partially: the older children picked out tight-fit containment as a distinct feature (looking longer at tight–in scenes than loose–in scenes during test) but did not do so for the loose fit feature. More specifically, children who were familiarized with a tight–in relation looked longer at the tight–in scenes during the test trials (demonstrating that they could pick out the tight-fit feature), but children who were familiarized with a loose–in relation could not differentiate between tight–in and loose–in during the test trials (demonstrating that they could not pick out loose fit as a distinctive feature). In contrast to English learners, 29-month-old Korean learners distinguished between the two relations in a categorical fashion. That is, 29-month-old Korean learners picked out both tight-fit and loose-fit containments as distinct features and distinguished one from the other. These cross-linguistic differences are in line with language-specific spatial semantics: in English, tight–in and loose–in form a single semantic category (i.e., "in"); thus, the two are *not* distinguished. By contrast in Korean, the two types of containment are semantically distinct: *kkita* refers to a tight-fit relation and contrasts with *nehta*, typically expressing a loose-fit relation.

The decrease in sensitivity in English toddlers and the maintenance of sensitivity in Korean toddlers suggest that language-specific spatial semantics begin to influence behaviors on nonlinguistic tasks some time between 24 and 29 months of age. This is a period when children begin to use spatial terms productively. Language surveys filled out by the mothers showed a significant increase from 24 to 29 months of age in the total number of words in their children's productive vocabularies. Also, the number of children who productively used the spatial word "in" (for English learners) and *kkita* (for Korean learners) increased significantly from 24 to 29 months (Choi, 2006a). More interestingly, a comparison between children's language and preferential looking data showed a significant effect of language (i.e., vocabulary level and the production of "in") on their preferential looking pattern: English-speaking children who had a high vocabulary level or produced "in" showed much less sensitivity to the difference between tight–in and loose–in than those who had a low vocabulary level or did not yet produce "in" (Choi, 2005, 2006a). These results strongly suggest that there is an intimate relation between vocabulary learning and nonlinguistic sensitivities in the spatial domain.

Our preferential looking data from preverbal to young learners of English on the containment relationship suggest that infants preverbally develop a larger set of spatial categories than may be required in the language they will learn. As children learn their language, their attention is channeled to linguistically relevant features (see section 7.4 for a discussion of this issue). In the case of English, as children build up their vocabulary (particularly in the domain of action and relational words) and learn the word "in," they start disregarding the difference between tight–in and loose–in. On the other hand, Korean learners whose language makes the distinction maintain the differentiation between the two types of containment. Given that preverbal infants make fine distinctions within the containment relation, what language does is tell the child how to package the preverbal categories to form language-specific semantic categories: either to maintain the fine preverbal categories as separate (in the case of Korean)[5] or to package them together (in the case of English).

But do all categories develop in this fashion? That is, is the role of language simply to repackage already established preverbal spatial categories? Or, does language in some cases engage in a more active role in young children's construction of spatial categories? Our recent data on categorization of support relations suggest that the latter is the case.

7.2.3 Categories of Loose and Tight Support Relation

Cross-linguistically, the semantic categories of support—the relation that English refers to as "on" (e.g., cup on table, ring on pole, Lego on another Lego, cap on bottle)—are extensively diverse, more so than the containment relation. In a recent cross-linguistic study, Levinson et al. (2003) examined spatial semantic categories in nine languages of different language families. In this study, speakers of different languages were shown 70 pictures of objects in various spatial relationships and configurations (e.g., apple in bowl, nail in wood, coat on hook, stamp on envelope, cap on bottle) and were asked to describe them in their language. Levinson et al. conducted a multidimensional cluster analysis on these elicitation data to examine which spatial relations were treated semantically similarly or semantically differently across languages. (Pictures ascribed to the same word were considered similar.) Overall, they found significant differences across the languages. This was particularly so in the domain of "support," as various types of "support" relations formed distinct clusters for many languages. (For containment relations, there was less variability across languages.) For example, the relations of "on top of," "on," "over," "attachment," "encirclement," and "covering" (all referred to as "on" in English) are categorized distinctly in different languages. Even what we call good instances of the "on" relation in English form distinct clusters in a cross-linguistic comparison: languages may treat "book on shelf," "table cloth on table," "tree on mountain," and "man on the roof " to be *distinct* from "cup on table," "cat on mat," or "pen on desk" on the basis of variables such as humanness, type of ground object, and amount of ground covered. Such cross-linguistic diversity for the "support" relation suggests that there are many different ways to conceptualize or classify various types of support, and language is one of the guiding principles for learners to select a particular way of categorizing them.

In a recent study, Choi (2006b) examined whether infants raised in either English or Korean environments could categorize the "support" category on the basis of difference in the tight-fit feature (i.e., loose-fit vs. tight-fit support). Recall that, in English grammar, no systematic distinction is made between loose and tight support, whereas in Korean, a systematic distinction is present: loose support is systematically termed *nohta*, and tight-fit support *kkita*. Using the same preferential looking method as McDonough et al. (2003), Choi (2006b) examined whether English- and Korean-raised children differentiate between loose support by a flat surface (e.g., putting a toy on the table), on the one hand, and tight support of various kinds, on the other (e.g., putting a Lego piece on another Lego, putting a bottle cap on bottle, putting a ring tightly on a cone-shaped pole).

Infants (9-, 11-, and 14-month-olds) were familiarized with one type of support relation: either tight–on relations (e.g., put Legos on other Legos) or loose–on relations (e.g., put toy cups on toy table). During the test trials, both familiarization groups were shown the same two test pairs, each pair consisting of one loose–on relation and one tight–on relation with novel objects.

Looking patterns during the test trials were analyzed. The results were surprising because they were different from the pattern we saw for the containment category: a cross-linguistically different pattern was shown from 11 months of age. The 11- and 14-month-old Korean-raised children preferred the tight–on scenes to the loose–on scenes significantly more than did the same-aged English-raised children. In fact, English-raised children did not differ in their looking preference to the tight–on versus loose–on relation, but Korean-raised children looked significantly longer at the tight–on relation than at the loose–on relation regardless of the familiarization category they saw. This suggests that Korean-raised children have a significantly higher interest in (or sensitivity to) the tight–on relation than do English-raised children.

These results show that tight–on is a salient relation for 11- and 14-month-old Korean-raised children. (One might argue that the tight–on test scenes were inherently more interesting than the loose–on test scenes for all children, but given that English-raised children did not show such preferences during the same test scenes, this interpretation is not likely. The objects in the test trials [i.e., sponge door clamps and thimbles] are fairly novel objects to infants in both cultures.) Why are Korean-raised children particularly interested in tight-fit support? We suggest that such interest is linguistically motivated. That is, this cross-linguistic difference for the "support" category can be explained by the differential linguistic input that the two groups receive: in English, the two relations are not distinguished, because both are expressed by a single spatial particle "on," whereas in Korean, they are semantically distinguished by two verbs: *kkita* for the tight-fit relation and *nohta* for the loose support relation. We propose that it is the verb *kkita* in the input that heightens the nonlinguistic sensitivity for the tight-fit relation in Korean-raised infants. Thus, in the case of the support relation, consisting of diverse relations such as attachment, encirclement, covering, and loose support, language-specific input guides spatial categories from early on (see section 7.5 for further discussion).

In fact, our data on containment and support, taken together, suggest that influences of language are multifaceted. On the one hand, language can tell young children to simply package preverbally established categories in different ways. But language can also highlight a relation that children have not paid attention to before, thus helping them develop a new category.

Now that we have presented our data, we begin our discussion of the mechanisms by which spatial categories for dynamic scenes can be formed during the preverbal stage, and how these categories interact with the particular language that is being learned.

7.3 IMAGE/EVENT SCHEMAS: THE BRIDGE BETWEEN PREVERBAL AND VERBAL THOUGHT

Most of the developmental research on categorization has been focused on object categories and how infants and young children use perceptual similarity to figure out which objects are the same kind of thing. The emphasis on similarity has been stressed to the extent that many researchers initially assumed that object categories are not only easier to learn but also the first to be acquired in all cultures (e.g., Gentner, 1982). Yet, judging similarity among objects is problematic because the basis for the judgment changes when expertise and task requirements change (McDonough, 2002b). More recently, researchers have considered two additional factors that influence the categorization of objects and that also play a role in the categorization of spatial relations. One is linguistic input. Findings suggest that learning basic-level nouns influences how object similarities are construed (e.g., Samuelson & Smith, 1999). The present chapter also focuses on the role of language, but the influence seen in the present data is on the relations among objects rather than the objects themselves. The second factor is the function of objects (e.g., Kemler Nelson, Egan, & Holt, 2004; Nelson, 1985). For example, containment not only is a spatial relation but also carries functional information about an object. Cups, boxes, and bowls can be classified as three different object categories or as one category based on containment.

Although functional information can be used to classify objects and spaces, understanding how people *represent* functional or spatial relational information poses a challenge. As adults, our understanding of what a cup looks like may give rise to thinking about containment relations, but just how we arrived at this understanding and how functional or spatial relations are represented appear to be more complex than simply conjuring up an image of a cup. Just as seeing a shelf is not sufficient for an understanding of support, seeing that an object is concave is not the same as understanding containment. Knowing what particular objects look like and bringing their images to mind does not provide functional information.

Cognitive linguists have proposed a solution to this problem, a solution that makes sense from a developmental perspective as well. They propose that the meanings underlying spatial terms can be decomposed into image schemas, universal to all languages (e.g., Fauconnier, 1985; Johnson, 1987; Lakoff, 1987; Lakoff & Nunoz, 2000). For example, when we see a cup sitting on a shelf, we can break this relation into smaller image schemas, such as an above schema (the cup is above the shelf), a contact schema (the cup is in contact with the shelf), and a support schema (the cup is supported by the shelf). Consider now the containment feature of the cup. To pour coffee into the cup, one views the coffee as following a trajectory (the path) from a coffee pot (the source location) and going into the interior of the cup (the goal). In these two examples (see Lakoff & Nunez, 2004, for more details), contact, support, containment, path, source, and goal are all schemas that are involved in understanding what in English would be labeled as "on" and "in" relations. The possibility of uncovering these and other meaningful image schemas (or what may be more aptly described as event or action schemas) is potentially within the grasp of developmental researchers studying spatial relations with preverbal infants (Mandler, 2004). By considering acquisition of spatial concepts in the manner proposed by cognitive linguists, we can then envision how infants and young children need to "package" image/event schemas to coordinate the meanings conveyed in the language they learn.

7.3.1 Distinguishing Image Schemas From Perceptual Images

As described in the above examples, an image/event schema is a hypothetical construct that provides a "grounding" for meanings that can be potentially expressed in widely varying languages (i.e., semantic concepts). The level of description (e.g., above or support) allows generalization across several contexts such that image schemas are not tightly associated with the perceptual details of objects. As such, image schemas are not like the images investigated by psychologists in mental imagery experiments in which rotation, direction taking, or descriptions of images of objects (or their prototypes) are tested. Instead, image or event schemas allow us to overlook the differences among toy boxes, drawers, cooking pots, cereal bowls, hands, and garages. All can be useful containers but understanding what they have in common is not obvious given how widely they vary in terms of their appearances and other related functions (e.g., hands are more than just containers). Yet once one observes the relational roles these objects can take in various events, what they share becomes more obvious. All can involve an object (notated either by a mass or count noun) being placed into other objects (e.g., boxes, drawers, cooking pots) that serve as containers. An analysis of the activity "going in" would provide an image/event schema for a containment relation. A containment image schema (or a "going in" image schema) allows this kind of understanding even though we are not consciously aware of the image/event schema itself.

The activity of seeing something going inside another object invites perceptual analysis of the difference between the beginning and end states (Mandler, 2004). The activity of being contained provides information about both noncontainment (the beginning state) and containment (the end state). Infants attend to motion, which provides information about change, for instance, an empty object becoming filled with another. Analysis of change provides the necessary functional information. Without observing change, infants may indeed perceive the concavity of objects, but concavity alone does not necessarily lead to an understanding of containment.[6]

The question that arises is how such an image schema is formed. We have long known that memory is not a veridical reflection of the world around us but is instead a construction based on our interpretation of experiences. However, one needs to form a foundation on which interpretations can be made. An analysis of dynamic events could provide a good start to this foundation. After all, we are endowed to attend to motion, although the ability to detect and track motion undergoes significant development in early infancy (e.g., von Hofsten & Rosander, 1998). Motion provides us with information about the manner and path of moving objects and also provides information about the function of objects. Motions, particularly those with clear end states such as the containment examples, invite what Mandler (2004) calls "perceptual meaning analysis," the mechanism by which we can construct potentially accessible concepts from perceptual arrays. The product of this kind of analysis is an image schema that is not dependent on any particular familiarity the infant may have with the object's appearance or the particular ongoing event (e.g., containment event) in which the object is seen.

What image/event schemas provide that perceptual images do not is an understanding of the relation one object has with another and the common activities between/among objects across numerous contexts. An example should be helpful to clarify how image schemas contrast with perceptual images. Suppose that the infant sees coffee being poured into a mug. The infant can learn the function of the mug by analyzing the liquid being poured into and being contained by the mug. The infant could also analyze the form of the mug such as its sides, bottom, and handle and then use this information to form a perceptual image of what coffee mugs look like. Two aspects of this event are observed: the function of the mug and the form of the mug. The analysis of the *function* of the mug aids in the formation of an image schema of the event, which in turn leads to the preverbal meaning of the object (i.e., the mug is a container). The analysis of the *form* of the object aids in the formation of a perceptual image of the object. Thus, image schemas provide information about pre- or nonverbal meanings such as the purposes or functions of objects, whereas perceptual images provide information about the appearances of objects. Of course, as adults we are "experts" when it comes to coffee mugs, so to think about what a mug looks like or to imagine its appearance may also lead to thinking about its function as a container. But infants are just learning about objects, so the appearance of an object does not lend information about its function, unless the function is already known and the object can be categorized in this instance as a "container." An analysis of the activity "going in" would provide an image or event schema for a containment relation, one that is clearly not limited to coffee mugs but also common to toys in a toy box, clothing into drawers, cooking pots in cupboards, a marble in a child's hand, and a car in a garage.

7.3.2 Memory for Motion versus Form

Another way to think about this issue is in terms of what is memorable about events. Given that motion attracts attention (and is difficult to ignore) and attention is a prerequisite to encoding, it makes sense that memory for motion may be more enduring than the static properties of an object. Just as the categorization of objects requires the learner to ignore variability among objects, categorization of motion events requires the learner to ignore variability among the different motions that involve placing one object in relation to another. For example, placing a toy into a cloth bag, pushing a block into a same-shaped opening in a box, or putting food into a pan all involve different directions of motion (as well as hand placement and orientation of objects). Yet, all result in the same effect—the placement of one object inside another. From positions A to B to C, the locations in space change and the paths between each of the points can be perceived or, if the motion is too quick to process or is not perceptually available (e.g., hidden), the paths might be inferred.

When we think about our representation of motion or about spatial relations, we generally also think about the object or objects involved as well. After all, motion events and relational information entail objects. Perhaps because of this, our early views of cognitive development posited that learning was context dependent: objects that are moving or are being manipulated were thought to be perceived holistically without parsing the movement or manipulation from what the object looked like (e.g., Werner & Kaplan, 1963). According to this view, it was presumed that learning an activity was linked to its associated context either narrowly defined in terms of a particular object or more broadly defined in terms of the larger environment in which the activity is learned. Although some research provides support for context specificity particularly as it relates to language acquisition (e.g., Bates, Thal, Whitesell, Fenson, & Oakes, 1989), it is important to consider the conditions under which object–action links are learned. Learning about a particular event that occurs repeatedly in a particular context

can lead to context-specific learning. For example, infants who are habitu-
ated to an event (either experimentally or in a natural environment) in
which one or a small selection of objects undergoes an activity may indeed
be coding actions and objects in context-specific ways. Evidence for context-
dependent learning is also found in adults (e.g., Endo & Takeda, 2004;
Godden & Baddeley, 1980).

Although no one has actually claimed that all learning in early infancy is
context dependent, much of the research has been interpreted as being consistent with this view. The challenge is then how to explain the processes
that allow generalization from one context to another. Habituation or
overlearning in a particular context can potentially obstruct generalization
abilities regardless of one's age because the representation of the action is
closely linked to the context in which it was learned. Thus, this kind of
learning is unlikely to show the same kind of robust generalization that
would be found if the infant (or adult for that matter) experiences the same
event with various objects or in differing contexts (see Landau & Shipley,
2001). Thus, any failure to generalize may be an artifact of a narrow learning situation. Another factor to be considered is what the learner encodes
and remembers about events.

Recent research suggests that memory for the perceptual details of objects is fleeting, while memory for actions (particularly those providing interesting outcomes) endures for longer periods of time. For example, Bahrick,
Gogate, and Ruiz (2002) have experimental evidence with 5-month-olds
showing that the properties of objects are less well encoded than the events
in which they are presented. They showed infants videos of actors (face
views only) each engaging in one of three different events: brushing teeth
with a toothbrush, blowing bubbles with a bubble wand, and brushing hair
with a hairbrush. The activities were remembered after delays as long as
7 weeks but the faces, and the objects in the activities were not remembered.
Infants may have forgotten the individual faces simply because they experience different people engaging in these activities. But infants did not remember the tools (toothbrush, bubble wand, and hairbrush), either.

The results from Bahrick et al. (2002) are consistent with Mandler and
McDonough's (2000) generalization research showing that infants as old as
14 months will overgeneralize activities to some inappropriate objects, such
as using a hairbrush to brush teeth or treating a bathtub as an appropriate
prop to demonstrate sleeping. The events are represented, but not the details of the objects used in the events. In more recent research, McDonough
(2004) showed that before their first birthdays, infants imitate and recall familiar actions with neutral objects such as wooden blocks as props (e.g.,
holding a wooden block to one's ear as if it were a telephone). At 9 months
of age, infants will occasionally imitate familiar actions with inappropriate
objects (e.g., using a toy car as if it was a telephone) even when the experimenter modeled actions with only appropriate objects. Data from several
other researchers have shown that well before their first birthdays, infants
make inferences about causality, self-propelled motion, contingent motion,

and agent–patient roles outside the context they normally occur (e.g., Gergely & Csibra, 1994; Leslie & Keeble, 1987; Rochat, Morgan, & Carpenter, 1997; Schlottman & Surian, 1999). Thus, actions can endure after lengthy delays and not be tightly linked (or even reliably associated) to the context in which they are learned. Image or event schemas are flexible enough to be possible representational formats for these kinds of activities.

In our studies on spatial categorization in infants, we used highly varied objects in the familiarization trials, yet infants could still pull out the relation common to the scenes. Whereas previous research shows that young infants can distinguish containment from noncontainment or support from nonsupport with a limited number of objects (Baillargeon, 2004; Hespos & Baillargeon, 2001; Needham & Baillargeon, 1993), our research demonstrated that slightly older infants can abstract a common relation that is demonstrated with perceptually varied objects using different hand orientations moving along both vertical and horizontal paths. This development can be thought of in terms of preverbal acquisition of image/event schemas, which are products of "meaning analyses" of dynamic events (Mandler, 2004) that are likely to be more memorable after long delays than the perceptual details of the objects that are associated with such events. Note that it is the details of the objects that are likely to be forgotten. This is consistent with the view that memory for objects may also be quite general. Thus, rather than remembering precise details, infants might simply remember whether or not objects are concave and useful as containers or whether or not they are smaller than a container such that they can fit inside. Such abstract properties could therefore guide object concepts, leading to the development of a "container" category.

But by the time language acquisition is well under way, form and motion are better coordinated such that infants can retain information about both. Linguistic evidence for the integration of form and motion can be found in languages such as Navajo (Young, Morgan, & Midgette, 1992), Atsugewi (Talmy, 1985), and Tzeltal (Brown, 1994), which semantically code the form of a moving object along with motion words. In Tzeltal, for example, there are several verbs meaning "be-located," and each verb specifies the shape and orientation of the object. For example, *waxal* means "be-located of tall oblong-shaped container (like a bottle) in the 'standing' position," where as *lechel* means "be-located of wide flat object (like a frying pan) lying flat" (Brown, 1994).

7.4 INTERACTION BETWEEN NONLINGUISTIC SPATIAL CATEGORIES AND LINGUISTIC INPUT

During the time that infants are forming image/event schemas, they are also becoming socialized into their own culture. An important aspect of this socialization process is the acquisition of language. Language is an intentional act, and infants are sensitive to intentionality from an early age (e.g., Carpenter, Nagell, & Tomasello, 1998). Language entails social interchanges where people share their experiences with others and, to the delight of older children and adults, infants provide an attentive audience. The kind of experiences shared and the language that accompanies these experiences often differ from one kind of activity to another. For example, in a book-reading context, mothers tend to label and point out objects, whereas in a toy-playing context, verbs and descriptions of the spatial array are often mentioned as the toys are being manipulated (Choi, 2000). In such situations where a speaker is directing attention to an event, it follows that language in general may highlight certain relational features that may otherwise not be picked up for category formation. In other words, language and the accompanying social context may actually "teach" infants to form spatial categories for semantic purposes.

We do not mean that infants learn the meaning of spatial terms such as "in" or *kkita* in any immediate sense on first hearing the terms used in an appropriate context, because knowing how such terms are to be extended will require several examples. But on hearing the varying prosodic cues that are well known to attract attention (Snow, 1972), infants will attend to an ongoing activity that is being highlighted in the eye gaze and speech of the knowing expert. In this way, linguistic input draws attention to the relevant properties that infants and young children will learn to express and semantically categorize in their particular native language.

We assume that these categories are within their conceptual reach to begin with. Evidence suggesting that language is influencing nonverbal categorization of spatial relations (in terms of tight-fit "on" relations from around 11–14 months in Korean infants and in terms of loose- vs. tight-fit "in" relations from around 24–29 months in English and Korean children) indicates that, whatever their influence may be, words are not automatically limited to or assumed to highlight objects alone. After all, infants do not know what language they are to acquire—one that categorizes containment events or tight-fitting events? Or one that denotes spatial relations with prepositions/particles or verbs? The point here is that the realization of which kind of category to be formed for the purposes of acquiring their native language is not immediately apparent to the young infant. But with an understanding of some spatial relations accompanied by extended linguistic experience, early categories of spatial relations begin to be molded to fit the communicative needs of the child growing up in a particular culture.

In summary, we propose that influences of language are multifaceted. On the one hand, language can tell young children to simply package preverbally established categories in different ways. But language can also highlight a relational aspect that children have not paid attention to before, thus helping them develop a new category.

7.5 CONCLUSIONS AND FUTURE DIRECTIONS

In this chapter, we suggest that (1) preverbal infants abstract relations across a variety of objects, (2) infants analyze events and form image/event schemas of spatial relations that are potentially accessible for the purposes of acquiring some rudimentary aspects of language (Mandler, 2004), and (3) language and the social contexts guide young children's attention to the boundaries of relational categories that are relevant in the language they are learning. However, language influences nonlinguistic sensitivity only partially; for instance, 29-month-old children learning English could categorize tight-fit containment relations when contrasted with a loose-fit containment event at testing but could not categorize loose-fit containment relations (Choi, 2006a)(see section 7.2.2). One possibility for this difficulty is that the degree to which the contained item is smaller than its container varies widely in loose-fitting relations. Young children may be sensitive to these differences, and they no longer consider loose fit as a coherent category as they once did at younger ages. At some point, English learners will attend much less to fit and will group containment relations together by noting them with the preposition "in."

Our findings suggest that language and cognitive development interact with each other in a bidirectional way. Cognition is needed in order to provide a basis so that language can be learned in a meaningful way, and language then fine-tunes cognition so that communication needs among those using the same language can be met. In so doing, some relations will be highlighted or differentiated into smaller categories, and others will be joined together to form larger ones. Thus, infants flexibly calibrate preverbal relations to the language they are learning.

We should note that much of the research on how language acquisition in young children guides their attention has focused on object labels. For example, Smith and colleagues have shown that the increase in object labels in a child's vocabulary is correlated with an increase in the use of overall shape information (Samuelson & Smith, 1999; Smith, Jones, Yoshida, & Colunga, 2003). That is, learning nouns tunes attention to object shape. In tasks designed to examine what cues children use to extend labels, novel labels and novel objects are introduced to children to see if their generalization choices are guided by shape cues. In the absence of functional information, children who have acquired a sizable noun vocabulary will generalize from one object to another based on shape similarities. Yet, during this same span of development when language is being acquired, children are also learning about the functions of objects and learning to parse global categories into basic-level ones (Kemler Nelson et al., 2004; Mandler & McDonough, 1998, 2000; McDonough, 2002a). Thus, the shape and function of objects both contribute to the acquisition of nouns. One possibility is that function plays a large role in guiding the acquisition of early labels, and then, as children begin to realize the correlation between function and shape, shape alone can assist them in their inferences of the extensions of newly learned labels. In light of evidence showing an enduring memory for motion that potentially provides insight to functional cues, as well as our findings on early comprehension and production of spatial terms, we think this possibility is worthy of further research (for research that examines the link between shape and motion, see chapter 8).

The case of spatial terms presents a slightly different scenario. The number of spatial terms is quite small relative to object labels, but children begin to comprehend and produce the few spatial terms they know in appropriate ways at an early age (Choi & Bowerman, 1991; Choi et al., 1999). We presented evidence suggesting that spatial terms found in the native language influence attention such that they shape nonverbal concepts between 24 and 29 months (Choi, 2006a) and may even influence preferential attention to the fit feature as young as 11 months, as shown in data with Korean infants (Choi, 2006b). These attentional preferences do not require a large productive vocabulary of spatial terms before an influence is evident. It appears that the spatial relations characterized by the semantics in the ambient language guide attention from the beginning. It becomes important to consider that an individual object can be manipulated in a variety of ways, giving rise to attention to functional information and object form (e.g., overall shape), but a given activity such as "putting in" can be also understood across a variety of objects. Differences in manner or trajectory of motion may be less relevant than the outcome of activities—the spatial relations themselves. When learning spatial relations, the constant is not the object class but the end point of the activity. Thus, language is not limited to guiding attention to objects and their shapes and features. It would appear that objects can be ignored (or simply forgotten) and regularities in relations can be attended to and encoded both in and out of linguistic context. But within a linguistic context, particular spatial relations can become more salient.

Given the diverse range of spatial categories across languages, it is obvious that the research on this topic has barely scratched the surface of what we still need to know about infants' and young children's understanding of spatial relations. For starters, we have yet to test whether infants understand containment as a single category that includes tight and loose fit. When we began our research, it was not clear that infants would be able to form abstract relational features such as tight containment or loose containment simply because the objects involved in such relations were perceptually diverse. When one considers the emphasis on perceptual similarity for category formation and then examines the range of objects involved in our tests, one might have thought we were being too ambitious. But given our findings, we are beginning to consider that perhaps we were not ambitious enough. It remains to be seen whether or not containment is a coherent category for infants and young children. This investigation is currently under way.

The category of support seems to follow a different pattern. In McDonough et al. (2003), support relations all involved placing items loosely on surfaces. More complex support relations such as encirclement and other such tight-fitting attachment relations were not included in the familiarization category. This suggests that a more general support category needs testing, as well. Yet, in subsequent experiments by Choi (2006b), the results suggest that 11- and 14-month-old preverbal infants in English environments have difficulties categorizing support on the basis of tight-fit support and distinguishing this category from loose-fit support. One might be inclined to think that these infants' difficulties with tests contrasting tight- and loose-fit support relations may be attributed to a different strategy from degree of fit. Although this has not been tested directly, we are inclined to believe that support may not be a coherent category in the same way containment seems to be.

The basis for the belief that containment but not support may be a coherent category goes as follows. Instances of containment relations are homogeneous (namely, putting X into an object with concavity) and thus may readily be grouped into a coherent category without much aid from language. Within this coherent category, infants can further subcategorize the relation based on the tight-fit (or loose-fit) feature. In contrast, instances of the "support" relation may be viewed as quite diverse in terms of the way "support" is configured between the figure and the ground object. For example, in the case of "putting a ring on a pole," the relationship of the figure ("ring") to the ground ("pole") is encirclement; for "putting a Lego piece on another," it is attachment, and for "putting a bottle cap on bottle," it is covering. In infants' minds, each of these configurations may be processed as distinct and object specific and may be more salient than the tight-fit support feature (see Bowerman & Choi, 2003; Choi & Casasola, 2005; Gentner, 2003; Levinson et al., 2003).

From our studies, it is clear that preverbal infants can extract relational commonalities across a number of events (e.g., X going tightly in Y) that involve a variety of objects. It is also clear to us that the repertoire of the relational concepts that infants develop can be fine grained or extensive (to include those *not* used in the ambient language). This suggests that there is no direct one-to-one mapping between preverbal concepts and linguistic categories. Rather, young children need to attend to the ambient language from early on either to repackage "already-established" preverbal categories or to develop sensitivity to "new" relational features to construct language-specific semantic categories. Thus, language shapes young children's semantic categories and even influences their level of nonlinguistic sensitivity to spatial features. But as found with our research with adults, language need not constrain thought in any absolute sense. Instead, language may guide adults' first construal of events, but even knowledgeable adults still need to be creative problem solvers when they are required to think beyond the habits that their particular language may entail.

NOTES

1. We refer to language as a "gentle" influence to contrast with claims that language places strong constraints on how the infant conceptualizes or categorizes a labeled object or event (e.g., Balaban & Waxman, 1997; Waxman & Markow, 1995). We view the influence as gentle because infants need to be flexible when figuring out the meaning of a word, particularly when it refers to a spatial relation. After all,

there are many different ways to divide up space, and the labeling of one spatial relation in the environment is insufficient to give infants a clue as to the way the language they are learning (whether it be English or Korean) categorizes the entire range of spatial relations.

2. *Kkita* is a spatial verb. In Korean, information about motion and path is systematically encoded by a set of spatial verbs, whereas in English it is encoded by motion verbs plus path particles, as in "put in" (Choi & Bowerman 1991; Talmy 1985).

3. English has words such as "tight" and "fit" to refer to tight fit. However, these words are not systematically used to refer to a tight fit relation as a result of a dynamic action, and their meanings are different from *kkita* in Korean. *Kkita* typically has to do with objects having complementary shapes that interlock tightly in a three-dimensional way. Thus, *kkita* cannot be used in expressions such as "this bed *fits* my size" or "these shoes *fit* loosely."

4. Of course, it is possible that English speakers can distinguish between tight–in and loose–in in other contexts. That is, they may not have completely lost the ability to distinguish between containment based on the tight-fit feature. Indeed, Choi (2005) has found that adult speakers of English are sensitive to the difference in certain contexts.

5. Note that *kkita* in Korean refers not only to tight-fit containment but also to tight-fit support (which includes tight-fit attachment, tight-fit encirclement, etc.). Thus, in the case of *kkita* in Korean, it is not a simple matter of repackaging preestablished categories of containment (see section 7.2.3 for further discussion).

6. Other researchers whose work is primarily focused on adult cognition and/or connectionist models (e.g., Lakoff & Nunez, 2000; Regier, 1996) have described image schemas that can be based on static information, such as seeing one object inside another. In this case, the container schema consists of an interior, boundary, and exterior, with the interior of the cup as the focus of attention. Yet these researchers also discuss the role of complex motor schemas that are used in reasoning about events leading to spatial relations such as containment (e.g., Narayanan, 1997).

REFERENCES

Aguiar, A. & Baillargeon, R. (1998). Eight-and-a-half-month-old infants' reasoning about containment events. *Child Development, 69, 3*, 636–653.

Bahrick, L. E., Gogate, L. J., & Ruiz, I. (2002). Attention and memory for faces and actions in infancy: The salience of actions over faces in dynamic events. *Child Development, 73*, 1629–1643.

Baillargeon, R. (1995). Physical reasoning in infancy. In M. S. Gazzaniga (Ed.), *The cognitive neurosciences* (pp. 181–204). Cambridge, MA: Bradford Press.

Baillargeon, R. (2004). Can 12 large clowns fit in a Mini Cooper? Or when are beliefs and reasoning explicit and conscious? *Developmental Science, 7*, 422–424.

Baillargeon, R., & Wang, S. (2002). Event categorization in infancy. *Trends in Cognitive Science, 6*, 85–93.

Balaban, M. T., & Waxman, S. R. (1997). Do words facilitate object categorization in 9-month-old infants? *Journal of Experimental Child Psychology, 64*, 3–26.

Bates, E., Thal, D., Whitesell, K., Fenson, L., & Oakes, L. (1989). Integrating language and gesture in infancy. *Developmental Psychology, 25*, 1004–1019.

Bowerman, M. (1996a). The origins of children's spatial semantic categories. In J. J. Gumperz & S. C. Levinson (Eds.), *Rethinking linguistic relativity* (pp. 145–176). New York: Cambridge University Press.

Bowerman, M. (1996b). Learning how to structure space for language: A crosslinguistic perspective. In P. Bloom, M. Peterson, L. Nadel, & M. Garrett (Eds.), *Language and space* (pp. 385–486). Cambridge, MA: MIT Press.

Bowerman, M., & Choi, S. (1994, January). *Linguistic and nonlinguistic determinants of spatial semantic development*. Paper presented at the Boston University Conference on Language Development, Boston, MA.

Bowerman, M., & Choi, S. (2001). Shaping meanings for language: Universal and language-specific in the acquisition of spatial semantic categories. In M. Bowerman & S. Levinson (Eds.), *Language acquisition and conceptual development* (pp. 475–511). Cambridge: Cambridge University Press.

Bowerman, M., & Choi, S. (2003). Space under construction: Language-specific spatial categorization in first language acquisition. In D. Gentner & S. Goldin-Meadow (Eds.), *Language in mind: Advances in the study of language and thought* (pp. 387–427). Cambridge, MA: MIT Press.

Bowerman, M., & Pederson, E. (1992, December). *Cross-linguistic perspectives on topological spatial relationships*. Paper presented at the annual meeting of the American Anthropological Association, San Francisco, CA.

Brown, P. (1994). The ins and ons of Tzeltal locative expressions: The semantics of static descriptions of location. *Linguistics, 32*, 743–790.

Carpenter, M., Nagell, K., & Tomasello, M. (1998). Social cognition, joint attention, and communicative competence from 9 to 15 months of age. *Monographs of the Society for Research in Child Development, 63* (Serial No. 255), 1–176.

Casasola, M., Cohen, L. B., & Chiarello, E. (2003). Six-month-old infants' categorization of containment spatial relations. *Child Development, 74*, 679–693.

Choi, S. (2000). Caregiver input in English and Korean: Use of nouns and verbs in book-reading and toy-play contexts. *Journal of Child Language, 27*, 69–96.

Choi, S. (2005). *Language-specific input and spatial cognition: Categories of containment*. Presented at the Society for Research in Child Development, Atlanta, GA.

Choi, S. (2006a). Influence of language-specific input on spatial cognition. Categories of containment. *First Language, 26*(2), 207–232.

Choi, S. (2006b). Preverbal spatial cognition and language-specific input: Categories of containment and support. In R. Golinkoff & K. Hirsh-Pasek (Eds.), *When action meets words: How children learn verbs* (pp. 191–207). New York: Oxford University Press.

Choi, S. (2005b). *Categorization of spatial relations in adult speakers of English and Korean in similarity judgment tasks*. Unpublished manuscript.

Choi, S., & Bowerman, M. (1991). Learning to express motion events in English and Korean: The influence of language-specific lexicalization patterns. *Cognition, 41*, 83–121.

Choi, S., & Casasola, M. (2005, April 7–10). *Preverbal categorization of support relations*. Paper presented at the Society for Research in Child Development, Atlanta, GA.

Choi, S., McDonough, L., Bowerman, M., & Mandler, J. M. (1999). Early sensitivity to language-specific spatial categories in English and Korean. *Cognitive Development, 14*, 241–268.

Endo, N., & Takeda, Y. (2004). Selective learning of spatial configuration and object identity in visual search. *Perception & Psychophysics*, *66*, 293–302.

Fauconnier, G. (1985). *Mental spaces: Aspects of meaning construction in natural language*. Cambridge, MA: MIT Press.

Gentner, D. (1982). Why nouns are learned before verbs: Linguistic relativity versus natural partitioning. In S. A. Kuczaj II (Ed.), *Language development: Vol. 2. Language, thought, and culture* (pp. 301–334). Hillsdale, NJ: Lawrence Erlbaum.

Gentner, D. (2003). Why we are so smart? In D. Gentner & S. Goldin-Meadow (Eds.), *Language in mind: Advances in the study of language and cognition* (pp. 387–428). Cambridge, MA: MIT Press.

Gergely, G., & Csibra, G. (1994). On the ascription of intentional content. *Cahiers de Psychologie Cognitiv/Current Psychology of Cognition*, *13*, 584–589.

Godden, D., & Baddeley, A. (1980). When does context influence recognition memory? *British Journal of Psychology*, *71*, 99–104.

Hespos, S. J., & Baillargeon, R. (2001). Reasoning about containment events in very young infants. *Cognition*, *78*, 207–245.

Hespos, S. J., & Spelke, E. S. (2004). Conceptual precursors to language. *Nature*, *430*, 453–456.

Johnson, M. (1987). *The body in the mind: The bodily basis of meaning, imagination, and reason*. Chicago, IL: University of Chicago Press.

Kemler Nelson, D. G., Egan, L. C., & Holt, M. B. (2004). When children ask "what is it?" what do they want to know about artifacts? *Psychological Science*, *15*, 384–389.

Lakoff, G. (1987). *Women, fire, and dangerous things: What categories reveal about the mind*. Chicago: University of Chicago Press.

Lakoff, G., & Nunoz, R. (2000). *Where mathematics comes from: How the embodied mind brings mathematics into being*. New York: Basic Books.

Landau, B., & Shipley, E. (2001). Object naming and category boundaries. *Developmental Science*, *4*(1), 109–118.

Leslie, A. M., & Keeble, S. (1987). Do six-month-old infants perceive causality? *Cognition*, *25*, 265–288.

Levinson, S., Meier, S. and the Language and Cognition Group (2003). "Natural concepts" in the spatial topological domain—adpositional meaning in crosslinguistic perspective: An exercise in semantic typology. *Language*, *79*, 485–516.

Mandler, J. M. (2004). *The foundations of mind: Origins of conceptual thought*. New York: Oxford University Press.

Mandler, J. M., & McDonough, L. (1998). Inductive inference in infancy. *Cognitive Psychology*, *37*, 60–96.

Mandler, J. M., & McDonough, L. (2000). Advancing downward to the basic level. *Journal of Cognition and Development*, *1*, 379–403.

McDonough, L. (2002a). Basic level nouns: First learned but misunderstood. *Journal of Child Language*, *29*, 357–378.

McDonough, L. (2002b). Early concepts and language acquistion: What does similarity have to do with either? In N. L. Stein, P. Bauer, & M. Rabinowitz (Eds.), *Representation, memory and development: Essays in honor of Jean Mandler* (pp. 115–143). Mahwah, NJ: Erlbaum.

McDonough, L. (May 2004). *Objects as symbols and/or actions as symbols: The development of early conceptual thought*. Talk given to the International Conference on Infant Studies, Chicago, IL.

McDonough, L., Choi, S., & Mandler, J. M. (2003). Understanding spatial relations: Flexible infants, lexical adults. *Cognitive Psychology*, *46*, 229–259.

Narayanan, S. (1997). *Embodiment in language understanding: Sensory-motor representations for metaphoric reasoning about event descriptions*. Unpublished Ph.D. dissertation, Department of Computer Science, University of California–Berkeley.

Needham, A., & Baillargeon, R. (1993). Intuitions about support in 4.5 month-old infants. *Cognition*, *47*, 121–148.

Nelson, K. (1985). *Making sense: The acquisition of shared meaning*. San Diego: Academic Press.

Regier, T. (1996). The human semantic potential: Spatial language and constrained connectionism, Cambridge, MA: MIT Press.

Rochat, P., Morgan, R., & Carpenter, M. (1997). Young infants' sensitivity to movement information specifying social causality. *Cognitive Development*, *12*, 537–561.

Samuelson, L., & Smith, L. B. (1999). Early noun vocabularies: Do ontology, category structure and syntax correspond? *Cognition*, *73*, 1–33.

Schlottmann, A., & Surian, L. (1999). Do 9-month-olds perceive causation-at-a-distance? *Perception*, *28*, 1105–1113.

Smith, L. B., Jones, S. S., Yoshida, H., & Colunga, E. (2003). Whose DAM account? Attentional learning explains Booth and Waxman. *Cognition*, *87*, 209–213.

Snow, C. (1972). Mother's speech to children learning language. *Child Development*, *43*, 549–565.

Talmy, L. (1985). Lexicalization patterns: Semantic structure in lexical forms. In T. Shopen (Ed.), *Language typology and syntactic description: Vol. 3. Grammatical categories and the lexicon* (pp. 57–149). Cambridge: Cambridge University Press.

Von Hofsten, C., & Rosander, K. (1998). The establishment of gaze control in early infancy. In F. Simion & G. Butterworth (Eds.), *The development of sensory, motor and cognitive capacities in early infancy: From perception to cognition* (pp. 49–66). Hove, UK: Psychology Press.

Waxman, S. R., & Markow, D. B. (1995). Words as invitations to form categories: Evidence from 12- to 13-month-old infants. *Cognitive Psychology*, *29*, 257–302.

Werner, H., & Kaplan, B. (1963). *Symbol formation: An organismic-developmental approach to language and the expression of thought*. New York: Wiley.

Young, R. W., Morgan, W., Sr., & Midgette, S. (1992). *Analytical lexicon of Navajo*. Albuquerque: University of New Mexico Press.

8

THE BODY
AND CHILDREN'S
WORD LEARNING

Linda B. Smith, Josita Maouene,
& Shohei Hidaka

The body is the conduit of experience into the mind and the final path-way through which ideas have their effect in the world. *Nothing* gets into or out of the cognitive system (or the brain) except through the surface structure of the body. Parts of the body—head, hands, legs, and feet—play a role in every experience, every second, every minute from birth to death. This raises the question of whether and how the morphology of the body—the front end to all cognition—matters to the nature of cognition itself.

Gordon Holmes (1922/1979) documented the representational role of the body early in the history of neuroscience, discovering the organiza-tional system known as the "neural map." This is a topographic array of nerve cells across which there is systematic variation in the value of some sensory-motor parameter. Maps organized by the body's surface are a par-ticularly common form of cortical representation (e.g., Grazianao, Cohen, & Botvinick, 2002; N. P. Holmes, Spence, Giard, & Wallace, 2004; Pen-field & Rasmussen, 1950). Studies of neurological disorders and functional brain imaging demonstrate important roles for these body maps in the per-ception of one's own body (N. P. Holmes et al., 2004), in the production of action (e.g., Gallese, Craighero, Fadiga, & Fogassi, 1999), in the under-standing of others' actions, and in the categorization of objects such as tools that are strongly linked to action by a particular body part (Hauk, Johnsrude, & Pulvermüller, 2004).

Studies of the world's languages also point to body parts as a universal representational medium (e.g., Heine, 1997; Svorou, 1993). Words derived from body parts are remarkably common in semantic domains of space, number, measurement, and emotion (de León, 1994; Lakoff & Johnson, 1980; Sakuragi & Fuller, 2003; Saxe, 1981, N. Yu, 2004). Indeed, researchers have proposed a universal semiotics of body parts to interpret and translate images and texts from ancient cultures (e.g., Bron, Corfu-Bratschi, & Maouene, 1989; see also Lakoff & Johnson, 1980). All this suggests that the body may be more than a mere interface between mind and world; rather, it may be central to the origin and representational basis of meaning.

Accordingly, this chapter considers the role of the body in children's early word learning. Children learn words in the here and now of physical space, through embodied actions of turning eyes and heads to look at things, through the movement of arms and hands to reach and act on things, and in the context of large body movements such as running and jumping. This chapter presents four examples of how processes of early word learning may be derived from and embedded in bodily action. Example 1 concerns the role of the body in the spatial organization of attention and, as a result, in the binding of internal cognitive contents to the external world. Example 2 concerns the role of the body in binding us to the attentional states of others. Example 3 concerns how bodily actions reveal and create meaning. Example 4 considers the role of the body—and its morphology—in the semantic structure of early learned verbs.

8.1 EXAMPLE 1: THE BODY AND SPATIAL ATTENTION

As J. J. Gibson (1979) argued, attention is fundamentally about bodily action in space, about orienting the sensors to pick up task-relevant information. The body's position in space—the direction we turn our heads, the bend of the body, the direction of eye gaze—determines the sensory information available. How one should *move* one's body to pick up the task-relevant information, however, depends both on where that information is in the world and on the current, momentary position of the body. This means that internal attentional and selective mechanisms must be dynamically coupled to the body's current position and, further, must be continuously updated with shifts in bodily orientation and with movement (e.g., Georgopoulos, 1997; Presson & Montello, 1994; Schutte, Spencer, & Schöner, 2003; see also Smith, Thelen, Titzer, & McLin, 1999). Considerable evidence from a variety of domains indicates that this relation between the spatial orientation of the body and what we perceive is so central to our everyday experience that it can be reliably used by the cognitive system to solve other cognitive problems (e.g., Grant & Spivey, 2003; Richardson & Kirkham, 2004; Spivey, Tanenhaus, Eberhard, & Sedivy, 2002). In particular, contemporary theories of attention, object tracking, and working memory incorporate the spatial direction of attention as a key binding mechanism (e.g., Ballard, Hayhoe, Pook, & Rao, 1997; Humphreys & Riddoch, 2003; Treisman, 1998). In these accounts, the direction of bodily attention is crucial to how we internally link the constituents of cognition to each other—the redness of a red square to its squareness, the goal of a reach to the motor plan or of a speaker to an utterance.

Ballard et al. (1997; see also Lesperance & Levesque, 1995) specifically propose that *bodily manifestations of direction of attention* work as tags (or "deictic pointers") to keep track of objects in the world and also in memory. This idea can be illustrated through the robotics research of Roy (2005). In one study, Roy presented the robot with multiple objects, for example, a green apple left of center on a table and a red cup right of center on the table. The physical *spatial* reality of the robot and the objects means that when the robot orients leftward, the sensory system picks up information about the green apple, and when it orients to the right, the sensory system picks up information about the red cup. This relation between where the robot looks and what the robot "sees" is a physical fact that the cognitive system can use to generate considerable intelligent behavior. Over the course of the task, the *act of looking left* (within the current frame of reference) will repeatedly yield a view of the green apple and will also activate memories of what was just previously seen (or heard) when attending to that spot. This activation of recent memories *indexed* by the direction of attention enables the robot to detect changes in the physical layout and to connect experiences that are *about* the same object but separated in time.

Experimental analyses of human behavior in block construction tasks (Ballard et al., 1997), in object recognition tasks (Chun & Jiang, 2001; Treisman, 1998), and in memory retrieval tasks (Richardson & Kirkham, 2004) support the "tagging" and "binding" roles of bodily orientation. For example, in the "Hollywood Squares" experiments of Richardson and Spivey (2000), people were presented with four different videos, each from a distinct spatial location. Later, with no videos present, the subjects were asked about the content of those videos. Eye-tracking cameras recorded where people looked when answering these questions, and the results showed that they systematically looked in the direction where the relevant information had been previously presented. *Looking* in a certain direction is linked to memories of the information that had been in those locations.

Children learn words in the physical reality of looking, reaching, and acting on things in space, and thus the tagging and binding mechanisms provided by the spatial orientation of attention should be relevant to word learning. We investigated this proposal using a task first introduced by Baldwin (1993) and illustrated in figure 8.1 (Smith, Samuelson, & Spencer, 2006). The task is structured to capture some of the complexities of real-world word learning. Multiple objects are presented amidst shifts in attention and shifts in bodily action, and most critically, objects and their names are not experienced at the same moment in time. The experimenter sits

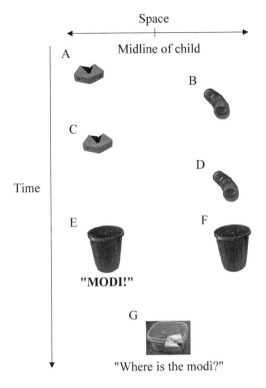

Figure 8.1 Elements of the task used by Smith et al. (2006). The vertical axis is time in the task. See text for a description of the task. See color insert.

before a child at a table and presents the child first with one object at one location (figure 8.1A), so that, for example, the child must turn and reach to the left to retrieve the object. Then the experimenter presents the second object at a second location (figure 8.1B), for example, on the right. In this way, the task creates directional shifts in attention that are associated with each object. These objects are each presented again, each at the same location as before (figure 8.1C, D). Then, out of sight of the child, the two objects are then put into containers and the two containers (figure 8.1E, F) are placed on the table. The experimenter directs the child's attention to one container by looking into it (figure 8.1E) and saying, "I see a modi in here." The experimenter does not show the child the object in the container. Later the objects are retrieved from the containers, placed in a new container, and presented in a neutral location (figure 8.1G). The child is asked which one is a "modi." Notice that the name and the object were never jointly experienced, yet as Baldwin (1993) first demonstrated and as Smith et al. (2006) replicated, children as young as 15 months link the name to the appropriate referent.

A series of subsequent experiments indicate that young children (15–24 months old) solve this problem much like Roy's robot might, binding an object to its name through the body's momentary disposition in space. In particular, success in this task requires the consistent presentation of the objects in space *prior to the naming event*. The linking of different objects to different locations enables children—through their own bodily direction of attention—to connect the object experienced at one moment in time with the name experienced at another. Further experiments show that one does not need containers or hidden objects for children to succeed in this task. One can merely present the target object on the right and have children attend to and play with it there, and then present the distracter object on the left and have children attend to and play with it there. Then, with all objects removed—with only an empty and uniform table surface in view—one can direct children's attention to one side (by a gesture in the air to the right or left) while saying the name children will consistently and reliably link the name to the object associated with that direction of attention. Other experiments show that the *momentary bodily direction of attention* is critical to this mechanism. If the child's posture or position is shifted *after* the objects are linked to directions of attention but *before* the naming event, children cannot use their own bodily direction of attention as a "pointer" to the memory, and they fail to make the link.

Children's solution in the Baldwin task, using the direction of bodily attention to bind recent memories to current experience, is a simple one that works in defined spaces *because* of the physical reality of objects and bodies in space. It is an elegant solution that falls out of the fundamental fact that the body's momentary position in space is the immediate source of all new information into that cognitive system. In this way, the body is foundational to all learning.

8.2 EXAMPLE 2: COUPLING LIKE MINDS THROUGH LIKE BODIES

Research also suggests that the social context of word learning is essential to children's success (Baldwin & Baird, 2001; P. Bloom, 2000; Tomasello, 2000). This social context is very much about the body (Smith, 2000a, 2000b; C. Yu, Ballard, & Aslin, 2005). Direction of eye gaze, posture, and hand gestures all inform others of attentional state (e.g., Goldin-Meadow, 2003; Langton, Watt, & Bruce, 2000; Lee, Eskritt, Symons, & Muir, 1998). Recent developmental research shows that infants are highly attentive to these cues (e.g., Baldwin, 1993; Tomasello, 2000). In one study, for example, Baldwin and Moses (1996) showed that 13-month-old infants give special weight to the speaker's gaze when determining the referent of a novel label. Their experiments showed that infants established a stable link between the novel label and the target toy only when that label was uttered by an adult who concurrently directed her/his attention (as indexed by gaze) toward the target.

Smith (2000a, 2000b) and C. Yu et al. (2005) have argued for an analysis of social cues in terms of the dynamic coupling of the child's own bodily gestures to those of the social partner. This construal reveals the potentially profound insight that through their bodily actions, mature so-cial partners might literally control the internal cognitive mechanisms of young learners. Quite simply, *where* young children look in the moment—how they turn their heads, their eyes, their bodies—will select and activate recent memories and bind them to the current input. And, where young children look is tightly tied to the *bodily* gestures—the eye gaze, head turn, hand movements—of the mature social partner. A mother's head turn and gesture to the right, for example, *causes* the child to look right, which causes the child to *see* a particular object or event and to *reactivate* memories re-cently associated with that bodily direction of attention. In this way, the so-cial partner, through her own bodily actions, can control the internal cogni-tive machinery of the learner.

Smith, Richardson, and Schuller (2006) demonstrated the real-world relevance of these ideas. Mothers were asked to teach 14-month-old chil-dren the names of two novel objects. Both objects were continually avail-able to the mother, and there were no constraints on how mothers distrib-uted time between the two objects. During the 5-minute teaching/play period, mothers typically shifted their attention many times between the two objects, handing one and then the other to the child, demonstrating actions with one and then with the other, all the while naming them re-peatedly. After this teaching and play period, the experimenter measured whether the child had learned the object names. She presented children (on a series of multiple test trials) with the objects and asked them to indicate the one named (e.g., "Where is the toma? Show me the toma"). The key re-sult lies in the relation between children's learning of the object names and the mothers' *spatially directed behavior* with regard to the two objects during the teaching/play period. Children of mothers who spatially segregated the objects through their own bodily gestures—tending to hold one object with one hand (right) and the other object with other hand (left), putting one object to rest on one side and gesturing to, looking at, and naming that object when it was on its most habitually presented side—learned the name. Children of mothers who did not spatially segregate the two objects through their bodily actions were much less likely to correctly map the names to the objects.

Figure 8.2 shows a brief period of activity for two different parents—one (figure 8.2A) who spatially segregated the objects and whose child learned the object names, and one (figure 8.2B) who did not consistently segregate the objects in space and whose child did not learn the object names. Both parents moved the objects, actively engaged with them, and often named them. And indeed, from the perspective of a casual observer, both parents and children appeared highly engaged in the task. But when the first parent named one object, it tended to be in her left hand and on her left side, and when she named the second object, it tended to be in her right hand, on the right side. In contrast, when the second parent named the ob-jects, they were in many different places and held by different hands. These differences mattered; an interaction pattern like the one depicted in the top

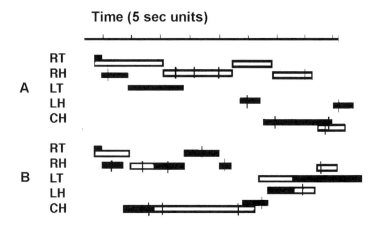

Figure 8.2 Two parents' interactions with objects with their children. White bars, object A; black bars, object B. RT/LT, right and left side of table; RH/LH, right and left hand of parent; CH, child's hands (children tended to hold all objects with both hands). Lines indicate naming of the object by the parent.

panel of figure 8, where the two objects tended to be spatially segregated, was more characteristic of the experiences that led children to learn the two names than was the pattern shown in the bottom panel of figure 8. Why is the first kind of experience better for learning a link between a name and a thing? Because in the here-and-now of real-time learning, the child will encounter the same object multiple times, often acquiring only partial information about the object, its name, or its function in a single encounter. Moreover, these multiple encounters with a single object are naturally interspersed with attention to other objects and other events. In the ecology of real-time learning, the child must shift attention among objects as the discourse shifts and must coherently bind events relevant to one object that are experienced at different times (and not bind them to the wrong object). The embodied nature of attention helps solve this problem. Attention and learning in the moment are tied to learner's body and its disposition in space; moreover, the learner's body is coupled to the bodily gestures of the mature social partner.

Coupled minds in coupled bodies is arguably *the* most important force on human intelligence. Minds are in bodies with a particular morphological structure. Our body's momentary disposition in space reflects and feeds back on our internal cognitions. The body's momentary disposition in space is also a clue to others about the own internal states of the actor. Further, this one mind in this one body is in a world that contains other *similar* bodies, with similar morphological structures, coupled to *similar* minds. This couples our mind, our cognitive system, to the minds and cognitive systems of others.

The coupling of like bodies (and in this way like minds) is evident from earliest infancy (e.g., Cohn & Tronick, 1988; Rogoff, 1990; Schaffer, 1996;

Trevarthen, 1988). Mothers' facial gestures and the sounds they make are tightly coupled to babies' behavior. When babies look into their mother's eyes, mothers look back and smile and offer a sound with rising pitch. When babies smile, mothers smile. When babies coo, mothers coo. These contingencies create a context for arousal and exploration and for learning how bodily gestures map to their effects in the world, and potentially for learning how one's own body maps to another's body. The physical and behavioral contingencies inherent in social interactions may provide the crucial structure for mapping like body parts to like body parts, and finally, these body mappings may yield inferences about other minds (see Smith & Breazeal, 2007).

Developing in a world of similarly structured minds coupled to similarly structured bodies in real time provides an additional level of higher order, multimodal correlations that may be responsible for notions of self, other, and intention (e.g., Leslie, Friedman, & German, 2004). Figure 8.3 illustrates how correlations emerging from coupled *like bodies* with *like internal cognitive systems* can create—through the body's external behaviors—ideas about the internal states of self and others. The key correlations are the correlations between the appearance of the self and the appearance of others (e.g., hands to hands, feet to feet), correlations between the behavior of the self and the behavior of others (looking to an object), correlations between one's own bodily behaviors and one's internal states (e.g., looking left and remembering what was on the left, maintaining the memory of a goal and looking in the direction of that goal), correlations between the external states of others and one's own internal states (where they look, where as a consequence one looks oneself, and thus what one sees and thinks about). The dynamic, socially embedded coupling of two intelligent systems—to each other through a similar body with similar body parts capable of doing similar things in the world—seems the likely origin of the very idea of mind.

In sum, our own body's orientation in space determines—moment to moment—what we experience and what we learn. Spatial direction of attention also serves as a pointing and tagging system for binding internal cognitive operations (including memories) to immediate experience. The outward manifestations of attention also provide others with information

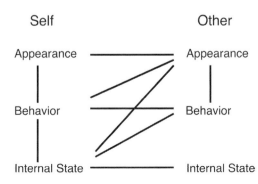

Figure 8.3 Higher order correlations available to the self from the coupling of behavior with a social other.

about our internal states, usable information that couples young learners to the internal states of mature social partners.

8.3 EXAMPLE 3: BODILY ACTIONS AND MEANINGS

Bodily actions make things happen in the world and, in so doing, create meaning. The body part most intimately involved in this meaning creation is the hands. As such, hands are near constants in children's visual fields as they learn about the world. Yoshida and Smith (2006) recently documented this by placing a small head camera with a wide-angle lens on 12- to 36-month-old children. Their goal was a description of the regularities in the visual field from the child's point of view. Analyses of these head-camera recordings suggest that *hands*—the child's or the mature social partner's—are in view in more than 80% of all frames, and this is so at every age. How might these hand actions—and the visual experience of them—create meaning?

Prior to word learning, the active manual exploration of objects provides infants with dynamically rich visual, proprioceptive, and haptic information about objects (Ruff & Lawson, 1990; Ruff & Rothbart, 1996). In one remarkably inventive experiment, Needham, Barrett, and Peterman (2002) fit 2- to 5-month-old infants with Velcro-covered "sticky mittens." These mittens enabled the infants (who were too young to reach for objects) to grab objects merely by swiping. Infants who were given 2 weeks of experiences with these mittens showed more sophisticated object exploration after these experiences *with the mittens off*. They looked at objects more, made more swipes at objects that were immediately preceded by visual contact, and produced more combined visual and oral exploration of objects than did control infants who had no exploratory experiences with "sticky mittens." Giving infants the ability to use their hands early enhances visual attention to objects.

Later in development, the integration of information from eyes and hands plays a formative role in category formation and in the selection and representation of visual properties. In one experiment, Smith (2005) presented children with the object shown in figure 8.4A. The children were told it was a "wug" and were then given the object to hold and shown how to it move up and down on a vertical path. The children then repeated this action three times. The experimental question was this: What other kinds of objects are also wugs? Children chose from new instances that were either elongated vertically or horizontally relative to the exemplar, as shown in figure 8.4B. Smith's conjecture was that children would be more likely to categorize the exemplar with the vertically rather than the horizontally extended alternative *because* of the experience of *manually* moving the object vertically. This conjecture is right, at least for 2- to 3-year-old children. Children who *acted* on an object by moving it up and down extended the name to vertically—but not horizontally—elongated objects. Children who

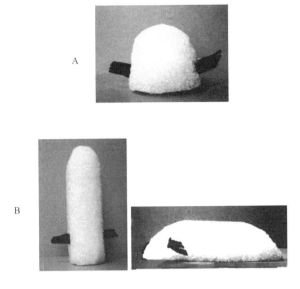

Figure 8.4   The exemplar (*A*) and two choice objects (*B*) used in Smith (2005).

acted on an object by moving it horizontally back and forth extended the name to horizontally but not vertically elongated objects. Children who only watched the experimenter perform the action but did not do the actions themselves did not prefer test objects elongated in the direction of the watched action.

The same point was made in a second study, illustrated in figure 8.5, which confirmed a relation between symmetrical hand actions and the perceived symmetry of an object. In the experiment, children were shown the exemplar in figure 8.5A and told its name ("This is a zup") and then were shown an action with the object and were asked to perform this action. Half the children performed an action that involved holding the object in one hand by one part and moving it back and forth (figure 8.5B, right). Half the children performed an action in which the two sides were held in the two hands and rotated about a central axis (figure 8.5B, left). The children in the first case extended the name to new instances less symmetrical in shape than the exemplar (figure 8.5C, left). The children in the second case extended the name to new instances more symmetrical in shape than the exemplar (figure 8.5C, right). Again, children who only watched these actions performed by the experimenter but did not perform them themselves did not show the effect. The implications of these results are clear: how one holds, uses, and acts on objects determines the aspects of shape considered relevant to categorization and naming. These experiments show a potentially direct effect of manual action on perceived shape.

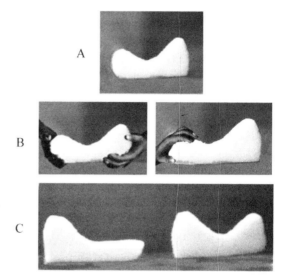

Figure 8.5 The exemplar (*A*), actions (*B*), and two choice objects (*C*) used in Experiment 2 of Smith (2005).

The role of hand actions in organizing visual perception is not just a characteristic of the developmentally immature. In one adult study, Freyd (1983) showed an effect on drawing on the perception of letterlike figures. Freyd taught adults to recognize new letterlike characters by having them watch a letter being drawn. Subjects watched characters drawn by one of two drawing methods. Figure 8.6 illustrates a character and the two drawing methods. Although the drawing methods differed, the final static characters that resulted from the drawing in the two conditions were identical. After training with one drawing method, subjects were presented with static representations and asked whether they were instances of the modeled character. Some of these test characters were "sloppily" drawn versions

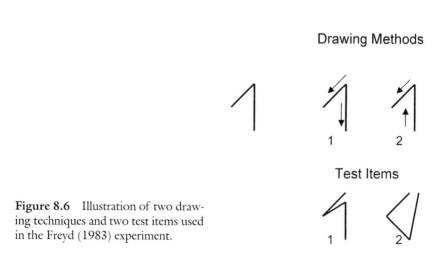

Figure 8.6 Illustration of two drawing techniques and two test items used in the Freyd (1983) experiment.

of the modeled character. Freyd found that subjects were reliably faster at recognizing static characters distorted in a manner consistent with the drawing method they observed during training than they were at recognizing equally distorted characters that were inconsistent with the observed drawing method. For example, subjects who observed drawing method 1 during training recognized test item 1 more rapidly than test item 2, whereas subjects who watched drawing method 2 recognized test item 2 more rapidly than test item 1. In brief, the static visual features that mattered for category membership were influenced by dynamic information about how those features were made in real time. Again, the coupling of vision and manual action yields visual percepts that are a blend, a joint product, of the multimodal experience.

In his theory of neural Darwinism, Edelman (1987) pointed to two principles of neural organization—degeneracy and reentrance—that are relevant to thinking about how coupled hands and eyes may create meaning and development. Neural degeneracy refers to how any single function may be carried out by more than one configuration of neural signals and to how different neural clusters often participate in a variety of different functions. Our multimodal sensory experience is a form of degeneracy. What we see and what we feel as we manually manipulate objects is a form of degeneracy—each modality is presenting overlapping and *partially* redundant information. This creates a potentially powerful source of learning whereby internal activity generated by one sensory (or motor) system may entrain the internal activity of another. Edelman calls this form of multimodal coupling *reentry*. Reentrance refers to the explicit interrelating of multiple simultaneous representations across modalities.

We can use these ideas to understand how action may inform visual perception in the action-shape and letter-writing experiments. For example, when a child held the "wug" and moved it up and down, the child generated a dynamic constellation of sensory experiences, including visual and proprioceptive. These multimodal experiences are time locked and correlated. Changes in the way the hand and arm feels as it moves the "zup" are time locked with activation produced in the visual stream by seeing the object move. The time-locked correlations potentially create a powerful learning mechanism, as illustrated in figure 8.7. The figure shows a physical object (the zup) and two modalities of interaction with the object.

One can describe these interactions in terms of a system of dynamic couplings. One coupling is between the physical properties of the zup as it moves and the neuronal activity in the visual system. Another coupling is between the physical properties of the zup and neuronal activity related to motor plans and felt movements. This coupling is bidirectional because the hand movements change the physical properties available to the sensory systems and because the activity in the sensory system is also a function of the momentary information presented by the object in its current position. The third and fourth couplings constitute what Edelman (1987) calls the reentrance: activity in the visual system is mapped to the motor system, and

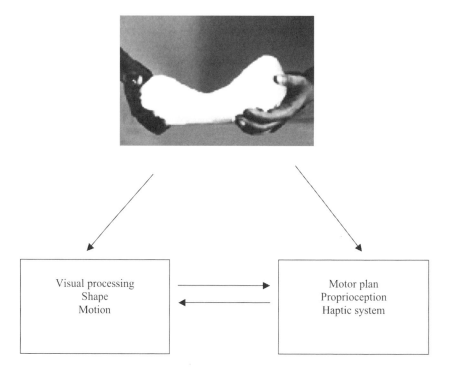

Figure 8.7   Reentrant mappings between visual and haptic, proprioceptive, and motor planning processes.

activity in the motor system is mapped to the visual system. Thus, the two different sources of information—the sight and the feel of the action—are correlated in real time and directly influence and educate each other. At the same time, the visual system is activated by time-varying changes in shading and texture, and collinear movement of points of the zup and arm, the motor and proprioceptive systems are activated by time-locked changes in pressures, velocities, and heft. At every step in real time, the activities in each of these heterogeneous processes are mapped to each other, melding information from one system into the other.

The regularities emergent in the reentrant coordination of vision and action have the power to potentially yield higher order and more abstract concepts. One potential example of how this might work is suggested by Kemler-Nelson and colleagues' programmatic series of experiments on young children's attention to function in forming categories that also illustrates the potential power of hands and action in the formation of categories. In one study (Kemler-Nelson, Russell, Duke, & Jones, 2000), 2-year-old children were presented with novel complex objects with multiple parts like those shown in figure 8.8. One object, the exemplar, was named with a novel name. In addition, the children were shown a function that depended on one of those parts. For example, they were shown how the hinged shape could open, close, and latch. They then manipulated the part causing the box to open and close. After seeing and manipulating the hinge, the children were more likely to extend the object name to the test objects that also had hinged parts rather than to those that were similar in global shape but lacked the hinge. How the children acted on the objects—and the outcomes generated by their actions—seem likely to have organized their attention to some aspects of the visual information over others, potentially changing how object shape itself was perceived. Multimodal regularities emergent in the coupling of vision and manual action may, in this way, create such abstract meanings as "open." If so, then much meaning may reside in the hands—in their actions on objects and in the dynamic visual trajectories they create.

In sum, example 3 illustrates how the body's physical interaction with things in the world may *create* new forms of multimodal input that may carry and create meaning.

8.4 EXAMPLE 4: BODY PARTS AND EARLY VERB MEANINGS

Developmentalists have long noted that children's early verb meanings seem to be about children's own actions (e.g., P. Bloom, 2000; Huttenlocher, Smiley, & Charney, 1983). L. Bloom (2000) in particular has argued that children learn and use words because they are relevant to their

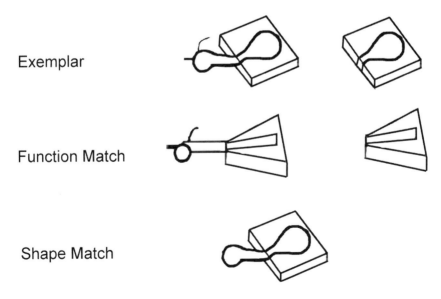

Figure 8.8 Illustration of the objects used by Kemler-Nelson et al. (2000). Shown are the exemplar in its closed and open form, the function-matching test object that closes and opens, and the shape-matching test object than cannot be opened.

own goals, desires, and actions. From this perspective, early verb meanings might be expected to be embedded in the child's bodily actions. Consistent with this idea is a landmark study by Huttenlocher et al. (1983) of young children's early comprehension and production of action words. These researchers found that young children were more likely to comprehend and produce words when they were about their own actions than about the actions of others. For example, children would say "kick" more frequently when they themselves were kicking than when they were watching someone else kick.

Self-action provides a richly interrelated set of immediate experiences out of which one might build meanings. As illustrated in figure 8.9, these include the agent's goal, the motor plan for a specific bodily action by a specific body part, the objects one acts on, as well as information about the effects of the action. Critically, it is the action *by a body part* that links these components, physically connecting goals to outcomes and realizing causes, effects, manners, and paths. Yet the role of the body in verb learning has rarely been considered.

As a first step in this direction, Maouene, Hidaka, and Smith (2006) asked adults how body parts link to the verbs that children learn early. We examined a corpus of 103 common English verbs that are normatively acquired by children by 36 months (Fenson et al., 1993). In a free association task, adults were asked to supply *one* body part associated with each verb. The participants were not told the reasoning behind the task and they were *not* asked for the body part associated with action; instead, participants were free to supply whatever body part popped into their heads for whatever reason. There were also no constraints on the scale of the body parts that might be offered: lips, gums, teeth, mouth, face, and so forth, were all possible associates. The rationale for this method was that if these verbs are associated with bodily actions done by particular body parts—and if this is

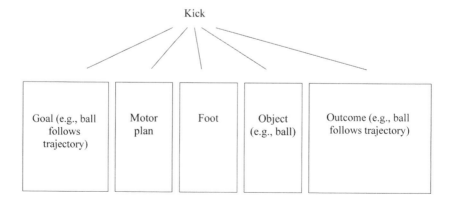

Figure 8.9 Verbs are linked to momentary events that include goals, motor plans, body parts, objects, and outcomes.

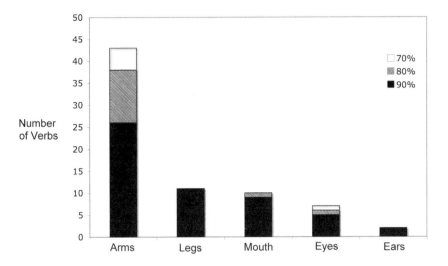

Figure 8.10   Number of verbs (of 103) that are associated to five body regions by more than 70%, 80%, or 90% of adult judges.

shared knowledge by mature speakers of English—then adults should systematically associate specific body parts with specific verbs and should agree with each other.

The results suggest, first, that adults do associate specific body parts with these common verbs. They readily generated body parts (more than 62 unique parts at multiple levels of scale) but generally agreed with each other as to which parts were relevant to specific verbs. Figure 8.10 shows the number of verbs associated by 70%, 80%, and 90% of the participants with one of five regions: arms, legs, mouth, eyes, and ears. The explicit body parts included in these five regions are subparts of the regions region (e.g., the arm region includes arm, elbow, hand, fingers, knuckles). Fifty-three of the total 103 verbs, slightly more than half, were associated with the same body region by 90% or more of the respondents. Only a very few more verbs are added if those associated with region by 70% are included. In brief, slightly more than half these verbs are overwhelmingly associated with a single body region.

Further analyses examined the semantic structure of these verbs through a statistical procedure known as correspondence analysis (a kind of principal component analysis for qualitative data). These analyses seek to find a smaller number of dimensions than the original set (of 103 verbs by 62 unique body parts) that nonetheless captures most of the variance in the data set. The input to the analysis was a matrix of 103 verbs by 62 body parts. As shown in figure 8.11, the analysis yielded a three-dimensional space in which verbs (indicated as a point) were clustered into four groups; each of these groups had an elongated, almost linear shape, in the multidimensional space. Accordingly, we will call each of these four elongated

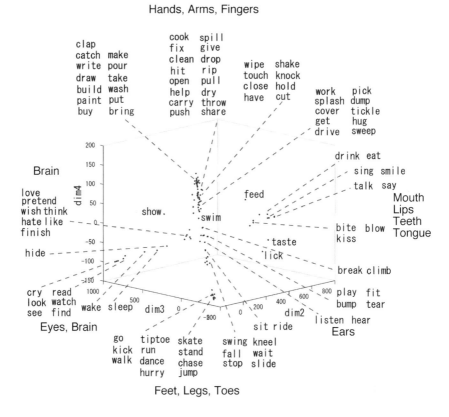

Figure 8.11   The structure of the 103 verbs and their body part associations in three dimensions. (Dimension 1 of the CA analysis segregated the two ear verbs from all other verbs. For clarity of the figure, this plane is not shown.)

clusters of verbs "arms." The verbs at the outer *extremities* of each arm are the ones most exclusively associated with a single body part by subjects.

The most vertically aligned arm in the figure contains verbs associated with hands, fingers, and arms. These include verbs obviously involving the hands such as *clap* and *write* but also verbs such as *give*, *buy*, and *share*, verbs that might be considered to be more abstract and relational in their meaning but that elicited hand as the primary associated body part (with arm as the remaining named part; e.g., the proportion of named body parts that were hand+arm were 82%, 90%, and 80% for *give*, *buy*, and *share*, respectively). As one moves downward in this cluster, the verbs become less exclusively associated with hands and associated primarily with arms (e.g., 94% and 70% for *hug* and *sweep*) or fingers (e.g., *tickle*, 60% fingers, 20% hand) or with a mixture of body parts with hands comprising a significant proportion of the body parts named (e.g., *work*, 54% hands, with no other body part named by more than 10% of the respondents). In total, 53 of the

103 verbs were associated by more than 50% of the adults with hands, arms, or fingers. Thirty-five were associated by more than 50% of the adults specifically with hands. In sum, many early verbs, including many with abstract relational meanings such as *put*, are strongly associated actions by hands. This is perhaps not surprising in that hands are how human bodies generally make things happen and, in particular, how they connect goals to objects.

The verbs on the lower vertical arm are associated with legs. For example, *stand*, *jump*, *chase*, and *kneel* were each associated by more than 96% of respondents with the legs (and leg parts, e.g., feet or thigh). But interestingly, *hurry* (65% legs, 32% feet) and *go* (54% legs, 40% feet) were also strongly associated with the legs. The verbs *stop*, *fall*, *swing*, and *wait* fell in a middle cluster on this arm; each of these verbs was associated with the legs or feet by more than 50% of the participants but was also associated by other participants with the whole body and/or the torso. The verbs in the center—*play*, *bump*, *fit*, *break*, and *climb*—fall between the verbs unambiguously associated with the hands and those unambiguously associated with the legs; that is, these middle cluster verbs are ones that were associated with both hands and legs. In total, only 14 of the 103 verbs were associated by more than 50% of the participants with the legs (and their subparts of feet, thigh, toe, and knee).

On the right side of the figure are a cluster of verbs strongly associated with the mouth. All verbs in this cluster were associated with the mouth (lips, tongue, or teeth) by more than 80% of the participants. *Feed*, which is by itself, was associated with the mouth by 60% of participants and with hands by the other 40%. On the left side are two clusters of verbs associated with eyes. At the extreme are verbs such as *cry*, *look*, *watch*, *find*, and *wake* that show a range of responses from those that were strongly associated with eyes by 98% of respondents (*cry*, *look*) to those verbs associated with eyes by 66% of respondents (*wake*). More internally on this arm are a cluster of verbs associated with both the eyes and the brain, mind, or head. These are the psychological verbs such as *pretend*, *wish*, *think*, and *hate*.

Overall, this correspondence analysis suggests that associations between the early-learned verbs and body parts are strong, coherent, and highly organized by four major bodily areas: the mouth, eyes (and also ears), legs and feet, and hands. Further, many of these individual verbs are systematically and strongly associated with a *single* area of the body. This result, although new and without precedent as far as we know, also makes sense. Most early verbs refer to physical actions by physical bodies and even those that do not, such as *pretend*, *wish*, *think*, and *hate*, lead to outward bodily behaviors that are visually perceptible and so associated with eyes.

Our further analyses suggest a relation among verbs, body parts and age of acquisition. We illustrate these relations in the body maps in figure 8.12. To generate these body-verb maps, a body-part meaning vector was created for each verb from the raw adult judgments. This vector represents

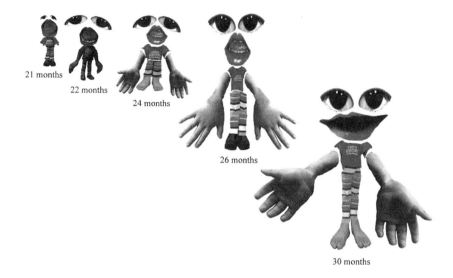

Figure 8.12 Body maps of body parts associated with typically known verbs at five ages. The size of each figure illustrates the number of known verbs at each age; the area of each body part region indicates percentage of associations (across all verbs known at that age). See color insert.

the percentage of adult judgers who listed each body part as associated with the verb. Nested body parts (e.g., lip, mouth, head) were treated separately. For example, the "meaning" vector for *bite* has these values within it: 58 mouth, 38 teeth, 2 head, and 2 lip, because these are the percentages of adults who listed each as the single body part most associated with *bite*. We then summed the vectors for all the verbs acquired by a given age, for example, summing all the vectors of all verbs normatively produced at 22 month of age. These summary vectors were used to generate the body-verb maps in figure 8.12. The size of the homunculus grows with the number of verbs normatively acquired by that age, and the size of a constituent body part grows with the number of verbs associated with that body part. For these figures, age of acquisition was defined by the age at which 80% of the children in the normative study (Fenson et al., 1993) have this verb in their productive vocabulary.

The smallest verb-body map is for a normative 21-month-old, the starting point in our analysis. Normatively, children this age have nine verbs in their productive vocabulary. Body maps for four subsequent ages are also shown: 22 months (21 verbs), 24 months (45 verbs), 26 months (74 verbs), and 30 months (96 verbs). As is apparent, verb acquisitions are clustered by body part. At every age, children add new verbs related to all body parts, but different body parts dominate earlier versus later acquisitions. At 21 months, verbs involving actions of the mouth and lips dominate, accounting for 47% of the body parts associated with verbs known at this age. Over the next month, verbs pertaining to the face region including the eyes (22% of the body parts associated with the new verbs) are added, as well actions by the limbs (52% of the body parts associated with the new verbs). Growth in new verbs from 22 to 24 months overwhelmingly (86% of all new meanings) concerns actions by the limbs. The predominant region of growth after this point is in verbs associated with the hands, accounting for 58% of new additions from 24 to 26 months and 59% of all new additions from 26 to 30 months. At 30 months, verbs associated hands and arms dominate, accounting for 51% of all verbs in children's total productive vocabulary at 30 months. Together, these body maps provide a developmental picture of verb learning that is strongly organized by dominant interactions of body parts with the world.

The observed pattern of acquisition is not easily explained by the frequency of individual verbs in the learning environment. We directly examined the potential role of frequency by measuring the occurrence of the each of the 100 verbs in the CHILDES (Child Data Language Exchange) corpus of parent speech to children (MacWhinney, 2001). The frequency of the verbs in this large sample of parent speech is not correlated with their normative age of acquisition ($r = -0.11$, not significant). Saliency of the relevant actions also seems an unlikely explanation because there is no evidence that we know of to suggest that young children have a greater interest in kissing than tickling or in biting than hitting.

The clustering of verb acquisitions by body part does fit previous descriptions of lexical development suggesting that once children learn a few words in a given domain, the rate of growth of new words in that same domain accelerates rapidly (Pollmann, 2003; Samuelson, 2002; Sandhofer & Smith, 1999; Yoshida & Smith, 2001). This pattern has been observed for object, color, number, and animal words. It appears that as children learn individual words, they also learn the more general parameters of meaning that distinguish words in that domain. Applying this idea to the present data suggests that *the body parts involved in the actions* define like kinds of verbs. There are a number of potential dimensions of meaning that are related to the body part region, including proximity of action to the body, the extent of the space in which the action may take place, and the variability of movements, as well as the objects involved.

There are strong associations between early-learned verbs and body parts. The strength, coherence, and apparent relation to acquisition of these associations fit the embodied reality of children's learning: children learn verbs as they move and act in the world. Not surprisingly, then, the body pervades representational systems.

8.5 BEYOND THE BODY: EXPANDING SPACES AND MEANING

Traditional theories of cognition segregate the mind from the body, from perception, and from action. Sensory systems are seen only as input devices and motor systems as output devices. There are grounds to reject outright this conceptualization of the cognitive system (see, e.g., Barsalou, 2003; Clark, 1997; Thelen & Smith, 1994); however, even within this traditional conceptualization, it seems highly likely that the body and its structure would leave its mark on internal cognitive processes and representations. Our own body—how it moves, the location of its parts and sensors, how those parts interact with the physical world and create change in the physical world—is the most pervasive regularity in experience. This very fact, however, makes it likely that mind (and brain) is not sequestered and not separate in mechanisms and processes from those of the body. The physical reality of the body in a physical world provides the cognitive system with mechanistic links to the world it can count on. The examples reviewed in this chapter, all focusing on how children learn words, suggest that these mechanistic links are crucial to attention, to solving the binding problem, and to understanding one's own mind and those of others, as well as to the discovery of meaning in the world and its representation.

In summary, then, understanding developmental process requires taking the physical reality of the body seriously. The body through its different sensory systems provides the developing organism with separate streams of information about the world, about the self, and about others—from hands, eyes, ears, and so forth. The multiple overlapping and time-locked sensory systems enable the developing system to educate itself—without defined external tasks or teachers—just by perceiving and acting in the world. Babies are physical beings in a physical world. Their own physical reality creates regularities (e.g., between how they move their hands and what they see, and between where they look and what they see). The physical world also offers on its own rich regularities that organize perception, action, and ultimately thought. The intelligence of babies not only resides inside them but also is distributed across their interactions and experiences in the physical world. Bodily action—in a moment, in a physical world—is what integrates different internal processes, is what couples the developing infant to social others—and in so doing may be crucial to the creation of higher order mental functions.

REFERENCES

Baldwin, D. A. (1993). Early referential understanding: Infants' ability to recognize referential acts for what they are. *Developmental Psychology, 29*, 832–843.

Baldwin, D. A., & Baird, J. (2001). Discerning intentions in dynamic human action. *Trends in Cognitive Science, 54*, 171–178.

Baldwin, D. A., & Moses, L. J. (1996). The ontogeny of social information gathering. *Child Development, 67*, 1915–1939.

Ballard, D. H., Hayhoe, M. M., Pook, P. K., & Rao, R. P. N. (1997). Deictic codes for the embodiment of cognition. *Behavioral & Brain Sciences, 20*, 723–767.

Barsalou, L. W. (2003). Abstraction in perceptual symbol systems. *Philosophical Transactions of the Royal Society of London: Biological Sciences, 358*, 1177–1187.

Bloom, L. (2000). Intentionality and theories of intentionality in development. *Human Development, 43,* 178–185.

Bloom, P. (2000). *How children learn the meanings of words.* Cambridge, MA: MIT Press.

Bron, C., Corfu-Bratschi, P., & Maouene, M. (1989). Hephaistos bacchant ou le cavalier comaste: simulation de raisonnement qualitatif par le langage informatique LISP. *Annali Istituto Universitario Orientale (Archeologia e Storia Antica), XII,* 155–172.

Chun, M. & Jiang, Y. (1998). Contextual cueing: Implicit learning and memory of visual context guides spatial attention. *Cognitive Psychhology, 36,* 28–71.

Clark, A. (1997). *Being there: Putting brain, body and world together.* Cambridge, MA: MIT Press.

Cohn, J. F., & Tronick, E. Z. (1988). Mother-infant face to face interaction: Influence is bi-directional and unrelated to periodic cycles in either partner's behaviour. *Developmental Psychology, 24,* 386–392.

Coulson, S., & Matlock, T. (2001). Metaphor and the space structuring model. *Metaphor & Symbol, 16,* 295–316.

de León, L. (1994). Exploration in the acquisition of geocentric location by Tzotzil children. *Linguistics, 32,* 857–884.

Edelman, G. (1987). *Neural Darwinism.* New York: Basic Books.

Fenson, L., Dale, P., Reznick, J. S., Thal, D., Bates, E., Hartung, J., Pethick, S., & Reilly, J. (1993). *The MacArthur Communicative Development Inventories: User's guide and technical manual.* San Diego: Singular Publishing.

Freyd, J. J. (1983). Representing the dynamics of a static form. *Memory & Cognition, 11,* 342–346.

Gallese, V., Craighero, L., Fadiga, L., & Fogassi, L. (1999, July). Perception through action. *Psyche: An Interdisciplinary Journal of Research on Consciousness, 5(21).* Retrieved from http://psyche.cs.monash.edu.au/v5/psyche-5-21-gallese .html Retrieved February 22, 2006.

Georgopoulos, A. (1997). Voluntary movement: Computational principles and neural mechanisms. In M. D. Rugg (Ed.), *Cognitive neuroscience: Studies in cognition* (pp. 131–168). Cambridge, MA: MIT Press.

Gibson, J. J. (1979). *The ecological approach to visual perception.* Boston, MA: Houghton Mifflin.

Goldin-Meadow, S. (2003). *Hearing gesture: How our hands help us think.* Cambridge, MA: Harvard University Press.

Grant, E. R., & Spivey, M. J. (2003). Eye movements and problem solving: Guiding attention guides thought. *Psychological Science, 14,* 462–466.

Graziano, M., Cohen, J. D., & Botvinick, M. (2002). How the brain represents the body. In W. Prinz & B. Hommel (Eds.), *Attention and performance: Vol. 19. Common mechanisms in perception and action* (p. 136–157). Oxford: Oxford University Press.

Hauk, O., Johnsrude, I., & Pulvermüller, F. (2004). Somatotopic representation of action words in human motor and premotor cortex. *Neuron, 41,* 301–307.

Heine, B. (1997). *Cognitive foundations of grammar.* Oxford: Oxford University Press.

Holmes, G. (1922/1979). The Croonian lectures on the clinical symptoms of cerebellar disease and their interpretation. *Lancet.* Reprinted in C. G. Phillips (Ed.), *Selected papers of Gordon Holmes* (pp. 186–247). Oxford: Oxford University Press.

Holmes, N. P., Spence, C., Giard, M., & Wallace, M. (2004). The body schema and multisensory representation(s) of peripersonal space. *Cognitive Processing*, *5*, 94–105.

Humphreys, G. W., & Riddoch, M. J. (2003). From what to where: Neuropsychological evidence for implicit interactions between object- and space-based attention. *Psychological Science*, *14*, 487–492.

Huttenlocher, J., Smiley, P., & Charney, R. (1983). Emergence of action categories in the child: Evidence from verb meanings. *Psychological Review*, *90*, 72–93.

Kemler-Nelson, D. G., Russell, R., Duke, N., & Jones, K. (2000). Two-year-olds will name artifacts by their functions. *Child Development, 18*, 1271–1288.

Lakoff, G., & Johnson, M. (1980). The metaphorical structure of the human conceptual system. *Cognitive Science*, *4*, 195–208.

Langton, S. R., Watt, R. J., & Bruce, V. (2000). Do the eyes have it? Cues to the direction of social attention. *Trends in Cognitive Neuroscience*, *4*, 50–59.

Lee, K., Eskritt, M., Symons, L. A., & Muir, D. (1998). Children's use of triadic eye gaze information for "mind reading." *Developmental Psychology*, *34*, 525–539.

Leslie, A. M., Friedman, O., & German, T. P. (2004). Core mechanisms in "theory of mind." *Trends in Cognitive Sciences*, *8*, 528–533.

Lesperance, Y., & Levesque, H. J. (1995). Indexical knowledge and robot action: A logical account. *Artificial Intelligence*, *73*, 69–115.

MacWhinney, B. (2001). From CHILDES to TalkBank. In M. Almgren, A. Barreña, M. Ezeizaberrena, I. Idiazabal & B. MacWhinney (Eds.), *Research on Child Language Acquisition* (pp. 17–34). Somerville, MA: Cascadilla.

Maouene, J., Hidaka, S., & Smith, L. B. (2006, May). *Body parts and early learned verbs*. Paper presented at the International Conference for Development and Learning, Bloomington, IN.

Needham, A., Barrett, T., & Peterman, K. (2002). A pick me up for infants' exploratory skills: Early simulated experiences reaching for objects using "sticky" mittens enhances young infants' object exploration skills. *Infant Behavior & Development*, *25*, 279–295.

Penfield, W., & Rasmussen, T. (1950). *The cerebral cortex of man: A clinical study of localization of function*. New York: Macmillan.

Pollmann, T. (2003). Some principles involved in the acquisition of number words. *Language Acquisition: A Journal of Developmental Linguistics*, *11*, 1–31.

Presson, C. C., & Montello, D. R. (1994). Updating after rotational and translational body movements: Coordinate structure of perspective space. *Perception*, *23*, 1447–1455.

Richardson, D. C., & Kirkham, N. Z. (2004). Multimodal events and moving locations: Eye movements of adults and 6-month-olds reveal dynamic spatial indexing. *Journal of Experimental Psychology: General*, *133*, 46–62.

Richardson, D., & Spivey, M. (2000). Representation, space and Hollywood Squares: Looking at things that aren't there anymore. *Cognition*, *76*, 269–295.

Rogoff, B. (1990). *Apprenticeship in thinking: Cognitive development in social context*. Oxford: Oxford University Press.

Roy, D. (2005). Semiotic schemas: A framework for grounding language in the action and perception. *Artificial Intelligence*, *167*, 170–205.

Ruff, H., & Lawson, K. (1990). Development of sustained, focused attention in young children during free play. *Developmental Psychology*, *26*, 85–93.

Ruff, H. A., & Rothbart, M. K. (1996). *Attention in early development: Themes and variations.* New York: Oxford University Press.

Sakuragi, T., & Fuller, J. W. (2003). Body-part metaphors: A cross-cultural survey of the perception of translatability among Americans and Japanese. *Journal of Psycholinguistic Research, 32,* 381–395.

Samuelson, L. K. (2002). Statistical regularities in vocabulary guide language acquisition in connectionist models and 15–20-month-olds. *Developmental Psychology, 38,* 1016–1037.

Sandhofer, C. M., & Smith, L. B. (1999). Learning color words involves learning a system of mappings. *Developmental Psychology, 35,* 668–679.

Saxe, G. B. (1981). Body parts as numerals: A developmental analysis of numeration among the Oksapmin in Papua New Guinea. *Child Development, 52,* 306–316.

Schaffer, H. R. (1996). *Social development.* Oxford: Blackwell.

Schutte, A. R., Spencer, J. P., & Schöner, G. (2003). Testing the dynamic field theory: Working memory for locations becomes more spatially precise over development. *Child Development, 74,* 1393–1417.

Smith, L. B. (2000a). How to learn words: An associative crane. In R. Golinkoff & K. Hirsh-Pasek (Eds.), *Breaking the word learning barrier* (pp. 51–80). Oxford: Oxford University Press.

Smith, L. B. (2000b). Avoiding association when it's behaviorism you really hate. In R. Golinkoff & K. Hirsh-Pasek (Eds.), *Breaking the word learning barrier* (pp. 169–174). Oxford: Oxford University Press.

Smith, L. B. & Breazeal, C. (2007). The dynamic lift of developmental process. *Developmental Science, 10,* 61–68.

Smith, L. B. (2005). Action alters perceived shape. *Cognitive Science, 29,* 665–679.

Smith, L. B., Richardson, A., & Schuller. D. (2006). *Mother's hands: Binding names to things.* Unpublished manuscript.

Smith, L. B., Samuelson, L. K., & Spencer, J. P. (2006). *The role of spatial attention in binding names to things.* Unpublished manuscript.

Smith, L. B., Thelen, E., Titzer, R., & McLin, D. (1999). Knowing in the context of acting: The task dynamics of the A-not-B error. *Psychological Review, 106,* 235–260.

Spivey, M. J., Tanenhaus, M. K., Eberhard, K. M., & Sedivy, J. C. (2002). Eye movements and spoken language comprehension: Effects of visual context on syntactic ambiguity resolution. *Cognitive Psychology, 45,* 447–81.

Svorou, S. (1993). *The grammar of space.* Amsterdam: John Benjamins.

Thelen, E., & Smith, L. B. (1994). *A dynamic systems approach to the development of cognition and action.* Cambridge, MA: MIT Press.

Tomasello, M. (2000). Perceiving intentions and learning words in the second year of life. In M. Bowerman & S. Levinson (Eds.), *Language acquisition and conceptual development* (pp. 111–128). Cambridge: Cambridge University Press.

Treisman, A. (1998). Features and objects: The fourteenth Bartlett memorial lecture. *Quarterly Journal of Experimental Psychology: Human Experimental Psychology, 40,* 201–237.

Trevarthen, C. (1988). Infants trying to talk. In R. Söderbergh (Ed.), *Children's creative communication* (pp. 9–31). Lund: Lund University Press.

Yoshida, H., & Smith, L. B. (2001). Early noun lexicons in English and Japanese. *Cognition, 82,* B63–B74.

Yoshida, H., & Smith, L. B. (2006). *Word learning from the child's point of view*. Unpublished manuscript.

Yu, C., Ballard, D. H., & Aslin, R. N. (2005). The role of embodied intention in early lexical acquisition. *Cognitive Science, 29*, 961–1005.

Yu, N. (2004). The eyes for sight and mind. *Journal of Pragmatics, 36*, 663–686.

9

DEVELOPMENTAL CHANGES IN CHILDREN'S UNDERSTANDING OF MAPS
What, When, and How?

LYNN S. LIBEN & LAUREN J. MYERS

In the comic strip *Rose Is Rose*, Pasquale is in the back seat of the family car, following along on a map, and suddenly cries out "Ona rong road!" [*sic*]. In the conversation that ensues with his parents, it becomes evident that Pasquale is distraught because the road on which they are driving is not red as is the road on the map. As adults, we are amused because we know that cartographic symbols do not necessarily resemble the referents for which they stand. That is, although some symbols may show strong, pictorial resemblance to their referents (i.e., *iconic* symbols, as in a drawing of the Empire State Building used to show its location on a map of New York City), others may bear no physical resemblance to the referent at all (i.e., *arbitrary* representations, as in a star used to indicate the state capital), and still others may combine both iconic and arbitrary qualities (e.g., a road line that is iconic insofar as it shares location and direction with the real road, but arbitrary insofar as its color carries meaning about road type only because it has been assigned to do so). In another comic strip, Dennis the Menace and his father, Hank, are seated in the living room, looking at a map to plan a trip. Hank shows Dennis where they will start and where they will end and tells Dennis that it will take about two days. Dennis, incredulous, responds "*Two days?* Just to go *three inches?*" We are amused because we have come to understand that map space (or representational space) is not identical to real space (or referential space). And in yet another comic strip, Born Loser stands in front of a locator map, sees an "X" labeled "You Are Here," turns quizzically to his friend and asks: "How do they know?"

These three cartoons, respectively, capture three important aspects of map understanding that develop during childhood. The first is understanding the referential meaning of map symbols (e.g., that squares on highway lines symbolize exits) referred to as understanding *representational correspondences* (Liben & Downs, 1989; Liben & Yekel, 1996), *identity correspondences* (Presson, 1982), or *object correspondences* (Uttal, Gregg, Tan, Chamberlin, & Sines, 2001). The second is understanding the links between spatial qualities of the referential space and spatial qualities of the map symbols (e.g., understanding how the location, size, and shape of a lake are symbolized by the location, size, and shape of the blue region on the map), referred to as *geometric correspondences* (Liben & Downs, 1989; Liben & Yekel, 1996) or *spatial correspondences* (Uttal et al., 2001). And the third is understanding one's own connection to the referential and representational space (e.g., coordinating where one is in the space and "on" the map so that one can use the map to navigate or to record information being gathered from the environment), referred to as the *self-space-map* relation (Liben, 2006; Liben & Downs, 1993).

In section 9.2, we provide a selective review of empirical work on children's developing understanding of these three aspects of maps and map use. In the course of reviewing *what* develops, we implicitly and simultaneously address the question of *when* understanding develops. It would be hard—probably impossible—to avoid doing so, because as developmental researchers, we routinely study progressive accomplishments in relation to chronological age. But chronological age alone does not explain developmental change; it is merely a marker for the factors that are critical for effecting progress. We focus explicitly on the question of *how* progress occurs in section 9.3. In the closing section (9.4), we offer brief suggestions about potential directions for future research.

Before turning to our descriptive review of what develops, in section 9.1 we define the particular kinds of maps we study, review some of their key qualities and the cognitive challenges entailed by those qualities, and comment briefly on the kinds of developmental spatial progressions that are relevant for understanding and using maps.

9.1 THE QUALITIES OF MAPS AND THE COGNITIVE CHALLENGES THEY PRESENT

9.1.1 Defining Maps

The word "map" has many meanings; thus, it is important to specify which one we are using. It can be used metaphorically, as in the phrase "Road Map to Peace" applied to the Israeli-Palestinian conflict. It can be used to refer to any kind of systematic relation between one thing and another, as in a mathematical mapping. The term may be used to refer to any kind of spatial-graphic representation of some physical entity, as in "brain maps" or "genome maps" (see Hall, 1992). In some graphics there are spatial iso-morphisms between the referent object and the representation so that there is a correspondence between the way that components are arrayed in the referent and the representation (e.g., distributions of locations in the brain represented by analogous distributions of locations on a functional MRI image). The maps we discuss in this chapter are graphics that honor this referent-to-representation spatial isomorphism. In addition, however, we constrain our topic further by including only those spatial-graphic repre-sentations whose referents are environments or spaces in which humans live and move (e.g., see Acredolo, 1981; Garling & Evans, 1991; Proshansky, Ittelson, & Rivlin, 1976). These are the kinds of maps used by geographers and historians, by geologists and surveyors. These are what are often re-ferred to by psychologists as "real" maps, in opposition to cognitive maps, metaphorical maps, or paper representations of table-top arrays of objects (Liben, 2001).

One way of capturing the core of meaning of "map" is to examine def-initions found in general reference sources. Illustrative is the following def-inition from the Milwaukee Public Museum, returned along with several others in response to entering the phrase "map definition" in a search en-gine (Google, 2005):

> A diagram, drawing or other graphic representation, usually on a flat surface, of selected physical features (natural, artificial, or both) of a part or the whole of the surface of the Earth or any desired surface or subsurface area, by means of signs and symbols and with the means of orientation indicated, so that the relative position and size of each feature on the map corresponds to its correct geographic situation ac-cording to a definite and established scale and projection.

9.1.2 The Cartographic Eye

As is clear from this as well as any other general definition of maps, spatial qualities are central. Three key spatial qualities of maps may be summarized by the three elements contained in the "cartographic eye" (Downs, 1981) reproduced in figure 9.1. One is *viewing distance* or *scale*, which refers to the ratio between environmental space and representational space (as in a 1:10,000 scale) and which thus is relevant to the metric features of the map. A second is *viewing angle*, which refers to the inclination from which the referent space is viewed. Viewing angles vary through 90°. At one ex-treme is a straight-down view (also referred to in cartography as a nadir, or-thogonal, or vertical view) that creates a "plan map" such as those com-monly used in municipal maps. When the angle is less extreme angle, for example, 45°, the map becomes an "oblique perspective map" such as the kind commonly found in city tourist maps, allowing visitors to see the to-pography of the landscape (e.g., the steep sections of San Francisco) and considerable detail about landmarks (e.g., a perspective drawing of the

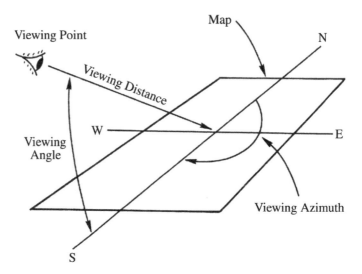

Figure 9.1 The cartographic eye showing the three dimensions of geometric correspondences: viewing distance, viewing angle, and viewing azimuth. From Downs (1981) with permission.

Golden Gate Bridge). Finally, at the other extreme, a 0° angle yields a straight-ahead, eye-level, or "elevation view" such as an architect's rendering of the front face of a building or a skyline photograph of a city. The third dimension of the cartographic eye is *viewing azimuth*, which refers to the direction from which the referent space is depicted (e.g., whether a continent is depicted with north or west at the top of the page).

When the environment being mapped is a relatively small, flat space such as a sparsely furnished laboratory room, cartographic variables have relatively minor effects on the map. For example, in the case of a room with, say, four boxes in it, maps at different scales will almost certainly vary only with respect to the overall ratio. That is, plan maps scaled to fit a standard piece of writing paper versus a poster would probably have the same symbols, varying only with respect to their precise sizes. In contrast, when the space being mapped is large and complex (e.g., a campus, town, country, or continent), cartographic decisions have a profound effect on the map's appearance. For example, a map of a state at two different scales would affect *which* referents could be included and at what level of categorization and with what symbolization (e.g., whether the map depicted individual local streets and small lakes, or only major highways and major bodies of water). Scale affects the details provided for any given feature. For example, shorelines would be shown as generalized coastal shapes in small-scale state maps but as detailed inlets in large-scale harbor maps designed for sailors.[1] When the referent space is three-dimensional (as is the oblate spheroid of Earth) rather than a flat surface (as a laboratory room floor), decisions about map projections also have profound effects on the appearance of the map and hence on the challenges presented to map users. That is, whenever one projects a three-dimensional object onto a two-dimensional surface, there must be distortion in size or angle, and the particulars of those distortions depend on which projection is employed. For example, the size and shape of Greenland appear markedly different on a Mercator projection than on an equal-area projection (see Liben, 2001). To interpret the referential meaning of "paper space" correctly, then, the map user must have some understanding of the way map projections function.

9.1.3 The Mind's Developing Spatial Eye

The preceding section focuses on the ways in which the space of reality is mapped onto the space of the representation. But cognitive qualities of map users also affect the information that is processed from a given map. Of particular relevance is what we call here the mind's spatial eye, a term meant to carry meaning about not only peripheral-level spatial perceptual skills but also higher order spatial concepts. It is thus shorthand for the "embodied" eye of an active, constructive knower whose developing cognitive processes are guided and constrained by the biological endowment of the species and of the individual (see Liben, in press). It would be impossible to try to review relevant developing spatial concepts fully here (indeed, that is one of the goals of this entire volume as well as of a number of others; see Eliot, 1987; Liben, Patterson, & Newcombe, 1981; Newcombe & Huttenlocher, 2000; for brief reviews, see Liben, 2001, 2006; Newcombe & Huttenlocher, 2006). However, just as it is useful to provide a structure for discussing the spatial qualities of maps (the cartographic eye), it is useful to provide a structure for discussing the spatial concepts of map users.

A structure we have found useful is the tripartite division into topological, projective, and Euclidean spatial concepts drawn from the early work of Piaget and Inhelder (1956). In brief, topological concepts are "rubber sheet" spatial relations that include concepts such as "next to" and "on" but do not conserve distance or angle. Projective concepts concern "point-of-view" relations, that is, those that depend upon viewing perspective, as in understanding that the top of a drinking glass would look round from directly above but elliptical from an oblique angle. Finally, Euclidean concepts are those linked to using a stable system (e.g., Cartesian coordinates) with which to represent space, thus permitting metric measurement and conservation of distance and angle. Piaget and Inhelder reported that topological concepts emerged during the preschool years and that projective and Euclidean concepts developed in tandem throughout early and later childhood. In later work, Piaget and Garcia (1989) substituted the concepts of intra-, inter-, and transfigural relations to describe the developmental progression. In a contemporary approach, Newcombe and Huttenlocher (2000) offered a developmental model of hierarchical spatial coding that begins by children conceptualizing locations with reference to general regions and landmarks, and later by fine-tuned metrics. Although the language differs across these various approaches, they share the notion that early spatial understanding relies on immediate relationships or regions (e.g., a toy is at the corner of a desk) whereas later spatial understanding makes use of precise frames of reference (e.g., locating a toy with respect to distances measured along two dimensions). Irrespective of the particular developmental system one might select, our theoretical approach to the development of children's map understanding assumes that map understanding rests on general spatial concepts that are themselves progressing over the course of childhood.

9.2 DEVELOPMENTAL ACHIEVEMENTS IN MAP MASTERY: WHAT DEVELOPS?

9.2.1 Understanding the Representational Nature of Maps and Map Symbols

At the most basic level, understanding the representational nature of maps means understanding that the two-dimensional graphic shows or stands for some environmental referent like a park, city, or continent. At a more specific level, it means interpreting the referential meaning of specific symbols such as understanding that blue areas stand for lakes, stars stand for state capitals, and planes stand for airports. These two categories of understanding have been referred to, respectively, as understanding at the *holistic* and *componential* levels (Liben & Downs, 1989).

To do either successfully, the child must first have the basic understanding that one thing can be used to stand for something else. Even this simple "stand-for" concept must develop, although it is usually in place by roughly 3 years of age (DeLoache, 1987). Consistent with the finding that children appreciate the general stand-for relation during the very early preschool years (e.g., DeLoache, 1987; Rochat & Callaghan, 2005; Troseth, 2003), 3- to 6-year-old children have generally been able to demonstrate their holistic understanding of maps. For example, when asked directly, many preschool children were able to articulate maps' meaning and function well, offering responses such as "something to look at to show you where to go" and "tells you where places are, where people live and different countries" (Liben & Yekel, 1996, p. 2786). Similarly, when given a variety of place representations such as oil company road maps and aerial photographs of cities and asked what they showed, preschool children were generally able to identify the environmental nature of the referent, offering identifications such as "states and stuff" or "a city" (Liben & Downs, 1991).

Not surprisingly, children were less successful in identifying the specific environmental referent. What is most telling in the errors, though, is not simply that children were unable to identify the specific environment (e.g., that it was a road map of Pennsylvania rather than, e.g., New Jersey or that it was a photograph of Chicago rather than, e.g., Los Angeles) but rather that they were often far afield with respect to the scope of the referential space. These scope errors reflect spatial understanding, and thus we postpone discussion of these until the next section. Before turning to spatial understanding, however, we address children's understanding of the symbolic meaning of maps at the componential level.

A basic challenge for interpreting specific map symbols is for children to learn to differentiate which qualities of the symbols carry meaning and which are simply incidental features of the symbols (Liben, 1999, 2001). Even in representational media that are arguably better known to children than maps, preschoolers show a tendency to overextend qualities of the symbols to the referent, or the reverse, as when preliterate children assume that the length of words carries meaning about the size of the objects they denote (Bialystok, Shenfield, & Codd, 2000) or when preschoolers expect a photograph of ice cream to be cold (Beilin & Pearlman, 1991).

Comparable kinds of expectations about a pervasive match between qualities of the symbol and qualities of the referent have been observed in the realm of maps, as implied by the *Rose Is Rose* cartoon with which we began this chapter. In this section, we focus on children's understanding of those components of symbols—such as color—that do not entail spatial concepts, postponing until the next section discussion of children's understanding of the components of symbols that do draw on spatial understanding.

There is ample evidence that the problem Pasquale encountered in his cartoon world is one that children encounter in the real world. For example, when we interviewed 3- to 6-year-old children about their understanding of a Rand McNally road map of Pennsylvania (Liben & Downs, 1989, 1991), we found similar kinds of overextension errors. Illustrative are the children who, like Pasquale, correctly interpreted red lines on the map as showing roads but went on to answer that the roads for which the lines stood would themselves be red, and children who interpreted the yellow areas (used to indicate highly populated areas) as "eggs" or "firecrackers." Similarly, children of this age rejected the suggestion that an area of a black-and-white aerial photograph of the local community could show grass because "it's not green."

In some cases, of course, symbol color does coincide with referent color, and in such cases, children's assumption about the match can help rather than hinder identification. For example, when we (Liben & Downs, 1989) asked preschool children if they could find a river on the Pennsylvania road map, children were frequently successful in picking out the Susquehanna River, explaining that they knew "because it's blue." In general, interpretations of a variety of symbols suggest that at least during the preschool and early elementary school years, children tend to be very literal, reifying the symbols so that they expect the symbol stands for what it looks like. In the same study, one preschool child interpreted an airplane symbol as meaning that there was an airplane on that particular location, and that if that particular plane flew away, there would no longer be an airplane drawing on the map. This finding might be a reflection of the observation that 3-to 5-year-old children expect that a drawing will "update" to match a changed referent (Thomas, Jolley, Robinson, & Champion, 1999), although it might also reflect the child's difficulty in interpreting any given symbol as a representation of a *category* rather than of an individual object. Confusions such as these are not overcome quickly. Even in the early elementary school years, children find it difficult to accept that an arbitrary symbol may be used to stand for a referent, as when children in a first-grade class laughed at the suggestion that asterisks be used to represent filing cabinets on a classroom map (Liben & Downs, 1994). By the late elementary school years, however, most children spontaneously produced arbitrary symbols for their class maps.

The assumption that symbolic and referential qualities will match may in part be overcome by the child's growing understanding that maps are designed intentionally by a creator seeking to communicate selective information about the referent space (e.g., information about physical features, political divisions, or land use). To begin to examine the possible relevance of children's understanding of map-makers' intent, Myers and Liben (2005) showed 5- and 6-year-old children two videotapes in which people enacted different intentions. In both, actors were shown adding dots to an oblique perspective map of a room. In one, the person demonstrated a symbolic intent by preceding the placement of each green dot by looking up as if to watch someone in the room, and then making a comment such as, "She put that one there in the room, so I should put my green dot here." In the other, the person demonstrated a nonsymbolic, aesthetic intent, preceding each placement of a red dot by looking only at the paper itself, and then making a comment such as, "This isn't colorful. I'll add a red dot here to make it prettier." After watching the videotapes, children were asked to explain what each person had been trying to do and then to select which of the two resulting images they would use to find hidden fire trucks. Although the majority of children could explain the actors' intentions correctly, almost all nevertheless incorrectly chose the drawing with red dots (even though the dots had been created to make the drawing "look pretty" rather than to show the location of hidden objects). Thus, even children who showed understanding of intention were unable to avoid being seduced by the color match between red dots and red fire trucks.

In summary, by the age of 3, children typically comprehend the general stand-for nature of maps, usually demonstrating holistic-level understanding that the referent is a spatial environment such as a town, city, or room. Children at this age, however, are less facile in their componential-level understanding. In part, their difficulty appears to be explained by their assumption that a symbol necessarily shares nonspatial qualities such as color with its referent. But in addition, their difficulty in understanding individual symbols may be attributed to constraints on their spatial concepts, discussed as one component of children's understanding of the spatial meaning of maps in the next section.

9.2.2 *Understanding the Spatial Meaning of Maps*

As implied by the definition of maps given above, spatial qualities are at the heart of any map, and therefore spatial concepts must be called upon whenever someone is asked to interpret or use a map in some way. To organize our review, we have divided our discussions into three major sections, each focusing on a different feature of the cartographic eye. We begin by discussing children's developing understanding of the correspondences between space and map that are related to scale or metrics more broadly, then turn to those related to angle, and finally discuss those related to azimuth. Within each section, we offer illustrative empirical research addressing children's understanding of individual components of the representation (e.g., the meaning of a map symbol or of a section of an environmental photograph) as well as research in which children are asked to use a map in some way (e.g., to indicate an object's location by placing a sticker on a map). In each section, too, we comment on ways in which children might draw on topological, projective, or Euclidean concepts when interpreting symbols or solving mapping task. We postpone for a separate section (9.2.3) discussion of tasks in which participants move within the space that is represented on the map.

9.2.2.1 VIEWING DISTANCE, SCALE, AND METRIC UNDERSTANDING   The viewing distance component of the cartographic eye is relevant for features of maps that are related to size in some way, and thus involves understanding scale in general, proportional ratios, and metric features or specific locations on maps.

At very young ages, children may completely fail to recognize the scale relation between a representation and its referent, as demonstrated by toddlers who try to sit down on tiny dollhouse chairs or get into tiny model cars (see DeLoache, Uttal, & Rosengren, 2004). However, typically by the age of 3, children do seem to appreciate that markings on something as small as a piece of paper can show something as large as a city. For example, as described above, when 3- to 6-year-old children were asked about an aerial photograph of Chicago or a state road map of Pennsylvania, they routinely identified the referents as real environments, and not, for example, as a model town (Liben & Downs, 1991). Under the umbrella of success in correctly identifying the referents as large environments, however, some children did evidence difficulty in interpreting the scope of the referential space. Illustrative were children who thought that the Chicago photograph depicted a far smaller referent such as a single building (e.g., identifying it as "a large big building" while gesturing to the whole image) or thought that it depicted a far larger referent (e.g., "That's the United States"). There were parallel interpretations for the Pennsylvania road map (e.g., respectively, "Indiana, PA" and "California, Canada, the West, and the North Coast").

The findings from interview studies also showed evidence of scale confusion at the level of interpreting individual symbols. Similar to the way that young children overinterpret the meaning of symbol color (as in assuming a red line depicts a red road), young children also overextend representational size to the referent, or the reverse. Shown the aerial photograph and state road map described above, some preschool children vehemently rejected correct identifications in ways that implied that they were confused about scale (Liben & Downs, 1989, 1991). Illustrative were a child's denial that a line shown on a road map could be a road because "it's not fat enough for two cars to go on," another child's assertion that a raised area of a plastic relief map could not be a mountain because "it's not high enough," and another's that a rectangular shape on an aerial photograph could not possibly be his father's office building because his building "is *huge!* It's as big as this whole map!" In addition, children spontaneously offered incorrect interpretations of individual symbols that also suggested scale confusions. Illustrative were children who identified road lines on the road map as "string," boats on a small-scale aerial photograph as "fish," and a baseball field on large-scale vertical aerial photograph as "an eye."

Subsequent research in which 4- to 5-year-old children were asked to identify referents of specific portions of a set of four aerial photographs (differing with respect to viewing distance and angle) revealed similar kinds of errors (see Liben, 2005). Illustrative were children's interpretations of a baseball field (which adults almost universally identified correctly). Although most (about 80%) of children's responses were either correct or reasonable errors with respect to the size and kind of referent (e.g., "pool," "helicopter landing area," "parking lot"), the remaining responses were dramatic scale confusions (e.g., "eyeball," "mushroom," "seashell"). Other investigators have also reported scale errors of these kinds. For example, Spencer, Harrison, and Darvizeh (1980) observed that "3 and 4 year olds do not feel constrained to maintain a size consistency within the one picture: they are quite happy to see hills as 'pebbles' along side water they have identified as the sea" (pp. 61–62). It should be noted, however, that even adults are not entirely immune to this problem. College faculty who teach remote sensing often comment on students' difficulty in maintaining a sense of scale in trying to interpret satellite images or other kinds of remote sensing images. Indeed, even when observing real environments from great viewing distances (e.g., from a plane), adults find it difficult to avoid scale errors in interpreting the objects below, perhaps in part because the visual experience does not fit embodied human action in the environment (see Liben, 2005, in press).

Another kind of evidence of the challenges of understanding scale comes from children's difficulty in identifying which specific symbol—among a number of similar symbols—represents a particular referent in the space. For example, consider a classroom that contains various pieces of furniture of the same general shape (e.g., rectangular bookcases, tables, benches, art shelves, and coat cubbies). If the furniture symbols are motivated spatially rather than semantically (e.g., representing the art table with a rectangle sized in proportion to the table top rather than with pictures of paint brushes), the task of discriminating the art-table rectangle from, say, the bench and bookcase rectangles, calls upon metric understanding (e.g., finding the largest of the rectangles, the one with the smallest side-to-end ratio, or perhaps the one that is about one-third of the way along the blackboard wall).

Consistent with the expectation that identifying the correct individual symbol among many similar ones should be especially difficult for those with limited understanding of Euclidean concepts and hence scale and measurement, preschool and kindergarten children have been found to have great difficulty in identifying the correct symbol on which to mark locations of objects on a plan map of their classroom (Liben & Downs, 1986; Liben & Yekel, 1996). Children in the early elementary grades are generally successful, at least when the map is aligned with the classroom (Liben & Downs, 1993). For example, asked to place stickers on a map of their classroom to show the locations of six objects in the room (e.g., a pencil sharpener), the average numbers of correct placements (within a sticker-size margin of error) for children in kindergarten, grade 1, and grade 2, respectively, were 3.0, 4.7, and 5.2 (Liben & Downs, 1986).

If children have difficulty in understanding the proportional relation between the referent space and the representation, they would also be expected to have difficulty in finding analogous locations between a map and space in areas in which distinctive, topological cues are unavailable (as when one is asked to identify analogous spots on undifferentiated regions of a floor or campus). Consistent with this expectation were findings from a study in which 4- to 6-year-old children first learned the locations of toy symbols on a map of a room and were then asked to place the real toys in the analogous locations in the real room (Uttal, 1996). Although the children were reasonably accurate in maintaining the correct configuration (pattern of toy placements) when they moved into the real room, they were generally inaccurate with respect to scaling up the configuration proportionately. The former but not the latter can be solved by using topological concepts alone.

Also consistent with the interpretation that young children have difficulty in scaling up to find analogous locations between undifferentiated regions of spaces and maps are findings from research in which children were asked to show on a map of their classroom the location of a person who stood at six different locations in the room (Liben & Downs, 1993). The average numbers of correct placements (within a sticker-size margin of error) for children in kindergarten, grade 1, grade 2, and grade 5/6, respectively were 2.6, 3.9, 5.0, and 5.1 (Liben & Downs, 1993). Importantly, performance tended to be far better when the person stood adjacent to a distinct piece of furniture (hence allowing solutions based on topological concepts) than when the person stood on more open areas of the floor. Similar patterns have been reported with other materials, as well. For example, first- and second-grade children were better able to find analogous locations between an aerial photograph and different-scale map of Chicago (both of which were in view throughout the task) when the locations were linked to distinct landmarks than when they were on less distinct areas that therefore required some use of metrics (and hence Euclidean concepts) to identify (Liben & Downs, 1991).

9.2.2.2 VIEWING ANGLE   Another map quality identified by the cartographic eye concerns viewing angle. Understanding representations that depict environments from directly overhead (i.e., vertical or 90° views) may be difficult because they go beyond the embodied experiences people have as they navigate through real environments (Liben, 2005, in press). The position that interpreting representations with vertical viewing angles draws on projective spatial concepts rather than simply on perceptual experience is bolstered by empirical work showing that young children have difficulty in deciphering the meaning of overhead perspectives.

Children's misinterpretations of individual components of environmental representations are again revealing. A number of spontaneous misinterpretations appear to be attributed to children's interpreting components of the representations as if they represented eye-level (straight ahead) rather than overhead viewing angles. For example, preschool children identified tennis courts on vertical aerial photographs as "doors" (Liben & Downs, 1991; Spencer et al., 1980), an interpretation also given to a double sink on a plan view map (Liben & Yekel, 1996). In both cases, if one assumes one is looking straight ahead rather than directly down on the referent, the rectangular shapes (made by the lines of the tennis courts and by the outlines of the sinks) might sensibly be interpreted as door panels. Other responses are also consistent with the idea that young children have difficulty using projective concepts when interpreting place representations, for example, preschoolers interpreting a triangular-shaped parking area as a "hill," a baseball field as an "eye," and trains lined up in parallel as "bookshelves" (Liben & Downs, 1991).

A second kind of evidence for the young child's difficulty in interpreting overhead views comes from data comparing preschoolers' performance on plan versus oblique representations. Direct comparisons have been made in studies in which preschool children were asked to show objects' locations on plan versus oblique perspective maps of their classroom or to identify a series of referents on nadir (straight-down) versus oblique aerial photographs of both unfamiliar and familiar environments. In the case of aerial photographs, oblique photographs elicited a higher number of correct identifications (Liben, 2005) and faster identifications (Blades, Spencer, Plester, & Desmond, 2004). In the case of maps, children were significantly better at making correct location responses on oblique than on plan maps (Liben & Yekel, 1996).

9.2.2.3 VIEWING AZIMUTH   Viewing azimuth refers to the bearing direction, typically described in relation to (clockwise) degrees deviation from north (defined as 0°). We use the term more generally to refer to the link between direction as indicated on a map and direction in the referential space. Understanding viewing direction also draws on projective concepts. Indeed, mapping tasks that tap an understanding of azimuth are much like the classic three-mountains task designed by Piaget and Inhelder (1956) to test children's ability to understand the way that an array looks depending on one's vantage point.

Consistent with the characterization that children do not master view-specific (projective) spatial concepts until the school years, early laboratory research established that preschoolers indeed showed far more success in finding locations in a room that had been indicated on an aligned map than on a map that had been rotated by 180° (Bluestein & Acredolo, 1979; Presson, 1982). This finding has been replicated in more recent work with the more complex spaces of children's own classrooms (Liben & Downs, 1993). In this study, children in kindergarten, grade 1, grade 2, and grade 5/6 were asked to place arrow stickers on their (aligned) classroom maps to show where a person was standing and which direction he was pointing. Under this aligned condition, performance was linked to age, increasing steadily from kindergarten through grade 2, at which point performance was approximately as high as it was in grade 5/6.

After completing this task, children were asked to complete the task again, but this time the map was rotated by 180° and children were required to leave the maps on their desk in this unaligned condition as they worked. In this unaligned condition, performance was significantly higher in older children. Furthermore, consistent with the position that most children do not develop flexible projective spatial concepts until roughly the age of 9 or 10, performance was significantly lower in the unaligned than aligned condition at all but the oldest grade tested (grade 5/6). Consistent with the hypothesized link to projective spatial concepts, children's performance on the mapping tasks was related to their performance on Piagetian spatial tasks, although the association was far from perfect (Liben & Downs, 1993).

The quality of errors also differed between aligned and unaligned conditions. To illustrate, figure 9.2 shows a composite of all the arrow responses under both aligned and unaligned conditions for a single item in one of the first-grade classrooms. It is striking that in the aligned condition (left panel), only one child placed an arrow sticker on an incorrect type of symbol (a furniture symbol). Most arrow placements were in the correct quadrant, and most were facing roughly the correct direction. The data from the unaligned condition (right panel) provide a sharp contrast: seven stickers are completely or partially on a furniture symbol, the modal placement is in the wrong quadrant of the room, and many of the arrows are 180° in error. One likely explanation of the modal erroneous responses (arrows off by 180° and placed in the room quadrant diagonally across from the correct one) is that children were placing arrows in relation to their own position relative to the room (e.g., "off to my upper left") without taking into account the relation between the map and room.

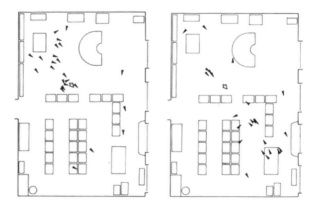

Figure 9.2   Map showing all arrow placements by children in one first-grade classroom. Children were asked to place arrows to show where a person was standing and the direction he was pointing, once when the map was aligned with the space (*left*) and once when it was 180° unaligned with the space (*right*). Correct answers are shown by open arrows. Based on Liben and Downs (1993).

The ability to understand one's own position and orientation in a space and, in turn, the ability to identify that position and orientation on a map are clearly at the heart of using a map for navigation or to record information on a map as one moves through an environment (e.g., as when a geologist records locations of outcrops or an ecologist records locations of animal nesting sites in the field). In the next section we discuss tasks in which the map user controls movement through the environment.

9.2.3 Understanding Self-Space-Map Relations

The final aspect of map understanding we discuss concerns children's ability to place themselves within the map and space. Understanding where you are "on the map" is critical when using a map to navigate or to record information gathered while moving through the environment. Successful performance depends not only on appreciating the representational and geometrical correspondences between map and space discussed above, but also on keeping track of one's own position in the space and on the map. What makes this particularly challenging from the perspective of projective spatial concepts is the fact that if one holds the map in a fixed position relative to the body and then turns in the environment, both the map-space relation and the self-space relation change. If, for example, someone is walking north while using a map in which north is at the top of the page, there is a match between the map orientation and walking direction. If the person turns left, the person is now facing west, but north remains straight ahead on the map. To adjust, the map user might physically (or mentally) rotate the map 90° clockwise so that now the map is aligned with the space, even though the map user is still facing west.

Illustrative of tasks requiring self-space-map understanding are two studies in which respondents moved through campus environments and were asked to locate themselves or objects they encountered on a map. In one study, 10-year-old children and college students were taken to various locations on a college campus and asked to show their current location and orientation on a campus map (plan or oblique perspective views) using arrow stickers (Liben, Kastens, & Stevenson, 2002). The 10-year-old children performed uniformly poorly, unable to even locate their stickers near the correct building representations. Performance was presumably so low on this task because of the complexity of the map and unfamiliarity of the environment. Although adults in general performed far better, some had difficulty finding correct locations and orienting their arrow stickers correctly. Interestingly, there was a significant relation between strategy use and accuracy of the arrow stickers' orientations: those participants who turned the map so that the map and space were aligned performed better than those who simply used the map in whatever orientation they happened to find it.

In another study, fourth-grade children were taken to either a rural or urban university campus (Kastens & Liben, 2004). Children were given a map, oriented to their current location and heading direction, and then allowed to explore the test area (with adults at the perimeter to keep them from wandering away from the designated portion of campus). Children were told they would find eight colored flags, and they were asked to indicate each flag's location by placing a sticker of the same color at the appropriate location on the map. Overall, this task was far more manageable than the one described above, presumably because children were oriented initially to the map and space, the area was smaller, and there were far fewer highly similar landmarks and map symbols. Children did particularly well when the flag was on a unique object that was represented by a unique map symbol. High levels of performance on these items are consistent with the notion that even relatively young children can solve mapping tasks that draw on topological concepts (e.g., "on the statue"). Children tended to do far worse for flag positions that called on either projective or metric spatial concepts. Illustrative of the former was a flag located on a building in the urban campus that was shaped like another building on the opposite side of the quadrangle. Children commonly placed their stickers on the mirror image building, apparently not taking into account the directions that they and the map were facing. Illustrative of the latter was a flag location along a road. For this item, children commonly placed their sticker on the correct road, but without metric precision so that responses were quite scattered. Composite maps of responses for the two rural campus locations are given in figure 9.3.

9.2.4 Summary of Developmental Achievements in Map Mastery

Taken together, the findings from a wide variety of tasks demonstrate that the process of becoming a skilled map user is a prolonged and challenging

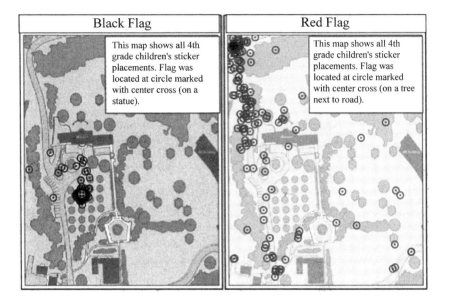

Figure 9.3   Maps showing composite of sticker placements by fourth-grade children asked to indicate the location of a flag on a statue (*left*) and on a tree along a road (*right*), and the correct location of the flag and tree (circles with a center cross). Data are from Kastens and Liben (2004). See color insert.

one. Even very young children have an understanding of the rudimentary concepts that are needed for map understanding. They understand the general "stand for" relation and appreciate that a flat piece of paper with marks and colors may stand for a large, three-dimensional environment through which they can navigate. At the same time, children are challenged in understanding both the representational and geometric correspondences that link the referent space and the representational space and do not consistently recognize the need to orient the map to the space physically or mentally before using it. The tripartite division of the cartographic eye—viewing distance, viewing angle, and viewing azimuth—provides a useful means of defining the spatial qualities of maps and some of the challenges maps present, and the tripartite division of children's developing spatial concepts—topological, projective, and Euclidean—provides a useful means of organizing the cognitive structures that are called upon in understanding them. Mapping tasks that require projective and Euclidean concepts are typically solved later than those that require only topological concepts. The early acquisition of topological concepts allows children to identify locations that can be defined as "on" or "next to" symbols, particularly those that can be identified by iconic resemblance (e.g., iconic symbols or oblique perspective line drawings rather than abstract, overhead plan views). Until projective and Euclidean concepts are more fully developed, however, it is difficult for children to interpret the changes in shape and direction that are entailed by changes in viewing angle and viewing azimuth. Similarly, Euclidean concepts are needed for children to understand the quantitative effects of changing scale and to understand the meaning of representational space (particularly when it carries different meaning across the paper as a consequence of some kinds of projections; see Liben, 2001).

9.3 DEVELOPMENTAL MECHANISMS: GETTING FROM HERE TO THERE

Our emphasis thus far has been on describing children's understanding and use of maps in relation to age. Given that most extant empirical work on the development of map understanding (including our own) has been cross-sectional rather than longitudinal, we can only infer individuals' age-linked developmental progress in map domains. At the broadest level, the map research illustrated by the studies described above leads to the unsurprising and uncontroversial conclusion that older children and adults perform better than younger children. In addition, the patterns of age-linked differences and of within-participant profiles of performance across tasks are consistent with (although do not prove) the theoretical position that map tasks drawing on topological concepts are solved earlier and more readily than are those drawing on projective Euclidean concepts.

At the same time, the investigations described above lead to another important conclusion—that map understanding does not emerge in a tightly age-locked manner, nor do adults demonstrate universally high levels of achievement. One illustration of variability in emergence may seen in the task described earlier in which children were asked to place arrows on a classroom map to show an adult's location and pointing direction. The mean numbers of correctly oriented arrows (highest possible number correct was six) increased from about one correct in kindergarten to about five correct in grade 5/6. At the level of individual behavior, though, what is remarkable is that a few children performed perfectly or nearly so even among kindergartners, for whom the modal response was zero correct (for precise distributions, see Liben & Downs, 1993).

An illustration of parallel variability among adults is evident in the study in which individuals were taken to various places on campus and asked to identify their location on the campus map (Liben, Kastens, & Stevenson, 2002). Although as a group adults fared far better than children, some adults were completely unable to locate themselves on the map. Indeed, even among adults, the distribution of the number of correct responses was normal, with some participants incorrect on every item and others correct on all. These data show that at least at the level of actual behavior (albeit perhaps not at the level of underlying conceptual competence), even adults do not necessarily demonstrate expertise in map understanding and use.

This conclusion is consistent with many adults' self-descriptions that they cannot read maps.

In addition to documenting remarkably good performance in some individual children and remarkably poor performance in some individual adults, research has revealed some intriguing variations in performance in spatial cognition in general and in map use, in particular, across various kinds of identified groups (Liben, 2006; National Research Council, 2006; Newcombe & Huttenlocher, 2006). For example, investigators have found that girls and women often perform worse on real or virtual reality mapping tasks than do boys and men, sometimes in interaction with age (e.g., Lawton & Morrin, 1999; Liben & Downs, 1993); that there is significant variation across socioeconomic groups in performance on spatial tasks, including those requiring aerial map interpretation (Levine, Vasilyeva, Lourenco, Newcombe, & Huttenlocher, 2005); and that people from some environments use different map strategies than do people from others (e.g., differential use of cardinal directions by Midwesterners accustomed to gridlike road layouts than by Northeasterners accustomed to spaghetti-like road layouts; Lawton, 2001). Group differences are useful in suggesting candidate factors that may play a role in the emergence of spatial skills. For example, factors that differ at the group level between males and females (e.g., the size of the "free range" that children are permitted to explore independently; see Hart, 1981) are candidate causal factors for within-sex variability.

Considered together, it is both the general order of emergence (success on tasks allowing topological solutions before those requiring projective and Euclidean concepts) and the variability within age groups that must be addressed by explanatory mechanisms. It would be impossible in just a few pages to try to cover the biological, experiential, and constructive explanatory mechanisms that may be at work. Thus, we consider explanatory mechanisms in fairly broad terms. To organize our comments, we use the embedded model from Liben (1999), reproduced in figure 9.4. This model was designed to identify the components and reciprocal interactions between the child and the environment (physical and social) involved in the developing understanding of spatial-graphic representations, of which maps are a quintessential example. As implied by the complexity of the figure, the embedded model holds that there are multiple, simultaneous, and reciprocally interacting factors, and thus that any attempt to dissect the model into components will in some sense be misleading. Nevertheless, because language (unlike graphic representation) is necessarily a sequential communication channel, it is necessary to discuss aspects of the model sequentially rather than simultaneously.

We begin by pointing to the construct labeled "child," which should be understood as the embodied child. It is in this aspect of the model that biological factors are particularly central. First, humans as a species have certain sensory, motor, and neuronal capacities that are relevant to spatial perceptual, motor, and cognitive experiences, which in turn are called upon for map understanding. Evolutionary psychologists present arguments for the

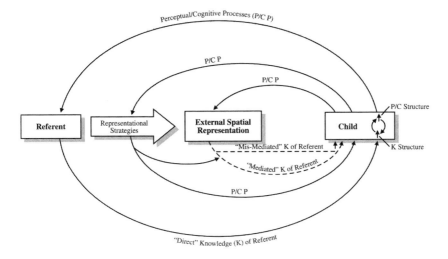

Figure 9.4   Embedded model of understanding spatial-graphic representations based on Liben (1999).

survival value of spatial abilities for the species in general and argue that the differential importance for survival for traveler-hunter males versus homebound child-rearing females can explain men's superior spatial skills (e.g., Gaulin, 1993). But whatever the explanation for human biological endowment at the level of the species, what is important for individual development is the fact that species inheritance endows individuals with bodies that support certain kinds of spatial experiences in moving about the world.

For example, and as discussed at greater length elsewhere (Liben, in press), what we see—from what height, direction, distance—and the neural systems that encode what we see are bound up in our bodies. Our musculoskeletal system affects what we encounter; our vestibular system helps us remain erect; we can walk on the ground but not the ceiling, and we cannot fly; the symmetries and asymmetries of our bodies affect the ease with which we differentiate up/down and in front/behind versus left/right (e.g., Franklin & Tversky, 1999); our brains appear to be prepared to perceive horizontals and verticals in some Euclidean world (O'Keefe & Nadel, 1978; although perhaps also in non-Euclidean space: see Koenderink, van Doorn, & Lappin, 2000); and so on. It is easy to link these kinds of spatial experiences in general to map understanding in particular. For example, the relatively greater ease of understanding oblique perspective maps than vertical plan maps described above may be linked to the greater similarity the former has to embodied experience (Liben, 2005, in press). That is, our ability to walk and climb allows us to see large environments obliquely from hilltops; our inability to fly precludes seeing large environments vertically. Within ontogenetic development, relevant physical changes occur as individuals grow taller and their visual and nervous systems mature; they acquire improved control over head and body movements, and they change the way they experience the environment as they learn to crawl, stand, walk, and so on. All of these developing systems are relevant for understanding space, individuals' place in space, and thus, we would argue, individuals' ability to use representations of space such as maps.

Biological factors do more than play a role at the level of the species; they also act at the level of each individual child. For example, in interaction with environmental experiences, each child is endowed with a genetic makeup that sets a context for levels of spatial abilities relevant for understanding and using maps (e.g., see Casey, 1996); each child has a prenatal history of testosterone exposure that has an impact on spatial behaviors (e.g., Resnick, Berenbaum, Gottesman, & Bouchard, 1986); each child has a pubertal timetable (again, in interaction with experiential factors, e.g., nutrition, exercise patterns, and stress) that affects levels of circulating sex steroids that may influence spatial functioning (e.g., Liben, Susman et al., 2002); and each child has a particular set of sensory sensitivities (e.g., visual acuity) or challenges (e.g., a visual impairment).

In addition to biological factors, the construct of the embodied child in figure 9.4 involves both "perceptual/cognitive" and "knowledge" structures. These are meant to imply that every action involved in the child's interaction with the surrounding environment rests on the current level of general perceptual-cognitive processes as well as on specific knowledge that has been stored as a result of prior experiences. The arrows going out from the embodied child are thus meant to suggest the constructive nature of the processes used to select from and process what is available in the external environment. Thus, what the child interacts with in the environment is not only a function of what is "out there" but also a function of the child's own interests, knowledge structure, cognitive skills, and so on. The arrows directed back to the embodied child are meant to suggest that these constructive experiences simultaneously feed back to the embodied child (much like the simultaneous and reciprocal processes of assimilation and accommodation in biological or cognitive-developmental theories).

Three additional constructs are central in figure 9.4 that, taken together, constitute the environmental content available as grist for the embodied child's constructive processes. The *referent* here refers to the physical environment itself. The embedded model holds that children's map understanding will be enhanced by interacting with various kinds of physical environments. For example, a child who has experience traveling on interstate highways is better equipped to interpret a cloverleaf intersection on an aerial photograph or a map; a child who has experience at a lake or ocean is better equipped to interpret symbols for bodies of water and coastlines on a map.

Experience with a range of different *external spatial representations*— here maps—is likewise presumed to enhance children's ability to understand and interpret them. In prior work (see Liben, 2006; Liben & Downs, 2001), we have suggested that children are advantaged by seeing the same referent space mapped in different orientations or azimuths (e.g., north at the left, right, or bottom of the page as well as the more canonical at the top), in different projections (e.g., a Mercator vs. an equal area projection), centered at different geographic locations (e.g., centered on North America vs. Antarctica), at different scales (large- vs. small-scale maps), using different graphic media (e.g., satellite imagery vs. perspective drawings vs. aerial photographs), and different symbol systems (e.g., using color vs. contour lines to indicate elevation; using red vs. black to indicate state highways). Exposure to varied maps is hypothesized to decrease children's tendency toward reified thinking such as assuming that blue necessarily means water or that the top of the page is necessarily north (see Liben & Downs, 1989).

Finally, the model proposes that children's map development is enhanced to the degree to which children have direct experience with *representational strategies*. This can include the experience of creating maps of different kinds, as well as using other representational media such as photography. Illustrative is an educational program called EarthKAM (Earth Knowledge Acquired by Middle School Students) sponsored by NASA. Middle school children may request that photographs be taken during Space Shuttle flights. To take and interpret images, they not only must learn something about the relation between the orbit of the Space Shuttle and Earth (e.g., how to calculate when the Shuttle will be located over the desired land or sea area, when it will be daytime at that location), but also must learn something about camera angle, azimuth, lenses, and so on. By seeing the images that result from their requests, children can learn not only something about the portion of Earth that they have photographed but also something about the process used to create those images (NASA, 2006).

Thus far, the discussion has concerned the availability and diversity of referent spaces, representations, and representational strategies encountered by the child. But it is not just what is available in the physical environment that matters: children's own motivations and interests affect engagement with actual and represented environments. Furthermore, the social context plays an important role in mediating these experiences. Consider, for example, a boy whose parents are planning a car trip for a vacation. Do his parents use multiple maps to discuss destinations and routes? Is he given access to these materials and involved in the discussions? Do parents guide him to see differences among maps (e.g., using and discussing road maps vs. hiking maps for driving to and then hiking through a state park)? Once on their way, does the child pay attention to twists and turns in the route, notice the sun's position in relation to the car and whether it changes as they travel? Does he, like Pasquale in the cartoon with which we opened this chapter, follow along on the map and, if so, draw on (successfully or unsuccessfully) mental rotation skills to mentally realign the map and landscape as they travel? Does he physically rotate the map instead? Do parents permit or even encourage him to act as the navigator for their trip? Do they perhaps pose questions along the way (e.g., What exit should we be coming to next? Can you find the nearest rest area?)? To our knowledge, there have not yet been observational studies examining parental guidance of map reading per se. There are, however, related studies of parent–child interactions with spatial graphic representations in book reading (Szechter & Liben, 2004), museum exhibits (Crowley et al., 2001), and instructional diagrams (Gauvain, 1993). This work shows that parents differ dramatically in the quality and quantity of spatial-graphic guidance they provide for their young children, and these differences relate to various measures of children's graphic understanding or spatial skills.

9.4 WHERE NEXT?

As should be evident from the preceding discussion, we view children's developing abilities to understand and use maps as a multifaceted achievement that draws on myriad more general developmental progressions. It is influenced by opportunities and constraints that are virtually universal in the maturing human body (e.g., developing systems of locomotion and vision) and in the normal human social environment (e.g., opportunities for exploration and motivations for symbolic communication). It draws from more general constructive processes associated with cognitive development, including spatial cognition in particular. At the same time, it is affected by individual children's particular genetic endowments and by the particular social and educational experiences available to shape and mediate those endowments.

   As noted in our introductory comments, the focus of our chapter is on research employing spaces and maps such as those encountered in daily life. This research converges on the conclusion that development of map understanding follows a prolonged path, a path that is not traversed easily by all individuals. Thus, although there is compelling evidence reviewed elsewhere in this volume that children—even infants—can exhibit many remarkable spatial competencies, it is also apparent that these basic, early competencies are not automatically translated into advanced levels of understanding and using maps. We would urge continued efforts at studying what experiences are linked to higher levels of map development in the natural ecology (e.g., studying parent–child interactions in the course of map use or wayfinding) as well as to developing and evaluating educational interventions aimed at enhancing ultimate outcomes. As argued elsewhere (Liben, 2006), educational programs that facilitate map development may be expected to have a positive impact on spatial thinking more generally, a kind of thinking not only that has been ignored too long but also that is becoming increasingly important as new spatial-graphic technologies become an ever more important part of our society. In short, we hope that increased attention to the development of map understanding will serve not only to advance the academic study of spatial development but also to enhance the quality and fluency of individuals' skills in using and thinking with spatial-graphic representations.

NOTE

1. In this chapter, we follow cartographic terminology in which "small-scale" and "large-scale" maps refer, respectively, to maps of large and small referent spaces. This usage is often reversed in the psychological literature.

ACKNOWLEDGMENTS   Portions of the research described here were supported by grants to the first author from the National Institute of Education (G-83-0025) and from the National Science Foundation (RED-9554504 and ESI 01-01758), although the opinions expressed here are not necessarily those of these agencies.

REFERENCES

Acredolo, L. P. (1981). Small- and large-scale spatial concepts in infancy and childhood. In L. S. Liben, A. H. Patterson, & N. Newcombe (Eds.), *Spatial representation and behavior across the life span: Theory and application* (pp. 63–81). New York: Academic Press.

Beilin, H., & Pearlman, E. G. (1991). Children's iconic realism: Object versus property realism. In: H.W. Reese (Ed.), *Advances in Child Development and Behavior, Vol. 23* (p. 73–111). San Diego, CA: Academic Press.

Bialystok, E., Shenfield, T., & Codd, J. (2000). Languages, scripts and the environment: Factors in developing concepts of print. *Developmental Psychology, 36*, 66–76.

Blades, M., Spencer, C., Plester, B., & Desmond, K. (2004). Young children's recognition and representation of urban landscapes. In G. L. Allen (Ed.), *Human spatial memory: Remembering where* (pp. 287–308). Mahwah, NJ: Lawrence Erlbaum.

Bluestein, N., & Acredolo, L. (1979). Developmental changes in map-reading skills. *Child Development, 50*, 691–697.

Casey, M. B. (1996). Understanding individual differences in spatial ability within females: A nature/nurture interactionist framework. *Developmental Review, 16*, 240–261.

Crowley, K., Callanan, M. A., Jipson, J. L., Galco, J., Topping, K., & Shrager, J. (2001). Shared scientific thinking in everyday parent-child activity. *Science Education, 85*, 712–732.

DeLoache, J. S. (1987). Rapid change in the symbolic functioning of very young children. *Science, 238*, 1556–1557.

DeLoache, J. S., Uttal, D. H., & Rosengren, K. S. (2004). Scale errors offer evidence for a perception-action dissociation early in life. *Science, 304*, 1027–1029.

Downs, R. M. (1981). Maps and mappings as metaphors for spatial representation. In L. S. Liben, A. H. Patterson, & N. Newcombe (Eds.), *Spatial representation and behavior across the life span: Theory and application* (pp. 143–166). New York: Academic Press.

Eliot, J. (1987). *Models of psychological space, psychometric, developmental, and experimental approaches.* New York: Springer-Verlag.

Franklin, N., & Tversky, B. (1990). Searching imagined environments. *Journal of Experimental Psychology: General, 119*, 63–76.

Garling, T., & Evans, G. (1991). *Environment, cognition, and action.* New York: Oxford University Press.

Gaulin, S. J. C. (1993). How and why sex differences evolve, with spatial ability as a paradigm example. In M. Haug, R. E. Whalen, C. Aron, & K. L. Olsen (Eds.), *The development of sex differences and similarities in behavior* (pp. 111–130). Dordrecht: Kluwer Academic.

Gauvain, M. (1993). The development of spatial thinking in everyday activity. *Developmental Review, 13*, 92–121.

Google. (2005, September 19). *Map definition*. Retrieved September 19, 2005, from http://www.google.com/search?hl=en&lr=&oi=defmore&q=define:map

Hall, S. S. (1992). *Mapping the next millennium*. New York: Random House.

Hart, R. A. (1981). Children's spatial representation of the landscape: Lessons and questions from a field study. In L. S. Liben, A. H. Patterson, & N. Newcombe (Eds.), *Spatial representation and behavior across the life span* (pp. 195–233). New York: Academic Press.

Kastens, K. A., & Liben, L. S. (2004, May). *Where are we? Understanding and improving how children translate from a map to the represented space and vice versa.* Poster presentation at the Instructional Materials Development PIs Meeting, National Science Foundation, Washington, DC.

Koenderink, J. J., van Doorn, A. J., & Lappin, J. S. (2000). Direct measurement of the curvature of visual space. *Perception, 29*, 69–79.

Lawton, C. A. (2001). Gender and regional differences in spatial referents used in direction giving. *Sex Roles, 44*, 321–337.

Lawton, C. A., & Morrin, K. A. (1999). Gender differences in pointing accuracy in computer-simulated 3D mazes. *Sex Roles, 40*, 73–92.

Levine, S. C., Vasilyeva, M., Lourenco, S. F., Newcombe, N. S., & Huttenlocher, J. (2005). Socioeconomic status modifies the sex difference in spatial skill. *Psychological Science, 16*, 841–845.

Liben, L. S. (1999). Developing an understanding of external spatial representations. In I. E. Sigel (Ed.), *Development of mental representation: Theories and applications* (pp. 297–321). Mahwah, NJ: Lawrence Erlbaum.

Liben, L. S. (2001). Thinking through maps. In M. Gattis (Ed.), *Spatial schemas and abstract thought* (pp. 44–77). Cambridge, MA: MIT Press.

Liben, L. S. (2005). The role of action in understanding and using environmental place representations. In. J. Rieser, J. Lockman, & C. Nelson (Eds.), *The Minnesota symposium on child development* (pp. 323–361). Mahwah, NJ: Lawrence Erlbaum.

Liben, L. S. (2006). Education for spatial thinking. In W. Damon & R. Lerner (Series Eds.) and K. A. Renninger & I. E. Sigel (Vol. Eds.), *Handbook of child psychology: Vol. 4. Child psychology in practice* (6th ed., pp. 197–247). Hoboken, NJ: Wiley.

Liben, L. S. (in press). Representational development and the embodied mind's eye. In W. F. Overton, U. Mueller, & J. Newman (Eds.), *Body in mind, mind in body: Developmental perspectives on embodiment and consciousness*. Mahwah, NJ: Lawrence Erlbaum.

Liben, L. S., & Downs, R. M. (1986). *Children's production and comprehension of maps: Increasing graphic literacy*. Final Report for Project #G83-0025. National Institute of Education.

Liben, L. S., & Downs, R. M. (1989). Understanding maps as symbols: The development of map concepts in children. In: H. W. Reese (Ed.), *Advances in child development and behavior* (Vol. 22, pp. 145–201). New York: Academic Press.

Liben, L. S., & Downs, R. M. (1991). The role of graphic representations in understanding the world. In R. M. Downs, L. S. Liben, & D. S. Palermo (Eds.), *Visions of aesthetics, the environment, and development: The legacy of Joachim Wohlwill* (pp. 139–180). Hillsdale, NJ: Lawrence Erlbaum.

Liben, L. S., & Downs, R. M. (1993). Understanding person-space-map relations: Cartographic and developmental perspectives. *Developmental Psychology, 29,* 739–752.

Liben, L. S., & Downs, R. M. (1994). Fostering geographic literacy from early childhood: The contributions of interdisciplinary research. *Journal of Applied Developmental Psychology, 15,* 549–569.

Liben, L. S., & Downs, R. M. (2001). Geography for young children: Maps as tools for learning environments. In S. L. Golbeck (Ed.), *Psychological perspectives on early childhood education* (pp. 220–252). Mahwah, NJ: Lawrence Erlbaum.

Liben, L. S., Kastens, K. A., & Stevenson, L. M. (2002). Real-world knowledge through real-world maps: A developmental guide for navigating the educational terrain. *Developmental Review, 22,* 267–322.

Liben, L. S., Patterson A. H., & Newcombe, N. (Eds.) (1981). *Spatial representation and behavior across the life span: Theory and application.* New York: Academic Press.

Liben, L. S., Susman, E. J., Finkelstein, J. W., Chinchilli, V. M., Kunselman, S. J., Schwab, J., Dubas, J. S., Demers, L. M., Lookingbill, G., D'Arcangelo, M. R., Krogh, H. R., & Kulin, H. E. (2002). The effects of sex steroids on spatial performance: A review and an experimental clinical investigation. *Developmental Psychology, 38,* 236–253.

Liben, L. S., & Yekel, C. A. (1996). Preschoolers' understanding of plan and oblique maps: The role of geometric and representational correspondence. *Child Development, 67,* 2780–2796.

Myers, L. J., & Liben, L. S. (2005, April). *Can you find it? Children's understanding of symbol-creators' intentions in graphic representations.* Poster presented at the biennial meetings of the Society for Research in Child Development, Atlanta, GA.

NASA. (2006, September 2). About ISS EarthKam. Retrieved February 11, 2006, from http://www.earthkam.ucsd.edu/public/about/index.shtml

National Research Council. (2006). *Learning to think spatially: GIS as a support system in the K-12 curriculum.* Washington, DC: National Academy Press.

Newcombe, N., & Huttenlocher, J. (2000). *Making space.* Cambridge, MA: MIT Press.

Newcombe, N. S., & Huttenlocher, J. (2006). Development of spatial cognition. In W. Damon & R. Lerner (Series Eds.) and D. Kuhn & R. S. Siegler (Vol. Eds.), *Handbook of child psychology: Vol. 2. Cognition, perception, and language* (6th ed., pp. 734–776). Hoboken, NJ: Wiley.

O'Keefe, J., & Nadel, L. (1978). *Hippocampus as a cognitive map.* Oxford, UK: Clarendon.

Piaget, J., & Garcia, R. (1989). *Psychogenesis and the history of science.* New York: Columbia University Press.

Piaget, J., & Inhelder, B. (1956). *The child's conception of space.* New York: Norton.

Presson, C. C. (1982). The development of map-reading skills. *Child Development, 53,* 196–199.

Proshansky, H. M., Ittelson, W. H., & Rivlin, L. G. (1976). *Environmental psychology: People and their physical settings.* New York: Holt.

Resnick, S. M., Berenbaum, S. A., Gottesman, I. I., & Bouchard, T. J. (1986). Early hormonal influences on cognitive functioning in congenial adrenal hyperplasia. *Developmental Psychology, 22,* 191–198.

Rochat, P., & Callaghan, T. C. (2005). What drives symbolic development? The case of pictorial comprehension and production. In L. Namy (Ed.), *Symbol use and symbolic representation: Developmental and comparative perspectives* (pp. 25–46). Mahwah, NJ: Lawrence Erlbaum.

Spencer, C., Harrison, N., & Darvizeh, Z. (1980). The development of iconic mapping ability in young children. *International Journal of Early Childhood, 12,* 57–64.

Szechter, L. E., & Liben, L. S. (2004). Parental guidance in preschoolers' understanding of spatial-graphic representations. *Child Development, 75,* 869–885.

Thomas, G. V., Jolley, R. P., Robinson, E. J., & Champion, H. (1999). Realist errors in children's responses to pictures and words as representations. *Journal of Experimental Child Psychology, 74,* 1–20.

Troseth, G. L. (2003). TV guide: Two-year-old children learn to use video as a source of information. *Developmental Psychology, 39,* 140–150.

Uttal, D. H. (1996). Angles and distances: Children's and adults' reconstructions and scaling of spatial configurations. *Child Development, 67,* 2763–2779.

Uttal, D. H., Gregg, V. H., Tan, L. S., Chamberlin, M. H., & Sines, A. (2001). Connecting the dots: Children's use of a systematic figure to facilitate mapping and search. *Developmental Psychology, 37,* 338–350.

10

MAP USE AND THE DEVELOPMENT OF SPATIAL COGNITION

CLARE DAVIES & DAVID H. UTTAL

This is what maps give us, *reality*, a reality that exceeds our vision, our reach, the span of our days, a reality we achieve no other way.
—Denis Wood, *The Power of Maps* (1992)

As the chapters in this volume indicate, interest and research in spatial cognition and its development have increased substantially in the past decade or two. However, it is fair to say that the vast majority has been conducted in relatively small spaces. For example, perhaps the most influential study of the development of spatial cognition that has been conducted in the past 20 years (Hermer & Spelke, 1994) was conducted in a space that was the size of a small closet (for an excellent critique of this study and evidence that room size matters, see chapter 3 this volume). Studies in small-scale space convey many advantages. In particular, they allow researchers to tightly control factors that may influence performance and hence to identify and isolate causal mechanisms. At the same time, studies that are limited to small spaces cannot investigate all that is interesting and important in the development of spatial cognition. Children in modern, Western society need to know about spaces at a variety of scales, from local scales right up to global scales.

For many years, researchers have argued that the perceptual and cognitive processes that are used in small-scale space may differ fundamentally from those used in large-scale space (Acredolo, 1977; Herman & Siegel, 1978; Montello, 1993). For example, small spaces can be experienced in a single glance, but larger spaces can be experienced directly only in "snapshots"

219

or sequential routes. Consequently, when we learn about a large-scale space from direct experience, we must *integrate* the various views into a coherent layout if we are asked to make judgments that require knowledge of relations among locations in the space, such as a route detour (Uttal, Fisher, & Taylor, 2006). Such judgments are often difficult for adults and are particularly difficult for young children (e.g., Siegel & White, 1975; Uttal et al., 2006). The need to learn about large-scale space and the challenges that such learning presents have led to the development of tools that facilitate the communication of spatial information. Maps are perhaps the best example.

A map is a unique form of symbolic representation. It forms a spatial one-to-one relationship with some, but not all, objects in the geographic landscape. By scaling them down to miniature size, it allows the viewer to see far more at one glance than could ever be possible from ground level. Maps are seen from a spatially realistic (but rarely viewed) aerial perspective, but not necessarily with any *pictorial* realism. Symbols replace and distinguish what is otherwise, say, in a suburban landscape, a mass of tiny rooftops and blobs. The result adds extra information as well as enhancing clarity, as shown in figure 10.1.

In this chapter, we argue that these features of maps may also play a role in the development of spatial cognition. We suggest that the use of maps may influence how children come to think about space beyond their immediate experience. This means, in part, that the development of cognition of large-scale space is symbolically mediated. Uttal (2000) has described the relationship between children and maps as a two-way street. Maps are tools that can be used by children to solve spatial problems but are also a potential accelerator for development, *if* their portrayal of spatial relations can help the child to think about space, and the correspondence between their own and external knowledge, in new ways.

Figure 10.1   An (edited and labeled) aerial photograph, and corresponding street map, of part of the Evanston neighborhood used in our research. (Reproduced with kind permission of the City of Evanston, IL.)

Our perspective on the relation between maps and the development of spatial cognition is aligned with that of other researchers who have stressed the influences of symbols. In particular, space beyond immediate experience is communicated and hence symbolically mediated by maps or language. Our perspective on the development of large-scale spatial cognition therefore stresses the role of symbols as tools for thought, following the tradition of Vygotsky (1978) and more recent researchers (e.g., Loewenstein & Gentner, 2005) who have stressed the influence of symbolically mediated information on cognitive development in general. Our contribution here is to bring the domain of large-scale spatial cognition under this general rubric. Because such space cannot be experienced directly without exerting great effort, people have traditionally relied on the information that others can provide through maps, directions, and other forms of communication. We hypothesize that these experiences with symbolic information then influence the development of large-scale spatial cognition.

This chapter describes some of the ideas and evidence from a research program that has investigated these possibilities. Such work is intimately tied to developmental and cognitive psychology, but also interfaces with other disciplines such as cartography, geography, and environmental psychology, and many contributions to our thinking come from researchers in those fields. Based partly on this body of knowledge and partly on our own research program, we will explore the apparent antecedents, challenges, task dependencies, and cognitive processes that impact children's effective use of maps, and the implications of these for our understanding of spatial cognitive development as it relates to large-scale space.

10.1 WHAT MAPS DO

Before discussing the development of map use, we focus on exactly what a map implies for cognition. It is clear from the modern urban street map shown in figure 10.1 that maps offer far more than a simple way to match locations on the map with locations in the world. In particular, maps offer the following:

1. A simplified "bird's-eye" visual image that *integrates multiple locations*, many of which can be experienced only separately on the ground, into a single structure.
2. Accurate (or at least, consistently distorted), easily perceptible information about the relative *distances and directions* between any two landmarks.
3. The opportunity to view whole *routes* between two distant points and to compare their relative lengths and complexity.
4. Representation of some invisible, *nonphysical elements* such as town boundaries, functions of land and buildings, and one-way traffic restrictions.

5. Depiction of the constrained *topology* of the street network, in effect highlighting where it is possible to walk or drive or cycle.
   Here, as we discuss further below, geometric shape and size are often less crucial than relative position and connection.
6. Pictorial or iconic *symbolization* of categories of real-life elements.
   Crosses may stand for churches, single lines for streets, squares or
   flags for schools, and so on.
7. Identification *labels* (using language) for many individual elements
   (e.g., street names and local landmarks).

Without a map or other representation, most of the items in this list would
have to be abstracted from the experience of navigating the real space itself.
For some items, particularly the first four, this is quite difficult and requires
multiple experiences. These items are also hard to communicate efficiently
through media other than a small-scale map, diagram, or model. In fact,
item 1, drawing on the precise geometry of a consistent map projection,
can generally *only* be shown by these means. Although maps of this kind
may thus seem unavoidable, this is certainly not the case since city maps
have tended to have this consistent geometry only since the Enlightenment.
During the eighteenth century, the now-common overhead "planimetric"
maps became gradually more common than the more aesthetic and easily
understood (but geometrically distorted) oblique views used in older city
maps (Elliot, 1987). Because the need for accurate configural knowledge
developed relatively late in civilization, we might expect its spontaneous appreciation by children to come relatively late in development. However,
this may not be the case.

In contrast to the first four items in the list above, one could convey the
later items through linguistic (e.g., a descriptive list) or pictorial means,
perhaps without any integrated plan. Symbolic representation of anything
carries with it the potential for alternative symbol systems, such as language, to do the job equally well. Therefore, only the earlier items in the list
may necessitate some specifically *spatial* cognitive processes when used in
problem solving. At the same time, one of the primary advantages of maps
is that they facilitate and promote this spatial reasoning. When looking at a
map, it is often possible to see, and hence to think about, the relations
among many locations simultaneously. We believe that depicting relational
information in this single visual array is a key feature of maps. Much of our
research has focused on the developing use of relational information to
strategically solve problems in situations where such information may use-
fully improve accuracy, speed, or cognitive efficiency.

It is important to note that not all map-reading tasks necessarily tap
into this specific function of maps, just as the maps themselves do not
"only" show an aerial view of space. For example, consider one commonly
used task: using a map or model to find a hidden toy. As Blades and Cooke
(1994) demonstrated, this task can be solved without thinking about the
spatial relations among multiple locations. Often it is possible for children

to find the hidden toy on the basis of a single correspondence between a depicted object and the corresponding real object in space.

In some situations, using a map may even hinder or limit cognitive flexibility, especially where mental rotation is required. Use of a map that is not aligned to one's direction of view or travel requires a second mental rotation, in addition to the rotation and translation already required to match the map's overhead view to one's ground-based, real-world viewpoint. Children, and also many adults, apparently find this extra rotation difficult, although they are still often able to do it in a simple environment (Vosmik & Presson, 2004). A map may also place other demands on cognition: the features that a particular map design emphasizes may not be those that are most salient to the user's interests or tasks; thus, the user might have a harder time extracting task-relevant features in the face of salient distracting information (Bertin, 1967/1983). Another potential source of cognitive load is what Gombrich (1977) called the "pathology" of symbols. Where map symbols are iconic rather than pictorial, people may be forced to interpret them via a less intuitive matching process, which can lead, at worst, to misconstruals or, at best, to some slower cognitive processing. It is not always clear, however, which aspects of a map may impair or enhance performance on a spatial task: sometimes the same aspect of a map may do both by enabling a more accurate solution but at the cost of greater mental effort.

Indeed, some tasks demand that children (or adults) exploit the special advantages that a map can provide. For example, one might expect tasks such as judging the spatial relation between two out-of-sight locations to be facilitated by looking at a map, because it allows a person to compare them independent of any experience of travel between them. Even when it exists, knowledge of a specific, navigable route between the two locations may not be relevant if a person needs to consider the true direction "as the crow flies." These tasks may require what is commonly referred to as *survey knowledge*, a mental representation that allows one to think about multiple relations among locations without calling on one's experience of navigation. Thinking about space in survey-like terms is greatly facilitated by looking at a map, because a map provides directly much of the information that would otherwise have to be acquired through exploration and mental integration of routes (Thorndyke & Hayes-Roth, 1982; Uttal, 2000).

We should be careful, however, not to simplify this notion of survey knowledge. The past two decades of research on human environmental cognition have suggested that even when we possess such knowledge about a geographic-scale space, it would be misleading to call that knowledge a "cognitive map," if a map implies a direct analog to the fixed two-dimensional paper artifacts designed by cartographers (e.g., Hirtle & Heidorn, 1993; Tversky, 1993). It is clear that high familiarity with an area allows us to mentally or physically visualize an overview of it, but it is not so clear that this overview is itself the form in which all of the information is stored. In particular, much evidence has demonstrated that such survey knowledge tends not to include metrically accurate representations of distance or direction. For example, even adults' judgments of distance are influenced by the semantic salience of landmarks (e.g., Tversky, 1992). Perhaps this is not surprising when we consider that even in smaller scale spaces such as rooms or tabletops, groups of objects tend to be encoded hierarchically to some extent, which biases our judgments of their relative locations (e.g., McNamara, 1986). Thus, another important potential use of a map is to correct or supplant these frequently incorrect estimates of spatial relations.

Arguably, to use a map or any other tool in problem solving, one must realize its potential value and relevance to the task, as well as be able to interpret it and incorporate it into the strategy one will follow. The task of judging the distance from one's current location to a distant location, for instance, may be solvable by mentally visualizing the route to the distant location and then making allowances for the difference between route and direct straight-line distances (e.g., in a regular urban street grid, by calculating the difference between the diagonal and the sum of two sides of a typical street block). It may also be solved—albeit not very accurately—by recalling how much effort or time it seemed to take the last time one traveled to the distant location. If one has not directly traveled there, then one may try to integrate separate portions of other routes, and so on. In other words, the strategic choice of operators in solving this type of problem will determine the accuracy of its outcome, and different strategies may "trade off" differently in terms of speed and mental effort. Therefore, in addition to realizing the relevance of a map to distance judgments, a child or adult must also judge that use of a map will be worthwhile, resulting in (usually) increased accuracy. To some extent, then, map use demands an appreciation that one's internal representation of a space may be poorer than an externally produced one, even though the former may seem more "real" and salient to us than the latter.

Even when a map is not physically present, it is logical to assume that one's memory for the spatial relations it depicts is likely to involve fewer distortions and biases than one's memory for the corresponding real-world space, if only because those relations could be taken in with just a few saccades over a single visual array. Therefore, if a child even subconsciously adopts a task strategy that exploits her/his memory of a map, rather than relying solely on her/his (probably) incomplete and highly distorted experience of the space, then this indicates an understanding that metric space is not the same as those experience-based internal representations. It suggests that children are willing to recognize that the correspondence from the map to some kind of objective reality is at least as strong as that from their own internal "reality" to that outside world. Once such notions of the utility of symbolic representations become established, many other types of problems may be more readily solved. The child is learning to truly *value* external spatial, symbolic information. When and how do children become ready to do this? As we describe in the next section, we have only indirect answers to this question at present.

10.2 CHILDREN'S RESPONSES TO MAPS

Imagine entertaining some visitors from a long-past century or a non-map-using culture who have never previously viewed a conventional map. They will be unfamiliar with its symbols and with its use for representing very large spaces. Yet they will not be entirely unfamiliar with its survey perspective—seeing an array of objects from above. As soon as children can view a backyard from an upstairs window or stand on a hilltop, they experience the outside landscape from an aerial view. Thus we should not be surprised that even 2- to 4-year-old children quickly grasp the nature and contents of an aerial photograph of both familiar and unfamiliar landscapes. Their initial recognition of the nature of the photograph, without being told, seems to vary between studies (Blades et al., 1998; Plester, Richards, Blades, & Spencer, 2002) but is successful around the age of 4–5 years. Once preschool children have identified or been told about the nature of an aerial photograph, they are generally able to run toy cars along its roads, correctly identify geographic features, and make route-planning decisions.

Children can also cope with some of the symbolic aspects of maps even at preschool age. Symbolic play is a regular feature of children's lives well before school age (Göncü & Klein, 2001), as is dealing with objects (toys) reduced and simplified to small-scale caricature. There is no reason to assume that the symbolic representation of a map, if it clearly indicates objects that are meaningful to a child, would not be understood as such within the first few years of life. A long line of studies has shown that this is indeed the case (e.g., Blades & Spencer, 1990; Blaut, McCleary, & Blaut, 1970; Presson, 1982): preschool children can correctly identify depicted landmarks in a room-sized space from their representations on a map. Nevertheless, children's willingness and ability to engage with maps and aerial photographs does not necessarily mean that they appreciate all of the potential problem-solving benefits of such representations (Uttal, 2000), nor that they can or want to apply the mental rotation and other transformations required to take advantage of them in many situations.

One potential impediment to early reliance on maps is the primacy of direct experience with spaces. Children's (and adults') internal representations of a known landscape, such as their home neighborhood, are built up mainly through the experience of wayfinding and being taken on journeys through it. However, people often do not extract multiple interroute relations (going from B to C having previously only been from A to B and from A to C) nor exact metric distances and directions from such spatial experiences (e.g., Hirtle & Jonides, 1985; Millar, 1994; Yeap & Jefferies, 2000). Instead, we make inconsistent and semantically biased judgments of distance and direction, based on such issues as salience, familiarity, and similarity. Lack of experience coupled with the relatively slow development of metacognitive skills could cause children to be unaware of this tendency in themselves, which could lead them to choose less effective and internally resourced strategies for spatial problem solving. In other words, even when a map is available to offer accurate multiple-object relations and even when a child *understands* the map, it may not appear better than his or her experience-based solutions when solving a problem that requires (geo)metric accuracy or a "survey" perspective.

In addition to a lack of metacognition, there are real challenges that children face when trying to apply maps to some tasks in a real space. In particular, the application of a map to a real space necessitates both a scale change and a mental rotation. The latter is trivial if the map is aligned with the child's viewpoint, involving only the change of view from overhead to ground level, but it can be quite complicated if not. At such times, the mental effort involved in these transformations is unlikely to encourage map use unless the gains are clearly apparent. Yet as children's spatial experience at the geographic scale grows, and as geometric representations become more familiar and offer a corrected view of the overall space, children may spontaneously realize the value of this. We might then see a greater tendency, as children grow older, to draw on less topological and more geometric solutions to spatial problems such as wayfinding and locating distant objects (Liben & Downs, 2001).

There is some evidence that even young children can use, learn, and remember quite precise spatial relations among multiple stimuli, when they are clearly aware that a task requires it (e.g., Sluzenski, Newcombe, & Satlow, 2004) and when no major scale transformations are involved (e.g., Uttal, 1996; Vasilyeva & Huttenlocher, 2004). Yet it might be expected that children may only gradually learn the value of external representations such as maps in enabling more accurate spatial judgments (e.g., of distance and direction), especially when such judgments can be approximated from experience.

Indeed, in most everyday real-world spaces and for many tasks including wayfinding, such accuracy is arguably *not* required, especially for sighted people. Within a room, playground, or street scene, it is relatively easy to judge distance and direction using direct visual cues. Physical constraints—doorways, hallways, stairs, a street network—strongly affect our experiences in space, and finding locations within such constrained spaces is greatly simplified by street addressing systems and other conventions, so accurate geometric knowledge is not always necessary. Even in rural areas, footpaths and fences may constrain movement to some extent, at least in most developed countries. Where such constraints allow a reliance on the topology rather than on the metrically scaled topography of the local landscape, it may be even more likely that map-based spatial solutions might be spontaneously appreciated relatively late in child development, since approximations are both possible and often "close enough." There is some evidence for this: children from rural areas who live in less spatially constrained environments, and also tend to have more freedom to explore them, outperform urban and suburban children on various spatial tasks, including map drawing (Norman, 1980).

To summarize, then, despite clearly being able to understand basic map concepts by the age of 5, and being able to use maps to locate items in simple room-sized spaces, it is less clear when or how well this "scales up" both to other tasks and other sizes of space. Map use is a choice when solving problems in large-scale spaces. It requires that children appreciate both the disparity between their internal and the map's external representation and the value of the latter. Map use also requires that children be proficient at relevant cognitive spatial skills (e.g., mental rotation, relative scaling of distances) so that the amount of effort required to derive a map-based solution to a spatial problem will not be too great. Otherwise, children are likely to select other strategies even if they know that the map holds more accurate information. For all of these reasons, it is helpful to examine what children choose to do with a map once they are at an age of being active navigators of geographic-scale environments, and hence potentially able to learn what maps can do.

In the remainder of this chapter, we will describe two lines of research that have helped us explore this question of the relations between children's developing understanding of maps and their internal, mental representations of space. The first concerns laboratory studies of children's map use, and the second is a new line of research that focuses on the use and influence of maps on children's thinking in a much larger and more naturalistic space, their neighborhood. Although these studies do not directly enable us to tease out the relationships among awareness, motivation, and cognitive skills, they take a step in this direction by examining when and how grade-school-age children take advantage of maps across various situations and tasks.

We have also attempted to take into account some of the dimensions on which situations and tasks vary. We focus on two dimensions in particular—environmental scale (the size of the space under consideration) and familiarity (of the child with the space). These factors are not always explicitly considered when making generalizations about children's "spatial abilities," but they may be critically important. For instance, laboratory studies of children reproducing object locations from simple maps (e.g., Vasilyeva & Huttenlocher, 2004) may involve different cognitive requirements from outdoor wayfinding and orientation (e.g., Anooshian & Young, 1981), which may be different again from tasks that probe knowledge of wider geographic regions such as across a whole city, country, or the world (e.g., Axia, Bremner, Deluca, & Andreasen, 1998). As an example, a room-sized space is at a scale that a child has, many times, appreciated within one single turn of the head (a "vista" space; see Montello, 1993) and may well have been seen from above (e.g., being held above an adult's head, or looking down from a balcony). It is therefore likely to be considerably easier to conceive of and apply a map of that space than a larger scale space such as a neighborhood (an "environmental" space) or country (a "geographical" space).

The level of familiarity has been varied in past research, particularly among outdoor-scale studies; however, it is not clear exactly how familiarity influences spatial performance across situations and tasks. Some studies have looked at children's knowledge of familiar environments such as their school grounds or home neighborhood (e.g., Anooshian & Young, 1981), while others have asked children to learn new environments (e.g., Cornell, Heth, & Skoczylas, 1999; Ambrose, 2000). Arguably, these studies could tap into different cognitive processes. For instance, the explicit learning of novel information for the sake of problem solving likely relies on processes that differ from those at work in incidental learning situations. Moreover, familiarity may interact with age in terms of children's spatial strategies and responses, even within one environment (e.g., Cousins, Siegel, & Maxwell, 1983; Lehnung, Leplow, Haaland, Mehdorn, & Ferstl, 2003).

10.3 CHILDREN, MAPS, AND ROOM-SIZED SPACES

In this section, we summarize results of three studies of the development of children's use of maps as spatial representations, that is, as visualizations that facilitate solving spatial problems and acquiring survey-like representations. In contrast to other studies of children's spatial reasoning, our focus was specifically on the relational, survey-like quality of maps and their relevance to spatial problems that may be harder to solve without them.

Our first study of children's acquisition of survey-like representations from maps (Uttal & Wellman, 1989) was conducted in an 18' × 12' playhouse. Even though this is a relatively small-scale space, our goal was to design a task that required children to think about spatial relations in survey-like ways. The space consisted of a 3 × 2 arrangement of small square rooms. Each room was identical except for the presence of a different animal. Thus, the individual rooms could be referred to as the dog's room, the cat's room, and so on. Children learned the layout of the space and then were asked to perform various spatial tasks to assess how they had mentally represented the information.

In the initial study, children 4–7 years of age were assigned randomly to learn the animals either from a map or from flashcards, so that they all learned "what" but only the map group learned "where" the animals were. The learning procedures and criteria were as similar as possible for the two conditions; in both cases, the children had to recall all the animals' names. In the map condition, the children also had to recall the animals' locations, by naming the correct animal when the experimenter pointed to its room. Once the children could recall all the animals twice in succession without error, the testing phase of the experiment began. The procedures were thus designed to ensure that children thoroughly knew the relevant information (the cards or the map) before we assessed their transfer of knowledge to the real environment.

At test, children were taken (without the map or cards) on a specific route through the actual playhouse and asked each time to state which animal lived in the next room before entering it. Children navigated this route until they could anticipate each animal twice in succession, without error. Perhaps surprisingly, even the younger children's responses demonstrated a substantial advantage of having learned the map. Overall, children in the map group were able to recall locations well and hence perform much better than those in the card group, particularly in the earlier rooms along the route.

In interpreting this finding, it is important to note that our tasks required the children to recall, translate (from the map, in that condition), and think about the spatial relations among locations within the playhouse. The route that we followed in the playhouse was never shown on the map, and hence the children had no basis for knowing which rooms we would enter or how we could get from room to room. Thus, the task required the sort of random access or *equiavailability* that is characteristic of a survey-like representation. Children could think about multiple relations among locations in a manner that was not tied to navigation of a specific route. Although the children did not perform perfectly, they performed about as well on any given spatial relation as on another.

Further evidence to support this claim came from a follow-up study in which we asked children to anticipate the identity of animals that were both on and off the route they followed through the playhouse after the initial learning phase (see Uttal & Wellman, 1989). That is, children were required to identify animals that were both ahead and to their left and right, relative to the direction in which they were traveling. The children did just as well on the left–right judgments as they did on the straight-ahead, and performance on the two measures was highly correlated. This result again reveals that the map-group children knew the relations among the locations and that they could exploit this knowledge in a navigation task.

For these reasons, we concluded that the best and most parsimonious explanation for the results was that the children viewing the map had acquired, and could reconstruct and manipulate, a survey-like representation of the space. The map helped them to think about multiple relations among locations, thus conferring one of the important advantages of using maps, even to 4-year-old children. Although performance did improve with age, even the 4-year-olds took advantage of the spatial relations on the map and used them to solve the spatial problem of identifying locations. Thus, this was one of the first studies to show that young children can use maps to solve the specific kinds of problems for which maps convey a special or even unique advantage.

We can therefore conclude that the basic skills of matching an overhead view to an immersed, ground-based one and accessing this spatial representation in a random, ad hoc order are already present in a typical American 4-year-old. However, it was still unclear whether it was the configural overview of the map itself that children were recalling, or only the individual items (pairwise spatial relations) conveyed within it. In the next section, we describe some more recent work that helps to clarify this point.

10.4 MAPS, WORDS, AND SPATIAL KNOWLEDGE
IN ROOM-SIZED SPACES

Uttal et al. (2006) recently investigated how children form mental representations from maps and from verbal directions. We began this research with the observation that in a verbal description, spatial information can be described only serially. That is, each spatial relation must be described individually; it is not possible to describe multiple relations simultaneously. In this regard, acquiring spatial information from a verbal description shares an important similarity with how we acquire spatial information while navigating in the world. In both cases, we encounter most of the relevant spatial relations (what follows from what) sequentially, while listening, reading, or traversing a route. To form a survey-like representation similar to that given by a map, a person would need to do more than simply remember the spatial information as it was encountered: the information must be integrated into a single structure. The person would need to hold each new relation in short-term memory, linking it to others to build a cohesive mental representation on the basis of either verbal descriptions or direct experience. It is likely that this would take place when first hearing the description, so that a mental image of the overall layout could be constructed and serve as a reference frame for information about individual locations within it. This is more cognitively economical than storing individual relations.

In general, such integration is easier with a map because it draws on basic integrative visual processes while actually viewing it. Multiple relations can be taken in with a single saccade, and the whole already exists as an integrated layout, so no "guesses" or estimates are required. One scans the map in the same way as any other tabletop array or picture; no physical turning or traveling is required. In the geographic-scale environment itself, however, this is rarely possible except when viewing from a highly elevated vantage point.

Nevertheless, research has suggested that adults do seem to form and use integrated surveys regardless of the form of the input. In one well-known study (Taylor & Tversky, 1992), adults either read or looked at a map of hypothetical places, such as a zoo. They were then asked to make judgments about spatial relations, some of which had not been included in the descriptions, and thus subjects had to infer them. This type of inference is clearly easier to solve if participants can recall or recreate a survey-like representation of the multiple locations. Therefore, one could have expected participants who learned from a map to do better regardless of the specific relations involved, as maps convey equiavailability of all spatial relations.

Surprisingly, Taylor and Tverksy (1992) found that the form of the input did *not* affect adults' judgments. Those participants who learned from descriptions did about as well as those who learned from a map, even for those spatial relations that were not explicitly described. Moreover, this finding held up even when the subjects were not informed beforehand that they would be asked to make judgments about spatial relations. These results suggest that adults can integrate spatial information into survey-like representations, regardless of the form of the input. Of course, in that study the complexities of the map and description were closely matched, which is likely not the case in most real-life situations. Nevertheless, it demonstrated that adults have the ability to effectively integrate spatial knowledge using verbal descriptions.

When do these abilities develop? Do children also integrate spatial information regardless of the form of the input? There is reason to believe that the answer might be no—that is, that the flexibility that adults demonstrate might have important developmental antecedents. For example, it has often been suggested that young children's recall of the locations of landmarks tends to be based on route knowledge, a representation that preserves the sequential ordering of landmarks but does not encode relations among locations that were not included on the same route (Allen, 1981; Siegel & White, 1975; but see also Anooshian & Young, 1981; Spencer, Blades, & Morsley, 1989; Yeap & Jefferies, 2000). Likewise, Plumert, Ewert, and Spear (1995) have shown that 3-year-old children sometimes focus on only one spatial relation at a time, even in situations where two simultaneous relations must be processed or described to avoid ambiguity (e.g., noting "It's in the bag by the chair" to disambiguate cases where there are two identical bags). For these reasons, we predicted that children's mental models of spatial information derived from verbal descriptions, or at least their use of those models in problem solving, might be more tied to the serial order of the information presented than are those of older children and adults.

To test this hypothesis, we set up an experiment that was in some ways akin to the original Uttal and Wellman (1989) work. As before, there were six rooms in a 2 × 3 layout, with a different toy animal in each room. In this case, however, half of the children (8 and 10 years of age) and adults learned the layout from a description. They were told, for example, that the bear was to the left of the frog and that the cat was to the left of the pig. We asked the children to repeat the descriptions from memory until they could say the entire set of relations two times in a row without error. The remaining participants memorized a map, following procedures similar to those used by Uttal and Wellman (1989).

After the participants had learned the layout, they completed two spatial tasks that were designed to assess how they had mentally represented the spatial information in the descriptions or on the maps. In the *model construction task*, the experimenter gave the children six cards (in random order), each with a photograph of an animal from the playhouse. The child was asked to arrange the cards to make a model of the layout of the playhouse. In the *pointing task*, the experimenter and participant entered a room into which a toy animal was placed. The experimenter than asked the participant to point to other animals' rooms. For example, the participant might be taken into "the pig's room" and asked to point to the bear's room and the cat's room. The pointing task thus demanded that children think about pairwise relations between locations, whereas the model task required the children to integrate those pairs into a coherent configuration.

The results revealed a distinct developmental transition in the integration of spatial information from descriptions. In general, the 8-year-olds did not appear to integrate the descriptions into survey-like representations. Their representations instead were based on the serial information in the descriptions and thus were akin to route-based representations. This was revealed particularly in their model constructions. Whereas most of the adults and many of the 10-year-olds placed the cards in the correct positions, the 8-year-olds did not. However, it was not the case that the 8-year-olds were simply bad at the task. Further examination revealed that almost all of the constructions preserved the *contiguity* relations between adjacent pairs of animals. In fact, on average, the children's constructions preserved at least five of the six contiguity relations that were described (but not their specific directions). Thus, the performance of 8-year-olds in the description condition was far from random, even though the constructions were inaccurate when assessed according to an absolute criterion. Their constructions (and their pointing) reflected the serial nature of the descriptions of spatial information in language.

In contrast to these findings from the description condition, all subjects performed very well when they learned from the maps, indicating, again, that maps can facilitate children's learning of spatial relations. The map allowed children to see and to think about the relations among all the locations.

In a follow-up experiment, we demonstrated that the advantage of using a map was not limited to having seen the exact location of each individual animal (avoiding the need to interpret left and right correctly from the descriptions), but was also related to the opportunity to learn the outline of the overall configuration. We tested whether providing this configuration in isolation would be sufficient to help young children perform better in the description condition. In particular, we created an outline map that showed only the overall layout, without the specific animals in the locations, and showed it to the children. We then had the participants (8-year-olds and adults) learn the descriptions, as in the first study. We hypothesized that seeing the outline map might give them the structure needed to integrate the descriptions into a cohesive, survey-like cognitive map, even though they would still need to learn the specific locations for each animal by correctly interpreting the relations they heard. This hypothesis was confirmed: 8-year-olds who saw the outline map and then heard the descriptions performed almost as well as those who learned from a complete map. This result demonstrates how maps can facilitate children's thinking about space: in addition to showing the individual relations between adjacent locations, the overall spatial *structure* is made clear and provides a reference frame for encoding those relations.

Taken together, these two studies demonstrate the role of maps in facilitating children's thinking about spatial relations. Maps can become "tools for thought" (Carey, 1990; Vygotsky, 1978), allowing children to encode spatial relations in an efficient, integrated manner that is difficult, and sometimes impossible, to gain from direct experience or from linguistic descriptions. In this way, maps make it relatively easy to see and judge the relations among multiple spatial locations.

10.5 MAPS, WORDS, AND SPATIAL KNOWLEDGE IN ENVIRONMENT-SIZED SPACES

As stated above, there is a relatively unexplored gap between findings from studies of children's spatial behavior in room-sized versus larger spaces. Thus, in this section, we discuss research that attempts to "scale up" from the laboratory studies described in the previous section to a larger and more familiar space—children's home neighborhoods. In particular, we used the central manipulation from Uttal et al. (2006) with an extended age range (7–10 years), to probe whether and when exposure to the configural information in maps would again facilitate spatial performance, in contrast to verbally presented information; however, there were two key differences. First, the space was outdoors, several hundred times bigger than the playhouse and much more complex (see figure 10.1). Second, the landmarks/objects probed in the study were already known to the children.

To investigate how exposure to maps versus verbal descriptions influences children's performance in a large-scale space, we conducted a partial microgenetic study of around one hundred children. First, we gathered data on each child's prior knowledge of (and emotional responses to) 18 landmarks across their neighborhood, coupled with a wealth of background data gathered via a structured interview with a parent or guardian. Immediately following this, we ran three weekly sessions with the child in which she or he was exposed to either a map or verbal descriptions of local geographic features. Children were also tested on spatial tasks at each session to assess learning from maps versus verbal descriptions.

This design allowed us to gradually expose children in the map condition to a local map, this time through a set of interactive activities rather than rote learning. Exposure to the map occurred through a set of activities that we called an indoor "information game." This centered around the locations of local landmarks and routes and also encouraged the use of symbolic representation. Children in the verbal condition received a similar set of information in an "information game" that, apart from one symbol-drawing activity, was performed using spoken and written descriptions rather than the map. There were five main tasks in this information game:

1. Solve a "Mystery Places" problem: match six dots on the map (or match six cards giving verbal descriptions) to six photographs of local landmarks.

2. Create a "Mystery Place" by marking a dot on the map (or providing a description) for their school in one session, and for their home in the other session.
3. Draw on the map (or on blank paper) symbols for a local post office, a church, the local canal and the railroad.
4. Draw on the map (or verbally describe) their usual route from home to school.
5. Report the names of three local friends and mark (or describe the location of) their homes, and say which lived closest and which farthest away from the children's own homes.

The study took place over two summers in Evanston and Wilmette, two suburbs in Illinois directly to the north of Chicago. Most of the children had lived most of their lives in the same neighborhood; we avoided testing children who were recent arrivals. We visited each child at his or her home on three weekly spaced occasions. During (usually) the first of these sessions, one experimenter interviewed the child's parent or guardian to gather background data, while in a separate room another experimenter asked the child to rate her or his familiarity with each of 18 local landmarks, to rate how much she or he liked the landmark (via a set of "smiley faces"), and to state whether each landmark was in what they thought of as "my neighborhood."

Then the child went outside and completed an *outdoor spatial performance test*. In this test, the child stood within sight of the street (usually on the sidewalk). The experimenter named a distant landmark and showed the child a picture of the landmark. Then, the child had to point straight toward the landmark. We told children to imagine they could travel straight through buildings and fences in order to go straight to the landmark (e.g., Cousins et al., 1983). Besides doing this for each of four landmarks, the child had to rank how far each of the same four landmarks was from the current location, by studying the photographs and successively eliminating the one closest to home. Given that there are alternative strategies children might use when judging distances and directions (especially from a familiar starting point such as home), we also included a "pretend" or "imagined" version of the pointing and distance-ranking tasks. Here the child had to imagine standing at one of the landmarks and to point to (and rank) the others in the set. Figure 10.2A shows a child performing the pointing task.

The second session started inside the home with the map or verbal "information game" activities. Then we took a walk through part of the neighborhood (navigated by the child as far as possible) to the landmark that the child had imagined standing at during the "pretend" spatial task in session 1. We then ran the outdoor spatial performance test again, at that location. This enabled us to see whether the children's (immediately previous) exposure to the map would help when they could less easily count on the familiarity of home as a potential spatial "anchor point."

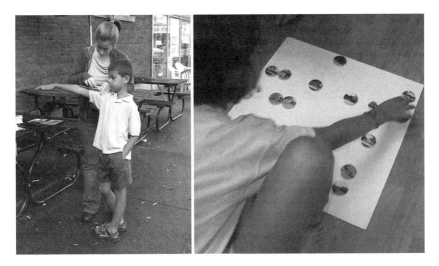

Figure 10.2   Children performing the pointing task (*left*) and the circles task (*right*) in the neighborhood study.

In the third session, we again conducted the map or verbal activities indoors in the child's home, and then tested the child on the outdoor spatial performance test. There was then a final task where the child had to construct a layout from memory of all 18 of the tested landmarks. We called this the "circles task" because the child was instructed to place circular foamboard cutouts, each showing the same photograph of a landmark that the child had seen earlier in the study, onto a large square sheet "as they are in real life" (see figure 10, left panel). It should be noted here that simply reproducing the earlier maps was not possible: the map layout was differently shaped and much larger, and only six of the landmarks had ever been shown on the earlier maps (the remaining six had never appeared at all). Thus, in both conditions, children had to integrate a configuration of landmarks that they had learned about (though at different times) with landmarks that had never been mentioned in the "information game." Because children in the map condition were effectively given a configuration in the information game that could act as a reference frame for placing the circles, we expected that children in the map condition would show a particular advantage on this critical task.

Below we briefly outline the findings of the two phases of this study. First, we discuss how children's prior experiences and knowledge of their neighborhood influenced their initial performance on the outdoor spatial performance test. This is of interest because, at present, very little is known about how children's experiences with real-world spaces lead to differences in the ability to make judgments about distance and direction, from either real or imagined viewpoints. This investigation provides an initial look at how particular experiences with a large-scale space are related to these spatial skills. Second, we focus on the central manipulation in this study and ask whether exposure to maps versus verbally presented information affected children's performance on the outdoor spatial tests and the final circles task.

10.5.1 The Influence of Prior Experience on Initial Spatial Performance

Besides our questions to the children about the familiarity and salience of the landmarks we used in the study, our interview with their parent included a range of other factors covering aspects of the child's local activities within the neighborhood, frequency of taking trips out by car or bicycle or on foot, experience (as far as the parent knew) of viewing various kinds of maps and learning other relevant information and skills, and the parent's assessment of the child's landmark familiarity (on the same rating scale as we used for the child). The latter was averaged with the child's ratings, to minimize the effect of situations where either the parent or the child confused one landmark for another, failed to recognize it, or forgot the extent to which the child would actually have visited or passed it. The parent was also asked to use a map-annotating task to indicate what area she or he thought the child would know well, the area where the child was free to go without adult accompaniment, and the places that the parent felt were potentially dangerous for the child (again, an aspect of salience, but this time via the parent's response to the place such as a verbal warning or ban). Some aspects of the parent's own knowledge were also examined: her or his own familiarity ratings of the 18 landmarks, the extent of what she or he would define as "my neighborhood," and the extent of her or his own activities around that neighborhood.

Given a sample size of approximately 100 children, it was possible to perform an exploratory multivariate analysis of these predictors to see which ones appeared related to the children's initial performance on the outdoor spatial test. In particular, we used canonical correlation analysis (following the methods of Thompson, 1984). This analysis technique is useful in that it allowed us to examine which of the above independent (predictor) variables contributed to which particular dependent (performance) measures—that is, how prior experiences are linked to specific aspects of spatial test performance. Canonical correlation analysis is thus one step beyond multiple regression: the latter relates the variance in a collection of predictor variables to the variance of a *single* dependent measure, while the former relates the predictors to a *set* of dependent measures. Canonical analysis results in a set of orthogonal (i.e., uncorrelated with one another) canonical *variates* (underlying dimensions or factors); each pair of these represents a specific relationship between the original sets of dependent and independent variables, in each case drawing on some of those variables more than others. As with related multivariate techniques (e.g., multiple regression or factor analysis), the correlations within successively extracted canonical variate pairs tend to decrease, representing successively less of the original variance. The overall significance of the analysis was tested and found to be high. The variates can be interpreted by examining the simple correlations of the original variables with the canonical variates (often called canonical factor *loadings*), in tandem with the statistical weights placed on each variable in contributing to each variate. Like most analysts, we also followed the convention of ignoring all correlations below 0.3 (i.e., representing less than 10% of the overall variance in the children's behavior).

The canonical correlation analysis of our data showed three significant factors that related background measures of children's everyday life (predictor variables) to their session 1 performance on the pointing and distance comparison tasks from a real and imagined starting location (dependent measures). Below, we discuss each factor in turn.

The first and strongest factor was linked to the child's pointing performance. Perhaps not surprisingly, the strongest predictor contribution to this factor came from a composite measure of the child's overall familiarity with the 18 landmarks and the space that encompassed them, based on the child and parent ratings and some related measures. The next strongest contribution came from what we labeled children's "problem-solving experience"—parents were asked to rate how often their children had ever personally navigated a route and given verbal route directions to someone else. Clearly, their having done this, and their knowing the overall space, allowed the children to develop what could loosely be termed a "sense of local orientation" that would be required for the pointing tasks. After this, the next strongest contribution was a composite measure of the child's previous exposure to various types of map (from fictional maps in adventure story books, up through various scales of real-world map). Children who had been exposed to maps either at home or at school (even though most parents and a schoolteacher felt that this had been minimal for most of them) were already performing better than their peers in local direction judgments. After that, the child's specific familiarity and "liking" of the specific set of four landmarks that they were pointing to were the next factors, followed by age, and then by their average "liking" of all the landmarks across the neighborhood.

Although these findings do not allow us to make a *strong* claim that map exposure and route-planning experience were more important than age in determining children's pointing performance, we can hypothesize that the common link here is most likely to be children's awareness and development of a spatial representation that is sufficiently "metric" (as opposed to loosely topological) to allow quite accurate estimates of relative direction even from a location where the child is not currently standing. It also suggests that children of grade-school age can utilize map-derived knowledge and strategies for making judgments in large real-world spaces (each of the two neighborhoods was 1–2 km across).

The second factor identified in the analysis was strongly linked to children's performance on the distance ranking task.[1] The predictors that influenced children's performance on this task appeared related to experiences, both direct and indirect, that could provide information about relative local distances. These included (in descending order of strength of contribution) the extent of the child's own participation in local activities (from shopping to sports), the various questions we asked the parents about their *own* local knowledge and activity, and then the child's age. Again, the child's experience of route planning tasks (navigating and giving directions) was also a factor. Interestingly, the specific salience (smiley-face "liking") of the specific landmarks in the session 1 set correlated *negatively* with the child's distance-ranking performance. As suggested previously, this may indicate that highly salient landmarks are judged to be nearer than they really are—a bias similar to that found in adults (e.g., Hirtle & Heidorn, 1993).

The third factor showing reasonably strong canonical coefficients was most strongly and positively linked to children's distance rankings from home and their "imagined" pointings, but was *negatively* linked to their "imagined" distance rankings. The strongest predictor of this factor was the extent of the child's freedom to roam unaccompanied by an adult (corrected for their age, with which it was strongly correlated), followed by their familiarity with the four specific landmarks. Problem-solving experience appeared to load *negatively* onto this factor.

At first sight, this is a counterintuitive result: we might not expect children's roaming experience to impact negatively on their ability to estimate distance in the "imagined" scenario. However, we interpret this as demonstrating a key point discussed earlier in this chapter—that it is possible for children (and adults) to try to solve large-scale spatial problems by relying solely on their personal navigational experience. Imagine a child who, having experience with roaming around the neighborhood, can recall or construct a vague and perhaps near-topological representation of the local neighborhood structure, but with little knowledge of the more accurate metric topography. Such a child may be able to use that personal wayfinding experience to estimate and compare distances from home to other places. This child would also perform much better at the imagined pointings if, from having traveled there, she or he knew exactly where the imagined starting location was. The pointing responses themselves would then draw on the child's semitopological awareness of the local layout, as would the direct pointings from home. However, for the imagined distance comparisons, he or she has no knowledge of metric distance to draw on unless through *direct travel between* the landmarks (which appeared to be unlikely in most cases: the landmarks tended to be single destinations in their own right).

These results underscore the mixed effects of reliance on personal wayfinding experience in children who probably possessed only vague topological knowledge of the neighborhood's spatial configuration. Reliance upon personal wayfinding knowledge helped with direct distance estimates and with indirect direction estimates, but it hurt indirect distance estimates where personal knowledge was simply unavailable. Yet, children who had greater experience with imagining locations and the spatial relations between them, as shown by our measure of prior spatial problem-solving experience, were presumably more likely to adopt an alternative strategy that was less based on physical navigation. Those children therefore showed the opposite pattern of results.

From a developmental perspective, it is worth noting that age was a significant contributor to both of the first two factors identified above, but in neither case was it the most significant factor in its own right. Nevertheless, on average, 7-year-old children pointed to each landmark with a median error of 48°, whereas 10-year olds' error averaged only 25°. This improvement over the age range roughly matches previous studies (Anooshian & Young, 1981; Herman, Heins, & Cohen, 1987; Lehnung et al., 2003), and the 10-year olds' accuracy is similar to that quite often found for adults (e.g., Davies & Pederson, 2001).

Although it is important to treat the results of multivariate analyses with caution, the above results are interesting given the relative rigor of canonical correlation, the reasonably sized sample, and the fact that these findings are consistent with our existing knowledge of spatial cognition in children and adults. The strong roles of previous spatial task performance, of local familiarity, and of past exposure to maps all suggest a link to the theoretical interpretations suggested above. These place an emphasis on the strategic and tool-using nature of children's spatial problem solving, and on the possible advantages conferred by appreciating and developing an integrated, relatively unbiased, survey-like representation of the space.

10.5.2 Children's Interactions with Maps and Their Impact on Subsequent Spatial Performance

Before turning to the central empirical question of this study—whether exposure to maps versus verbal information influenced children's performance in the outdoor and circles tests as it had in the previous laboratory setting—we first evaluated children's performance in the information game. This was important to check, given previous predictions that children will show only gradual development in map interpretation skills via a series of approximate stages (Liben, 1999). If children were indeed unable to cope with interpreting more "real-world" maps in the information game, then we could not expect the maps to influence their spatial test performance. However, there were no significant age differences or apparent "stages" in children's performance in the information game. Rather, children found the matching, drawing, tracing, and interpreting tasks easy and fun, although their accuracy was not always perfect and they were not always familiar with all of the landmarks. A few children even made comments that might have placed them near the highest level in Liben's proposed stage theory, by critiquing the content and design of the map itself as if recognizing that alternatives were also possible.

In general, children coped very well with the "Mystery Places" game— very few made more than a handful of errors over the two sessions. Children's drawings and map annotations also demonstrated that they had no trouble understanding either the symbolic or spatial aspects of the map. Examples are shown in figure 10.3. When spatial errors occurred in placing landmarks such as the child's home or a local church, these tended to be within a block of the correct location. Moreover, children's symbols (in both conditions) ranged imaginatively from a simple cross or envelope up to quite detailed buildings, but there was no apparent systematic increase or decrease in symbolism with age. For the railroad or canal, although the children were often able to draw only a small portion of the line due to ignorance of its route, they had no trouble drawing a simplified railroad track or wave patterns to signify them. Age also had no discernable effect on the correctness of the children's placement of these symbols in the map condition or on their placement of their own home and school.

Overall, then, all symbolic and basic spatial aspects of the information game seemed quite easy. This was the case even for 7-year-olds and even though most of the children had never previously seen any spatial representations of their local area (and few maps in general). This matches other research suggesting that children's approach to the symbolic aspects of maps is largely mature by the age of 6 (Lee & Karmiloff-Smith, 1996). It also helps to explain why some children's previous exposure to maps had apparently benefited their initial spatial test performance (at least on the pointing tasks), as described above. As far as we could ascertain, none of the children had received any actual formal training in map interpretation. It makes

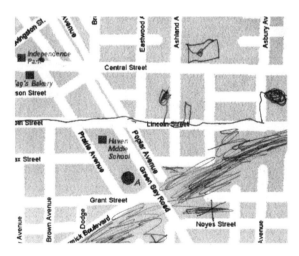

Figure 10.3   Excerpt from a 7-year-old's map in the information game. The child has drawn the canal in the right area (scribbles) and drawn an envelope to symbolize the post office (near top right), although this is in the wrong place. The line across the middle is part of the child's route to his school, which is on the far right (corrected twice by child). The circle marked "A" is one of the six premarked Mystery Places.

sense to assume that if prior map exposure was able to influence children's spatial performance even before we showed them our map stimuli, then they already had sufficient spatial cognitive skills to be able to understand our (relatively simplified) maps, too.

At the same time, it is important to note that children in the verbal condition were *equally* able to perform the tasks in the information game: the two groups of children were equally successful at matching the landmark locations to their photographs. This suggests that the children were just as comfortable with using approximate, verbally described information as with the accurate metric and configurational representation of the map.

With this background, we turn to the question of whether the knowledge gained from the information game would and could be used by children in the outdoor spatial performance and circles tests. With regard to the outdoor tests, there was some evidence that the map benefited children more in the "imagined" pointing and distance tasks than in the "real" ones, especially when performing them both at home in session 3. This again appears to suggest that the value of such "survey-based strategies" in solving spatial tasks lies where they are clearly the best way of solving the problem with any degree of accuracy—their influence appears less critical when direct personal experience can be recalled to help calculate direct distances and directions. As with the laboratory study described above (Uttal et al., 2006), children's performance on the more basic pointing and distance comparison tasks was also aided by the verbal condition (as shown by a similar improvement between sessions 1 and 3). We can conclude that children were again able to learn pairwise spatial relations from verbal stimuli, but these were (again) insufficient when an integrated and geometrically accurate configuration was required—which was the case in the "imagined" tasks.

Again, as with the model construction task in the Uttal et al. (2006) study, success on the "circles" task depends heavily on such a configuration being available; simple pairwise knowledge of distances and directions is clearly inadequate for constructing an integrated model of a space. Almost all the children tackled the circles task with enthusiasm, and most seemed quite confident in the layouts they produced, even though some differed wildly from geometric reality. As might be expected, children's mean placement accuracy in this task gave the strongest statistical difference between the two groups, with the map group clearly performing better. Additionally, there was a gradual increase in performance on the circles task with age in the map condition, before apparently leveling off around age 9. In the verbal condition, by contrast, performance actually *worsened* with age for the 7- to 9-year-olds before making a dramatic improvement around age 10. In terms of difference between the two conditions, this meant that 9-year-olds showed the strongest effect, with those who had played the verbal information game producing the worst overall performance on the circles task, while those who played the map information game produced the best (in terms of mean error of placement when compared to an "ideal" layout).

There was no difference among 10-year-olds in the two conditions, perhaps because their local knowledge had matured to the point of being able to re-call or reconstruct a fully integrated "survey" representation of their own (which is supported by our earlier observation that their pointing and dis-tance accuracies were close to those of adults).

It is important to note that, as in earlier experiments, the children were never explicitly encouraged to learn or transfer knowledge from one task to another; it was up to them to decide which of our "games" with them were helpful to other tasks. In this study, the only task for which the children were given feedback on their performance was the information game, to ensure that they always had a chance to learn the correct matchings and lo-cations. However, there was no explicit suggestion that we wanted them to learn the correct solutions for later use in other tasks. Unlike the earlier ex-periments, there was no repetitive rote learning of the spatial representa-tions: the children learned through interaction with them, and any commit-tal to memory was up to them. Nevertheless, playing the "game" did affect children's spatial responses in other tasks. Despite the complexity and mul-tiple sources of bias that are present in cognitive models of real-world spaces, both phases of the above analysis demonstrate that the chance to view a consistent Euclidean representation of the space does facilitate more accurate spatial problem solving where such geometric factors are impor-tant, particularly for tasks where other strategies cannot easily be applied.

10.6 CHILDREN AND MAPS: CONCLUSIONS AND RECOMMENDATIONS

At the start of this chapter, we outlined the types of information that a map gives to its user, placing special significance on the spatial configuration as the main feature of maps that cannot be easily supplied in any other form. That configuration, we pointed out, is also likely to be a more accurate spa-tial representation in terms of Euclidean geometry than the mental repre-sentations we generate as a result of real-world spatial experience. How-ever, we also cautioned that a child must be able to appreciate the value of such a representation and its superiority (in geometric terms, at least) over his or her own imperfect spatial knowledge, before she or he is likely to choose to use a map in a task where alternative strategies are possible. This may be particularly true in circumstances where maps are harder to use or apply, and also where accurate metrics are less important in solving com-mon spatial problems such as locating landmarks or planning routes.

Our laboratory studies avoided these issues by constraining the task such that no alternative was possible that would allow successful problem solving within the artificial space; the child had no other prior experience of it. In this way, we were able to demonstrate that children from 4 years of age are at least *capable* of utilizing a map within a large-scale environment, for encoding and recalling spatial relations (and that 8-year-olds can do this even when those spatial relations are not explicitly shown on the map). We also saw that the spatial knowledge children gained from descriptions was insufficient for a configural task such as model construction. When we scaled up the task to study children's map use within their familiar local neighborhood, where past direct and indirect experience offered even more alternative strategies for spatial problem solving, we again found that maps made a difference primarily for tasks where it was difficult for a child to use any alternative strategy, such as in the "imagined" pointings and distance rankings, and the circles task.

We also found that past exposure to maps, with no formal training in their use, had apparently contributed meaningfully to children's initial ability to make direction judgments, which suggested that they might in fact be spontaneously appreciating the value of these integrated "survey-like" representations. That same analysis also showed that having already tried to solve spatial problems, such as route planning, appeared to be strongly linked to children's initial spatial performance, although, of course, we cannot be sure of the direction of causality: perhaps children with better spatial skills are more likely to play at being "back seat drivers" and explorers. At the same time, familiarity with the landmarks was crucial to general pointing and distance estimation ability, as was their personal salience to the child. Yet specifically salient landmarks appeared to negatively affect distance estimates, possibly due to bias. It also appeared that some children may have been depending on their physical experience of traveling to the landmarks, which improved their distance estimates *to* them from home but worsened their ability to make such estimates *among* them. This demonstrates the importance of an integrated "survey" reference frame in solving some, but not all, spatial tasks. Where this frame is absent or incomplete, performance worsens on tasks that demand it, but not on simple spatial estimates of distance or direction.

Age tended to be a significant but nondominating factor in these analyses, suggesting that it may be appropriate to consider this type of task more in terms of children's opportunities to learn from experiences than as something dependent on an invariant developmental "stage" (although this could still, theoretically, underlie the differences among children by affecting their ability to respond to those experiences with optimal effectiveness). Rather, a more parsimonious theoretical framework, for interpreting our and much other work on children's responses to maps, is Vygotsky's (1978) notion of "proximal development." Under this interpretation, children take advantage of the tools to which they are exposed, where the tools often include experiences of local spatial relations as well as map representations that can help them to integrate those experiences together into a usable framework for spatial reasoning.

Since these studies demonstrate clearly that first-grade children are capable of understanding and using the symbolic aspects of maps, we suggest that greater exposure to them at this age, along with some encouragement to improve mental rotation skills and to interpret the less pictorial and more iconic symbolism that many maps rely on, could help children of this age group toward maximal effectiveness and confidence in the use of maps and other spatial representations. This is a useful skill in several subjects later on in the school curriculum, and indeed across the life span.

To summarize, our research suggests that exposure to survey representations such as maps induces spontaneous use in some types of spatial problem-solving by the age of 7–10 years, at least for children living in a midwestern U.S. suburban area. This implies that making maps available to children by this age can encourage their use and appreciation of such external representations.

NOTE

1. We had used a relative rather than an absolute task here, owing to concerns about the artifactual nature of most large-scale distance estimate tools used with children in previous studies. If the child has to scale down the distance artificially to a straight-line rule or row of lights, this adds a level of artifice and transformation to the task that may confound the results. Children's ranking scores were then weighted by difficulty (i.e., according to the size of the actual difference in distances to the two landmarks).

REFERENCES

Acredolo, L. P. (1977). Developmental-changes in ability to coordinate perspectives of a large-scale space. *Developmental Psychology, 13*(1), 1–8.

Allen, G. L. (1981). A developmental perspective on the effects of "subdividing" macrospatial experience. *Journal of Experimental Psychology: Human Learning & Memory, 7*(2), 120–132.

Ambrose, G. V. (2000). Sighted children's knowledge of environmental concepts and ability to orient in an unfamiliar residential environment. *Journal of Visual Impairment & Blindness, 94*(8), 509–521.

Anooshian, L. J., & Young, D. (1981). Developmental changes in cognitive maps of a familiar neighborhood. *Child Development, 52,* 341–348.

Axia, G., Bremner, J. G., Deluca, P., & Andreasen, G. (1998). Children drawing Europe: The effects of nationality, age and teaching. *British Journal of Developmental Psychology, 16,* 423–437.

Bertin, J. (1967). *Semiologie graphique: Les diagrammes, les réseaux, les cartes.* Paris: Mouton & Gauthier-Villars.

Bertin, J. (1983). *The semiology of graphics* (W. J. Berg, trans.). Madison: University of Wisconsin Press.

Blades, M., Blaut, J. M., Darvizeh, Z., Elguea, S., Sowden, S., Soni, D., et al. (1998). A cross-cultural study of young children's mapping abilities. *Transactions of the Institute of British Geographers (New Series), 23,* 269–277.

Blades, M., & Cooke, Z. (1994). Young children's ability to understand a model as a spatial representation. *Journal of Genetic Psychology, 155*(2), 201–218.

Blades, M., & Spencer, C. (1990). The development of 3- to 6-year-olds' map using ability: The relative importance of landmarks and map alignment. *Journal of Genetic Psychology, 151*(2), 181–194.

Blaut, J. M., McCleary, G. F., & Blaut, A. S. (1970). Environmental mapping in young children. *Environment & Behavior, 2*, 335–349.

Carey, S. (1990). Cognitive development. In D. N. Osherson & E. E. Smith (Eds.), *Thinking: An invitation to cognitive science* (Vol. 3, pp. 147–172). Cambridge, MA: MIT Press.

Cornell, E. H., Heth, C. D., & Skoczylas, M. J. (1999). The nature and use of route expectancies following incidental learning. *Journal of Environmental Psychology, 19*(3), 209–229.

Cousins, J. H., Siegel, A. W., & Maxwell, S. E. (1983). Way finding and cognitive mapping in large-scale environments: A test of a developmental model. *Journal of Experimental Child Psychology, 35*, 1–20.

Davies, C., & Pederson, E. (2001). Grid patterns and cultural expectations in urban wayfinding. In D. R. Montello (Ed.), *Spatial information theory: Foundations of geographic information science. International conference, COSIT 2001, proceedings* (pp. 400–414). Berlin: Springer.

Elliot, J. (1987). *The city in maps: Urban mapping to 1900*. London: British Library.

Gombrich, E. H. (1977). *Art and illusion: A study in the psychology of pictorial representation* (5th ed.). London: Phaidon Press.

Göncü, A., & Klein, E. L. (Eds.). (2001). *Children in play, story and school*. New York: Guilford Press.

Herman, J. F., Heins, J. A., & Cohen, D. S. (1987). Children's spatial knowledge of their neighborhood environment. *Journal of Applied Developmental Psychology, 8*(1), 1–15.

Herman, J. F., & Siegel, A. W. (1978). Development of cognitive mapping of the large-scale environment. *Journal of Experimental Child Psychology, 26*(3), 389–406.

Hermer, L., & Spelke, E. S. (1994, July 7). A geometric process for spatial re-orientation in young children. *Nature, 370*, 57–59.

Hirtle, S., & Heidorn, P. (1993). The structure of cognitive maps: Representations and processes. In T. M. Gärling & R. G. Golledge (Eds.), *Behavior and Environment: Psychological and geographical approaches* (pp. 170–192). Amsterdam: Elsevier.

Hirtle, S., & Jonides, J. (1985). Evidence of hierarchies in cognitive maps. *Memory & Cognition, 13*(3), 208–217.

Lee, K., & Karmiloff-Smith, A. (1996). The development of external symbol systems: The child as notator. In R. Gelman & T. K.-F. Au (Eds.), *Perceptual and cognitive development* (pp. 185–211). San Diego, CA: Academic Press.

Lehnung, M., Leplow, B., Haaland, V. O., Mehdorn, M., & Ferstl, R. (2003). Pointing accuracy in children is dependent on age, sex and experience. *Journal of Environmental Psychology, 23*(4), 419–425.

Liben, L. S. (1999). Developing an understanding of external spatial representations. In I. E. Sigel (Ed.), *Development of mental representation: Theories and applications* (pp. 297–321). Mahwah, NJ: Lawrence Erlbaum.

Liben, L. S., & Downs, R. M. (2001). Geography for young children: Maps as tools for learning environments. In S. L. Golbeck (Ed.), *Psychological perspectives on early childhood education: Reframing dilemmas in research and practice* (pp. 220–252). Mahwah, NJ: Lawrence Erlbaum.

Loewenstein, J., & Gentner, D. (2005). Relational language and the development of relational mapping. *Cognitive Psychology, 50*, 315–353.

McNamara, T. (1986). Mental representations of spatial relations. *Cognitive Psychology, 18*, 87–121.

Millar, S. (1994). *Understanding and representing space: Theory and evidence from studies with blind and sighted children*. Oxford: Clarendon Press.

Montello, D. (1993). Scale and multiple psychologies of space. In A. U. Frank & I. Campari (Eds.), *Spatial information theory: A theoretical basis for GIS. Proceedings of COSIT '93* (Lecture Notes in Computer Science Vol. 716, pp. 312–321). Berlin: Springer-Verlag.

Norman, D. K. (1980). A comparison of children's spatial reasoning: Rural Appalachia, suburban, and urban New England. *Child Development, 51*, 288–291.

Plester, B., Richards, J., Blades, M., & Spencer, C. (2002). Young children's ability to use aerial photographs as maps. *Journal of Environmental Psychology, 22*(1–2), 29–47.

Plumert, J. M., Ewert, K., & Spear, S. J. (1995). The early development of children's communication about nested spatial relations. *Child Development, 66*, 959–969.

Presson, C. C. (1982). The development of map-reading skills. *Child Development, 53*(1), 196–199.

Siegel, A. W., & White, S. H. (1975). The development of spatial representations of large-scale environments. In H. W. Reese (Ed.), *Advances in child development and behavior* (Vol. 10, pp. 9–55). New York: Academic Press.

Sluzenski, J., Newcombe, N. S., & Satlow, E. (2004). Knowing where things are in the second year of life: Implications for hippocampal development. *Journal of Cognitive Neuroscience, 16*(8), 1443–1451.

Spencer, C., Blades, M., & Morsley, K. (1989). *The child in the physical environment: The development of spatial knowledge and cognition*. Chichester: John Wiley & Sons.

Taylor, H., & Tversky, B. (1992). Spatial mental models derived from survey and route descriptions. *Journal of Memory & Language, 31*(2), 261–292.

Thompson, B. (1984). *Canonical correlation analysis: Uses and interpretation*. Beverly Hills, CA: Sage.

Thorndyke, P., & Hayes-Roth, B. (1982). Differences in spatial knowledge acquired from maps and navigation. *Cognitive Psychology, 14*, 560–589.

Tversky, B. (1992). Distortions in cognitive maps. *Geoforum, 23*(2), 131–138.

Tversky, B. (1993). Cognitive maps, cognitive collages, and spatial mental models. In A. U. Frank & I. Campari (Eds.), *Spatial information theory: A theoretical basis for GIS. Proceedings of COSIT '93* (Lecture Notes in Computer Science Vol. 716, pp. 14–24). Berlin: Springer-Verlag.

Uttal, D. H. (1996). Angles and distances: Children's and adults' reconstruction and scaling of spatial configurations. *Child Development, 67*, 2763–2779.

Uttal, D. H. (2000). Seeing the big picture: Map use and the development of spatial cognition. *Developmental Science, 3*(3), 247–264 (including commentaries and response: 247–286).

Uttal, D. H., Fisher, J. A., & Taylor, H. A. (2006). Words and maps: Developmental changes in mental models of spatial information acquired from descriptions and depictions. *Developmental Science, 9*(2), 221–235.

Uttal, D. H., & Wellman, H. M. (1989). Young children's representation of spatial information acquired from maps. *Developmental Psychology, 25*(1), 128–138.

Vasilyeva, M., & Huttenlocher, J. (2004). Early development of scaling ability. *Developmental Psychology, 40*(5), 682–690.

Vosmik, J. R., & Presson, C. C. (2004). Children's response to natural map misalignment during wayfinding. *Journal of Cognition & Development*, 5(3), 317–336.

Vygotsky, L. S. (1978). *Mind in society: The development of higher psychological processes* (M. Cole, V. John-Steiner, S. Scribner, & E. Souberman, Eds.). Cambridge, MA: Harvard University Press.

Yeap, W. K., & Jefferies, M. E. (2000). On early cognitive mapping. *Spatial Cognition & Computation*, 2(2), 85–116.

11

COMMENTARY: LINKING INTERNAL REPRESENTATIONS TO THE EXTERNAL WORLD VIA SPATIAL RELATIONS

Laura Carlson

The spatial relations among objects, people, and places are critical for a wide variety of daily tasks. Consider, for example, the activities that are involved in preparing for your child to attend a friend's birthday party. First, you need to get a present. This may involve looking up in the Yellow Pages the location of the new toy store just constructed across town and reading the map listed in its advertisement. Next you need to generate a route from your home to the toy store, and update your position as you navigate along this route. Once you are at the toy store, you and your child need to pick out a present. This will undoubtedly involve many endless repetitions of pointing out to your child a candidate object on a shelf and asking, "What about this [name of toy] as a present?" Once you get home, you need to wrap the present. This involves estimating the size of the present and cutting the appropriate amount of wrapping paper. Because your child wants to help put on the tape, this involves specifying the location of the tape dispenser in the desk drawer so that your child can retrieve it, and then conveying how much tape to use and where to put it.

Within each of these activities, the usefulness of spatial information depends upon a connection between an underlying internal spatial representation and the external information available in the world. For example, in reading a map, one must link the symbols and relations that are specified

248

Table 11.1 Spatial Information and Cognitive Processes Involved in a Common Activity

Activity	Spatial Information	Cognitive Process	Chapter
Reading the map in the toy store advertisement	Symbols on map and their relations	Connecting map symbols and real-world entities	Chapter 9
Driving to the toy store	Location of store and home	Updating one's position while navigating from home to store	Chapter 10
Indicating a present	Location of present relative to other objects and to the shelves	Identifying objects by their locations	Chapter 8
Cutting the wrapping paper	Size of paper and size of present	Estimating and comparing spatial features	Chapter 6
Getting the tape	Memory for location of tape	Formulating a spatial description that specifies the correct drawer containing tape	Chapter 7

This table provides a list of possible activities related to sending your child to a friend's birthday party, a sample of the type of spatial information and cognitive processes at work within these activities, and the chapters that are loosely affiliated with these representations and processes.

on the map to their corresponding entities and relations in the world. In navigating, the appearance of various landmarks must be used to mentally update one's position along the route. In pointing and labeling a possible present on the shelf in the toy store, one must link the spatial gesture and the object name to the correct target. In cutting the wrapping paper, one must visually compare the spatial features of the present and the paper. Finally, when the tape is needed, one must translate knowledge of its spatial location into a verbal description that enables the child to find it. Table 11.1 summarizes each of these activities and provides an example of the type of critical spatial information and the cognitive process that operates on such information that is necessary to accomplish each of these activities.

Each of the chapters in this section focuses on the developmental changes and underlying mechanisms at work in linking an underlying spatial representation with external information. Indeed, each chapter can be loosely affiliated with one of the processes listed in Table 11.1. In chapter 9, Liben and Myers focus on the link between components on a map and components of real-world space. In the activity described above, reading the map in the toy store advertisement corresponds to the processes by which the symbols and spatial features on the map would be interpreted, and the manner in which they would be linked to objects and relations in the environment.

Davies and Uttal in chapter 10 focus on the interfaces among navigation, written descriptions, and map use. One central point in this work is that learning is restricted in navigation to serial input, much like learning from a set of spatial descriptions; in contrast, learning with maps bypasses this restriction because maps present information about multiple spatial relations simultaneously. In the above activity, such a distinction is relevant to representing the location of the toy store on a map rather than simply providing a street address or a list of directions to its location.

In chapter 8, Smith, Maouene, and Hidaka focus on the role that location plays in binding names to objects. They argue that the use of the spatial information (e.g., the body's orientation in space) is a critical bootstrapping technique that facilitates learning. In the activity described above, this process is presumably at play when you gesture to an object and ask whether it would be a suitable present. The gesture highlights the object's location and assists in mapping an unfamiliar name onto the object.

Quinn in chapter 6 focuses on the categorization of spatial features in displays. Specifically, in a familiarization phase, he presents preverbal infants with sequences of displays that are similar with respect to certain spatial features but different with respect to other spatial features. For example, the displays may show objects in various locations above a reference line. In a test phase, he then shows infants novel displays that illustrate the same spatial relation (*above*) or a different spatial relation (*below*). Based on infants' preferences for novel displays, he can infer the type of spatial features that are encoded and compared across displays. In the above activity, this is similar in spirit to encoding and mentally comparing the spatial features related to the size of the present and the spatial dimensions of the wrapping paper. Note that the features under examination in Quinn's work and in the sample activity are perceptual, and although the particular features at work are different (features defining above vs. size), the focus is on the representation of these perceptual features and the ability to apply the representation to other situations. In Quinn's paradigm, this means applying the representation encoded during familiarization to test trials; in the sample activity this would be analogous to applying the representation of the size of the present to the rolled out wrapping paper to determine where to cut.

Finally, in chapter 7, Choi and McDonough focus on the spatial features that are explicitly encoded in a language and the spatial features that define spatial categories. In the sample described above, the child's ability to successfully find the tape dispenser will depend in part upon the linguistic description of its location. This is because the linguistic description will necessarily highlight certain features at the expense of other features. If the features that are highlighted linguistically are compatible with the features that are present in the child's representation of the kitchen, drawers, and tape, then the description should facilitate search.

In the remainder of this commentary, I evaluate one example of the link between the underlying spatial representation and the external information that is presented in each chapter, addressing the developmental changes that take place. Specifically, for chapter 9, I focus on the features of maps that affect learning; for chapter 10, on spatial perspective; for chapter 8, on the use of location information to assist identification; for chapter 6, on the representation of the spatial features that give rise to spatial categories for projective relations such as *above* and *below*; and for chapter 7, on the relation between linguistic features and the spatial features that define containment and support categories. Within each section, I highlight the issues that offer a useful contribution to researchers in adult spatial cognition and point out issues from the adult spatial cognition literature that could be profitably examined developmentally.

11.1 CHAPTER 9: PERCEPTUAL AND SPATIAL CORRESPONDENCES

Liben and Myers describe an extensive and impressive body of work on the development of children's understanding of maps. They focus on three types of correspondences: (1) representational correspondences, such as linking a cross symbol on a map to a church in the world; (2) geometric correspondences, such as negotiating differences on the map and in the world with respect to scale, viewing angle, and viewing azimuth; and (3) self-space-map relations, such as linking where you are on the map to where you are in the world. Throughout, the authors assess map learning with natural large-scale environments, consistent with their model in which the developmental trajectories of the various aspects of map learning are affected by cognitive, social, experiential, and physical/biological components, encapsulated in the idea of the "embodied" child.

One important question stemming from this work is why children find it so hard to establish the link between a map and a large-scale, natural environment. An interesting research avenue related to correctly linking information from a map to the external world would be to assess the extent to which various features of the maps being learned affect the ability to establish these correspondences. For example, the distortions in perception and memory for maps in which relations are regularized (e.g., Tversky & Schiano, 1989) may cause difficulty in linking to the real-world relations that may not be as regularized. Another important feature might be the scale of the map. For example, in the adult spatial language literature, there is a preference to describe some environments (e.g., apartments that can be viewed from a single vantage point) using a gaze tour perspective (Ullmer-Ehrich, 1982), a perspective that differs in fundamental ways from a route or survey perspective (Taylor & Tversky, 1996). More generally, when the features of a given environment encourage the use of particular perspectives, does the ability to establish representational, geometric, and map-space-self correspondences change? Finally, as Liben and Myers point out at the end of chapter 9, important work in this area will link the competencies in representing spatial relations observed for infants by Quinn (chapter 6), Choi and McDonough (chapter 7), and Smith et al. (chapter 8) to the more complex domain of map learning by older children.

11.2 CHAPTER 10: SPATIAL PERSPECTIVE

Our direct experience of a given space is both simultaneous, with respect to the objects and relations within our immediate line of sight, and sequential, with respect to our need to move our heads and bodies in order to bring nonvisible objects into view. In a similar manner, space can be represented in a simultaneous fashion or a sequential fashion. For example, the most common type of map portrays information about an environment from a *survey* perspective, a bird's-eye view of objects and their relations, most typically from an aerial viewpoint that is outside of the environment. Davies and Uttal argue in chapter 10 that the relational information provided by such maps may be particularly useful because maps convey multiple relations among objects simultaneously. In contrast, verbal descriptions of space are sequential, relating one object to another in a serial fashion. Davies and Uttal make the interesting point that navigation through space is similarly sequential, in that relational information is obtained in a serial fashion. The authors focus on the simultaneous presentation of multiple object relations as a key benefit of maps. Specifically, they examine the developmental trajectory of the use of maps to solve various problem-solving tasks and describe lab-based and field-based experiments that demonstrate a benefit in various spatial tasks when information is learned via a map as opposed to via a set of written descriptions. This benefit is attributed in part to the simultaneous presentation of spatial relations in the maps that enables a better link between the external world and its internal representation.

Two questions follow from this result, one based on the type of written descriptions that were used, and one based on the spatial tasks used to assess learning. There are different types of written descriptions that present spatial information sequentially but from different perspectives. For example, descriptions can adopt a *survey* perspective that is outside of the environment, such as, "The house is to the north of the mountains and to the west of the river." In contrast, a description can adopt a *route* perspective that is within the scene, presenting information as it is experienced while navigating through space. Such information is inherently tied to one's movement and one's own perspective within the environment, and is thus arguably experienced in a serial fashion. For example, the description "The house is to the left of the grocery store" is a route perspective because one needs to know the vantage point of the person producing the description in order to correctly interpret the projective term "left" (Levelt, 1984; Taylor & Tversky, 1992). The written descriptions that were used in the studies described by Davies and Uttal seem to be route based (e.g., "The bear is to the left of the frog" in Uttal, Fisher, & Taylor, 2006). Thus, one reason that the learning by written descriptions condition may have been difficult (relative to the map learning condition) is because the descriptions required converting from a route perspective to a survey perspective.

It is interesting to note that Taylor and Tversky (1992) have shown that adults can successfully convert from a route to survey perspective. Thus, one contribution of the results of Uttal et al. (2006) is to indicate the point at which children can similarly integrate information from a set of descriptions into a survey perspective. More generally, the benefit observed from learning from maps relative to written descriptions makes an important contribution to the adult literature, where the question of how survey and route representations develop (route first then survey, or both simultaneously) remains unanswered (for discussion, see Taylor, Naylor, & Chechile, 1999).

It is important to note, however, that such a trajectory does not necessarily indicate a priority for survey information over route information, such that once the ability to integrate across descriptions is established, this then becomes the default or preferred representation. Rather, it seems more likely that the acquisition of the ability to integrate information enables flexibility in the type of representation that can be created during learning. Such flexibility would be important because different spatial tasks seem to require different types of spatial information. Indeed, research on adults has shown that navigation through an environment facilitates performance on some spatial tasks (i.e., estimates of route distances and degree of change in orientation needed to see certain objects), whereas learning from a map facilitates performance on other spatial tasks (i.e., estimates of relative position) (Thorndyke & Hayes-Roth, 1982). In addition, Sholl (1987) found that relations among objects were equally accessible when learned from a map, consistent with the idea that maps present such information simultaneously. However, when learned via navigation, objects imagined in the direction of the visual field were more accessible, consistent with the idea that locations were encoded with respect to how they were encountered and perceived. Finally, Taylor et al. (1999) showed that learning condition, spatial goals, and type of perspective task (route or survey) strongly influenced performance.

Thus, with respect to the spatial tasks used to assess learning, it may also be possible that the benefit from learning information from maps relative to written descriptions observed by Uttal et al. (2006) is due to the selection of tasks (i.e., pointing and model construction) that are best solved on the basis of survey rather than route information. If that is the case, then one might expect to see a benefit for learning from descriptions rather than learning from maps when spatial tasks are selected that can best be solved on the basis of route information. More generally, given the flexibility exhibited within the adult literature, an important developmental question would be how children learn to shift flexibly between route and survey representations. In particular, how do they identify and use cues from goals, the learning environment, and task to effectively select the most appropriate representation? Are there differences in the ability to link to these different types of representations based on the cues that are provided from the external world?

11.3 CHAPTER 8: USING LOCATION
FOR IDENTIFICATION

Smith, Maouene, and Hidaka focus on the way in which the body assists in the processes and representations that are critical for early word learning. Of particular interest is the description of the research of Smith, Samuelson, and Spencer (2006), in which the body's orientation in space facilitates linking the name of an object with the object in the real world. In this study, a novel object is presented to a child to play with; this object is located on one side of the child (e.g., left). The child is then presented with a second novel object to play with, located on the other side (e.g., right). These objects are never named for the child. The experimenter then takes the objects away, and out of sight puts them into containers. The containers are then placed in front of the child, one on the left and one on the right. The experimenter then looks into one of the containers (e.g., left) and labels the object (i.e., "I see a modi"). Critically, the child never sees the object in the container while hearing the label. Later, in a test phase, both objects are placed in a neutral location with additional objects, and the child is asked to pick up the modi. If the child encoded the object's location as a critical feature, the child should infer that the container on the left holds that particular object. If this is the case, then the child should be more likely to select that object than the object that was played with on the right, despite never seeing the object and hearing its name at the same time. Smith, Samuelson, and Spencer (2006) found that with consistent presentation of the object to a particular side prior to the test phase, children were more likely to pick the same-side object, indicating a mapping based on a spatial feature.

One interesting question is the nature of this spatial feature. In chapter 8, Smith, Maouene, and Hidaka interpret the feature as linked to the body's orientation in space and subsequent allocation of attention to that side rather than as a spatial feature per se. For example, they describe other experiments that show that large movements disrupt the linking, indicating that the name is not linked generally to an egocentric direction. For example, if the child is turned prior to the test phase, the label is not linked instead to whatever new object now appears on the left. Nor is it linked to an objective location in space. Rather, it seems that the body's current position in space provides a set of temporary cues with which one may represent the location of surrounding objects; however, when the body moves, these cues seem to be replaced by ones defined by the new position.

This work has implications for the adult literature on spatial language use because it suggests that temporary episodic representations mediate the link between the external world and internal representations. That is, this link is not simply a transfer of information from one form (perceptual) to another (conceptual). Rather, the physical body that is experiencing the external world and internally representing it has a direct role in defining the way in which the information is encoded and ultimately represented, consistent with Barsalou's (1999) ideas on perceptual symbol systems. Nevertheless, internal representations are ultimately constructed that are enduring and that are not limited to current body position. Future adult work needs to focus on the way in which the momentary experience of objects and their spatial relations is abstracted from these transitory representations to a longer lasting internal representation.

11.4 CHAPTER 6: SPATIAL FEATURES FOR PROJECTIVE RELATIONS

Quinn focuses on infants' prelinguistic concepts of spatial relations, the perceptual spatial features that underlie spatial concept formation, and the implications that these features may have for later spatial language learning. In his tasks, he familiarizes infants to a particular spatial relation (e.g., *above*) by showing them displays containing lines and various geometric stimuli (i.e., diamond, arrow, plus) in a given spatial configuration (e.g., diamond above the line). He then provides two displays, a novel display that depicts the familiarized relation (i.e., *above*) and a novel display that depicts a new relation (e.g., *below*). If infants can represent the spatial relation *above* on the basis of the familiarization phase, then they should show a preference for the display depicting the novel spatial relation (in this case, *below*). Such a preference is taken to mean that the infant has formed a category corresponding to the spatial relation *above* and is able to successfully discriminate that category from one corresponding to *below*. The lack of such a preference is taken to mean that the relation was not initially learned during the familiarization phase—in that case, both test stimuli would be seen as novel, with no ensuing preference for one over another.

In a series of studies using this paradigm, Quinn observed three patterns. First, simple relations (e.g., *above*) are learned before compound relations (e.g., *above-left*). Second, one-object (landmark) relations (e.g., *above*) are learned before two-object (framework) relations (e.g., *between*). Third, there is a shift in learning from concrete information to abstract information, such that initial category learning is tied to the specific geometric stimuli that are presented, with generalization to novel geometric stimuli occurring later.

These findings have important implications for adult work in spatial language, particularly for research that examines the formulation of spatial descriptions. For example, Carlson and Hill (in press) summarize three studies in which adults were presented with displays of objects and asked to produce spatial descriptions in response to queries about the location of one of the objects in the display. The spatial relations among the objects were manipulated across displays, and the preferences for using different types of spatial terms were assessed. For example, descriptions were coded as to whether objects were related with a simple relation such as above versus a complex relation such as above and left. One key finding was that simple descriptions are largely preferred over complex descriptions (see also Munnich, Landau, & Dosher, 2001), consistent with Quinn's developmental progression. It would be of interest to determine whether Quinn's other progressions are mirrored in adults' preferences for spatial descriptions. This may be the case. For example, Plumert, Carswell, DeVet, and Ihrig (1995) found that adults mirrored young children's preferences in using the terms "on" and "in" over the term "by." Note, however, that this does not have to be the case. Once both simple and complex are acquired, adults may have no strong preference for the earlier acquired relation, but rather use the one that seems most appropriate. Interestingly, data from Carlson and Hill (2006) indicate a preference for using a between relation for certain displays containing three objects arranged in arrowhead configuration (i.e., ">" or ">"), with the top and bottom objects vertically aligned, positioned on the outer edge of the arrow and the middle object placed at the point of the arrow.

One question for infant work that emerges from the adult literature is to examine whether the spatial categories that infants acquire are based on the same types of spatial features as adult categories of space. Spatial terms such as *above* and *below* are defined with respect to a reference frame, a conceptual representation consisting of axes that serves to map the linguistic spatial term onto space. This representation contains a number of parameters whose values configure the space (Logan & Sadler, 1996; for evidence for each parameter, see Carlson, 2003). For example, the orientation parameter defines the axes as vertical (above/below) or horizontal (front/back or left/right). The direction parameter defines the endpoints of each axis (above vs. below). These parameters are hierarchical in nature and are thought to be represented separately (Hoffman, Landau & Pagani, 2003; Landau & Hoffman, 2005; Logan, 1995; McCloskey & Rapp, 2000). For example, Hoffman et al. (2003) observed that patients with Williams syndrome have impaired representation of direction but not axial structure in a block construction task, more often placing blocks at the opposite endpoint within the correct axis (e.g., below rather than above) than on a different axis (e.g., left rather than above). Thus, it would be interesting to determine whether infants acquire categories that are differentiated by axis (e.g., above vs. right) before they acquire categories that are on the same axis but differentiated by the endpoints (e.g., above vs. below or left vs. right). This would indicate that particular features of the external world (e.g., object relations corresponding to axes) may be easier to link to internal representations than others (e.g., endpoint relations).

11.5 CHAPTER 7: SPATIAL FEATURES FOR CONTAINMENT AND SUPPORT

While Quinn focuses on the linking between an internal preverbal spatial concept acquired on the basis of perceptual features in chapter 6, in chapter 7 Choi and McDonough focus on the role of language in mediating this relationship. They start from a similar position as Quinn—that acquisition of linguistic spatial categories is predicated on an underlying spatial concept that is acquired preverbally. In support of this idea, they discuss data that illustrate that preverbal infants can distinguish between two types of containment, tight fitting and loose fitting. This finding is observed regardless of whether the ambient language that surrounds the infant linguistically makes this distinction (as is the case in Korean) or does not make this distinction (as is the case in English) (McDonough, Choi, & Mandler, 2003). Thus, preverbal infants (around 9–14 months old) seem to be quite flexible in the categories that they can develop. Choi and McDonough argue further that the language being acquired has an additional influence on these categories, prioritizing some over others, such that at a subsequent developmental stage, attention is biased toward spatial features that correspond to linguistic distinctions. For example, English children around 24–29 months show a loss of sensitivity to the tight-fitting versus loose-fitting distinction, while such sensitivity is maintained by Korean children at this age (Choi, in press). Moreover, there is some evidence that adults may not spontaneously attend to features that are not consistent with distinctions in their language (McDonough et al., 2003).

One might ask whether this argument leads to an assumption that the spatial categories underlying language and perception are the same. Within the adult spatial language literature, this has been a somewhat controversial claim, at least with respect to projective relations (for extended discussions, see Crawford, Regier, & Huttenlocher, 2000; Hayward & Tarr, 1995). At a minimum, it seems to assume a common set of features that are derived from the external world and possibly integrated into a single representation. Yet, how does one derive the set of features? One could follow the approach in chapter 7, starting with the contrasts that are marked in a language and then assessing whether those contrasts are attended in a nonlinguistic task (for excellent work in this tradition, see Levinson, 2003). However, the failure to obtain evidence for the contrast in a nonlinguistic task does not necessarily mean that such a feature is not represented or cannot be represented, as Choi and McDonough acknowledge. Rather than start with the contrasts marked explicitly in the language, another approach to deriving the set of features could be to start with the underlying semantics of the spatial relations as analyzed by linguists and psycholinguists (e.g., Coventry & Garrod, 2004; Langacker, 1987; Miller & Johnson-Laird, 1976, pp. 374–410; Regier, 1996; Talmy, 1983). One potential problem is that it is not always clear whether these features would correspond to a single underlying category or a set of subcategories. Indeed, spatial terms are notoriously polysemous, making it difficult to come up with one common underlying set of features (e.g., for the case of "over"; see Brugman, 1988). Thus, I would endorse the suggestion for future work in this area proposed by Choi and McDonough of uncovering the underlying semantic categories for these spatial relations. This work would presumably occur at the adult level to define the established categories and their structure. It would also be important that this be done separately for different languages. Then, once these established categories are better understood, the features that are derived from them can be effectively tested developmentally and contrasted cross-linguistically. This is similar in spirit to Quinn's approach, in which one starts with the nonlinguistic spatial categories and then later maps these to language. Regardless of the approach at deriving the set of features, such a set is a fundamental component of the linkage between the internal representation and the external world.

11.6 CONCLUSIONS

The chapters in this section represent the current state of research investigating our understanding of thinking and talking about spatial relations. The chapters are united in that they all focus on spatial features that assist in the links between cognitive representations and the external world. One could think of the spatial features as a set of parameters that are represented internally; the link would be the assignment of a value to the parameters from within a set of alternatives. For example, the spatial relation between two objects might be represented internally with respect to a spatial category, such as above, but the link to the external world would provide additional specifics about this relation (e.g., distance, angular direction, and so on; see Carlson & Van Deman, 2004). For example, prepositions such as "above" convey information about the direction of one object with respect to another; nevertheless, during the encoding of this information, the distance between the two objects that is present in the external world is also represented. The goal of future research in this area should be to further examine which set of critical features best mediate the link between the external world and internal representations, to examine how this set changes as a function of task (map learning, navigation, spatial descriptions), and to determine the developmental progression of the acquisition of such features.

REFERENCES

Barsalou, L. W. (1999). Perceptual symbol systems. *Behavioral & Brain Sciences*, 22, 577–660.
Brugman, C. (1988). *The story of "over": Polysemy, semantics, and the structure of the lexicon*. New York: Garland Press.
Carlson, L. A. (2003). Using spatial language. *Psychology of Learning & Motivation*, 43, 127–158.
Carlson, L. A., & Hill, P. L. (in press). *Formulating spatial descriptions across various dialogue contexts*. In K. Coventry, J. Bateman, & T. Tenbrink (Eds.), *Spatial language and dialogue*. Oxford: Oxford University Press.
Carlson, L. A. & Hill, P. L. (2006). *Spatial descriptions of targets in multiple object scenes*. Unpublished manuscript.
Carlson, L. A., & Van Deman, S. R. (2004). The space in spatial language. *Journal of Memory & Language*, 51, 418–436.
Choi, S. (2006). Influence of language-specific input on spatial cognition. Categories of containment. *First Language*, 26(2), 207–232.

Coventry, K. R., & Garrod, S. C. (2004). *Saying, seeing and acting: The psychological semantics of spatial prepositions*. New York: Psychology Press.

Crawford, L. E., Regier, T., & Huttenlocher, J. (2000). Linguistic and non-linguistic spatial categorization. *Cognition, 75*, 209–235.

Hayward, W. G., & Tarr, M. J. (1995). Spatial language and spatial representation. *Cognition, 55*, 39–84.

Hoffman, J. E., Landau, B., & Pagani, B. (2003). Spatial breakdown in spatial construction: Evidence from eye fixations in children with Williams syndrome. *Cognitive Psychology, 46*, 260–301.

Landau, B., & Hoffman, J. E. (2005). Parallels between spatial cognition and spatial language: Evidence from William's syndrome. *Journal of Memory & Language, 53*, 163–185.

Langacker, R. W. (1987). *Foundations of cognitive grammar: Vol. 1. Theoretical prerequisites*. Stanford, CA: Stanford University Press.

Levelt, W. J. M. (1984). Some perceptual limitations on talking about space. In A. J. van Doorn, W. A. van der Grind, & J. J. Koenderink (Eds.), *Limits in perception* (pp. 323–358). Utrecht: VNU Science Press.

Levinson, S. C. (2003). *Space in language and cognition*. Cambridge: Cambridge University Press.

Logan, G. D. (1995). Linguistic and conceptual control of visual spatial attention. *Cognitive Psychology, 28*, 103–174.

Logan, G. D., & Sadler, D. D. (1996). A computational analysis of the apprehension of spatial relations. In P. Bloom, M. A. Peterson, L. Nadel, & M. Garrett (Eds.), *Language and space* (pp. 493–529). Cambridge, MA: MIT Press.

McCloskey, M., & Rapp, B. (2000). Attention-referenced visual representations: Evidence from impaired visual localization. *Journal of Experimental Psychology: Human Perception & Performance, 26*, 917–933.

McDonough, L., Choi, S., & Mandler, J. M. (2003). Understanding spatial relations: Flexible infants, lexical adults. *Cognitive Psychology, 46*, 229–259.

Miller, G. A., & Johnson-Laird, P. N. (1976). *Language and perception*. Cambridge, MA: Harvard University Press.

Munnich, E., Landau, B., & Dosher, B. (2001). Spatial language and spatial representation: a cross-linguistic comparison. *Cognition, 81*, 171–207.

Plumert, J. M., Carswell, C., DeVet, K., & Ihrig, D. (1995). The content and organization of communication about object locations. *Journal of Memory & Language, 34*, 477–498.

Regier, T. (1996). *The human semantic potential: Spatial language and constrained connectionism*. Cambridge, MA: MIT Press.

Sholl, M. J. (1987). Cognitive maps are orienting schemata. *Journal of Experimental Psychology: Learning, Memory & Cognition, 13*, 615–628.

Smith, L. B., Samuelson, L. K., & Spencer, J. P. (2006). *The role of spatial attention in binding names to things*. Unpublished manuscript.

Talmy, L. (1983). How language structures space. In H. L. Pick & L. P. Acredolo (Eds.), *Spatial orientation: Theory, research and application* (pp. 225–282). New York: Plenum Press.

Taylor, H. A., Naylor, S. J., & Chechile, N. A. (1999). Goal-specific influences on the representation of spatial perspective. *Memory & Cognition, 27*, 309–319.

Taylor, H., & Tversky, B. (1992). Spatial mental models derived from survey and route descriptions. *Journal of Memory & Language, 31*, 261–292.

Taylor, H., & Tversky, B. (1996). Perspective in spatial descriptions. *Journal of Memory & Language*, *35*, 371–391.

Thorndyke, P., & Hayes-Roth, B. (1982). Differences in spatial knowledge acquired from maps and navigation. *Cognitive Psychology*, *14*, 560–589.

Tversky, B., & Schiano, D. (1989). Perceptual and conceptual factors in distortions in memory for graphs and maps. *Journal of Experimental Psychology: General*, *118*, 387–398.

Ullmer-Ehrich, V. (1982). The structure of living space descriptions. In R. J. Jarvella & W. Klein (Eds.), *Speech, place and action* (pp. 219–249). Chichester: John Wiley & Sons.

Uttal, D. H., Fisher, J. A., & Taylor, H. A. (2006). Words and maps: Developmental changes in mental models of spatial information. *Developmental Science*, *9*, 221–235.

III

MAPPING THE NEUROPSYCHOLOGICAL BASES OF SPATIAL DEVELOPMENT

12

EFFECTS OF BLINDNESS AND DEAFNESS ON THE DEVELOPMENT OF SPATIAL PERCEPTION AND COGNITION

Teresa V. Mitchell

Spatial perception and cognition depend on multimodal sources of information (e.g., auditory, visual, vibrotactile, and olfactory information). To behave adaptively in the environment, one must determine where in space these sources of information originate. If they originate from a shared location, the response may be to orient toward that location to identify and possibly respond to the object or event in that location. One must also learn to discriminate and identify objects at a distance on the basis of sometimes significantly limited information, and one must learn how to construct a unified representation of the spatial environment from the disparate information provided by each sensory modality. All of these aspects of spatial perception and cognition—orienting to locations, discriminating and identifying the contents of those locations, and constructing integrated spatial representations—are carried out nearly constantly, more often in parallel than not, and generally highly accurately.

Given the typically multimodal nature of spatial information, what happens when input to one sensory modality is deficient? In this chapter, I consider the consequences of blindness and deafness on spatial perception and cognition. A critical question is whether three-dimensional spatial representations can be developed in the absence of auditory or visual input that are sufficient to support accurate spatial perception and cognition. If not, what suffers in the absence of visual or auditory information? Do the differences between organisms with unimodal sensory loss and those with intact sensory modalities illuminate boundary conditions and other characteristics of spatial cognition, and do they inform our understanding of how spatial perception and cognition unfold during typical development?

12.1 CHARACTERISTICS OF VISUAL AND AUDITORY SPACE

Human beings are overwhelmingly visual creatures. A greater proportion of our brain is devoted to processing visual input than to processing any other sensory modality. Vision is particularly efficient for perceiving space. Several short exposures to an environment, allowing for foveation of multiple regions of the scene, provide enough geometric information to establish a three-dimensional representation that includes information about object number, color, size, texture, distance, and layout. Visual attention research suggests that object localization in the visual field can be rapidly achieved, while object identification occurs only after localization in a serial, deliberate fashion (Kahneman Treisman, & Gibbs, 1992; Treisman, Vieira, & Hayes, 1992). An important limitation of vision is that objects that are outside the visual field or are occluded within it cannot be visually apprehended.

The auditory system, by contrast, does not encode the location of an event or stimulus. It encodes the presence of particular stimulus frequencies, and the location of those frequencies is then derived by integrating responses over many neurons (Recanzone, 2000). Interaural time differences, intensity differences, and spectral differences are computed across input from the two ears, yielding spatial localization of much lower resolution than the visual system (Recanzone, 2003). Audition has one advantage over vision in that it can apprehend events outside of the visual field, as well as occluded objects or events.

As described in the following sections, the reliance of humans on visual information for spatial perception and cognition has driven the types of studies conducted. Most studies of blind humans focus on whether auditory spatial input is sufficient to support behaviors such as localization and locomotion. Studies of deaf humans, on the other hand, focus on questions of visual attention, such as its distribution and effectiveness—not questions of whether input is sufficient, but questions of whether input is efficient.

One theoretical perspective posits that each individual sensory modality dominates those perceptual processes for which it is best suited. This "modality appropriateness" hypothesis posits that vision typically dominates spatial processing because it has greater spatial acuity than audition (Welch & Warren, 1980). By contrast, audition tends to dominate temporal processing because it has greater temporal acuity than vision. Evidence relevant to this hypothesis is provided throughout this chapter. In the final section, I address the implications of unimodal sensory deprivation for this hypothesis.

12.2 NEURAL REPRESENTATIONS OF VISUAL AND AUDITORY SPACE

Animal studies have provided detailed characterizations of the neural representations of auditory and visual space. Neurons in maps of auditory space are arranged according to their sensitivity to sound localization cues like interaural time differences (Moiseff, 1989), while neurons in maps of visual space, by contrast, are organized on the basis of the location of their receptive field, so that neighboring cells also have neighboring receptive fields. These maps exist in subcortical structures (Knudsen & Brainard, 1991), as well as in sensory (Law, Zahs, & Stryker, 1988) and association cortices (Rauschecker & Korte, 1993). The purpose of these maps is to guide the organism's behavior in the spatial environment so that the better tuned the maps are, the better the organism's ability to localize and respond to events in space.

One subcortical structure, the superior colliculus (SC), is a site of very early, basic representation and processing of both auditory and visual space. The auditory and visual maps within this structure are aligned such that a single auditory-visual event will activate a functionally correlated group of auditory and visual neurons in the SC. Studies of barn owls show that manipulations of visual input affect the normal alignment of the auditory and visual maps in the SC. In one study, infant barn owls were fitted with prism spectacles that displaced only the central visual field by 23–34° (Knudsen & Brainard, 1991). After approximately 70 days of experience with the prism spectacles, their visual and auditory maps were examined using single-unit electrophysiology. Alignment of visual and auditory responses to peripheral stimuli was relatively intact. In contrast, visual responses to central stimuli were misaligned to a degree similar to the prismatic offset. Moreover, the auditory neurons responded to a broader range of spatial locations than is normally observed. The authors concluded that in normal development, vision "teaches" auditory spatial localization by narrowing the spatial receptive field of auditory neurons.

Data contradictory to this "teaching hypothesis" have been reported, however. A comparable line of research on ferrets demonstrated that auditory maps in the SC can develop in the absence of visual input. Ferrets acutely and binocularly deprived of visual input prior to eye opening still developed auditory maps in the SC that had normal spatial tuning (King & Carlile, 1993). Furthermore, ferrets binocularly deprived for 6 months or more, regardless of whether the deprivation occurred in infancy or adulthood, showed *better* auditory spatial acuity in the horizontal plane than did sighted ferrets, particularly in response to laterally presented stimuli (King & Parsons, 1999). These results strongly suggest that, while visual input may dominate auditory localization when both sensory modalities are intact, visual input is not *required* in order to establish a valid auditory representation of space in the SC. The fact that spatial acuity was actually higher in the binocularly deprived ferrets suggests that the typical dominance of visual input in spatial localization may, in some instances, serve to suppress the development of auditory spatial acuity.

The principles of creation and calibration of spatial maps in subcortical structures described above also generalize to some extent to maps in cortical regions. Studies of cat auditory localization have focused on properties of the anterior ectosylvian area, a cortical association area that processes visual, auditory, and somatosensory stimuli. In cats binocularly deprived of vision, the relative representation of these sensory modalities in this cortical area shifts. The number of auditory cells that are spatially tuned is much higher than in normally sighted cats (Korte & Rauschecker, 1993), as is the number of somatosensory neurons (Rauschecker & Korte, 1993). This is accompanied by a decrease in the number of visually responsive cells in the anterior ectosylvian area. Finally, binocularly visually deprived cats also show an accompanying enhancement in auditory localization skills that is largest for sounds presented in the periphery and behind the animal (Rauschecker & Kniepert, 1994). Thus, auditory neurons in the cortex, like their counterparts in the SC, do not require visual input to accurately represent space. The fact that auditory localization was superior in visually deprived cats provides further support for the notion that the typical dominance of vision in spatial localization suppresses the development of spatial tuning in auditory neurons, at least in some instances.

Together, these studies show that sensory input is constantly calibrating and recalibrating visual and auditory spatial maps and the correspondence between them. This inherent plasticity allows the organism to develop spatial representations that fit its niche. In typical development, when vision and audition are intact, they work together to create a representation of space that is highly plastic. Short-term manipulations of sensory input (e.g., visual displacement prisms) result in plasticity of spatial processes that, in turn, allow the organism to adapt quickly and efficiently to the new experience. The literature with blind and deaf humans reviewed in this chapter documents the longer term effects of these short-term plasticity mechanisms and ultimately shows how organisms successfully adapt to atypical experience.

The following sections address questions of cross-modal effects on spatial perception and cognition in human children and adults. What happens when input from one modality is deprived? Are spatial maps less precise? Does the precision of the mapping directly correlate with the precision of perception and cognition? If not, what does that tell us about normal spatial processing?

12.3 BLINDNESS

In this section I review studies that address the hypothesis that vision is the "teacher" in spatial computation, which is to say that visual input is necessary for the fidelity of auditory spatial processes (Knudsen & Brainard, 1991). If vision is necessary, then blindness should negatively affect auditory skills such as localization. If vision is not necessary, then blindness should not negatively affect auditory skills. Finally, if auditory localization skills are plastic, then blindness could result in compensatory changes that result in supranormal spatial acuity and localization skills.

12.3.1 Auditory Spatial Acuity and Localization

In the absence of vision, spatial perception and cognition are turned over in large part to the auditory modality. This raises two important questions: (1) whether blindness reduces, enhances, or produces no effect at all on auditory spatial acuity, and (2) how blindness affects auditory localization. Some of the research on neural maps of space outlined above would predict that auditory acuity and localization should require visual input as a guide and would therefore suffer in the absence of vision, while other studies show evidence of auditory compensation as a result of visual deprivation.

Ashmead et al. (1998b) assessed auditory acuity and localization skills in children and adults 6–20 years of age with varying degrees of vision loss, including 22 with congenital blindness. These researchers also studied a comparison group of typically sighted children and adults. All subjects were tested blindfolded in tasks assessing minimal audible angles (i.e., the minimum discriminable distance between two successive auditory stimuli) and in tasks involving reaching and walking to auditory targets. The minimum audible angle in the vertical dimension (elevation) was smaller in visually impaired children than in either sighted children or adults. When subjects were seated 45° from the 0° reference stimulus, minimum audible angles in the horizontal dimension (azimuth) were similar across the three groups. When subjects directly faced the 0° reference, minimum audible angles in the horizontal dimension (azimuth) were smaller in visually impaired than sighted children, but similar to those of sighted adults.

Results from localization tasks that required reaching to an auditory target showed that the three subject groups showed similar reaching errors in elevation and azimuth, but visually impaired children showed smaller reaching errors in the distance dimension. Results from a localization task that required walking to an auditory target indicated that visually impaired children were as good as sighted adults when starting from a stationary position but were better at walking to an auditory target when already in motion. This difference suggests that blind children may be particularly sensitive to dynamic auditory information provided during locomotion. The overall pattern of group differences also held across all analyses when the visually impaired group was restricted to only congenitally blind subjects, suggesting that auditory compensation occurs even when visual experience is absent from birth.

In all, these results strongly support the hypothesis that blindness can result in enhanced auditory perception of spatial information. The fact that enhanced localization skills were documented in young blind children suggests that the functional pressures placed on the auditory system to achieve accurate spatial localization are strong enough to result in early compensatory changes.

12.3.2 Central and Peripheral Space

Further study of auditory localization in the blind has been conducted using both behavioral and event-related potential (ERP) measures. Previous research has shown that sighted individuals are better at localizing auditory events that occur in front of them than at localizing events in the auditory periphery (Teder-Salejarvi, Hillyard, Röder, & Neville, 1999). In essence, there is a gradual decrease in spatial "tuning," or precision of localization, from the center to the periphery. Röder et al. (1999) designed an experiment to test the hypothesis that congenitally blind individuals would have sharper auditory spatial tuning than sighted individuals and that ERP results would indicate activity across posterior (typically visual) brain regions. They employed a free-field auditory apparatus, shown in figure 12.1, that consisted of four speakers in front of the subject (0°, 6°, 12°, and 18° along the azimuth) and four speakers to the right of the subject (72°, 78°, 84°, and 90°). Two short noise bursts were presented, one a frequent "standard" stimulus presented 84% of the time, the second an infrequent "target" stimulus presented 16% of the time. In one block, stimuli were presented in equal distribution across all four frontward speakers, but the subject was directed to respond only to targets that sounded from the 0° location. In another block, stimuli were presented in equal distribution across all four rightward speakers, but subjects were to respond only to target stimuli presented at the 90° location. Head movements were monitored and discouraged throughout the procedure. The dependent measures were correct responses in locating the target sound to the 0° or 90° speakers, and false alarms in incorrectly locating a target that was actually presented at 0° or 90° to the neighboring speakers.

Eight sighted control adults wearing blindfolds and eight congenitally blind adults were tested. Behavioral results showed that blindfolded, sighted adults were better than blind adults at localizing target stimuli to the attended speaker at 0°, but the two groups showed similar spatial "tuning" across the four front speakers, as evidenced by few false alarms. When attending to the 90° speaker, blind and sighted adults were equally good at locating sounds to the 90° speaker, but spatial tuning differed significantly between the two groups. Sighted adults mislocated sounds presented at the attended speaker to the neighboring speakers more often than blind adults did and were more likely to mislocate those sounds to the 72° and 78° speakers than were blind adults. Thus, spatial tuning in the center was similar for the two groups but was sharper in the periphery for blind than sighted adults.

Analyses of the ERP waveforms focused on the N1, a negative component 100–200 milliseconds poststimulus that is known to vary in amplitude and latency with attention. Results showed that N1 amplitudes decreased

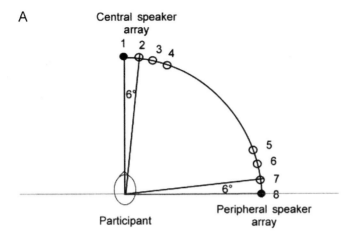

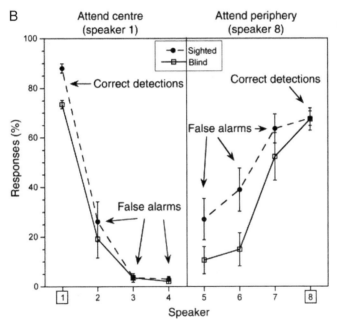

Figure 12.1 Speaker layout and response gradients. (*A*) Central and peripheral speaker arrays. Participants had to detect rare deviants at speaker 1 (attend center condition) or speaker 8 (attend periphery condition). (*B*) Gradients of the percentage of detection responses (mean ± standard error) to deviants at the central speakers 1–4 and peripheral speakers 5–8 when the subject's task was to attend to the center speaker 1 and to attend to the peripheral speaker 8, respectively. Responses to deviants at locations 1 and 8 were classified as correct responses, whereas responses to the remaining locations were considered false alarms. Response rates to deviants in the unattended speaker array were negligible and are not shown. Blind participants showed a more sharply tuned gradient of attention than sighted subjects in the attend periphery condition. (Reprinted from "Improved auditory spatial tuning in blind humans," by Röder et al., 1999, *Nature, 400*: 162–166, with permission from Macmillan Publishers Ltd.)

with increasing distance from the attended speakers. This decrease was sharper when subjects attended to the center than the periphery and was sharper for blind than sighted individuals when attending to the periphery. Finally, the spatial distribution of the N1 across the scalp was more posterior for blind than sighted subjects, suggesting possible activation of visual cortical areas during this auditory localization task. Thus, both behavioral and ERP data indicated that blind adults differentiated between the four peripheral speakers with finer spatial resolution than did sighted adults, and the ERP results suggested that visual cortical regions may be activated in an auditory localization task. The pattern of performance in response to the central array of speakers further suggests that greater acuity in the periphery may come at the cost of acuity in the center. I return to this point further below.

Recent positron emission tomography (PET) results demonstrate that early onset of blindness may be necessary for recruitment of visual regions into auditory processing. During a monaural sound localization task, PET activation foci were observed in occipital cortex only for those early blind participants who were better at localization than were sighted individuals (Gougoux, Zatorre, Lassonde, Voss, & Lepore, 2005). Moreover, the strength of activation was correlated with accuracy. Neither sighted nor early blind participants with similar or poorer localization accuracies than the sighted participants activated occipital cortex. Thus, there was a functional correlation between the occipital cortex activation and greater localization accuracy. These findings support the idea of a "sensitive period" during which the visual cortex must be deprived of input early in life for cross-modal plasticity of the visual system to occur.

Superior localization performance in the blind is not always observed, however. Zweirs, Van Opstal, and Cruysberg (2001) conducted an auditory localization task in which subjects made head turns toward a target sound played from a single movable speaker placed along the elevation (vertical dimension) and azimuth (horizontal dimension). Throughout the task, background auditory noise was presented from an array of six speakers equidistant from the subject. Localization in elevation deteriorated at a lower noise level than in the azimuth for all subjects. Localization in elevation also deteriorated at a lower noise level for blind than for sighted subjects. Localization along the azimuth did not differ between the two subject groups. The lack of agreement between these results and those reviewed above are likely due to task differences. In the Zwiers et al. (2001) study, subjects localized a single target in the presence of noise and all the stimuli were presented within 50° of the center of auditory space. It is possible that compensatory effects could have been observed with more peripherally presented stimuli, as in the Röder et al. (1999) study reviewed above. Zwiers et al. (2001) concluded that the addition of environmental noise attenuated the enhanced localization abilities documented in other studies, and they suggested that visual experience may be important in calibrating auditory spatial cues in the presence of noise. These subtle task differences, and the resulting differences in population effects observed, suggest that compensatory auditory plasticity may be specific to some processes and not others and that this specificity may yield clues about mechanisms of plasticity.

To summarize, findings from auditory localization studies show that blindness enhances simple localization of sounds in the periphery of auditory space, but not in the center. These studies also document cross-modal plasticity of visual areas as a result of blindness. This activation of visual areas is correlated with behavioral function, and there may be a sensitive period in early development during which visual brain regions may be recruited for auditory processing. Finally, variation in compensatory effects across task demands may provide clues as to which auditory functions may be more or less susceptible to visual deprivation.

12.3.3 The Challenge of Locomotion

The absence of vision poses significant challenges for locomotion. Many of the obstacles we must avoid do not emit any sound and therefore are difficult to perceive without vision. One solution to this problem has been to train individuals with visual impairment to attend to reverberated sounds, such as those created by cane tapping, and how those sounds relay information about objects and features of the spatial layout. In this section, I consider whether there is sufficient information readily available in the auditory environment that can guide locomotion.

Ashmead et al. (1998a) investigated whether ambient noise varies around major landmarks and obstacles in the spatial environment and whether any observable variations can be used to guide blind locomotion. The authors measured ambient noise in a room (average 38 dBA) and observed that low-frequency ambient sound increased nonlinearly in pitch with decreasing distance to large objects or features. The authors then tested the hypothesis that this information could inform locomotion. Blind subjects 7–18 years of age were asked to walk down hallways while several measurements were taken of their path. Subjects were asked not to create any sounds (e.g., finger snaps) and to walk shoeless so that the only available auditory information was the ambient sound. They either were allowed normal access to the ambient sound in the hallway or wore earphones connected to a microphone placed elsewhere within the room. There were three hallways, one narrow, one medium, and one wide. Subjects were placed slightly off center at the beginning of each trial walk, and their path down the hallway was measured with optical sensors and video. Subjects walked straighter and faster with free access to ambient sound in the hallway than with sound through the headphones. This was particularly true for the medium-width hallway. The authors concluded that the subjects were using the gradient in ambient sound to avoid touching the walls of the hallway and that this gradient was most readily available within 1–2 meters of the walls.

A follow-up experiment investigated whether access to ambient sound must be binaural to efficiently guide locomotion. Subjects walked down a hallway under four listening conditions: (1) unoccluded hearing, (2) left ear occluded, (3) right ear occluded, and (4) both ears occluded. Paths were straightest and walking was fastest with unoccluded hearing. When one ear was occluded, subjects more frequently contacted the wall on the same side as the occluded ear than the opposite wall, and they made more overall wall contacts in this condition than when hearing was unoccluded. Poorest performance was observed when both ears were occluded. Thus, while available ambient sound can be perceived with one ear, binaural access is optimal.

The final experiment presented blind children with hallways that varied in width and straightness and again measured their paths for straightness, speed, and frequency of wall contacts. Ears were occluded in the same manner as in the previous experiment. Results showed that subjects were sensitive to changes in the width or straightness of the hallway if the change occurred on the side of the unoccluded ear. The results of these experiments strongly suggest that blind individuals can perceive the naturally occurring gradient of ambient sound, that binaural access to this sound is optimal, and that it can guide locomotion in the blind. Subjects in this study had never received training in this behavior. Therefore the ability to use gradients in ambient sound to guide locomotion may emerge with experience in blind individuals.

These findings suggest that the functional needs of the blind human—to move through space with limited knowledge about the geometric layout—enhance attention to ambient sound so that variations in that sound have functional consequences for locomotion. They also illustrate how heightened attention to peripheral stimuli is adaptive not only for localizing objects in space but also for localizing one's *self* in relation to other objects and surfaces in space. These findings also raise the question of whether sighted humans can similarly attend to and perceive ambient sound. The decibel level of the ambient sound indicates that it should be perceptible to all, but the lack of functional pressure to rely on this information could mean that sighted individuals would not use the information to guide locomotion without being trained to do so.

12.3.4 Building Spatial Representations

Navigation tasks are a useful method for illuminating how spatial layouts are represented and abstracted. The research covered in this section addresses whether auditory and tactile spatial information gives rise to representations of three-dimensional space that are comparable to those representations that result from visual input.

An early study of gesturing in blind children suggests that they build abstract representations of space in a piecemeal fashion. Gestures and verbal descriptions of four blind boys 10–12 years of age were compared to those of 20 normally sighted children 10–12 years of age (half of whom were tested while blindfolded) during a Piagetian conservation task, a direction-giving task, and a narrative task (Iverson & Goldin-Meadow, 1997). Blind subjects produced more words across the three tasks but a similar frequency of gestures, demonstrating that gesturing itself occurs in the absence of a visual model. All subjects gestured most during the conservation task and least during the narrative task, and the three groups produced highly similar gestures in these settings. Blind children gestured less during the direction-giving task than did sighted and blindfolded children, and blind children described highly segmented paths compared to sighted and blindfolded children. When blind children gave directions, they provided step-by-step, turn-by-turn directions from the navigator's perspective in very short, detailed segments and used very little gesture. By contrast, sighted children—whether blindfolded or not—gave less detailed directions that were accompanied by lots of gestures. The authors concluded that blind children represent spatial layouts in a more segmented fashion than do sighted children and therefore describe them in a much more sequential manner and rely minimally upon gesture. These detailed descriptions may arise from extensive experience verbally describing spatial layouts and routes or from relying more on locomotive than on visual input in constructing spatial representations (for related ideas, see chapter 4).

In a follow-up study, 12 congenitally blind children 9 and 10 years old and 24 sighted subjects 9–17 years old (half of whom were tested blindfolded) described known and learned routes (Iverson, 1999). In the route description task, subjects were asked to describe well-known routes within their school. In the small-scale path description task, they were presented with a small Lego model of a building and later were asked to describe routes through this building from memory. This small-scale model was employed to reduce reliance of blind subjects on the "segmenting strategy" described in the Iverson and Goldin-Meadow (1997) study and to increase use of gesture. Blind and blindfolded children explored the Lego model haptically, and sighted children explored it visually. Then a path through the model was laid down using a chain that was also explored visually or haptically. A total of four paths were explored and described from memory. Results from the route directions task replicated the Iverson and Goldin-Meadow study, with blind children producing significantly more speech, fewer gestures, and more landmarks than did sighted or blindfolded children. By contrast, in the small-scale path task, the three groups of subjects produced similar frequencies of speech, but blind children again produced fewer gestures (although all subjects gestured more in the small scale than the route directions task). Finally, the small-scale landscape essentially deleted the use of landmarks in the descriptions of all subjects. Overall, regardless of visual status, information about direction and location are more easily communicated in gesture than speech. The stimulus manipulations reduced the piecemeal fashion of blind children's route descriptions somewhat, but not completely.

Considered together, these studies suggest that mental representations of spatial layouts can be established even in the absence of vision, but that some aspects of space may not be as well represented. Blind children's highly segmented path descriptions demonstrate a heavy reliance on an egocentric frame of reference, while sighted children's path descriptions demonstrate reliance on both egocentric and allocentric frames of reference. Similar characteristics of spatial representations have been documented in blind adults compared to sighted adults (Klatzky & Golledge, 1995; Rieser, Lockman, & Pick, 1980). When presented with novel spatial layouts, few differences are observed between blind and sighted adults as they locomote to targets, but blind subjects are poorer at devising shortcuts, suggesting limitations in spatial representations created on the basis of locomotion. When asked to devise routes in well-known layouts, however, blind adults perform as well as sighted adults and are as capable of devising shortcuts (Rieser, Guth, & Hill, 1982). Thus, what tend to be weak in the way that blind individuals represent spatial layouts are geometric relationships between objects and locations in a spatial layout, although these relationships are not completely absent. This raises the possibility that auditory, locomotive, and tactile spatial input are poorer sources of survey spatial knowledge than is visual input but are sufficient sources of egocentric, path-oriented knowledge. This difference may arise because of the more serial nature of auditory, locomotive, and tactile spatial perception and the more parallel nature of visual spatial perception.

12.3.5 Spatial Perception and Cognition of Tactile/Haptic Input

Blindness affects not only auditory processing but also the processing of tactile stimuli. Visual and tactile sensation are considerably different from one another, the former being the transduction of light, the latter being the transduction of pressure. Given that the nature of the signal itself is so different for the two sensory modalities, is it possible to arrive at the same percept of spatial information from either visual or tactile input alone?

This question has been addressed in a series of studies that investigated whether a classic visual illusion, the Müller-Lyer illusion shown in figure 12.2, can also result from tactile input. Researchers have long speculated that this illusion depends upon perception of linear perspective in visual line drawings and therefore should not be observed in the tactile modality or in individuals who have not had visual experience. Heller et al. (2002) tested sighted, late-blinded, and congenitally blind adults using raised-line drawings of Müller-Lyer figures with varying lengths of line and varying endpoint segments (none, tangential, obtuse, and acute angles). Using a sliding ruler, subjects reproduced the length of the line they perceived haptically (i.e., through touch with movement) from the raised-line drawing. All subjects showed a robust Müller-Lyer effect—the length of line configurations with

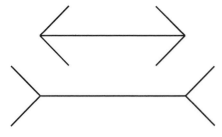

Figure 12.2 The Müller-Lyer illusion. The bottom figure is judged to be longer than the top figure, regardless of whether they are perceived visually or haptically.

"wings in" were reliably judged to be shortest, and those with "wings out" were perceived to be longest. A second experiment presented subjects with varying sizes of angles at the endpoints and found that smaller angles induced a larger illusion. One explanation of this result is that angular endpoint segments interfere with perception of the line segment, either because they mislead the observer as to which endpoints should be attended or because the observer averages lengths across all segments of the line and angles. These types of errors in spatial perception are easily transferable and highly comparable between visual and tactile modalities.

These results strongly suggest that theoretical explanations of the Müller-Lyer effect must take into account the fact that visual input and experience are not necessary for the illusion to be perceived. Importantly, late-blinded and congenitally blind subjects performed similarly, indicating that timing or length of visual experience does not affect perception of the illusion. Finally, the original hypothesis that the Müller-Lyer illusion depends upon perception of linear perspective may still hold true. Heller, Calcaterra, Tyler, and Burson (1996) have shown that blind subjects can perceive and produce elements of linear perspective in raised line drawings.

Mental rotation tasks similarly ask whether haptic information can produce perceptual and cognitive effects similar to those produced by visual information. In a visual mental rotation task, subjects are presented with pictures of three-dimensional objects and then are asked which of several test pictures represents the original object rotated in space. In a haptic mental rotation task, subjects are allowed to explore three-dimensional objects or raised drawings or letters and then are asked which of several test items match the original stimulus rotated in space. All studies report that blind individuals are fully capable of mentally rotating objects and raised line stimuli and that they show typical effects of mental rotation, including a linear increase in reaction time with increasing degree of rotation. Some studies report that blind subjects are slower and somewhat less accurate than are sighted subjects (Marmor & Zabeck, 1976), while others report similar performance for the two groups (Klatzky & Golledge, 1995; Röder, Rosler, & Henninghausen, 1997). Studies employing the ERP technique report that activity over occipital brain areas in blind adults during mental rotation tasks varies with processing load (Röder et al., 1997). In all, these findings from mental rotation tasks provide further support for the notion that sight is not a prerequisite for spatial computation and that haptic and tactile sensation can result in the same percepts as visual information.

These studies demonstrate that blindness affects perception of tactile and haptic information. They further suggest that the visual system in blind individuals can be recruited for tactile and haptic as well as auditory perception of spatial information, as reviewed above. In this instance, early onset of blindness may not be necessary for visual regions to be recruited for tactile and haptic processing of spatial information, but more research is needed. Finally, the fact that spatial analysis of tactile input can give rise to the same percepts as spatial analysis of visual input is strong evidence that either (1) spatial analyses are "amodal" processes that operate independently of the nature of the sensory input, or (2) the sensory modalities arrive at similar percepts regardless of their inherent differences because they are operating in the same spatial environment in both real and developmental time.

12.3.6 Summary

Blindness presents significant challenges in spatial perception and cognition. Vision typically dominates spatial processing because visual spatial acuity is greater than auditory spatial acuity. In the absence of vision, however, the organism must rely on auditory information to localize objects and events. The evidence reviewed in this section shows that this increased functional reliance on auditory information leads in some instances to compensatory plasticity such that auditory localization in blind individuals is better than that of sighted individuals. Thus, in the absence of visual input, auditory spatial processing develops to a level beyond what is typically observed in the presence of visual input. This raises the possibility that sensory dominance in spatial processing is not biologically determined but is determined dynamically from the capabilities of each modality, the task, and the environment such that the spatial acuity of the most "appropriate" sensory modality increases over time and experience.

Research with young blind children indicates that plasticity in those processes required for spatial navigation occurs early in development. Moreover, in the case of attention to ambient sound, such plasticity occurs in the absence of direct instruction and training. More developmental studies are needed to understand which plastic effects require early-onset blindness and which effects require many years of experience to emerge.

Studies of blind humans have also shown that analysis of spatial information derived from haptic and locomotive experience gives rise to similar percepts as the analysis of visual information. There is also strong evidence across studies, tasks, and modalities to suggest that visual brain regions in the blind are recruited into auditory, tactile, and spatial processing. Thus, the challenges posed by the absence of vision are managed by enhancing functional capabilities of existing sensory modalities. This is accomplished, in part, by the cross-modal plasticity of visual brain regions.

12.4 DEAFNESS

Deafness presents a very different set of problems for perceiving space than does blindness. One problem is how to distribute visual attention across the visual field. Deaf individuals have instantaneous, parallel, holistic access to the visual spatial environment but cannot perceive events that are not visually available. Objects that are hidden by occluders or objects that are either too peripheral or too distant to be within the visual field are not perceived, even if they emit sound. In addition to these "availability" limitations are limitations of attention. Individuals with intact hearing can focus visual attention on one object or region with little or no "cost." For them, visual information about unattended, peripheral events can be obtained by redirecting the fovea or the attentional spotlight, while auditory information about these events can be obtained simultaneously with no need for redirection of the fovea or spatial attention. By contrast, highly focused visual attention may in fact be too costly for deaf individuals to maintain because it severely limits their ability to monitor the surroundings. In this section I review studies that shed light on the distribution of visual attention in the absence of auditory information and whether cross-modal plasticity results from deafness as it does from blindness.

Spatial processing can also be affected in deaf individuals for a very different reason: the use of a visuospatial language. American Sign Language (ASL) takes advantage of the parallel, holistic nature of vision as its modality, which stands in stark contrast to the linear nature of speech. One well-articulated sign can convey what requires three or four words to convey. Furthermore, the ASL analog of phonological processing requires difficult on-line discriminations of handshape, path of motion, manner of motion, and sign placement. Fine discriminations within and between each of these dimensions are necessary for comprehension because all of these factors convey crucial aspects of meaning and syntax in ASL. The increased functional significance of these fine spatial discriminations has led several researchers to ask whether ASL fluency, particularly native acquisition of ASL, affects the spatial distribution of visual attention and its neural underpinnings.

12.4.1 Central and Peripheral Space

In the section on blindness, I reviewed studies showing that the processing of central auditory space is unaffected by visual deprivation but the processing of peripheral auditory space is enhanced under certain circumstances. Does deafness affect the processing of visual space in the same way as blindness affects the processing of auditory space? An early study showed that deafness, like blindness, selectively affects the processing of peripheral visual space. Neville and Lawson (1987a, b, c) presented subjects with small white rectangles either in the center of a computer monitor or 18° to the left or right periphery. These "standard" stimuli were presented on 80%

of the trials. On the other 20% of the trials, the white rectangles produced apparent motion in one of eight different directions; these were referred to as "target" stimuli. Standard stimuli could appear in any location, but subjects were instructed to attend to only one location at a time and to press a button to indicate the direction of motion of the target stimuli. Reaction times and accuracies in response to target stimuli and ERPs in response to standards were recorded throughout the task. Data were collected from typically hearing adults, from congenitally, genetically deaf adults, and from hearing adults for whom ASL was their native language, learned from their deaf parents. Hearing signers were included to separate effects of auditory deprivation from effects of ASL use. If hearing signers performed like deaf individuals but different from hearing nonsigners, then the observed population effect could be traced to ASL use. On the other hand, if hearing signers performed like hearing nonsigners but different from deaf signers, then the observed population effect would be traced to deafness itself.

All three groups performed similarly when attending to the central stimulus, but deaf adults were better than either hearing signers or nonsigners at detecting the direction of motion of the peripheral stimuli. ERP data were largely in line with these behavioral results. The main analysis centered on the degree to which attention to a location affected the amplitude and latency of the N1 waveform, a negative component that peaks 150–200 milliseconds poststimulus. Central standard stimuli elicited similar attentional effects on the N1 across the three subject groups. Attention to peripheral standard stimuli, by contrast, evoked a significantly larger amplitude N1 in deaf subjects than in hearing signers or nonsigners. This pattern indicates that deafness itself, rather than sign language use, drives the increase in attention to the periphery. The overall scalp distribution of the N1 was more anterior in deaf than hearing signers or nonsigners, which the authors hypothesized may indicate recruitment of primary auditory or auditory association cortices for visual processing in deaf subjects. These ERP effects, along with the behavioral results, suggest that auditory deprivation enhances processing of visual events in the periphery of space much like visual deprivation enhances the processing of auditory events in the periphery.

Analogous results have been documented using functional MRI. Congenitally, genetically deaf adults and hearing adults viewed fields of moving dots and attended to brief changes in luminance of the dots that occurred either in the center, in the periphery, or across the entire field of dots (Bavelier et al., 2000, 2001). Analyses focused on activity in the middle temporal gyrus (area MT), a region typically highly responsive to visual motion (e.g., Tootell et al., 1995). When subjects attended to the center or to the entire field at once, similar activation was observed in the two groups. When attention was directed to the periphery, however, greater activation was observed in area MT for deaf compared to hearing subjects. Peripheral motion also elicited activation in the superior temporal gyrus, a region typically activated by biological motion (e.g., Puce & Perrett, 2003). As in the ERP research described above, this enhanced processing of motion in the periphery appears to be driven by auditory deprivation rather than native use of ASL; hearing individuals who learned ASL from their deaf parents produced activation patterns like those of hearing nonsigners, not like those of deaf signers (Bavelier et al., 2001). Functional MRI studies have also shown that visual motion in the periphery elicits activation in temporal brain areas in deaf adults (Bavelier et al., 2001; Fine, Finney, Boynton, & Dobkins, 2005; Finney, Fine, & Dobkins, 2001). This temporal cortex activation is also not observed in hearing signers, which further supports the hypothesis that deafness drives the increase in attention to peripheral visual motion and recruits temporal auditory brain regions for the processing of visual motion.

Additional behavioral studies have reported enhanced processing of stimuli in the periphery of the visual field. One study tested the hypothesis that deaf individuals would be more "alert" in their responses to peripheral stimuli than would hearing individuals but that the two groups would be similarly "alert" to central stimuli (Loke & Song, 1991). Teenaged and young adult deaf and hearing subjects were presented with a single digit in the center of a computer screen. This digit was followed by an asterisk, which appeared near the centrally presented digit or 25° to the left or right. All trials were viewed monocularly with the subject's dominant eye. Subjects were asked to respond when they detected the asterisk, and then to recall the identity of the digit presented at the beginning of the trial. All subjects were faster to respond to asterisks presented in the center than the periphery, but deaf subjects were significantly faster than hearing subjects when attending to peripheral asterisks. These data show that motion is not required for peripheral visual events to be processed more quickly in deaf than hearing adults.

A second behavioral study employed a Posner-type task (Posner, 1980) involving centrally presented stimuli that either cued the spatial location of a subsequent peripheral target or cued the opposite location (Parasnis & Samar, 1985). Deaf college students were better than hearing college students at disengaging attention from an incongruently cued location to the correct target location. These and other studies (Reynolds, 1993) support the notion that deafness increases attention to peripheral visual stimuli and suggest that this may be enabled by faster disengagement of focused, central attention.

Proksch and Bavelier (2002) took these ideas further and asked whether this increase in attention to peripheral events reduces attentional resources available to central events. Congenitally, genetically deaf college students who were native ASL users, hearing college students with no sign language experience, and hearing college students with native ASL experience completed a visual search task. Subjects viewed a ring of six circles and responded to a target shape that appeared in any of the possible locations. Attentional load was manipulated by presenting irrelevant shape stimuli inside none to five of the remaining circles. Competing distracter stimuli that were either the same or a different shape as the target appeared either in the center of the ring or outside the ring. Results showed that attentional load and eccentricity of the distracter stimulus affected the two groups differently. Hearing nonsigners were more affected by attentional load when the distracter stimulus was presented in the periphery, while deaf subjects were more affected by attentional load when the distracter stimulus was presented in the center. The authors concluded that deaf individuals distribute more attentional resources to the visual periphery but at the cost of reduced attentional resources in the center. Hearing native signers performed like hearing nonsigners, which again suggests that this change in the distribution of attentional resources is due to auditory deprivation and not to the use of a signed language. These results support the notion that spatial attention is a limited resource such that an increase in its distribution to the periphery results in a decrease in available resources in the center.

How does the spatial distribution of attention change with age in the deaf? Mitchell and colleagues investigated whether deafness would enhance attention to physical changes in a visual array such that suppressing attention to those changes would be more difficult for deaf than for hearing children (Mitchell, 1996; Mitchell & Smith, 1996). Prelingually, profoundly deaf signing 6- to 7-year-olds, 9- to 10-year-olds, and adults along with their hearing, nonsigning counterparts completed two experiments. In the first experiment, the two groups performed similarly on a visual search task for a uniquely shaped target. Reaction times were not affected by display size, indicating "pop-out" of the uniquely shaped distracter. Thus, simple visual search did not differ between deaf and hearing children and adults. Subjects then completed a second task in which either the target or the distracter included an irrelevant stimulus dimension—color or apparent motion. Deaf and hearing children did not differ, but deaf adults were more affected by the presence of any irrelevant stimulus dimension than were hearing adults. Deaf adults were faster to respond than were hearing adults when the target varied along the irrelevant dimension ("target" trials) and were slower to respond when a distracter varied ("distracter" trials). Thus, visual search only differed in adults and only when there was an irrelevant stimulus dimension to be ignored.

In a second experiment, more stimuli were presented and the stimulus array extended to the edges of the computer screen. As in the first experiment, deaf adults were more affected by the irrelevant dimension than were hearing adults. The largest difference was observed on "distracter" trials, indicating that attention was captured more often by the irrelevantly varying distracter in deaf than in hearing adults. Importantly, significant differences were also observed between deaf and hearing children in this second experiment. Deaf children were more attentive to the irrelevant stimulus dimensions than were hearing children, especially on "target" trials. Furthermore, search times of deaf children were more affected by display size than were search times of hearing children. Performance of the 9- to 10-year-olds in

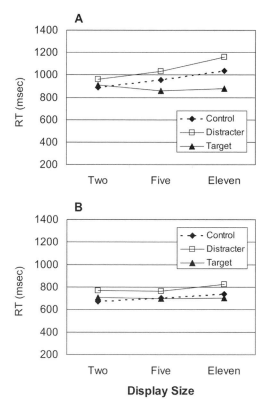

Figure 12.3 Reaction times (RT) of 9- to 10-year-old subjects in the visual search task with motion as the irrelevant stimulus dimension, plotted as a function of display size and trial type. Deaf subjects (*A*) were speeded when the target moved and slowed when a distracter moved more than were hearing subjects (*B*). All subjects were slower on the color condition, but a similar pattern of group differences was observed.

the motion task is presented in figure 12.3; deaf and hearing subjects at this age did not differ in the first experiment but differed significantly with the larger stimulus array. Overall, simple visual search was very similar in young deaf and hearing children, but expansion of the stimulus arrays into peripheral space revealed early effects of deafness on visual search. By adulthood, this increased attention to featural changes can be observed in response to events across the entire visual field.

Overall, these studies suggest that deaf individuals allocate and redirect attention to peripheral locations more efficiently than do hearing individuals. Some studies suggest that this increased distribution of spatial attention to peripheral regions comes at a cost of spatial attention to central regions. Recent research suggests that this cost may be observed only when subjects must balance spatial attention across central and peripheral events. When featural search is restricted to the center of the visual field and no peripheral distracters are presented, deaf adults outperform hearing adults (Stivalet, Moreno, Richard, Barraud, & Raphel, 1998). Thus, attention across the visual field may be a limited resource, and the absence of auditory input results in a different balance between central and peripheral events in visual attention. This balance must be flexible and adaptive in order to maintain attention to task demands while monitoring the environment for ongoing events.

12.4.2 Mental Rotation and Spatial Transformation

The work reviewed above clearly shows that deafness influences the allocation of visuospatial attention above and beyond any influence of sign language use. This raises a critical question: does sign language use itself also have an influence on spatial perception and cognition that is separable from the effects of deafness? American Sign Language (ASL) has been shown to reorganize certain aspects of brain function. For example, native ASL use shifts the hemispheric asymmetry of attention to motion from the typical right hemisphere/left visual field advantage to a left hemisphere/right visual field advantage, regardless of whether the signer is hearing or deaf (Bavelier et al., 2001; Bosworth & Dobkins, 2002; Brozinsky & Bavelier, 2004; Neville & Lawson, 1987b, c), although this difference in asymmetry is not observed when spatial attention is broadly distributed over several locations (Armstrong, Neville, Hillyard, & Mitchell, 2002). It is thought that this difference in hemispheric asymmetry stems from the visuospatial nature of ASL. Because ASL relies heavily on path and manner of motion for both semantic and syntactical information, left hemisphere language areas may increase their sensitivity to all forms of visual motion to an extent that they surpass typical right hemisphere involvement. Native ASL use also reorganizes the neural substrates of language. Canonical left hemisphere regions such as Broca's area and Wernicke's area are involved in ASL production and perception, as are analogous regions in the right hemisphere (Bavelier et al., 1998; Newman, Bavelier, Corina, Jezzard, & Neville, 2002). This is thought to arise from the complex spatial analysis required in ASL; right hemisphere structures that are typically strongly involved in spatial analysis become selectively involved in processing the visuospatial language.

The complex spatial nature of ASL may give rise over time to spatial analysis skills that generalize to nonlinguistic spatial tasks. For instance, ASL conversations always involve face-to-face interactions, and the observer often must spatially transform signs produced by the signer. For example, spatial layouts and routes within those layouts are described from the perspective of the *signer*, not the observer. Thus, if a signer describes a room and then a leftward route through that room, the described route is actually toward the observer's right. To accurately comprehend the description, the observer must rotate the signing space into his own perspective. Several studies have tested the hypothesis that ASL use affects mental transformation skills. Emmorey, Kosslyn, and Bellugi (1993) presented deaf signers, hearing signers, and hearing nonsigners with two two-dimensional shapes and then asked them whether the two shapes were the same or were mirror images of each other. Some shapes were rotated in space 90°, 135°, or 180°. Both deaf and hearing signers responded more quickly than hearing nonsigners, at all levels of spatial rotation. Hearing individuals with 6 years of ASL interpreter training also outperform hearing individuals who have no ASL knowledge in a task requiring mental rotation of drawings of three-dimensional objects (Talbot & Haude, 1993). These results strongly suggest that ASL use, not auditory deprivation, is the driving factor behind superior mental transformation skills. The fact that late learners of ASL also show highly developed mental rotation skills suggests that the effects are highly plastic and may not depend upon early acquisition of sign language.

Additional research has investigated how the mental transformations that deaf individuals apply to sign language discourse itself might differ from the transformations they apply to objects. Emmorey, Klima, and Hickok (1998) asked deaf signers to match video of a real room to signed descriptions of a room that were either produced from the typical signer's perspective or from the atypical viewer's perspective. Deaf signers were more accurate when the description was signed from the signer's perspective than when it was signed from the viewer's perspective, even though the signer's perspective required a spatial transformation. In this same study, deaf signers and hearing nonsigners were then compared in a nonlinguistic task in which they had to reproduce movements and appearances of objects, either in the same orientation or at 180° of rotation. All subjects were better at reproducing the events in the given orientation than in the 180° condition, but deaf signers were better than hearing nonsigners at remembering the orientation of objects during the task. The deaf signers then completed a second linguistic task in which the same object movements were described in ASL, either from the typical signer's perspective or from the atypical viewer's perspective, and the signers reproduced what was described to them. Deaf signers were worse in this condition than in the nonlinguistic task but were uninfluenced by rotation. Thus, the signed description moderated the rotation effect observed in the nonlinguistic task. The results of this study suggest that spatial transformation of signs may automatize with signing expertise, but typical accuracy decreases and reaction time increases are still observed with greater degree of rotation.

12.4.3 Summary

Deafness results in an enhancement of attention to peripheral events. Some evidence suggests that it may come at the cost of limiting central attention, but these limits may be observed only when events occur simultaneously in central and peripheral locations. No studies document that deafness affects spatial acuity per se, but a ceiling effect could be observed due to the fact that spatial acuity in vision is typically quite high. For deaf individuals, the challenges of attending to the world without auditory input are solved with the flexible deployment of attention across the visual field.

Deafness also results in the reorganization of the neural substrates of visual motion perception. Visual motion activates the typical neural substrate of visual motion perception in deaf individuals, but to a greater extent. Temporal auditory brain regions in deaf adults are also activated by peripheral visual motion.

The research reviewed here also shows that not only sensory experience but also language experience can affect spatial cognition. In particular, the on-line mental rotation and spatial transformation skills involved in the comprehension of sign language generalizes to other objects and spatial layouts. Interestingly, this effect does not appear to require early onset of sign language use, which suggests that mental rotation and spatial transformation are highly plastic processes.

The few studies of spatial perception and cognition in young deaf children suggest that enhancements of peripheral attention can be observed in elementary school years, but that many years of cumulative experience is necessary for effects of deafness to stabilize. Much more research is needed to understand the developmental aspects of this plasticity.

12.5 CONCLUSION

The research reviewed in this chapter demonstrates that representations of three-dimensional space can be developed in the absence of visual or auditory input that are sufficient to support adaptive spatial perception and cognition. Basic spatial perception and cognition are intact in blind and deaf individuals. Furthermore, in those instances when blind and deaf individuals are outperformed by sighted or hearing individuals, performance is not disordered or severely limited. Thus, the research reviewed here demonstrates that spatial perception and cognition are highly plastic and capable of reorganization—and sometimes compensation—in the absence of significant input from one modality. Developmental research documents that some aspects of spatial perception and cognition, such as sound localization, typically develop slowly across infancy and into late childhood (Litovsky & Ashmead, 1997). Perhaps it is this protracted developmental time course that allows compensatory effects to emerge in remaining modalities after early sensory deprivation.

Deafness and blindness both give rise to enhanced perception of information in the spatial periphery. It is important to note that even when all sensory systems are intact, localization and discrimination of stimuli are poorer in the periphery of space than in the center of space. This inherent superiority of processing in the center means that there may be a ceiling effect on performance in central spatial conditions and little room for improvement. By contrast, the typical decrement in performance with increasing spatial eccentricity means that there is plenty of room to improve perception and cognition of peripheral stimuli under exceptional circumstances. For deaf and blind individuals, the absence of significant information about the spatial layout increases pressure on the remaining senses to monitor the environment. This monitoring often means alerting the system to new stimuli and events entering the auditory or visual field, thereby increasing the importance of peripheral events. This behavioral need may interact with developmental processes of longer time courses to push attentional resources to compensate by increasing their distribution to the periphery of space.

The spatial transformation skills observed in both blind and deaf individuals may be explained by a similar confluence of pressures. Mental rotation and other spatial transformations are typically difficult and slow for adults, in part because there are few daily behaviors that require such spatial analysis. Functional needs of blind and deaf individuals, however, place increased pressure on spatial cognition to solve problems of navigation and language, respectively. Blind individuals must compute detailed spatial information from auditory and locomotive experience to successfully build representations of the spatial layout. This strongly suggests that vision is not privileged in this process and that other sensory modalities can result in similarly accurate representations. Deaf individuals must extract semantic and syntactic information conveyed through facial expressions, handshapes, locations of signs, and manner and path of motion. This functional pressure results in the development of spatial transformation skills that surpass those typically observed in hearing individuals. Deafness may result in supranormal spatial transformation skills because these functional pressures are imposed upon vision, the typically dominant spatial modality.

Plasticity of spatial perception and cognition in both blind and deaf individuals is enabled by changes in the neural substrates of auditory and visual spatial processing. In the case of blindness, activation of occipital visual brain areas by a wide variety of tasks, from auditory localization (Gougoux et al., 2005; Röder et al., 1999) to mental rotation (Röder et al., 1997), suggests that adaptive and flexible attention can be achieved in part by expansion of the neural substrates devoted to spatial processing. In the case of deafness, enhanced processing of peripheral motion is achieved in part by the recruitment of temporal auditory brain regions (Bavelier et al., 2001; Fine et al., 2005; Finney et al., 2001). There is also evidence that sensory deprivation changes the functional connectivity within typical neural networks (Bavelier et al., 2000). Overall, it is clear that auditory and visual cortical brain areas are not "silent" in the absence of auditory and visual input, respectively, but are actively engaged in the adaptation of the organism to its environment. Additional neural plasticity occurs within association cortices, which are typically activated by multiple sensory systems. In unimodal sensory deprivation, activity in association cortices becomes dominated over time by the intact sensory modalities because of the lack of competitive activity from the deprived sensory modality (e.g., Rauschecker & Korte, 1993). Thus, experience drives the expansion of neural substrates. This expansion, in turn, supports the development of adaptive behaviors.

Some questions raised by this body of research remain unanswered. For example, how do two different sensory modalities (e.g., vision and touch) that arise from completely different sources of energy and are transduced completely differently arrive at the same percept? Are there "amodal" properties of the input, such as location, intensity, or rhythm that are similar enough to give rise to the same percept? Or do vision and touch pass their information on to brain regions downstream that combine the disparate sources of information into the same percept? Cognitive neuroscience techniques can shed light on the neural underpinnings of the processes central to multimodal integration, while developmental approaches to these questions are crucial for ultimately understanding the origins of these processes.

Similarly, a developmental approach is needed to understand how the modulation of spatial attention across central and peripheral regions occurs. This requires an understanding of how the unique behavioral challenges facing deaf and blind individuals interact with mechanisms of neural plasticity over longer time scales. For instance, over the course of typical development, the precision of spatial processing increases such that the "spotlight" of attention narrows around the attentional target, to enable enhanced processing of the target and to decrease attention to peripheral, distracting information (for related ideas, see Schutte, Spencer, & Schoner, 2003; see also chapter 14 of this volume). Results from deaf and blind humans suggest that when one sensory modality is absent, it is not adaptive to develop spatial attention that is strongly selective and biased to the center of space because the loss of information in the periphery is too great. In unimodal sensory deprivation, flexible deployment of attention across the visual field allows for an adaptive balance between focused, task-oriented attention and stimulus-driven environmental monitoring. When all sensory modalities are intact, the development of precisely focused attention is similarly driven by experience, but the inclusion of input from all modalities results in highly precise visual attention because audition is available for the monitoring of peripheral events. Thus, the development of visual-spatial attention can be best understood as part of a larger, multimodal phenomenon that recalibrates itself in real time in response to task demands and that continues to change over developmental time as skills develop, knowledge accumulates, and spatial representations achieve greater complexity.

REFERENCES

Armstrong, B., Neville, H., Hillyard, S., & Mitchell, T. (2002). Auditory deprivation affects processing of motion, but not color. *Cognitive Brain Research*, *14*, 422–434.

Ashmead, D. H., Wall, R. S., Eaton, S. B., Ebinger, K. A., Snook-Hill, M.-M., Guth, D. A., & Yang, X. (1998a). Echolocation reconsidered: Using spatial variations in the ambient sound field to guide locomotion. *Journal of Visual Impairment & Blindness*, *92*(9), 615–632.

Ashmead, D. H., Wall, R. S., Ebinger, K. A., Eaton, S. B., Snook-Hill, M.-M., & Yang, Y. (1998b). Spatial hearing in children with visual disabilities. *Perception*, *27*(1), 105–122.

Bavelier, D., Brozinsky, C., Tomann, A., Mitchell, T., Neville, H., & Liu, G. (2001). Impact of early deafness and early exposure to sign language on the cerebral organization for motion processing. *Journal of Neuroscience*, *21*(22), 8931–8942.

Bavelier, D., Corina, D., Jezzard, P., Clark, V., Karni, A., Lalwani, A., Rauschecker, J. P., Braun, A., Turner, R., & Neville, H. J. (1998). Hemispheric specialization for English and ASL: Left invariance-right variability. *Neuroreport, 9*(7), 1537–1542.

Bavelier, D., Tomann, A., Hutton, C., Mitchell, T., Corina, D., & Neville, H. (2000). Visual attention to the periphery is enhanced in congenitally deaf individuals. *Journal of Neuroscience, 20*(RC93), 1–6.

Bosworth, R. G., & Dobkins, K. R. (2002). Visual field asymmetries for motion processing in deaf and hearing signers. *Brain & Cognition, 49*, 170–181.

Brozinsky, C. J., & Bavelier, D. (2004). Motion velocity thresholds in deaf signers: Changes in lateralization but not in overall sensitivity. *Cognitive Brain Research, 21*(1), 1–10.

Emmorey, K., Klima, E., & Hickok, G. (1998). Mental rotation within linguistic and non-linguistic domains in users of American Sign Language. *Cognition, 68*(3), 221–246.

Emmorey, K., Kosslyn, S. M., & Bellugi, U. (1993). Visual imagery and visual-spatial language: Enhanced imagery abilities in deaf and hearing ASL signers. *Cognition, 46*(2), 139–181.

Fine, I., Finney, E. M., Boynton, G. M., & Dobkins, K. R. (2005). Comparing the effects of auditory deprivation and sign language within the auditory and visual cortex. *Journal Cognitive Neuroscience, 17*(10), 1621–1637.

Finney, E. M., Fine, I., & Dobkins, K. R. (2001). Visual stimuli activate auditory cortex in the deaf. *Nature Neuroscience, 4*(12), 1171–1173.

Gougoux, F., Zatorre, R. J., Lassonde, M., Voss, P., & Lepore, F. (2005). A functional neuroimaging study of sound localization: Visual cortex activity predicts performance in early-blind individuals. *Public Library of Science: Biology, 3*(2), 324–333.

Heller, M. A., Brackett, D. D., Wilson, K., Yoneama, K., Boyer, A., & Steffen, H. (2002). The haptic Mueller-Lyer illusion in sighted and blind people. *Perception, 31*(10), 1263–1274.

Heller, M. A., Calcaterra, J. A., Tyler, L. A., & Burson, L. L. (1996). Production and interpretation of perspective drawings by blind and sighted people. *Perception, 25*(3), 321–334.

Iverson, J. M. (1999). How to get to the cafeteria: Gesture and speech in blind and sighted children's spatial descriptions. *Developmental Psychology, 35*(4), 1132–1142.

Iverson, J. M., & Goldin-Meadow, S. (1997). What's communication got to do with it? *Developmental Psychology, 33*(3), 453–467.

Kahneman, D., Treisman, A., & Gibbs, B. J. (1992). The reviewing of object files: Object-specific integration of information. *Cognitive Psychology, 24*(2), 175–219.

King, A. J., & Carlile, S. (1993). Changes induced in the representation of auditory space in the superior colliculus by rearing ferrets with binocular eyelid suture. *Experimental Brain Research, 94*(3), 444–455.

King, A. J., & Parsons, C. H. (1999). Improved auditory spatial acuity in visually deprived ferrets. *European Journal of Neuroscience, 11*(11), 3945–3956.

Klatzky, R. L., & Golledge, R. G. (1995). Performance of blind and sighted persons on spatial tasks. *Journal of Visual Impairment & Blindness, American Foundation for the Blind, 89*, 70.

Knudsen, E. I., & Brainard, M. S. (1991). Visual instruction of the neural map of auditory space in the developing optic tectum. *Science, 253*, 85–87.

Korte, M., & Rauschecker, J. P. (1993). Auditory spatial tuning of cortical neurons is sharpened in cats with early blindness. *Journal of Neurophysiology*, *70*(4), 1717–1721.

Law, M. I., Zahs, K. R., & Stryker, M. P. (1988). Organization of primary visual cortex (area 17) in the ferret. *Journal of Comparative Neurology*, *278*(2), 157–180.

Litovsky, R. Y., & Ashmead, D. H. (1997). Development of binaural and spatial hearing in infants and children. In R. H. Gilkey & T. R. Anderson (Eds.), *Binaural and spatial hearing in real and virtual environments* (pp. 571–592). Hillsdale, NJ: Lawrence Erlbaum.

Loke, W. H., & Song, S. (1991). Central and peripheral visual processing in hearing and nonhearing individuals. *Bulletin of the Psychonomic Society*, *29*(5), 437–440.

Marmor, G. S., & Zabeck, L. A. (1976). Mental rotation by the blind: Does mental rotation depend on visual imagery? *Journal of Experimental Psychology: Human Perception & Performance*, *2*, 515–521.

Mitchell, T. V. (1996). *How audition shapes visual attention*. Bloomington, IN: Indiana University Department of Psychology.

Mitchell, T. V., & Smith, L. B. (1996). Deafness drives development of attention to change. In G. Cottrell (Ed.), *Proceedings of the Eighteenth Annual Conference of the Cognitive Science Society* (pp. 627–632) Mahwah, NJ: Erlbaum.

Moiseff, A. (1989). Bi-coordinate sound localization by the barn owl. *Journal of Comparative Physiology A Sensory Neural & Behavioral Physiology*, *164*(5), 637–644.

Neville, H. J., & Lawson, D. (1987a). Attention to central and peripheral visual space in a movement detection task: An event-related potential and behavioral study. I. Normal hearing adults. *Brain Research*, *405*, 253–267.

Neville, H. J., & Lawson, D. (1987b). Attention to central and peripheral visual space in a movement detection task: An event-related potential and behavioral study. II. Congenitally deaf adults. *Brain Research*, *405*, 268–283.

Neville, H. J., & Lawson, D. (1987c). Attention to central and peripheral visual space in a movement detection task: An event-related potential and behavioral study. III. Separate effects of auditory deprivation and acquisition of a visual language. *Brain Research*, *405*, 284–294.

Newman, A. J., Bavelier, D., Corina, D., Jezzard, P., & Neville, H. J. (2002). A critical period for right hemisphere recruitment in American Sign Language processing. *Nature Neuroscience*, *5*(1), 76–80.

Parasnis, I., & Samar, V. J. (1985). Parafoveal attention in congenitally deaf and hearing young adults. *Brain & Cognition*, *4*(3), 313–327.

Posner, M. I. (1980). Orienting of attention. *Quarterly Journal of Experimental Psychology*, *32A*, 3–25.

Proksch, J., & Bavelier, D. (2002). Changes in the spatial distribution of visual attention after early deafness. *Journal of Cognitive Neuroscience*, *14*(5), 687–701.

Puce, A., & Perrett, D. (2003). Electrophysiology and brain imaging of biological motion. *Philosophical Transactions of the Royal Society of London Series B: Biological Sciences*, *358*(1431), 435–445.

Rauschecker, J. P., & Kniepert, U. (1994). Auditory localization behaviour in visually deprived cats. *European Journal of Neuroscience*, *6*(1), 149–160.

Rauschecker, J. P., & Korte, M. (1993). Auditory compensation for early blindness in cat cerebral cortex. *Journal of Neuroscience*, *13*(10), 4538–4548.

Recanzone, G. H. (2000). Spatial processing in the auditory cortex of the macaque monkey. *Proceedings of the National Academy of Sciences of the United States of America*, *97*(22), 11829–11835.

Recanzone, G. H. (2003). Auditory influences on visual temporal rate perception. *Journal of Neurophysiology*, *89*(2), 1078–1093.

Reynolds, H. N. (1993). Effects of foveal stimulation on peripheral visual processing and laterality in deaf and hearing subjects. *American Journal of Psychology*, *106*(4), 523–540.

Rieser, J. J., Guth, D. A., & Hill, E. W. (1982). Mental processes mediating independent travel: Implications for orientation and mobility. *Journal of Visual Impairment & Blindness*, *76*(6), 213–218.

Rieser, J. J., Lockman, J. J., & Pick, H. L. (1980). The role of visual experience in knowledge of spatial layout. *Perception & Psychophysics*, *28*(3), 185–190.

Röder, B., Rosler, F., & Henninghausen, E. (1997). Different cortical activation patterns in blind and sighted humans during encoding and transformation of haptic images. *Psychophysiology*, *34*, 292–307.

Röder, B., Teder-Salejarvi, W., Sterr, A., Rosler, F., Hillyard, S. A., & Neville, H. J. (1999). Improved auditory spatial tuning in blind humans. *Nature*, *400*, 162–166.

Schutte, A. R., Spencer, J. P., & Schöner, G. (2003). Testing the dynamic field theory: Working memory for locations becomes more spatially precise over development. *Child Development*, *74*, 1393–1417.

Stivalet, P., Moreno, Y., Richard, J., Barraud, P.-A., & Raphel, C. (1998). Differences in visual search tasks between congenitally deaf and normally hearing adults. *Cognitive Brain Research*, *6*(3), 227–232.

Talbot, K. F., & Haude, R. H. (1993). The relationship between sign language skill and spatial visualization ability: Mental rotation of three-dimensional objects. *Perceptual & Motor Skills*, *77*(3), 1387–1391.

Teder-Salejarvi, W. A., Hillyard, S., Röder, B., & Neville, H. J. (1999). Spatial attention to central and peripheral auditory stimuli as indexed by event-related potentials (ERPs). *Cognitive Brain Research*, *8*(3), 213–227.

Tootell, R. B. H., Reppas, J. B., Kwong, K. K., Malach, R., Born, R. T., Brady, T. J., Rosen, B. R., & Belliveau, J. W. (1995). Functional analysis of human MT and related visual cortical areas using magnetic resonance imaging. *Journal of Neuroscience*, *15*(4), 3215–3230.

Treisman, A., Vieira, A., & Hayes, A. (1992). Automaticity and preattentive processing. *American Journal of Psychology*, *105*(2), 341–362.

Welch, R. B., & Warren, D. H. (1980). Immediate perceptual response to intersensory discrepancy. *Psychological Bulletin*, *88*, 638–667.

Zwiers, M. P., Van Opstal, A. J., & Cruysberg, J. R. (2001). A spatial hearing deficit in early-blind humans. *Journal of Neuroscience*, *21*(9), 1–5.

13

EXPLAINING SELECTIVE SPATIAL BREAKDOWN IN WILLIAMS SYNDROME
Four Principles of Normal Spatial Development and Why They Matter

BARBARA LANDAU & JAMES E. HOFFMAN

The phenomenon that motivates this chapter is simple to describe: people with Williams syndrome (WS)—a rare genetic deficit caused by missing a handful of genes—are severely impaired in carrying out a class of tasks commonly called "visual-spatial construction" tasks. These tasks require people to copy spatial patterns, either by drawing or by assembling individual blocks to form an overall design. The difficulties shown by people with WS are so serious that even adults with the syndrome produce drawings like the ones shown in figure 13.1A, and copies of block patterns like those shown in figure 13.1B. Standardized measures show that people with WS typically score in the first or second percentile for their age on these tasks. Adults perform at the rough age equivalence of normally developing 4-year-old children. Thus, the overt manifestation of the spatial deficit is not subtle. We do not need more than a paper and pencil or a set of blocks to show that a person with WS has severe difficulty in visual-spatial construction tasks, and we do not need statistical tests to determine whether his or her performance is dramatically worse than it should be.

But explaining this severe impairment is not so simple. In fact, it is decidedly complex and rather subtle. It is also important. The questions that are raised by the case of WS are no less than whether there is specialization in cognition, how developmental mechanisms interact with cognitive and

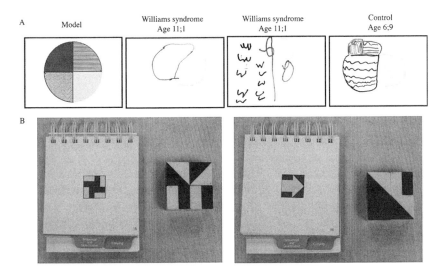

Figure 13.1. (*A*) Copies of a model by two children with WS (age 11) and one normally developing child (age 6, control). (*B*) Two samples of a model pattern (left in each picture) and the copy produced by an adult with WS. See color insert.

neural structures, and whether and how genetic changes come to have impact on the structure of knowledge in the human mind. For these reasons, understanding spatial impairment in WS holds the promise not only of understanding this particular syndrome, but—equally important—of understanding the nature of normal development of mind and brain.

The goal of this chapter is to propose an explanation of the spatial impairment in WS that depends heavily on our understanding of normal spatial development. We proceed as follows. First, we propose four principles underlying the normal development of human spatial representations. The first three are (1) specialization of function, (2) constraint within each specialized system, and (3) the importance of timing in the emergence of brain and cognitive systems. We add to this a fourth principle that must be invoked in order to understand how a genetic deficit can result in specific spatial impairments: (4) genes can target cognitive systems. That is, even though genetic mechanisms have proximal effects that might be best understood at a molecular level, genes can also have effects on higher levels of organization, in this case, spatial organization.

We then discuss three salient characteristics of the WS spatial profile and document these characteristics with evidence from studies in our lab as well as other labs. In brief, the WS profile (a) is uneven across different kinds of spatial representation, (b) is strongly constrained within each domain of knowledge, and (c) shows a somewhat unusual timing profile. It is uneven because certain areas of spatial representation in WS are not impaired or only minimally impaired, whereas others are severely impaired.

It is strongly constrained because the detailed patterns of performance for each type of spatial task show significant and highly specific internal structure. It reflects an unusual timing profile because people with WS perform like normal people of the same chronological age on some tasks, like normal people of the same mental age (but much younger chronological age) on other tasks, and like normal children who are much younger than mental age matches on yet other tasks. As we discuss these aspects of the profile, we propose that they map onto the first three principles of normal spatial organization and development, providing an explanation within normal spatial development for why the WS profile is the way it is. We conclude with a speculative hypothesis based on the four principles. Specifically, we discuss the relationships among genes, brains, and minds and how they can account for the spatial profile of WS in the context of normal human spatial representation and its development.

13.1 FOUR ORGANIZING PRINCIPLES OF SPATIAL REPRESENTATION AND ITS DEVELOPMENT

13.1.1 There Is Specialization of Function Within Spatial Domains

Any explanation of a naturally occurring human spatial impairment will have to confront the question of what human spatial knowledge *is*. If a system of knowledge can be severely impaired by the absence of a small set of genes (as is the case with WS), then what is it that is actually impaired? The outward manifestation of the WS spatial impairment—failure in copying and other visual construction tasks—is unlikely to reflect a single, uniform aspect of spatial knowledge or a single core knowledge domain such as the domain of language, number, or objects, because construction tasks are surprisingly complex and tap into multiple spatial processes. That is, there is not likely to be any single spatial capacity whose impairment results in failure to copy patterns. Rather, failure in this class of tasks is likely to be due to a variety of factors such as impairments in spatial attention, visual-spatial memory, object representation, and other spatial systems, each of which might contribute to the solution of construction tasks (see Hoffman, Landau, & Pagani, 2003). For this reason, it is unlikely that we will make much progress in understanding the WS spatial impairment if we look for "the visual-spatial construction task" system. Rather, we must look to more fundamental aspects of spatial representation in order to understand what has gone wrong.

Basic research in cognitive science, neuroscience, and psychology shows that spatial cognition is not a single monolithic system with a single set of principles, but rather is a set of systems, specialized by nature to solve different kinds of tasks that we carry out in space (Epstein & Kanwisher, 1998; Gallistel, 1990; Hermer & Spelke, 1996; Kanwisher, McDermott, & Chun, 1997; see Landau, 2002, for review). The existence of specialization of function in the *normal* spatial system raises the possibility that the same types of specialization will be observed in cases of genetic deficit such as WS. In particular, we might expect highly selective impairment or breakdown, because some spatial systems might be more vulnerable than others. We present evidence for this possibility, because people with WS show an *uneven* spatial profile, with some systems relatively damaged and others spared.

13.1.2 Each Specialized Subsystem Has a Highly Constrained Architecture

Evidence and arguments also suggest that the internal architecture of each specialized subsystem—that is, the representations and algorithms for operating on these representations—is distinct. This is perhaps not surprising since the computational problems that each must solve are quite different. For example, the internal architecture and computations used to recognize objects are quite different from those used to perceive biological motion or to navigate in space. The existence of these different sets of constraints provides a powerful tool for cognitive scientists to determine whether genetic differences lead to qualitative differences in cognitive organization or only quantitative ones. This is because a high degree of constraint within each subsystem predicts that all spatial representations should reflect the same strong internal structure, which might be robust across variation in genetic endowment or environmental conditions. Alternatively, it is possible that genetic deficits—or any highly unusual circumstances of development—result in cognitive structures that are qualitatively different from the norm.

One manifestation of a qualitative change in cognitive processes would be an unusual pattern of errors across conditions or an atypical sequence of responses, such as eye movements, during performance of a task, even when it is done accurately. If performance patterns and patterns of errors look the same across normal and unusual development, we can tentatively conclude that the internal structure of the representations being studied is the same in both cases (i.e., no qualitative change). As we show when we discuss the constrained profile, even in cases where individuals with WS perform far worse than their chronological age mates, their performance accuracy and the details of they how they achieved that performance are highly similar to those of normal children at some earlier developmental point.

13.1.3 Timing Matters

A rock-bottom assumption of normal development is that the time of appearance of cognitive functions is significant. Deviations from the normal sequence of development can take several forms. Onset of cognitive functions can be delayed with later catch-up (e.g., in adulthood). Alternatively, there may be developmental arrest, that is, persistent performance at an early developmental point with no later catch-up. A combination of these two deficits can also occur, as appears to be the case for language in people with WS. Their acquisition of language is delayed (see Mervis et al., 2003) and never reaches normal levels in adulthood. In addition, these deficits in timing may be uniform across cognitive domains or they may be selective, affecting some areas of cognition and not others.

What comparisons will shed light on these questions? In the typical study of unusual developmental populations, children are matched in some way to normally developing children of various ages (i.e., children with no known impairment), and the sameness or difference in profile tells us whether and where there are differences. People with WS are typically moderately re-tarded, and researchers often try to account for the effects of retardation by matching to normal individuals on the basis of either chronological age (CA) matches (for whom overall IQ will surely be higher) or "mental age" (MA) matches. MA matches are usually determined by equivalent perfor-mance on some presumed independent test (usually an IQ test). Typically, matches for retarded individuals will get the same raw score on some target test, but they are likely to be chronologically younger than the individuals with WS and have a higher overall IQ. If the individuals with WS are iden-tical to CA matches, we might conclude there is no impairment, as has been shown for some aspects of face perception (Tager-Flusberg, Plesa-Skwerer, Faja, & Joseph, 2003). If they are no different from MA matches (who are typically younger but are of the same "mental age"), then we might once again conclude that there is no impairment because performance is what one would expect given overall mental age. If individuals perform worse than MA matches, then there is clearly some impairment, since perfor-mance is worse than one would expect even after equating for mental age.

Although this approach is quite common, there is a serious question of whether matching on the basis of "mental age" makes sense, given that we know precious little about what either overall IQ or mental age actually measures. We believe that a better solution is to simply generate normal de-velopmental curves for different aspects of cognition and then map the WS profile onto the normal developmental curves. From this, we can gain insight into the overall pattern of performance across different kinds of knowl-edge. This is particularly important in the case of a broad investigation into spatial representations, because different spatial subsystems might develop normally at different rates and therefore might mature at different points in developmental time. Without knowing whether different spatial functions are normally acquired at different times, we cannot really evaluate the na-ture or meaning of an unusual pattern of performance.

This approach further requires that we think about how to organize our developmental timeline. What task comparisons should be made, and how should we group tasks? We offer two possibilities, both of which de-pend on hypotheses about normal spatial development. One possibility is to consider each spatial subsystem (e.g., face perception, object representa-tion, navigation, etc.) and decide on a system-by-system basis how the WS profile compares to the normal profile. This is the approach taken by several investigators who have evaluated face perception (Dereulle, Mancini, Livet,

Casse-Perrot, & de Schonen, 1999; Tager-Flusberg et al., 2003), object perception (Landau, Hoffman, & Kurz, 2006), and motion perception (Atkinson et al., 1997; Atkinson, Braddick, & Anker, 2003; Jordan, Reiss, Hoffman, & Landau, 2002; Reiss, Hoffman, & Landau, 2005).

A second approach is to group different spatial systems at a more molar level. One important grouping at this level corresponds roughly to different streams of processing in the brain, which also map onto different regions of the brain. The most widely discussed division of labor within the visual system is that between the ventral and dorsal streams. Several researchers have suggested that the differences therein may be functionally important for development and that the two streams may develop at different rates (Johnson, 2004; Neville & Bavelier, 2000). Within each stream, it is possible that different functions and regions also normally develop at different rates and times. For example, we might find that tasks normally engaging inferotemporal regions of the ventral stream (e.g., object or face recognition) result in different performance profiles than tasks normally engaging dorsal and parietal regions (e.g., on-line visual–manual action, modulation of attention, or mental rotation). Within each region, we might further find differences in different functions (object vs. face recognition, or manual action vs. mental rotation).

Grouping at these more molar levels may provide an important foundation for understanding both normal and unusual development. For example, different streams of processing in the brain may undergo different developmental time courses, relative to each other in normal development. If one stream of processing lags further behind the other in abnormal development, then we might see an uneven profile of spatial functions that exaggerates the profile seen in normal development. In the section on timing, we speculate that the uneven spatial profile observed in WS may reflect early developmental arrest interacting with an exaggeration of the normal differences in the rate of development of the dorsal and ventral visual pathways.

13.1.4 Genes Can Target Cognitive Systems

The fourth principle matters for explaining how genetic deficits come to have cognitive consequences. Williams syndrome is a genetic deficit, caused by the absence of roughly 1.6 contiguous megabytes of DNA that normally span approximately 28 genes (Hoogenraad, Akhmanova, Galjart, & De Zeeuw, 2004; Meyer-Lindenberg, Mervis, & Berman, 2006). Studies of familial patterning, analysis of unusual human cases in which only a few genes in this region are affected, and studies of knockout mice have converged to suggest that the cognitive symptoms of WS are likely to be linked to a small set of candidate genes (Hoogenraad et al., 2004; Frangiskakis et al., 1996). Studies of knockout mice further suggest that some of these genes are involved in the development of dendritic spine morphology: mice that lack one of the candidate genes (*LIMK-1*) show no change in the number of synapses or their baseline functioning, but they do show abnormal structure and some associated abnormalities in spatial learning (Weeber, Levenson, & Sweatt, 2002). Missing genes clearly result in changes to the developing brain, due to a variety of molecular actions that are part of the intricate chain of mechanisms that lead from DNA to the development of organs.

But this raises a difficult and subtle problem: how do missing genes come to have effects on cognitive systems? How can a few genes act to cause cognitive deficits? There are two strong views on this issue. One is that developmental genetic deficits will inevitably result in widespread subtle anomalies in cognition, shown by a variety of abnormalities and, in particular, qualitative differences in cognitive structures (e.g., Karmiloff-Smith, 1998). The rationale behind this view is that genetic defects have ubiquitous effects on brain development, and therefore, there is a strong likelihood that cognition across the board will develop abnormally. A hallmark of abnormal cognition would be qualitative differences in the cognitive structures that emerge over time. For example, Dereulle et al. (1999) propose that people with WS do not process faces holistically, as is true of typical adults. Similarly, Karmiloff-Smith et al. (1997) proposed that children with WS do not follow the same rules of morphology as do typical children. These are qualitative differences that range across cognitive domains and are consistent with the idea that damage is not specifically targeted.

Our view is quite different: we believe that genes can indeed target specific cognitive systems. If genes can have highly specific effects on the micromechanisms of development, with a single gene responsible for producing the right proteins for healthy red blood cells (absent in sickle-cell anemia) and a different gene playing a crucial role in the normal development of the vertebrate eye (Bailey et al., 2004), then we believe it is also possible for a mere handful of genes to be responsible for a specific spatial impairment.

Importantly, this claim requires that we step away from simplistic explanations of the relationship between genes and cognition and that we acknowledge the importance of explanation at the cognitive level. Much of the literature on genes and cognition tends to "explain" cognitive deficits in terms of "a gene or genes" (see Marcus, 2004, for discussion). The problem here is that we are nowhere near understanding the proximal (i.e., molecular) effects of genes, much less how these ultimately lead to cognitive structure. As John Morton (2004) has emphasized, it is crucial to separate levels of explanation and lay out the nature of cognition before making pronouncements about the effects of gene deletions. Here, we can use guidance from the idea of specialization of function in normal populations. A targeted impairment in the spatial system could manifest itself in a number of different ways. It could result in a single impaired subsystem (e.g., face processing), with little repercussion for other spatial systems. Or it could target an entire set of spatial functions that are carried out in a particular region of the brain. As we discuss below, parietal regions of the brain are likely to be compromised in WS, and these regions could guide a variety of spatial subsystems.

The proof is in the pudding. We assume that explaining the WS spatial deficit must ultimately include an understanding of how a handful of missing genes can result in impaired spatial representation. However, the crucial step in developing this understanding is determining the nature of spatial cognitive impairments. To address this issue, the bulk of our work is carried out at the level of cognition, in trying to understand how a cognitive system can come undone. Eventually, this cognitive profile of deficit and sparing will have to be merged with an explanation at many levels, including specification of how molecular changes produced by missing genes might culminate in a highly unusual profile of the mind. We speculate on this more toward the end of the chapter.

13.2 THE SPATIAL DEFICIT IN WS

Williams syndrome was first brought to the attention of cognitive scientists by Bellugi, Sabo, and Vaid (1988), who provided evidence for a strikingly uneven cognitive profile that included strength in language and severe weakness in visual-spatial construction tasks. The combined language–space profile suggested the strong hypothesis that genetic deficits could target some domains of knowledge while leaving others spared (Bellugi et al., 1988; Pinker, 1994). Explaining the spatial impairment itself gave rise to the hypothesis of a deficit in "global processing" (Bihrle, Bellugi, Delis, & Marks, 1989), that is, the claim that people with WS process local features of objects correctly but are impaired in integrating these features into a global percept. Such a deficit could, in principle, explain the great difficulty these people have in the hallmark tasks of reassembling local elements of a pattern into a global form.

The global processing deficit has, however, been ruled out by a number of findings. In visual search, for example, normal adults find it easy to locate a target when it is presented in isolation from a set of confusable distractors because the display is organized as two distinct groups, with the target being easy to see as an element different from the distractors. Pani, Mervis, and Robinson (1999) reported that adults with WS showed the same effect, demonstrating their normal use of the gestalt law of "grouping by proximity." Recent research has further shown that children and adults with WS are susceptible to visual illusions to the same degree as normal adults (Ogbonna, Palomares, Landau, Hoffman, & Egeth, 2004; Palomares, Ogbonna, Landau, & Egeth, 2006). Perception of visual illusions is produced by obligatory visual grouping processes, and the normal susceptibility to illusions in WS therefore argues strongly against a global processing deficit in perception. Finally, studies by Farran, Jarrold, and Gathercole (2003) have directly contrasted tasks requiring drawing of global patterns from local parts to those requiring perceptual matching for global patterns composed of local parts. These studies show deficits only in the drawing tasks, showing that the severe spatial impairment cannot be explained by faulty perception.

More recently, a different kind of hypothesis has been offered to explain the impairment. Wang, Doherty, Rourke, and Bellugi (1995) first suggested that the overall pattern of spatial impairment across a variety of tasks might be caused by damage to the dorsal stream of the brain with relative sparing of ventral stream functions. They tested individuals with WS on a range of spatial tasks and found the typical severe deficit on construction tasks, but less of a deficit (relative to controls who had Down syndrome) on tasks of face perception or tasks requiring identification of objects from noncanonical perspectives. Since object and face recognition are thought to be carried out by the ventral stream, Wang et al. reasoned that the WS deficit might be specific to the dorsal stream.

Atkinson et al. (2003) offered a similar hypothesis, specifically, that the deficit was produced by damage to a cortical circuit consisting of dorsal and frontal (executive) areas that operate on spatial information. Atkinson et al. (2003) reported several pieces of evidence in favor of this hypothesis, including deficits in people with WS on a Stroop test that used spatial stimuli, deficits in a visual-motor task (see section 13.2.1.2), and deficits in some aspects of motion processing (see section 13.2.1.1). The hypothesis of generalized dorsal stream deficit has recently been challenged by evidence that perception of motion coherence—a putative dorsal stream function—is not impaired in children and adults with WS (Reiss et al., 2005; see section 13.2.1.2). However, recent functional MRI studies show that people with WS exhibit hypoactivation of parietal areas when they are engaged in visual-spatial construction tasks (Meyer-Lindenberg et al., 2004). This abnormal hypoactivation is provided as direct evidence of deficits in parietal areas of the dorsal stream.

The hypothesis of dorsal stream deficits possibly localized to areas of the parietal lobe gains plausibility on a number of other grounds, as we discuss below. However, as we stress in our introduction, we believe that deep understanding of the spatial deficit in WS requires detailed studies of the nature of spatial representation. For this reason, we now turn to our own studies of the WS profile, showing that it has the three characteristics discussed above: it is uneven, it is constrained, and it has an unusual set of timing characteristics.

13.2.1 The Uneven Profile: Robustness and Fragility

Despite the severe deficit shown by people with WS in construction and drawing tasks, we have found quite remarkable robustness in several spatial domains that have complex and highly specific computational characteristics and are governed by specific areas of the brain. These contrast with areas of clear fragility. Below, we report briefly on areas of robust representation (object representation, biological motion perception, spatial language) and areas of fragility (attentional object tracking, coordination of reference frames, visual–manual guided action).

13.2.1.1 ROBUST REPRESENTATION

13.2.1.1.1 Objects Although object recognition can sometimes be achieved on the basis of color or surface texture (bananas are yellow; artifacts often have smooth surfaces), one spatial property—object shape—is arguably the most important property used by the visual system for recognition. The computational solution to recognizing objects is complex because objects need to be identified regardless of changes in viewpoint, size, lighting, and so on (see Palmieri & Gauthier, 2004, for a review). In addition, many objects such as bears, trees, and people are nonrigid and therefore can change shape from one occasion to another. Object recognition processes must somehow pick out the invariant characteristics of object shape and discard the results of these irrelevant transformations. Object recognition in adults also occurs extremely rapidly. Recent evidence shows that we identify objects at about the same time as we realize that we have seen them (Grill-Spector & Kanwisher, 2005).

In a series of experiments, we asked whether children with WS could accurately recognize (and identify) common objects when presented briefly (500 msec each), and under a variety of challenging conditions (Landau et al., 2006). In one condition, we presented full-color objects either in canonical or unusual orientations. Canonical orientations exposed many large and diagnostic parts of objects, whereas unusual orientations showed highly atypical views with few diagnostic parts (see figure 13.2). Overall, children with WS were comparable to mental-age–matched controls (MA) and only slightly worse than normally developing children of the same age (CA controls), primarily in the unusual views condition. In order to make sure that the good performance of children with WS was not based on non-shape features such as color or texture, we also tested them on line drawings of the same objects (see, e.g., figure 13.2B). The results were similar, with comparable performance for WS and MA controls and a small advantage for the CA group, mainly on objects shown in unusual views. The good performance of children with WS stands in marked contrast to their difficulty in block construction and drawing tasks and indicates that their object recognition processes are largely spared (see Landau et al., 2006, for full discussion).

13.2.1.1.2 Biological Motion and Other Motion Processing Motion processing in people with WS has also been of interest, primarily because evidence suggests that various components of the motion processing system reside in the dorsal stream, and therefore, deficits in motion processing might provide evidence for dorsal stream impairments. However, the motion processing system is itself specialized: biological motion processing, motion coherence, and form-from-motion appear to be dissociable from each other (for evidence from single-cell recording in monkeys, see Maunsell & Van

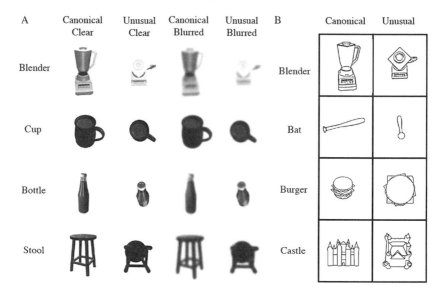

Figure 13.2 (*A*) Examples of full-color objects used in an experiment on object recognition. Objects were shown in four different conditions, crossing viewpoint (canonical or unusual) with clarity of image (clear or blurred). (*B*) Examples of line-drawn objects used in a second experiment on object recognition. Objects were shown in two different conditions varying viewpoint (canonical or unusual). Objects are representative of the stimuli used in Landau, Hoffman, and Kurz (2006). See color insert.

Essen, 1983; for evidence in human patients, see Cowey & Vaina, 2000; Vaina, Lemay, Bienfang, & Choi, 1990). We took advantage of this fact and studied whether any aspects of motion processing are selectively impaired in WS.

A particularly compelling example of seeing shapes based on motion is biological motion perception in which observers are able to quickly perceive a walking person based only on the motion of lights attached to the major joints (Johansson, 1973). This kind of motion perception involves the *global integration* of the local motion paths traced out by each of the joints. Taken singly, these local motion paths do not lead to a perception of biological motion. People with WS, who have sometimes been characterized as having deficits in the ability to see global shapes, might be expected to have difficulty with this task. However, we found that children with WS were comparable to and, in some cases, better than MA controls in discriminating the direction of locomotion of a point-light-walker embedded in dynamic noise (Jordan, et al., 2002).

The robustness of biological motion perception is consistent with the idea of specialization within spatial systems. In order to further probe robust representation in other systems of motion perception, we examined performance of people with WS in a variety of motion perception tasks, including motion coherence, biological motion, and two-dimensional form-from-motion (Reiss et al., 2005). People with WS were impaired (relative to MA matches) only in the two-dimensional form-from-motion task. Interestingly, this task was similar to one used by Atkinson et al. (1997), who also reported a motion processing deficit. We also found that the relative difficulties with the form-from-motion task persisted into adulthood, with adults with WS failing to perform at levels beyond that of a normal 6-year-old child.

These results show that biological motion is not the only motion task that is preserved in people with WS; motion coherence is, as well, and evidence from animals suggests that this is processed in dorsal stream region V5/MT (Newsome & Pare, 1988). This finding is important because it suggests that people with WS do not have a "generalized" dorsal stream deficit but are impaired in only certain kinds of motion tasks that are thought to engage the dorsal stream.

The underlying cause of difficulty in the two-dimensional form-from-motion task remains to be determined, but one possibility is that this task places a premium on the ability to segment a noisy signal from its background. People with WS seem to have difficulty with segmentation of a part from a surrounding whole. For example, Hoffman et al. (2003) found that performance in the block construction task by both normally developing and children with WS improved when the blocks making up the model were separated from each other. Even here, however, children with WS continued to show a deleterious effect of the surrounding blocks, reflecting an inability to effectively separate individual blocks from their surrounding context.

13.2.1.1.3 Spatial Language: Motion Events   Mapping spatial experience into linguistic forms engages a distinctly different kind of system from either object recognition or motion perception. One must, of course, perceive objects and their motions in order to say what has occurred in any motion event. But talking about what we see further requires that we map these percepts into a linguistic structure that obeys syntactic and semantic constraints on the expression of motion events (Jackendoff, 1983; Talmy, 1978).

In two series of experiments, we probed the spatial-linguistic knowledge of people with WS, testing whether they obeyed the constraints of English in describing simple motion events. In the first series, we showed children a series of brief animated motion events, for example, a doll hopping into a small ring or a toy cow falling off the back of a wagon. After people viewed each event, they were asked to tell us "what happened" (Landau & Zukowski, 2003). Descriptions were analyzed in terms of both semantic and syntactic content, emphasizing the encoding of three key elements of the motion events that are encoded in languages of the world: the *figure* (a noun phrase in English, e.g., "a girl"), the *motion* (usually a verb, e.g., "hopped"), and the *path expression*, a combination of a path function (usually a preposition, e.g., "into") and a reference object (a noun phrase, e.g., "a small ring"). Importantly, the path expressions in English and other languages have significant internal structure. For example, paths are differentiated into three types: goal paths (for figures moving toward a reference object), source paths (figures moving away from a reference object), and via paths (figures moving past the reference object). Different terms must be used for different path types (e.g., *to* or *into* for goal paths, *off of* or *away from* for source paths). Moreover, one must differentiate between types of reference object in choosing a specific path term. Terms such as *on* or *off* are used when the surface of a reference object is pertinent; terms such as *in* or *out* are used when containment is pertinent.

We found that children with WS performed no differently from normally developing MA-matched children in their production of terms for the figure, motion, or path expressions, as long as the path was a "goal path"—one in which the figure moves *to* a reference object. For events in which the figure moved *away from* the reference object (source path expressions), we found that children with WS again produced well-formed expressions, but they omitted the entire path expression reliably more often than did their MA matches. Importantly, sentences produced without source path expressions were still grammatical. For example, a child with WS might tend to describe an event as "the girl fell" rather than "the girl fell off the swing." The only difference was the lower frequency with which children with WS included source path expressions.

These findings strongly suggest that there is sparing of the internal semantic and syntactic structure of spatial language among children with WS. Lakusta and Landau (2005) provided further extensive evidence for this conclusion in a series of experiments examining the structure of path expressions for different event types, including manner of motion events, change of state events, transfer events, and attachment/detachment events. In each case, children with WS were no different from MA-matched controls, and both groups showed significant and appropriate modulation of both syntax and semantics, varying with event type. Moreover, Lakusta and Landau found that the pattern of dropping source paths is common across all event types and occurs frequently in young normally developing children as young as age 3. Dropping source paths does not result in an ungrammatical utterance or a pragmatically odd one; it is simply an option to encode the source path or not. The fact that young children and people with WS tend to omit source paths may be the result of a bias to represent and remember events in terms of their goal structure (see discussion in Lakusta & Landau, 2005) but does not represent a *linguistic* deficit of any kind. Thus, we conclude that the control of linguistic structures required for the language of motion events—as well as language for other event types—is not impaired in children with WS.

13.2.1.2 FRAGILITY   In contrast to our findings of robust representation, we have found significant impairment in areas that we conjecture are related to the functioning of the dorsal stream and, more specifically, parietal areas. The clearest evidence for specific impairment in the brain is the study by Meyer-Lindenberg et al. (2004), who showed hypoactivation in the parietal areas of people with WS when they carry out visual spatial construction tasks. We hypothesize that these tasks engage many component processes that may normally demand participation of the parietal areas. Results for three candidate components are described below.

13.2.1.2.1 Object Tracking One plausible contributor to poor performance in construction tasks is the obvious need to keep track of which block in the model is being duplicated in the copy space. Keeping track of this is crucial since the task requires continuous looking back and forth between model and copy to check the identity of target model blocks and their correct locations in the copy (see, e.g., figure 13.3A). Several researchers have suggested that people typically keep track of relevant blocks and their locations by an unconscious strategy in which deictic visual "pointers" are deployed via fixations to mark each block (Ballard, Hayhoe, Pook, & Rao, 1997; Pylyshyn, 2000). Such a visual "indexing" mechanisms could provide a kind of "direct access" to objects in the world, one that is not mediated by identity or conceptual knowledge (Pylyshyn, 2000).

We asked whether such indexes could be faulty in WS, possibly accounting in part for failure in the block task. We adapted the multiple-object–tracking (MOT) task of Pylyshyn and Storm (1988). In this task, observers are cued to track a subset of identical objects while they move randomly around a display. After a motion interval lasting several seconds, people are asked to indicate which elements belong to the original cued set. This task can only be accomplished by continually tracking the objects during the motion phase because targets and distractors are not otherwise distinguishable. Normal adult observers can track approximately four or five target objects with high accuracy, but performance drops precipitously with more targets. Pylyshyn and Storm suggested that this limit on tracking accuracy reflected a similar limit on the number of visual indices that can be simultaneously deployed.

O'Hearn, Landau, and Hoffman (2005) directly examined the indexing mechanism in people with WS using this tracking task (see, figure 13.3B). Performance in the MOT task was compared to a control task in which the objects remained stationary for the entire trial. Compared to MA-matched controls, children and adults with WS were impaired on the MOT task but not the control task. In order to see where people with WS fell on a normal developmental curve, we also assessed performance across a range of ages in normally developing children. People with WS, who had an average chronological age of 18, were comparable to 5-year-old, normally developing children on the static control task but performed like 4-year-olds on the MOT task. This difference is important because large improvements were observed in MOT for normally developing children between the ages of

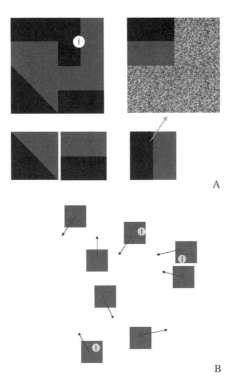

Figure 13.3 (*A*) Illustration of the role of indexes in block construction. The observer is moving a block into the copy area and will need to make an eye movement back to the model to retrieve its location. That location has been marked by an index (circle with "I" in the center), facilitating an eye movement to the block's location without the need to store that information in working memory (for discussion, see text and Hoffman et al., 2003). (*B*) Illustration of the role of indexes in multiple object tracking (MOT). The observer is tracking three objects in a display of eight identical objects each moving along an independent motion path (arrows). Indexes allow multiple objects to be tracked in parallel without the need to store explicit location information in working memory. Errors can arise, however, when a distractor passes too close to a target and captures its index. The beginning of this kind of error is illustrated by the two objects on the right of the display. This type of error accounts for the majority of errors committed both by children and adults with WS and by normal children between the ages of 4 and 7 (for discussion, see text and O'Hearn et al., 2005).

4 and 5. The results suggest that there is rapid development in indexing ability during the first 6 years of life and that people with WS are delayed and/or arrested in their development of this skill. It is interesting to note that imaging research suggests that the neural substrate of object tracking is located in parietal and frontal cortex (Culham et al., 1998), and these areas are known to show a protracted period of development.

13.2.1.2.2 Coordinating Frames of Reference to Represent Location Another plausible contributor to failure in visual construction tasks is the need
to transfer spatial information from one reference system (centered on the
model) to another, separate reference system at another location (the copy
area). Once information is transferred to the new reference system, the person needs to place each copied component of the model at the "same place"
in the copy area.

Abundant evidence from neuroscience shows that the coordination of
frames of reference of various types occurs in frontal and parietal areas of
the brain (Andersen & Zipser, 1988; Colby & Goldberg, 1999). For example, the transformation from retinocentric to egocentric frames of reference,
required for accurate updating of eye movements, engages these areas. Developmental evidence suggests that toddlers with WS may be impaired in
the updating of eye movements (Brown et al., 2003). Moreover, the clear
difficulties that people with WS experience when they try to place individual blocks into parallel locations in a copy space suggests that they have difficulty in establishing parallels between the model's reference system and
that of the copy area (Hoffman et al., 2003).

In order to directly examine difficulties in coordinating the reference
systems for two different spaces, Landau and Hoffman (2005) asked children with WS to match a sample array (a square with a dot nearby) to its
identical copy. The sample was always shown in the center of one sheet of
paper, and the test items (same, different) were shown on a sheet of paper
placed below the sample sheet, with the test items shown to the left and
right of the sample (see figure 13.4). "Same" items were always identical to
the sample, and the "different" items portrayed the dot moved by a small

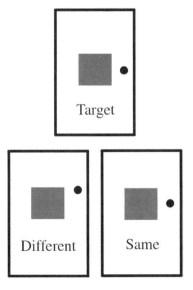

Figure 13.4 Sample arrays from experiments on coordinating reference systems.
People are instructed to observe the location
of the dot relative to the square in the top
panel, and then select which of the two bottom panels shows the dot in the same location relative to the square. Test locations
were distributed around the square, with
dot locations varying in distance and direction from the center of the square (for discussion, see text and Landau & Hoffman,
2005).

amount. The entire set of test items sampled a wide range of locations relative to the square, including locations that fell at varying distances on the extension of the square's vertical and horizontal axes, or along the extension of the square's oblique axes.

Results showed that children with WS could coordinate the two reference frames as well as MA-matched children, but only for certain locations (see figure 13.5). For example, all locations in which the dot contacted the square were accurate at ceiling levels. In addition, locations close to the square but along the extension of the vertical or horizontal axes were also matched at very high levels of accuracy. Two major and important differences did emerge, however. First, children with WS were reliably worse than MA matches for dots located at larger distances from the square, suggesting that representing locations in a single reference frame and/or translating one location via the coordination of two reference frames is quite fragile, breaking down with any substantial distance from the reference object (see chapter 14 for ideas on calibrating reference frames). Second, although both normal and children with WS performed worse for locations along the horizontal axis than along the vertical axis, children with WS suffered more, again suggesting a fragile reference system.

These results are consistent with the difficulty that children with WS have in putting blocks into the "same" location in a copy area after having inspected a model. The reference system seems to have normal structure

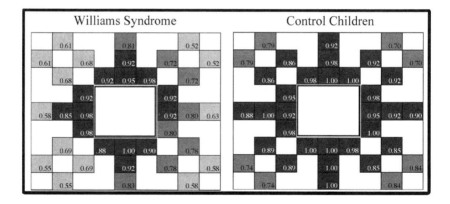

Figure 13.5 Pattern of performance by children with WS and normal MA-matched children. Accuracy is coded by shades, with darker regions corresponding to higher accuracy. Percent correct for each target location is indicated inside each box. Both groups of children perform at ceiling for locations in contact with the square reference object (at center), and both groups show higher accuracy for locations along the vertical and horizontal extensions of the square's axis. However, children with WS break down more rapidly with increasing distance from the reference object and show lower accuracy for horizontal axes than do normal children (for discussion, see text and Landau and Hoffman, 2005).

(i.e., two orthogonal axes), but these systems are fragile. This fragility carries over into tasks requiring that one location be mapped onto another in a different reference system—a requirement for any copying task. Given the evidence for parietal involvement in the coordination of reference frames, these findings again suggest that dorsal and particularly parietal functions may be impaired in WS.

13.2.1.2.3 Visual–Manual Action A final mechanism required in the construction task is the manual placement of copy blocks into their target locations. Areas of the motor cortex and, more generally, the dorsal stream have been implicated in the ability to carry out visually directed actions. One widely cited analysis was offered by Milner and Goodale (1995), who described a patient who had sustained cortical damage due to carbon monoxide poisoning. This woman was severely impaired in a task requiring her to judge the orientation of a slot in a box but was able to post a letter into the same slot. This and other cases led Milner and Goodale to propose that two separate functions are carried by two different streams of processing in the brain. The "what" system engages the ventral stream of the brain, supporting tasks such as perception and object identification. The "how" system is located in the dorsal stream of the brain, supporting tasks such as grasping, posting, and other visual–manual actions that require online continuous updating of the effectors relative to a stable target as the action is carried out.

We adapted Milner and Goodale's (1995) tasks for use with children and adults with WS, as well as MA-matched children (who were approximately 6 years of age) and other normal children who were younger than these MA matches (approximately 4 years of age; Dilks, Landau, & Hoffman, 2005; see also Atkinson et al., 2003, for a similar task). In the action task, we asked people to pick up a "dollar bill" and insert it into a "piggy bank" whose slot could be oriented at any of four different angles. In the perceptual matching task, we asked people to judge whether a manikin hand holding the dollar bill was "ready to put the dollar into the slot," using the same test angles.

In the perceptual matching task, all performances were highly accurate, with the performances of people with WS and those of MA matches closely comparable to each other. Even 4-year-olds performed very accurately, indicating that the task tapped into a function that develops rapidly and is close to mature by this age. In contrast, the action task showed large differences across groups. The MA matches performed reliably better than did the people with WS (both children and adults), who performed at the level of 4-year-old normal children. These results reveal that there is significant development in visually guided action among normally developing children between ages 4 and 6. In addition, the results showed that the participants with WS (mean age of children = 12 years, mean age of adults = 23) were basically stuck at the level of 4-year-old, normally developing children. The pattern of performance across the different groups was similar, with high accuracy on vertical and horizontal target orientations and error-prone performance on obliques, suggesting a common, underlying representation of orientation.

These results suggest fragility in the visual–manual action system among people with WS, with disproportionate error around targets in the posting (action) task. The 4-year-old age equivalence for individuals with WS was the same in both the perception and action tasks, but importantly, the perception task was close to maturity in normal children by age 4, whereas the action task showed significant growth among normal children between ages 4 and 6. Individuals with WS appear to perform about like 4-year-olds in both tasks, suggesting the possibility of arrest at this developmental level.

13.2.2 The Constrained Profile

In the foregoing discussion, we have presented evidence on overall robustness or impairment but have said little about the nature of the underlying cognitive processes supporting this performance. If normally developing children's spatial representations have internal structure, then we can ask whether people with WS show the same internal structure. Detailed error analyses can tell us whether any fragility or impairment is a qualitative or quantitative phenomenon.

Across many studies from our lab, patterns of performance and error analyses show that people with WS possess the same internal structure for various domains as normally developing people at *some* developmental point. In the preceding sections, we reported that people with WS performed sometimes at the same level as CA matches (object identification with canonical and full-color objects), sometimes at the same level as MA matches (object identification with unusual views and line drawings, biological motion, language of events), and sometimes worse than the MA matches (MOT, coordination of reference frames, visual–manual posting). In some of these cases, we also know that the individuals with WS perform at the same level as normally developing 4-year-olds (MOT, posting). As it turns out, whatever the overall performance level (hence whatever the average age equivalence), error profiles of individuals with WS look the same as those of normal individuals. There is insufficient space in this chapter to detail all of the error analyses we have carried out. Thus, we highlight several examples to make the point, and we urge readers to consult our publications for further information (see, e.g., Lakusta & Landau, 2005; Landau & Hoffman, 2005; Landau et al, 2006; O'Hearn et al., 2005).

In our studies of object identification, we found similar distributions of responses across all age groups tested. For example, errors tended to be shape related (e.g., calling a cheeseburger viewed from above "the sun," or an upright piano a "desk"). Because the objects were briefly presented (500 msec), it is likely that the overall shape of the objects played a large role in guiding guesses among all participants, including normal adults.

In addition, we ranked the relative difficulty of all 80 objects we used as test items and found very high correlations across all groups in the relative degrees of difficulty. In other words, an object that was incorrectly named by a normal adult was also likely to be labeled incorrectly by the children with WS as well as normally developing children.

In the studies of spatial language, we already noted that the primary difference between people with WS and normal controls was the tendency for people with WS to omit source path expressions. However, Lakusta and Landau (2005) found that this tendency to omit source paths also occurs regularly among 3- to 4-year-old normally developing children; moreover, this profile of "source vulnerability" appears across a variety of different event types. We found additional error patterns that reinforced the notion of source vulnerability. For example, young children occasionally substituted a goal path term for a source path term ("the girl got the ball *to* the boy," meaning "got *from*") but never the reverse. These errors were also found among participants with WS.

In the MOT task, the participants with WS (children and adults) performed overall like 4-year-olds in the moving condition, which is most diagnostic of the mechanism of "indexing." Our analysis of error patterns revealed that all groups showed a tendency toward "slippery indexes" in which distractors that passed close to a target object during the tracking phase were often designated as targets at the end of the trial—as if the indexes "slipped off" the targets while they were moving, landing on a spatial neighbor. This pattern accounted for the majority of errors in all groups. The similarity of performance across groups suggests that development of indexing ability, and its impairment in WS, may not involve a reorganization of how the task is accomplished as much as an improvement in the ability to deploy multiple indexes (and possibly an increase in the number of indexes) and resist their capture by nearby distractors. Finally, as we noted above in our discussion of the visual–manual "posting" task, we tested people on four different orientations of the slot and found more errors and variability for oblique targets than for vertical or horizontal ones. Crucially, however, the degree of error at each orientation was no different between participants with WS and the 4-year-old normally developing children, suggesting once more that the fine-grained pattern of performance was the same in these two groups.

Thus, in the four examples we have discussed (object identification, spatial language, MOT, visual–manual action), we have found consistent and considerable evidence for sameness in the internal architecture of performance. Even detailed analyses of copying—a task that always shows severe deficit—reveals strong similarities between individuals with WS and their MA matches, suggesting that the breakdown observed is more likely to be the product of normal development at some point than a qualitative reorganization in the system (Bertrand, Mervis, & Eisenberg, 1997; Georgopoulos, Georgopoulos, Kurz, & Landau, 2004).

13.2.3 The Unusual Timing Profile (and the Importance of Normal Development)

One of the most persistent puzzles about WS is the unusual profile of combined strengths and weaknesses—both across aspects of spatial representation and across different knowledge domains. The earliest and most compelling description of WS still holds: people with WS have surprisingly strong language, both in an absolute and relative sense. In an absolute sense, people with WS can make accurate judgments about the grammaticality of complex sentences (Bellugi et al., 1988), and they can produce very complex sentences such as those with both object and subject-relative clauses (Zukowski, 2001). These structures are very complex, and highly internally constrained; accurate production by people whose average overall IQ is 70 is surprising to even the strongest skeptic. Language is definitely a strength, especially relative to the severe impairment on block construction tasks.

But there is another sense of "relative" strength that is also important. How does the language profile of a child with WS compare to that of a normally developing child? Are complex structures such as object-relatives accurately produced at age 4? At age 7? At age 18? Depending on the answer, we may have a very different picture of the developmental mechanisms at work.

Thinking about strength and fragility in spatial representation requires a similar analysis. Surely block construction is a weakness, and we have argued that people with WS also show special weakness in other spatial tasks such as multiple-object tracking, visual–manual action, and recognizing objects shown in unusual perspectives. We have also argued that people with WS show relative strengths in other classes of spatial tasks, including recognition of objects shown in canonical perspectives, perception of biological motion and motion coherence, and spatial language. But how do these profiles of strength and fragility look when they are compared to the normal developmental profile? Are there normally differences in the developmental trajectory of these tasks? Surely the WS spatial profile is unusual for a normal adolescent or adult. But is this profile completely different from what we would see in normal development at *any* age?

We speculate that the unusual spatial profile seen in WS is a consequence of two effects. First, the two sets of tasks we have used may map onto two different systems or pathways in the brain, with the ventral stream developing early and the dorsal stream having a more protracted course of development. This predicts that younger normal children will show an imbalance in which cognitive functions that depend on the ventral stream may be stronger than those that depend on the dorsal stream. Older children will have a more balanced set of abilities as both systems approach maturity.

The second effect is particular to WS. We speculate that people with WS undergo very slow development of both streams and that there is premature developmental arrest at the functional level of a normally developing

4-year-old child. This arrest could take place because of the early onset of puberty (Partsch et al., 1999), which might create changes in the efficiency of biological learning mechanisms. Such prolonged growth followed by functional arrest would result in the spatial imbalance characteristic of a 4-year-old: good performance in ventral stream tasks with relative weakness in tasks that depend on the immature dorsal system. Of course, this pattern occurs for WS in a much older child, or an adult, and this will present as a seriously abnormal imbalance.

The basis for our speculation is the overall profile of strengths and fragility across the different aspects of spatial representation we have examined. As we have reported, people with WS perform worse than MA matches (approximately 6-year-olds) on tasks such as block construction and drawing (Georgopoulos et al., 2004; Hoffman et al., 2003), coordination of reference frames (Landau & Hoffman, 2005), MOT (O'Hearn et al., 2005), and visual–manual action ("posting"; Dilks et al., 2005). At the same time, we have stressed that the overall performance and detailed internal structure of the performance of people with WS on these tasks is quite similar to 4-year-old normally developing children. This suggests that the people with WS we have tested (usually 10 or more years of age) have reached the functional level of a normal 4-year-old for these tasks.

In contrast, we have also reported that people with WS perform at the same level or better than MA matches in tasks tapping perception of biological motion and motion coherence (Reiss et al., 2005), object recognition under canonical or unusual views (Landau et al., 2006), and spatial language (Lakusta & Landau, 2005). Perceptual matching of orientation is almost equivalent to MA matches, even though visual–manual action using the same stimuli is much worse (Dilks, Reiss, Hoffman, & Landau, 2004).

But what is the normal trajectory for these capacities that are robust in people with WS? We currently have only preliminary evidence on this question, but we speculate that these capacities normally emerge quite early. Consider object identification from canonical perspectives. People with WS recognize and accurately identify objects at close to ceiling levels and do not differ from either MA or CA matches in this regard. This is clearly a strength. But suppose normal 4-year-olds show the same levels of performance. Then the WS strength in object recognition relative to the weakness in block construction would have a very different interpretation: it would suggest performance across both tasks that is about comparable to that of a 4-year-old normally developing child. Preliminary evidence from our studies of normally developing 4-year-olds suggests that this is the correct interpretation. If confirmed, this would suggest a different kind of spatial profile—one in which strengths appear in those areas that are normally early-developing. Other comparisons from our lab are also consistent with this picture. For example, the crucial syntactic and semantic properties of spatial language for motion events are normally mastered by age 4, and people with WS show strength in these properties. Tasks requiring simple perceptual matching of two oriented lines elicit strong performance by normal 4-year-olds, and there is little development between age 4 and 6. People with WS perform about like both 4- and 6-year-olds, showing strength, especially in comparison to parallel tasks requiring visual–manual action (Dilks et al., 2005).

These cases can be contrasted with spatial capacities that normally undergo more prolonged development. One example is object identification from unusual perspectives. Normal children show substantial development between ages 6 and 12, according to our data (Landau et al., 2006). People with WS show performance no different from 6-year-olds (also their MA matches) but worse performance than 12-year-olds. This ability clearly undergoes prolonged development in normal children, and individuals with WS do not ever seem to reach the same level as normal 12-year-olds. We do not yet know whether there is also normal development in recognition from unusual perspectives between ages 4 and 6. If there is growth in this age range, then this would suggest that people with WS have strength relative to normal 4-year-olds, contrasting with the cases discussed above. But if there is no developmental change between ages 4 and 6, then it would appear that people with WS hit the functional level of a 4-year-old normal child, and grow no further.

We can idealize these different views of the unusual timing profile in two different ways, illustrated in figure 13.6. An assumption of both possibilities is that normally there are different developmental trajectories—or rates of development—for each of the two streams of visual-spatial processing, dorsal and ventral. Various researchers have hypothesized that the ventral stream undergoes more rapid development than the dorsal stream, with the latter also more vulnerable to developmental abnormalities (Neville & Bavelier, 2000). Figure 13.6A idealizes the situation in which relative shapes of the two trajectories (dorsal and ventral streams) are the same for people with WS and normal children, but there is an overall slower rate of development for people with WS relative to normal children. Another way of saying this is that the differences between the rates of development for the two streams is roughly equal, despite the overall slowing down of development in the case of WS. For sake of argument, the WS rate is shown as half the rate (twice as slow) as normal children. This is shown by the difference in chronological ages for the two groups along the x-axis. If we combine this profile with early arrest (due to puberty, perhaps), we would place the profile of the person with WS at roughly the level of a 4-year-old normally developing child (shown as the vertical line in figure 13.6A). Thus, the ventral and dorsal streams in people with WS might develop until they reach the functional level of a normal 4-year-old child and then slow down or stop completely. Their profile would look like that of a normal 4-year-old but it would, of course, look very unusual in a 12- or 20-year-old person.

Figure 13.6B idealizes a different picture of timing, in which the relative shapes of the trajectories for the two streams are different for normal children than for people with WS. In the hypothetical curves shown, the

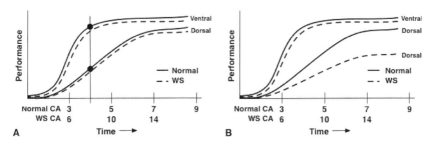

Figure 13.6 Two hypothetical views of the timing relationships between dorsal and ventral streams for normally developing children and individuals with WS. Both views assume that there are differences in rates of development between the dorsal and ventral streams. (A) The relative shapes of the two trajectories (dorsal, ventral) are the same for people with WS and normal children, although there is overall slower development with WS, leading to different age profiles (shown along the x-axis in hypothetical chronological ages). This profile, combined with early arrest, would lead to a profile that resembles that of a normally developing 4-year-old child, with strength in ventral stream functions and weakness in dorsal functions, as indicated by the vertical line crossing the two streams. (B) The relative shapes of the two trajectories are different for WS and normal individuals, with the WS dorsal trajectory much flatter than the normal one. Even without early arrest, this profile would lead to persistent and permanent immaturity in dorsal stream functions but relative strength in ventral stream functions. See text for further discussion.

dorsal stream in WS undergoes development that is even slower than that of the ventral stream, increasing the difference in early developmental profile between functions of the two streams. This situation would lead to an even greater lag in dorsal stream functions (relative to ventral functions) for people with WS compared to normally developing people. Even if there were no arrest at the functional level of a 4-year-old, the dorsal stream functions would never reach normal levels, resulting in permanent developmental deficits in these functions.

Figure 13.6B is obviously a simplification. For example, detection of coherent motion and perception of biological motion are both, at least partly, dorsal stream functions but ones that develop early. Generally, early developing systems are ones that appear to be primarily "bottom-up" or automatic and consist of dedicated computational and neural machinery of great complexity, designed to carry out specific cognitive tasks given the right input (e.g., object recognition from canonical perspectives, or language acquisition). People with WS perform at the level of MA matches or better on these tasks (we have yet to determine whether 4-year-old, normally developing children also perform at these levels). In contrast, tasks that are not likely to be carried out by such dedicated neural machinery, such as recognizing objects from unusual perspectives, appear to call on dorsal stream activation, particularly various areas of the parietal lobe.

It should be noted that the parietal lobe plays an important role in co-ordinating various frames of reference, and this may provide a clue as to why this area has a protracted course of development and is important in situations requiring flexibility in response. First, because the size of the body is changing over the course of development, the relationship between perception and action must constantly be updated. Second, because different reference frames may be important for different tasks, choice and flexibility are important requirements for the kinds of computations carried out in this area. These properties may help explain why the parietal lobe is an important area for controlling visual attention and why it may have a protracted course of development.

We speculate that tasks having a protracted course of development are those that require flexibility and control and therefore require attention that can be flexibly modulated. This includes attentive MOT, visual–manual action requiring some precision (e.g., the posting task), and object recognition from unusual perspectives. Note that a system such as visual attention is likely important for a wide range of very different tasks and that deficits in this system will show up in a variety of different contexts from block construction to spatial language.

Interestingly, in this view, some apparent exceptions to the rule that we have observed make sense. For example, despite overall strength in spatial language, people with WS have difficulty encoding direction in spatial terms (e.g., above/below, right/left). This is an area of spatial language that develops at around age 6 or 7 in normal children, and we have found that even adults with WS still make systematic confusion errors between right and left (Landau & Hoffman, 2005). Although this is a language task (hence a putative ventral stream function), talking about left and right requires that a person accurately represent directional differences along an axis (the horizontal for left/right). Such differences are also involved in recognition of mirror-image differences. There is evidence that discrimination between mirror-image versions of objects depends on parietal areas. For example, damage to these areas in human adults leads to difficulties distinguishing mirror-image objects from each other (Priftis, Rusconi, Umilta, & Zorzi, 2003; Warrington & Taylor, 1973). Not surprisingly, our WS group is also impaired (relative to MA matches) at matching under brief delay in the context of mirror-image objects (Hoffman & Landau, 2006).

In sum, we speculate that normal differences in the time of emergence for different aspects of spatial representation can shed light on the WS spatial impairment. Early-emerging spatial capacities seem to draw on primarily ventral functions, and these capacities would be important for tasks such as object recognition from canonical viewpoints, biological motion, and much of spatial language. Those capacities that appear to have a more protracted developmental course are likely to be the province of the dorsal stream, particularly parietal areas. These capacities underlie tasks such as MOT, visual–manual action, and object recognition from unusual perspectives.

We can add to these the classic tasks that are diagnostic of WS—block construction and drawing. Above we suggested that these tasks reflect many different kinds of spatial capacities. But they also seem to have a protracted developmental curve, and people with WS typically perform at the level of a normal 4-year-old child. Perhaps not coincidentally, these tasks appear to tap many spatial capacities that involve the parietal areas of the brain. Given recent evidence that people with WS may have parietal damage (Meyer-Lindenberg et al., 2004), it is perhaps not surprising that their performance on these tasks shows massive impairment.

13.3 GENES, BRAINS, AND MINDS: EXPLAINING THE SPATIAL DEFICIT IN WS

Above, we outlined four principles of human spatial development: specialization of function, constraints within each specialized system, differences in developmental timing across different systems, and the idea that genes can target specific areas of cognition. We believe that these four principles taken together with the evidence reviewed above point to an explanation of sparing and breakdown in WS that brings together otherwise diverse phenomena. But how does this explanation start with genes and end up with effects on cognitive systems? We assume that genes have (at least) proximal effects, for instance, effects that result in altering the production of proteins involved in early development, the development of neurons, and connectivity among them. These molecular effects could play a role in slowing down the cascade of developmental events that accompanies development of the brain. These proximal effects might also give rise to differences in the rate of development of the two major streams of processing in the visual brain. The differences in rate of development could then result in a profile of strengths and fragility that mimics the functional level of a 4-year-old, or perhaps even more imbalance in the relative strength and fragility of functions carried out by the two streams. In this way, the unusual profile of a person with WS might actually be a consequence of normal developmental process and mechanism, combined with slow growth and arrest at an early functional level. The unusual profile would be a consequence of timing differences but would not result in compromise of the core properties of spatial representational systems, including specialization of function and internal cognitive architectural characteristics.

Although our explanation is clearly speculative, it satisfies a number of desirable criteria. First, it preserves the computational distinctions among different spatial functions by proposing that the breakdown is specialized, respecting normal aspects of spatial architecture. Second, it preserves the idea that there are strong internal constraints on learning in any domain—in this case, the multiple domains of spatial representation—and proposes that these constraints are obeyed even in cases of unusual or abnormal development. Third, it preserves the idea that spatial specialization is reflected in the functioning of different areas of the brain or, more generally, different streams of processing. Fourth, it unites normal developmental process with impairment due to genetic deficit. And finally, it preserves the idea that, even though genes clearly have proximal effects, they can also target specific cognitive systems.

ACKNOWLEDGMENTS   This work is supported by March of Dimes grant 04-78, National Science Foundation BCS 0117744, and National Institute of Neurological Disorders and Stroke RO1 NINDS RO1 NS 050876. We thank Whitney Street for her assistance in preparation of the manuscript.

REFERENCES

Andersen, R. A., & Zipser, D. (1988). The role of the posterior parietal cortex in coordinate transformations for visual-motor integration. *Canadian Journal of Physiology & Pharmacology, 66*, 488–501.

Atkinson, J., Braddick, O., & Anker, S. (2003). Neurobiological models of visuospatial cognition in children with Williams syndrome: Measures of dorsal-stream and frontal function. *Developmental Neuropsychology, 23*, 139–172.

Atkinson, J., King, J., Braddick, O., Nokes, L., Anker, S., & Braddick, F. (1997). A specific deficit of dorsal stream function in William's syndrome. *Neuroreport: An International Journal for the Rapid Communication of Research in Neuroscience, 8*, 1919–1922.

Bailey, T. J., El-Hodiri, H., Zhang, L., Shah, R., Mathers, P. H., & Jamrich, M. (2004). Regulation of vertebrate eye development by Rx genes. *International Journal of Developmental Biology, 48*, 761–770.

Ballard, D. H., Hayhoe, M. M., Pook, P. K., & Rao, R. P. N. (1997). Deictic codes for the embodiment of cognition. *Behavioral & Brain Sciences, 20*, 723–767.

Bellugi, U., Sabo, H., & Vaid, J. (1988). Spatial deficits in children with Williams syndrome. In J. Stiles-Davis, M. Kritchevsky, & U. Bellugi (Eds.), *Spatial cognition, brain bases, and development* (pp. 273–298). Hillsdale, NJ: Lawrence Erlbaum.

Bertrand, J., Mervis, C. B., & Eisenberg, J. D. (1997). Drawing by children with Williams syndrome: A developmental perspective. *Developmental Neuropsychology, 13*, 41–67.

Bihrle, A. M., Bellugi, U., Delis, D. C., & Marks, S. (1989). Seeing either the forest or the trees: Dissociation in visuospatial processing. *Brain & Cognition, 11*, 37–49.

Brown, J. H., Johnson, M. H., Paterson, S. J., Gilmore, R., Longhi, E., & Karmiloff-Smith, A. (2003). Spatial representation and attention in toddlers with Williams syndrome and Down syndrome. *Neuropsychologia, 41*, 1037–1046.

Colby, C. L., & Goldberg, M. E. (1999). Space and attention in parietal cortex. *Annual Review of Neuroscience, 22*, 319–349.

Cowey, A., & Vaina, L. M. (2000). Blindness to form from motion despite intact static form perception and motion detection. *Neuropsychologia, 38*, 566–578.

Culham, J. C., Brandt, S. A., Cavanagh, P., Kanwisher, N. G., Dale, A. M., & Tootell, R. B. H. (1998). Cortical fMRI activation produced by attentive tracking of moving targets. *Journal of Neurophysiology, 80*, 2657–2670.

Deruelle, C., Mancini, J., Livet, M. O., Casse-Perrot, C., & de Schonen, S. (1999). Configural and local processing of faces in children with Williams syndrome. *Brain & Cognition, 41*, 276–298.

Dilks, D., Landau, B., & Hoffman, J. (2005). *Vision for perception and vision for action: Normal and unusual development*. Unpublished manuscript.

Dilks, D., Reiss, J., Hoffman, J. E., & Landau, B. (2004, November). *Representation of orientation in Williams syndrome*. Paper presented at the annual meeting of the Psychonomics Society, Minneapolis, MN.

Epstein, R., & Kanwisher, N. (1998). A cortical representation of the local visual environment. *Nature, 392,* 590–601.

Farran, E. K., Jarrold, C., & Gathercole, S. E. (2003). Divided attention, selective attention and drawing: Processing preferences in Williams syndrome are dependent on the task administered. *Neuropsychologia, 41,* 676–687.

Frangiskakis, J. M., Ewart, A. K., Morris, C. A., et al. (1996). LIM-kinase1 hemizygosity implicated in impaired visuospatial constructive cognition. *Cell, 86,* 59–69.

Gallistel, C. R. (1990). *The organization of learning.* Cambridge, MA: MIT Press.

Georgopoulos, M. A., Georgopoulos, A. P., Kurz, N., & Landau, B. (2004). Figure copying in Williams syndrome and normal subjects. *Experimental Brain Research, 157,* 137–146.

Grill-Spector, K., & Kanwisher, N. (2005). Visual recognition. As soon as you know it is there, you know what it is. *Psychological Science, 16*(2), 152–160.

Hermer, L., & Spelke, E. (1996). Modularity and development: The case of spatial reorientation. *Cognition, 61,* 195–232.

Hoffman, J. E., & Landau, B. (2006). *Mirror image recognition and errors in people with Williams syndrome.* Unpublished manuscript.

Hoffman, J. E., Landau, B., & Pagani, B. (2003). Spatial breakdown in spatial construction: Evidence from eye fixations in children with Williams syndrome. *Cognitive Psychology, 46,* 260–301.

Hoogenraad, C. C., Akhmanova, A., Galjart, N., & De Zeeuw, C. I. (2004). LIMK1 and CLIP-115: Linking cytoskeletal defects to Williams syndrome. *Bioessays, 26,* 141–150.

Jackendoff, R. (1983). *Semantics and cognition.* Cambridge, MA: MIT Press.

Johansson, G. (1973). Visual perception of biological motion and a model for its analysis. *Perception & Psychophysics, 14,* 201–211.

Johnson, M. (2004). *Developmental cognitive neuroscience.* London: Blackwell.

Jordan, H., Reiss, J. E., Hoffman, J. E., & Landau, B. (2002). Intact perception of biological motion in the face of profound spatial deficits: Williams syndrome. *Psychological Science, 13,* 162–167.

Kanwisher, N., McDermott, J., & Chun, M. M. (1997). The fusiform face area: A module in human extrastriate cortex specialized for face perception. *Journal of Neuroscience, 17,* 4302–4311.

Karmiloff-Smith, A. (1998). Development itself is the key to understanding developmental disorders. *Trends in Cognitive Sciences, 2,* 389–398.

Karmiloff-Smith, A., Grant, J., Berthoud, I., Davies, M., Howlin, P., & Udwin, O. (1997). Language and Williams syndrome: How intact is intact? *Child Development, 68*(2), 246–262.

Lakusta, L., & Landau, B. (2005). Starting at the end: The importance of goals in spatial language. *Cognition, 96,* 1–33.

Landau, B. (2002). Spatial cognition. In V. Ramachandran (Ed.), *Encyclopedia of the human brain* (Vol. 4, pp. 395–418). San Diego, CA: Academic Press.

Landau, B., & Hoffman, J. E. (2005). Parallels between spatial cognition and spatial language: Evidence from Williams syndrome. *Journal of Memory & Language, 53,* 163–185.

Landau, B., Hoffman, J. E., & Kurz, N. (2006). Object recognition with severe spatial deficits in Williams syndrome: sparing and breakdown. *Cognition, 100*(3), 483–510.

Landau, B., & Zukowski, A. (2003). Objects, motions, and paths: Spatial language in children with Williams syndrome. *Developmental Neuropsychology, 23,* 105–137.

Marcus, G. (2004). *The Birth of the Mind: How a Tiny Number of Genes Creates the Complexities of Human Thought.* New York: Basic Books, 2004.

Maunsell, J. H., & Van Essen, D. C. (1983). The connections of the middle temporal visual area (MT) and their relationship to a cortical hierarchy in the macaque monkey. *Journal of Neuroscience, 3,* 2563–2586.

Mervis, C. B., Morris, C. A., Klein-Tasman, B. P., et al. (2003). Attentional characteristics of infants and toddlers with Williams syndrome during triadic interactions. *Developmental Neuropsychology, 23,* 243–268.

Meyer-Lindenberg, A., Kohn, P., Mervis, C. B., et al. (2004). Neural basis of genetically determined visuospatial construction deficit in Williams syndrome. *Neuron, 43,* 623–631.

Meyer-Lindenberg, A., Mervis, C. B., & Berman, K. F. (2006). Neural mechanisms in Williams syndrome: A unique window to genetic influences on cognition and behaviour. *Nature Reviews: Neuroscience, 7*(5), 380–393.

Milner A. D., & Goodale, M. A. (1995). *The visual brain in action.* New York: Oxford University Press.

Morton, J. (2004). *Understanding developmental disorders: A causal modelling approach.* Malden, MA: Blackwell Publishing.

Neville, H., & Bavelier, D. (2000). Specificity and plasticity in neurocognitive development in humans. In M. S. Gazzaniga (Ed.), *New cognitive neurosciences* (2nd ed., pp. 251–271). Cambridge, MA: MIT Press.

Newsome, W. T., & Pare, E. B. (1988). A selective impairment of motion perception following lesions of the middle temporal visual area (MT). *Journal of Neuroscience, 8,* 2201–2211.

Ogbonna, C., Palomares, M., Landau, B., Hoffman, J., & Egeth, H. (2004, May). *The perception of visual illusions in Williams syndrome.* Paper presented at the annual meeting of the Vision Sciences Society, Sarasota, FL.

O'Hearn, K., Landau, B., & Hoffman, J. E. (2005). Multiple object tracking in normally developing children and people with Williams syndrome. *Psychological Science, 16*(11), 905–912.

Palmieri, T. J., & Gauthier, I. (2004). Visual object understanding. *Nature Reviews: Neuroscience, 5,* 291–304.

Palomares, M., Ogbonna, C., Landau, B., & Egeth, H. (2006). *Normal susceptibility to visual illusions in abnormal development: Evidence from Williams syndrome.* Unpublished manuscript.

Pani, J. R., Mervis, C. B., & Robinson, B. F. (1999). Global spatial organization by individuals with Williams syndrome. *Psychological Science, 10,* 453–458.

Partsch, C. J., Dreyer, G., Goesch, A., et al. (1999). Longitudinal evaluation of growth, puberty, and bone maturation in children with Williams syndrome. *Journal of Pediatrics, 134*(1), 82–89.

Pinker, S. (1994). *The language instinct.* New York: William Morrow & Co.

Priftis, K., Rusconi, E., Umilta, C., & Zorzi, M. (2003). Pure agnosia for mirror stimuli after right inferior parietal lesion. *Brain, 126,* 908–919.

Pylyshyn, Z. W. (2000). Situating the world in vision. *Trends in Cognitive Science, 4,* 197–204.

Pylyshyn, Z. W., & Storm, R. W. (1988). Tracking multiple independent targets: Evidence for a parallel tracking mechanism. *Spatial Vision, 3,* 179–197.

Reiss, J., Hoffman, J. E., & Landau, B. (2005). Motion processing specialization in Williams syndrome. *Vision Research, 45,* 3379–3390.

Tager-Flusberg, H., Plesa-Skwerer, D., Faja, S., & Joseph, R. M. (2003). People with Williams syndrome process faces holistically. *Cognition, 89,* 11–24.

Talmy, L. (1978). Lexicalization patterns: Semantic structure in lexical forms. In T. Shopen et al. (Eds.), *Language typology and syntactic description* (Vol. 3, pp. 57–149). New York: Cambridge University Press.

Vaina, L. M., Lemay, M., Bienfang, D. C., & Choi, A. Y. (1990). Intact "biological motion" and "structure from motion" perception in a patient with impaired motion mechanisms: A case study. *Visual Neuroscience, 5,* 353–369.

Wang, P. P., Doherty, S., Rourke, S. B., & Bellugi, U. (1995). Unique profile of visuo-perceptual skills in a genetic syndrome. *Brain & Cognition, 29,* 54–65.

Warrington, E. K., & Taylor, A. M. (1973). The contribution of the right parietal lobe to object recognition. *Cortex, 9,* 152–164.

Weeber, E. J., Levenson, J. M., & Sweatt, J. D. (2002). Molecular genetics of human cognition. *Molecular Interventions, 2*(6), 376–391.

Zukowski, A. (2001). *Uncovering grammatical competence in children with Williams syndrome.* Unpublished dissertation thesis, Boston University, Boston, MA.

14

WHAT DOES THEORETICAL NEUROSCIENCE HAVE TO OFFER THE STUDY OF BEHAVIORAL DEVELOPMENT?

Insights from a Dynamic Field Theory of Spatial Cognition

JOHN P. SPENCER, VANESSA R. SIMMERING,
ANNE R. SCHUTTE, & GREGOR SCHÖNER

The chapters in this edited volume address two questions central to discussions of the emerging spatial mind: *what* changes in spatial cognition occur over development, and *how* these changes come about. By our read of the literature, decades of research on the development of spatial cognitive abilities have yielded many clear answers to the first question but rather limited insights into the second. To illustrate, consider the following three lines of research examining the *what* question. First, evidence shows that the precision of spatial memory changes systematically over development. For instance, there is an increase in the metric precision of children's responses over a broad age range—from 2 to 11 years—in tasks where children either search for objects hidden in a homogeneous space (e.g., Schutte, Spencer, & Schöner, 2003; Spencer & Hund, 2003) or replace objects in previously learned locations (Hund & Plumert, 2002, 2003, 2005; Hund, Plumert, & Benney, 2002; Plumert & Hund, 2001).

Second, there are clear developmental changes in children's ability to coordinate/update spatial reference frames. Three-month-old infants appear to encode locations egocentrically, showing initial evidence of using a world-centered reference frame by 6 months (Gilmore & Johnson, 1997). Beyond infancy, children rely more and more on world-centered reference frames (e.g., Newcombe & Huttenlocher, 2000) but alter how these frames are used. For instance, between 3 and 6 years of age, there is a qualitative shift in children's recall accuracy near symmetry axes such that young children are biased *toward* axes of symmetry while older children are biased *away from* such axes (Schutte, 2004; Schutte & Spencer, 2002).

Third, research demonstrates that children develop the ability to think about space in increasingly complex ways. For instance, according to De-Loache's dual representation hypothesis, there is a dramatic improvement in 2.5- to 3.5-year-olds' ability to think about a scale model both as an object in and of itself and as a symbol for an identical but larger space (see DeLoache, 2004, for review).

In all of these examples, there is a clear understanding—grounded in a rich empirical database and strong theories—of *what* is changing over development. Less clear is *how* these changes take place. For instance, our spatial precision hypothesis (Schutte et al., 2003; Spencer & Hund, 2003) effectively captures the systematic improvement in spatial memory accuracy over development across a range of tasks (see section 14.5). But this hypothesis fails to explain how changes in spatial precision arise over development. Similarly, J. Huttenlocher, Hedges, and Duncan (1991) have proposed a model to explain the shift in children's use of symmetry axes/category boundaries, but this model fails to explain how this shift occurs. Finally, the dual representation hypothesis effectively brings together a diverse set of empirical findings and has generated several counterintuitive predictions (DeLoache, 2004), but this hypothesis says little about how the posited developmental change occurs.

We contend that this state of affairs is not unique to the domain of spatial cognition. Rather, developmental science in general has made relatively modest progress on specifying the mechanisms that underlie behavioral change. In McClelland and Siegler's recent volume *Mechanisms of Cognitive Development*, for instance, Posner (2001) offers the following synthesis of candidate mechanisms: (1) strategic activation of brain regions/circuits, (2) automation, (3) changes in synaptic connections in the brain, (4) changes in cortical maps, and (5) creation of new neural networks. Each of these "mechanisms" was motivated by a rich set of empirical and theoretical work using multiple techniques (e.g., behavioral work, functional MRI [fMRI], computational modeling), many of which explicitly probe brain–behavior relations. And in each case, the proposed mechanisms offer insights about development.

But also in each case, there is a clear tension: as researchers explore/ explain the longer time scales of learning and development, it becomes harder and harder to offer a detailed, process-based account of real-time behavior. For instance, many of the advances in our understanding of how synaptic connections contribute to behavioral change come from work with connectionist models (e.g., McClelland & Jenkins, 1991). Although such work has led to fundamental insights about how nonlinear change can emerge from distributed activation in neural networks using relatively simple learning rules (see Munakata & McClelland, 2003, for a review), such models are often weakly linked to the real-time behavior of children in real tasks (see Spencer & Schöner, 2003, for a more detailed discussion). Because such models are often loosely tied to behavior, they can become demonstration proofs of the power of synaptic changes over learning rather than formal theories of particular types of developmental change (see Rogers & McClelland, 2004, for an exception).

A second example further highlights the tension between explanations of real-time and learning/developmental processes. Research by Stiles, Bates, Thal, Trauner, and Reilly (1998) has shown profound reorganization of cortical circuits following brain damage in early development (e.g., during infancy), with impressive recovery of function by 6 years of age. Although there are some constraints on such reorganization (see Stiles et al., 1998, for a discussion), this demonstrates an impressive capacity to recruit new neural networks over the longer time scales of development. Critically, though, we know relatively little about how this is done and how the recruitment/establishment of new networks in the brain emerges from the real-time behavioral experiences of children.

We want to stress that the work we have reviewed thus far has contributed fundamental insights into changes in spatial cognitive development as well as potential mechanisms of development. Our point here is to draw attention to two themes in the literature on the *how* of development: (1) there is a growing trend to search for mechanisms of development in brain–behavior relations, and (2) as researchers explore the longer time scales of learning and development, this often comes at the cost of real-time details. Combining these two themes sets up a key challenge for future work: to develop theories of development grounded in a rich understanding of brain–behavior relations that handles the dual challenges of offering a detailed account of real-time behavior but also incorporates the longer time scales of learning and development.

In this chapter, we describe our pursuit of this goal that integrates empirical work with a theoretical neuroscience perspective. In particular, we describe a dynamic field theory (DFT) of spatial cognition that is grounded in a rich understanding of brain–behavior relations, offers a detailed account of the real-time processes underlying many spatial behaviors, and provides insights into the link between behavior in the moment and learning/ development. Although our efforts to integrate short and long time scales are still limited in important respects (see section 14.6), we emphasize two insights in the present chapter. First, we have uncovered a rich array of behavioral and theoretical constraints because processes that "live" at different time scales in our theory constrain one another. Second, our theory captures a host of developmental changes in spatial cognition with a relatively simple and neurally plausible hypothesis. This has led to the insight that less is required of developmental processes when they are coupled to the complex dynamics at shorter time scales.

The next section provides an overview of the spatial cognitive phenomena we set out to capture with the DFT. Then, we describe how the DFT offers a detailed, constrained view of the real-time and learning-time (e.g., trial-to-trial) processes that underlie spatial performance in multiple tasks. In addition, we discuss how the DFT is constrained not just by behavioral data but also by a rich understanding of brain–behavior relations. These sections highlight that our theory is both task specific and task general. Task specificity is needed for strong ties to the real-time details of behavior. Task generality is needed for generalization across different experiences, which, we contend, plays a role in another type of generalization—generalization over development.

We then tackle the longer time scale of development by discussing our *spatial precision hypothesis*. This relatively simple hypothesis—that neural interactions become stronger and more spatially precise over development—has captured both quantitative and qualitative changes in performance in several tasks, shedding light on both how children use available perceptual structure in spatial tasks and how children construct long-term memories of specific locations in the world. We conclude by discussing the challenges that lie ahead. One critical next step is to "close the loop" on development (see Simon, 1962)—to explain how the spatial precision hypothesis emerges from the reciprocal coupling of processes that live at different time scales. More concretely, we must explain the developmental mechanisms that—in conjunction with real- and learning-time processes—cause developmental change. We speculate on these mechanisms at the end of our chapter and highlight what a theoretical neuroscience perspective can contribute to the more general search for the *how* of development.

14.1 WHAT NEEDS TO BE EXPLAINED IN SPATIAL COGNITION?

The theory that we describe in the present chapter focuses on the dynamics of spatial cognition, that is, the time-dependent processes that underlie coordinated spatial behavior. Such behavior requires that people remember the locations of important objects in the local surrounds with enough fidelity to coordinate a myriad of second-to-second decisions, actions, and attentional shifts. Moreover, the local "map" that is used in one workspace must be coordinated with other maps as people move from context to context—from the office desk, to the office filing cabinet, to the desk at home. This requires the real-time, contextually specific integration of past and present, of long-term memory with short-term memory.

To illustrate the many challenges involved in achieving coordinated spatial behavior in complex, real-world environments, consider the challenges facing a child during her first day at daycare. When she walks into her "home" room for the first time, she is surrounded by a myriad of new toys, cribs pushed against a wall, a table, some chairs stacked in the corner, and balls hanging in a bag by the door. How is she going to make sense of all of this? She needs to keep in mind and, ultimately, to learn where these objects are in the room, which toys are the really fun ones, and so on. But a static "map" will not do. Rather, her knowledge needs to cope with repeated changes in the local layout of objects in the room as toys are played with, moved, and (sometimes) put back, with changes in the global layout as cribs are moved in and out of place during naptime and chairs are rearranged for snack time, and with changes in the "virtual" layout as some toys became off limits in some contexts (e.g., shakers only available during music). Finally, she needs to learn the layout of separate spaces—the collective play area and the all-important outside play area—each of which share the dynamic properties of the "home" room.

How do people acquire such spatially grounded knowledge? To answer this question, we must first appreciate that people acquire knowledge by interacting with and exploring the world through a richly structured sensorimotor system. This sets up several key challenges. First, people must calibrate/coordinate reference frames in real time. In particular, they must keep egocentric reference frames in register with allocentric or world-centered frames as they move around. This is critical to remembering, for instance, that the books are on the upper shelf of the bookcase currently over to the left. This sets up a related challenge: encoding/remembering the locations of particular items relative to a reference frame. Although it might be useful to know that there is a red ball somewhere in this room, it is much more useful to know that the red ball is in the bag by the door. Finally, remembering the spatial characteristics of many objects can be a daunting task. Thus, people form spatial categories to reduce memory demands, to help them generalize, and to help them retrieve information reliably because categories offer a consistent retrieval cue.

The issue of forming spatial categories highlights that, although the challenges above are all linked to the formation of spatial knowledge in real time, these challenges must be solved in a way that extends beyond initial interactions with objects in the room. In particular, spatial knowledge must be "stored" in a way that it can be successfully retrieved and linked to the current context when the child reenters the "home" room each morning. This involves activating the "right" memories based on, for instance, the spatial layout of landmarks in the room (i.e., the child must recall object locations from memories of the "home" room and not the play room) and bringing these memories into register with the current scene (e.g., the child might have to mentally rotate retrieved information because she previously viewed objects in the room from a different vantage point).

Finally, we can extend all of the challenges above to the longer time scales of learning and development. These time scales present their own unique challenges. The first is generalization: how does the child generalize knowledge across tasks and contexts to form, for instance, a survey representation of the layout of rooms in a house or town? Similarly, how are developmental changes in spatial cognition linked to the striking array of other interconnected skills that come "on-line" during, for instance, infancy and early childhood: social skills (e.g., which things are off limits in certain situations), language skills (e.g., use of spatial relational terms and object names), and motor skills (e.g., reaching, walking, tool use).

The daycare example does a particularly good job highlighting that the challenges above are real challenges, because it is often painfully evident with children that learning to skillfully interact with the world is hard: they forget where objects are, they go to the wrong room of the house, and so on. But these challenges are not isolated to early development. They emerge when children and adults are taxed in controlled, experimental settings. And they resurface in the behavior of disordered populations across a broad range of development (Barnett et al., 2001; Karatekin & Asarnow, 1998; Landau, 2003; Lawrence, Watkins, Sahakian, Hodges, & Robbins, 2000).

Given the complexity of the spatial challenges people face in real-world situations, it is not surprising that, to date, no theory effectively explains how people handle these challenges. Thus, the goal of our theoretical efforts was to take a first step toward a formal model of spatial cognition capable of integrating some of the diverse processes that underlie spatially grounded behavior. We focused on four "core" aspects of spatial cognition discussed below: (1) how people form metric or "fine-grained" location memories, (2) how people link metric spatial information to particular reference frames and form "geometric" categories, (3) how people integrate spatial information perceived and remembered in the here-and-now with long-term memories that can be reactivated in context, and (4) how people achieve behavioral flexibility, which, we contend, is related to the generalization of spatial knowledge across tasks.

To facilitate our discussion of these core aspects of spatial cognition and our presentation of the DFT (see section 14.2), we focus primarily on empirical results from studies using our "spaceship" task. Figure 14.1 shows an image of the spaceship table we use in our laboratory (e.g., Spencer & Hund, 2002), with a frame of reference centered at a "start" location directly in front of where participants sit. Within this frame, 180° is along the midline of the task space projecting away from the start location through a second reference dot, with 90° to the right and 270° to the left. Figure 14.1 also shows a sample target (a triangular "spaceship") at 220°. To study the characteristics of spatial cognition, we have used relatively simple tasks in this task space. For instance, in our spatial recall task, the spaceship appears on the table, then it disappears, there is a short delay (0–20 seconds), and then participants move a mouse cursor from the start location to the remembered location. As we describe below, even this

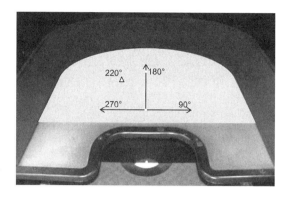

Figure 14.1 The "spaceship" table used in our laboratory. Two dots mark the midline symmetry axis, which corresponds to 180° in the model, with 90° to the right and 270° to the left. A sample triangular "spaceship" target is shown at 220°.

simple task can reveal key characteristics of the processes that underlie spatial cognition.

14.1.1 Metric Memory for Locations

To successfully act in the world, one must remember relatively precise, spatially continuous, metric information—not just qualitative, categorical information. Evidence suggests that children and adults can remember many types of metric information—direction and distance in a polar coordinate frame (McIntyre, Stratta, & Lacquaniti, 1998), x and y coordinates within a rectangular frame (J. Huttenlocher, Newcombe, & Sandberg, 1994), and so on. Given that spatial memory must be linked to multiple sensory and motor systems as well as to other internal processes (e.g., those dealing with reference frames), and given that the state of these multiple subsystems may vary in time due to the complex behavior of the organism in changing environments, the maintenance of spatial information in working memory requires processes that stabilize metric information in the face of both internal and external perturbations (Spencer & Schöner, 2003).

Although remembering precise metric information seems relatively straightforward for adults, this is not the case for children. Early in development, infants and young children do not always succeed in stabilizing memorized information in our spaceship task. For instance, when 3.5-year-olds were asked to remember a spaceship location to the left of the midline symmetry axis, they "forgot" the location on about 10% of all trials and responded to a target to the right of midline that they had seen on the just-previous trial (Schutte, 2004). What is so striking about these errors is that the memory delay was only 10 seconds and the right target was 80° away (for related effects with infants, see Smith, Thelen, Titzer, & McLin, 1999; Thelen, Schöner, Scheier, & Smith, 2001).

Insufficient stability of spatial memory manifests itself in more subtle ways later in development—even into adulthood. For instance, 6- and 11-year-old children and adults showed a systematic, delay-dependent increase in bias relative to midline in the spaceship task during 0- to 20-second delays (Spencer & Hund, 2002, 2003). In particular, memory responses to targets to the left of midline showed an increase in leftward errors over delays (e.g., responses to the 220° target were accurate at no delay but were shifted leftward by 4°—to 224°—by the 20-second delay), while targets to the right of midline showed an increase in rightward errors over delays. Responses showed a systematic, delay-dependent increase in variance as well. Thus, in the absence of any perceptual markers indicating the location of a target, children and adults remember roughly where the target is located, but the metric content of this memory is systematically distorted over time.

14.1.2 Metric Memory Relative to Reference Frames and Geometric Categories

A central challenge for any theory of spatial cognition is to explain how metric information remains calibrated and updated within a frame of reference. On one hand, this challenge requires keeping metric information calibrated with on-line changes in sensorimotor reference frames as people move their eyes, head, and body through space over time (e.g., Graziano, Hu, & Gross, 1997; Soechting & Flanders, 1991; see also chapter 4). Similarly, one must keep metric information grounded in external reference frames—the edges of a table, the boundaries of an object, and so on (J. Huttenlocher et al., 1991; Newcombe & Huttenlocher, 2000; Tversky & Schiano, 1989). Several neural mechanisms have been proposed to transform information from one frame into another frame (Deneve & Pouget, 2003; Pouget, Deneve, & Duhamel, 2002). Less understood is how such calibration processes are linked to processes that deal with recognition of reference frames and the real-time maintenance of metric information in memory.

Although the processes that link frames of reference to metric memories are poorly understood, there is strong evidence that metric memory is grounded in perceived reference frames. For instance, studies have shown that adults' memory for precise, metric information is biased away from the visible edges of L- and V-shaped frames, as well as their symmetry axes (Engebretson & Huttenlocher, 1996; Schiano & Tversky, 1992, experiments 1 & 2; Tversky & Schiano, 1989). The "midline" biases discussed above provide a concrete example of this type of error (see also J. Huttenlocher, Hedges, Corrigan, & Crawford, 2004; J. Huttenlocher et al., 1991; Plumert & Hund, 2001; Sandberg, Huttenlocher, & Newcombe, 1996). Such biases have been referred to as *geometric category biases* to highlight that use of visible edges and axes of symmetry carves up space into smaller regions that can help keep metric memory contained within the correct spatial region.

A central question in this domain is how people decide where to put or "impose" category boundaries. Our view is that geometric category boundaries are *always tied to perceived reference frames*. Adults' use of visible edges in the context of L- and V-shaped frames clearly fits with this picture. But what about the use of symmetry axes such as the midline symmetry axis of the spaceship table? After all, symmetry axes are not visible per se. Although this is certainly the case, evidence from the perceptual literature suggests that symmetry axes are perceived like weak visible lines (Wenderoth & van der Zwan, 1991). Moreover, the accuracy with which people perceive symmetry axes increases with the salience of visible cues (Beh, Wenderoth, & Purcell, 1971; Li & Westheimer, 1997; Simmering, Spencer, & Schöner, 2006). Finally, data suggest that symmetry axes have a special developmental status in that the ability to perceive symmetry develops quite early (3- to 4-month-old infants are capable of perceiving vertical symmetry; see Quinn, 2000).

More direct evidence that spatial category boundaries are grounded in perceived reference frames comes from a recent study from our laboratory (Simmering & Spencer, 2006a). We asked adults to reproduce a target location to the left of a virtual axis defined by two dots. This axis was parallel to the midline symmetry axis of the task space but translated to the right by 15 cm (imagine the two dots in figure 14.1 translated to the right). As in previous studies, responses to the left target were biased leftward after a 10-second delay. By contrast, when we removed the dots, responses to the same target location were biased rightward—away from the midline axis. Critically, this happened on a trial-by-trial basis, even when participants were instructed to "act as if the dots are there on every trial" and even when the trial with the dots "off" was preceded by five trials in a row with the dots "on". Furthermore, none of the participants mentioned using the midline symmetry axis in a postexperiment questionnaire, suggesting that participants were spontaneously locking onto whatever visible structure was present in the task space with little awareness that they were doing so.

14.1.3 Integration of Short-Term and Long-Term Spatial Memories

Thus far, we have focused on a very basic issue: perception of and memory for individual locations over short-term delays within a calibrated reference frame. How are such memories linked to performance over a longer time scale; that is, how are short-term memories integrated with long-term spatial memory?

Work in our laboratory has demonstrated that a simple mechanism can bridge these two time scales: as people remember individual locations over short-term delays, this activity leaves a trace of activation in long-term memory. Such traces can then bias performance toward these previously visited locations on subsequent trials. For instance, older children (6 and 11 years) and adults show biases toward an average remembered location. In particular, when children and adults are asked to repeatedly remember a small set of close locations (e.g., three targets separated by 20°), they show biases toward the central target (Spencer & Hund, 2002, 2003). These biases can be systematically distorted toward one of the outer targets by increasing the frequency with which people visit an outer target relative to the other two (Hund et al., 2002; Hund & Spencer, 2003). Such distortions in short-term memory toward information in long-term memory are often referred to as *experience-dependent category biases* (for related effects, see Schutte et al., 2003; Smith et al., 1999; Spencer, Smith, & Thelen, 2001; Thelen et al., 2001).[1]

14.1.4 Task Generality and Behavioral Flexibility

The final "core" issue we sought to tackle provides a bridge from task-specific behavior toward more task-general behavior. Very few theories have attempted to capture generalization across diverse experiences. This is not surprising because what is carried from one experience to the next is rarely transparent. This is true even if we ignore the complexity of generalizing across experiences in different spaces. For instance, what should generalize across the following three experiences? (1) A child puts down her red, plastic party cup, turns to look at the television, and then turns back a second later to find that Mom has placed an identical red cup next to hers, but she identifies the correct cup. (2) The child leaves the room, but forgets her cup; she then asks her Mom to bring the cup and verbally specifies its location. (3) The child returns to the room; the cup is in a new location, but she quickly recalls where it is and walks over to the television to retrieve her drink. These three experiences require a largely perceptually based "same/different" decision, the generation of a linguistic description, and a recall-based motor response, respectively. What should the child "take" from these experiences? Should they all be "bound" together since they are grounded in the same spatial array? Should they all be isolated because they tap into what have been characterized as different spatial systems (see, e.g., Bridgeman, 1999; Bridgeman, Gemmer, Forsman, & Huemer, 2000; Brungart, Rabinowitz, & Durlach, 2000)?

One way to foster generalization across diverse experiences would be to have a system that is behaviorally flexible—that can generate different types of responses and configure itself to solve multiple tasks as the situation demands. This would naturally lead to some form of generalization because the same spatial system would be involved in multiple behaviors. We have begun to probe this possibility empirically by asking a simple question: how is performance in one spatial task linked to performance in another spatial task? For instance, rather than asking participants to recall a remembered location on our spaceship table, we showed them two dots in quick succession (500 msec apart) and asked them whether the dots were in the "same" or a "different" position (Simmering et al., 2006). Importantly, we found that discrimination responses showed evidence of "fast repulsion" from midline: discrimination abilities were impaired when the second dot was presented away from midline relative to the first, that is, in the direction of bias observed in our studies of spatial recall (for related effects, see Werner & Diedrichsen, 2002). Specifically, our data suggest that the memory of the first dot drifted away from midline during the 500 msec delay. Consequently, when the second dot was presented away from midline relative to the first, the memory of the first dot blended with the presentation of the second dot, and people erroneously said they were in the "same" position. Although this highlights that the use of a midline reference frame has consequences for both recall and discrimination, it has a positive influence, as well: discrimination abilities showed an overall enhancement when the stimuli were presented closer rather than farther from midline (for a second example that probes task generality, see Spencer, Simmering, & Schutte, 2006). These data suggest that a shared spatial system might handle the generation of these different response types, even though, to date, spatial recall and position discrimination have been treated as separate literatures captured by different classes of models (for a discussion, see Simmering & Spencer, 2006b).

14.2 A DYNAMIC FIELD THEORY OF SPATIAL COGNITION

Figure 14.2 shows a simulation that implements our DFT.[2] This simulation consists of seven layers: a perceptual field in an egocentric frame of reference (PF_{ego}; figure 14.2A), a system that transforms activation in an egocentric reference frame into an object-centered frame (shift; figure 14.2B), a perceptual field in an object-centered frame (PF_{obj}; figure 14.2C), a long-term memory field associated with the object-centered perceptual field (LTM_{PFobj}; figure 14.2D), a layer of (inhibitory) interneurons ($Inhib_{obj}$; figure 14.2E), a spatial working memory field in an object-centered frame (SWM_{obj}; figure 14.2F), and a long-term memory field associated with the working memory field (LTM_{SWMobj}; figure 14.2G).

In this section, we step through key characteristics of the theory and how it provides a neurally plausible account of each aspect of spatial cognition discussed above. We first cover some of the basic principles of dynamic fields and how such fields capture short-term "working" memory for locations. Second, we discuss our approach to the dynamics of reference frame calibration, which involves the top four layers of the model (figure 14.2A–D). We then turn our attention to three central layers of the model (figure 14.2C,E,F), showing how our theory accounts for location memory relative to a perceived reference frame and geometric category biases. Third, we discuss how the DFT integrates short-term and long-term time scales through the coupling of two long-term memory fields to PF_{obj} and SWM_{obj} (in figure 14.2C,D,F,G). Fourth, we discuss how this theory captures aspects of task generality and behavioral flexibility.

Note that, although we discuss different aspects of the model in turn, we emphasize that the system shown in figure 14.2 is a single, integrated, dynamical system. As an example, consider the two layers shown in figure 14.2, C and D (PF_{obj} and LTM_{PFobj}). These two fields participate in refer-

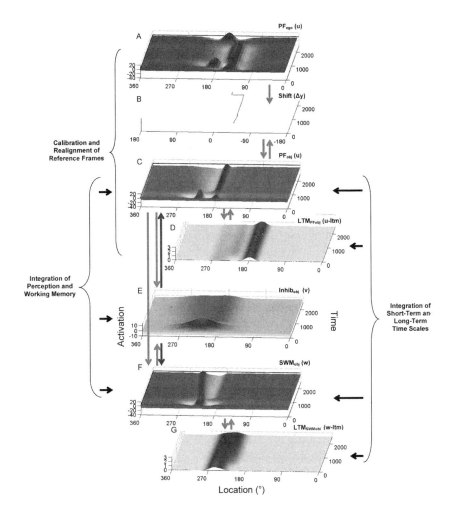

Figure 14.2 A simulation of the DFT performing one spatial recall trial. In each panel, location is across the x-axis, activation on the y-axis, and time on the z-axis. The model consists of seven layers: (*A*) a perceptual field in an egocentric reference frame, (*B*) a system that transforms locations from egocentric to an object-centered frame, (*C*) a perceptual field in the object-centered reference frame, (*D*) a long-term memory field associated with this perceptual field, (*E*) a shared layer of (inhibitory) interneurons, (*F*) a spatial working memory field in the object-centered reference frame, and (*G*) a long-term memory field associated with the spatial working memory field. Light gray arrows show excitatory connections between layers, and dark gray arrows show inhibitory connections between layers. Brackets describe the behavioral functions of subsets of the layers. See text for additional details. See color insert.

ence frame calibration, the real-time coupling of perception and working memory, and the integration of spatial information across short and long time scales. This highlights that our theory does not consist of specialized modules/boxes typical in many models. That said, the different layers do serve conceptually different functions—most of the time! Again, focusing on figure 14.2C, we note up-front that although we call this a perceptual field (PF_{obj}), we can generate behavioral flexibility by having this field serve a decision-making/working memory function during the test phase in specific types of tasks (e.g., position discrimination). This flexibility arises, in part, due to the reciprocal interconnections among the layers. Importantly, such dense interconnection is inspired by the densely connected, reentrant nervous system we are trying to model. Although this presents some theoretical challenges, we contend that thinking of the brain as an integrated dynamical system offers new insights into task generality, behavioral flexibility, and, ultimately, development (for related ideas, see Skarda & Freeman, 1987).

14.2.1 Metric Memory for Locations

There is general agreement that some form of sustained activation is the most plausible neuronal substrate for short-term spatial memory (Constantinidis & Steinmetz, 1996; Fuster, 1995; Miller, Erickson, & Desimone, 1996). This substrate involves graded, metric representations that evolve continuously in time under the influence of current sensory information as well as the current activation state (Constantinidis & Steinmetz, 1996; Rao, Rainer, & Miller, 1997; Smyrnis, Taira, Ashe, & Georgopoulos, 1992). Exactly how sustained activation is neurally realized, however, is not clear. One class of models achieves a stable memory state using bistable networks in which a stable state of sustained activation or "on" state coexists with an "off" state (Amari, 1989; Amari & Arbib, 1977; Compte, Brunel, Goldman-Rakic, & Wang, 2000). Within the "on" state, locally excitatory and laterally inhibitory interactions among neurons create sustained activation patterns.

The DFT is in this class of neural networks (see also Erlhagen & Schöner, 2002; Thelen et al., 2001). To describe the theory, consider an activation field defined over a metric spatial dimension, x (e.g., the angular location of a target). The continuous evolution of the activation field is described by an activation dynamics, that is, a differential equation that generates the temporal evolution of the field by specifying a rate of change, $dw(x,t)/dt$, for every activation level, $w(x,t)$, at every field location, x, and at any moment in time, t. The field achieves stable patterns of activation through time via the inverse relationship between the rate of change and the current level of activation (for a discussion of related dynamic systems concepts, see Braun, 1994). This means that at high levels of activation, negative rates of change drive activation down, while at low levels, positive rates of change drive activation up.

The activation level that emerges from this basic stabilization mechanism is a function of the balance of different inputs to the field (e.g., perceptual inputs) and neural interactions within the field. We use a locally excitatory/laterally inhibitory form of interaction depicted in figure 14.3A. According to this type of interaction, neurons that "code" for similar values along the spatial dimension, x (e.g., similar locations in space), excite one another, while neurons that code for very different values (e.g., different locations in space) inhibit one another. Note that only sufficiently activated sites contribute to interaction. This is achieved by passing activation levels through the sigmoidal function shown in figure 14.3B. According to this function, highly active neurons contribute fully to interaction (they are weighted by a value of 1), while inactive neurons do not participate (they are weighted by a value of 0). Such threshold functions are necessarily nonlinear to achieve the co-existing "on" and "off" states central to bistable networks.

Figure 14.4 shows two simulations (A–C and D–F) that illustrate the consequences of combining these concepts in a dynamic field. In each panel of this figure, the angular location of targets in the task space is along x (recall that $180°$ is along the midline of the task space), y shows the activation of each site in the field, and z captures time from the start (front of the figure) to the end of a spatial recall trial (1 time step = 5 msec). In figure 14.4, A and D show activation in an input field, whereas B, C, E, and F show activation in a two-layered dynamic field. Because cortical neurons never project both excitatorily and inhibitorily onto target neurons, lateral inhibition must be mediated through an ensemble of interneurons. A generic formulation (Amari & Arbib, 1977) is to introduce a second, inhibitory activation

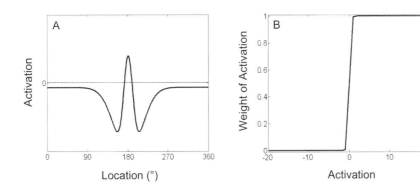

Figure 14.3   Two mathematical functions that govern neural interactions in the DFT. (*A*) A local excitation/lateral inhibition function where neurons that code for similar locations excite one another (positive activation) while neurons that code for dissimilar locations inhibit one another. (*B*) A sigmoidal function that determines which neurons participate in interaction: highly active neurons contribute fully to interaction (weighted by 1), while inactive neurons do not participate (weighted by 0).

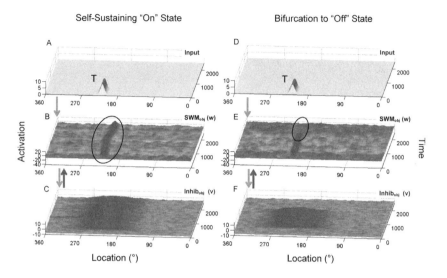

Figure 14.4 The dynamics of the DFT yield qualitatively different attractor states. The simulation in *A–C* shows the self-sustaining "on" state. The target (T) is presented at 220° in an input field (*A*), which leads to a peak of activation in the spatial working memory field (*B*), which is sustained during the memory delay (see oval) via locally excitatory and laterally inhibitory interactions with the inhibitory field (*C*). Because the system is close to the transition between the "on" and "off" states with this parameter setting, the simulation in *D–F* shows a spontaneous bifurcation to the "off" state during the memory delay (see oval in *E*) with the same parameters and input (see *D*). In *A–F*, location is across the x-axis, activation on the y-axis, and time on the z-axis. Arrows indicate excitatory (light gray) and inhibitory (dark gray) connections among layers. See color insert.

field, $v(x,t)$ (figure 14.4C,F), which receives input from the excitatory activation field, $w(x,t)$ (figure 14.4B,E), and in turn inhibits that field. These reciprocal interactions are captured by the arrows connecting paired fields (e.g., between panels B and C).

The dynamic interaction among the w and v layers combined with a nonlinear threshold function yields bistability—the potential to be in either an "on" or an "off" state. The simulation in figure 14.4A–C shows the "on" state. At the start of this simulation, neurons in the w and v layers are at a homogeneous resting level. Next, a target appears in the task space at 220° for 2 seconds, creating the activation profile shown in the input field (T in figure 14.4A). This event provides localized input to those neurons in the w field spatially tuned to this location, building a "peak" of activation centered at the target location. Next, the target is turned off; nevertheless, neurons in the w field remain in the "on" state—the field actively (and stably!) maintains a "working" memory of the location for the entire 10 second

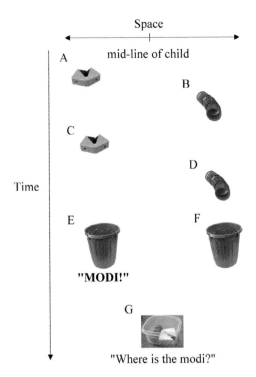

Space

mid-line of child

A

B

C

D

Time

E

F

"MODI!"

G

"Where is the modi?"

Figure 8.1 Elements of the task used by Smith et al. (2006). The vertical axis is time in the task. See text for a description of the task.

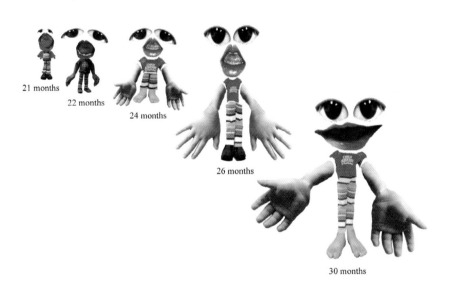

21 months

22 months

24 months

26 months

30 months

Figure 8.12 Body maps of body parts associated with typically known verbs at five ages. The size of each figure illustrates the number of known verbs at each age; the area of each body part region indicates percentage of associations (across all verbs known at that age).

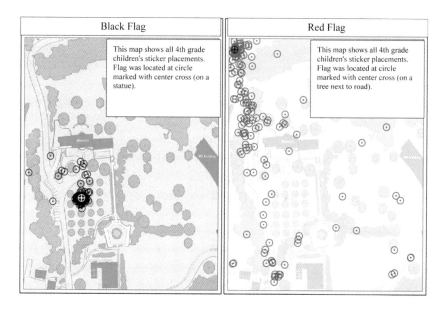

Figure 9.3 Maps showing composite of sticker placements by fourth-grade children asked to indicate the location of a flag on a statue (*left*) and on a tree along a road (*right*), and the correct location of the flag and tree (circles with a center cross). Data are from Kastens and Liben (2004).

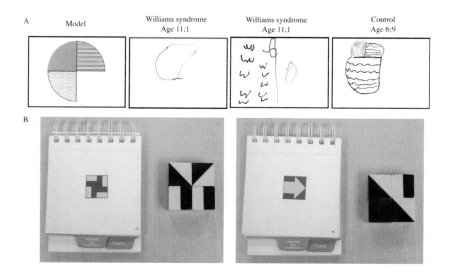

Figure 13.1. (*A*) Copies of a model by two children with WS (age 11) and one normally developing child (age 6, control). (*B*) Two samples of a model pattern (left in each picture) and the copy produced by an adult with WS.

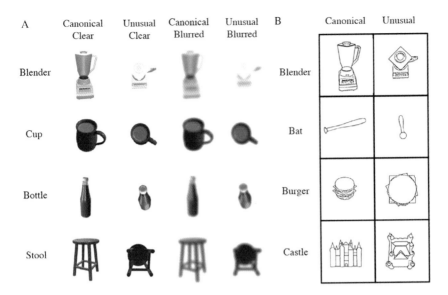

Figure 13.2 (*A*) Examples of full-color objects used in an experiment on object recognition. Objects were shown in four different conditions, crossing viewpoint (canonical or unusual) with clarity of image (clear or blurred). (*B*) Examples of line-drawn objects used in a second experiment on object recognition. Objects were shown in two different conditions varying viewpoint (canonical or unusual). Objects are representative of the stimuli used in Landau, Hoffman, and Kurz (2006).

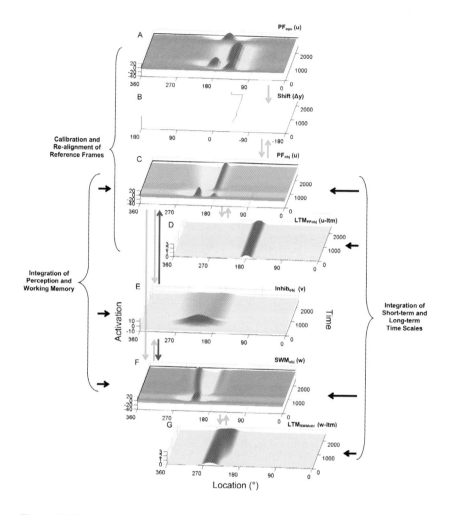

Figure 14.2 A simulation of the DFT performing one spatial recall trial. In each panel, location is across the x-axis, activation on the y-axis, and time on the z-axis. The model consists of seven layers: (*A*) a perceptual field in an egocentric reference frame, (*B*) a system that transforms locations from egocentric to an object-centered frame, (*C*) a perceptual field in the object-centered reference frame, (*D*) a long-term memory field associated with this perceptual field, (*E*) a shared layer of (inhibitory) interneurons, (*F*) a spatial working memory field in the object-centered reference frame, and (*G*) a long-term memory field associated with the spatial working memory field. Green arrows show excitatory connections between layers, and red arrows show inhibitory connections between layers. Brackets describe the behavioral functions of subsets of the layers. See text for additional details.

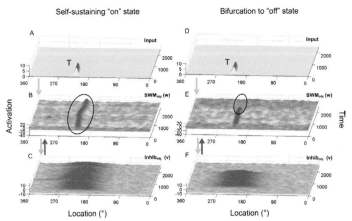

Figure 14.4 The dynamics of the DFT yield qualitatively different attractor states. The simulation in *A–C* shows the self-sustaining "on" state. The target (T) is presented at 220° in an input field (*A*), which leads to a peak of activation in the spatial working memory field (*B*), which is sustained during the memory delay (see oval) via locally excitatory and laterally inhibitory interactions with the inhibitory field (*C*). Because the system is close to the transition between the "on" and "off" states with this parameter setting, the simulation in *D–F* shows a spontaneous bifurcation to the "off" state during the memory delay (see oval in *E*) with the same parameters and input (see *D*). In *A–F*, location is across the x-axis, activation on the y-axis, and time on the z-axis. Arrows indicate excitatory (green) and inhibitory (red) connections among layers.

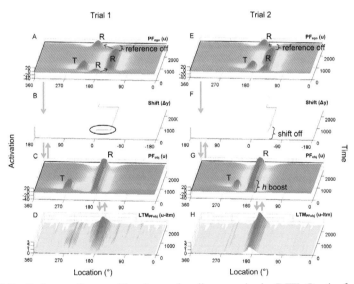

Figure 14.5 Reference frame calibration and realignment in the DFT. On the first trial (*A–D*), activation from the reference frame (R) is originally presented at 180° in the egocentric perceptual field (*A*). Across eye movements (indicated by arrows in *A*), the reference frame and target inputs (T; presented 40° from the reference) shift; this shift in the egocentric frame is corrected (*B*) to bring the reference frame input into 180° in the object-centered perceptual field (*C*). The continued activation of the object-centered reference frame leaves a trace in long-term memory (*D*). The second trial (*E–H*) begins with a resting level boost (*h*-boost in *G*), which creates a peak in the object-centered field (*G*) due to input from long-term memory (*H*). After a brief interval when the shift mechanism is off (*F*), reference input in the egocentric perceptual field (*E*) is realigned (*F*) with the reference from the previous trial. Axes and arrows are as in figure 14.4.

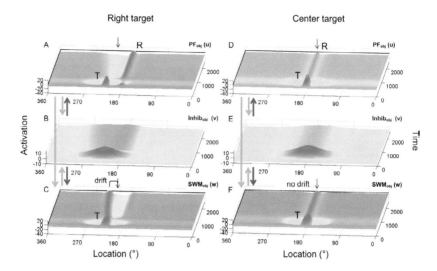

Figure 14.6   Spatial working memory within a stable reference frame. The perceptual field (*A*) maintains the reference frame (R) throughout the trial, leaving an inhibitory trace in (*B*). The target (T), presented at 220°, forms a self-sustaining peak in spatial working memory (*C*); this peak drifts away from 180° (see "drift" in *C*) over delay due to the inhibition associated with the reference frame. In contrast, when the target is presented at 180° (*D–F*), activation from the reference frame in the perceptual field (*D*) aligns with the target peak in spatial working memory (*F*); this peak does not drift over delay (*F*). Rather the peak is stabilized by excitatory input (green arrow) from the perceptual field (*D*). Axes and arrows are as in figure 14.4.

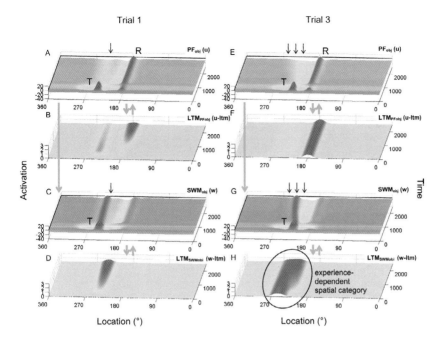

Figure 14.7 Integration of short-term and long-term spatial memories in the DFT. On the first trial (*A–D*), the perceptual field (*A*) maintains the reference frame (R) throughout the trial. Activation from both the target (T) and the reference leave traces in the associated long-term memory field (*B*). The target, presented at 240°, forms a self-sustaining peak in spatial working memory (*C*), which drifts away from midline over delay. The peak in spatial working memory leaves a trace of activation in the associated long-term memory field (*D*). By the third trial (*E–H*), the repeated activation from the reference frame in the perceptual field (*E*) has left a robust memory for the reference in long-term memory (*F*). The target, presented at 220°, still drifts away from midline in spatial working memory (*G*), but now long-term memory (*H*) shows traces of three target locations—an experience-dependent spatial category. Axes and arrows are as in figure 14.4.

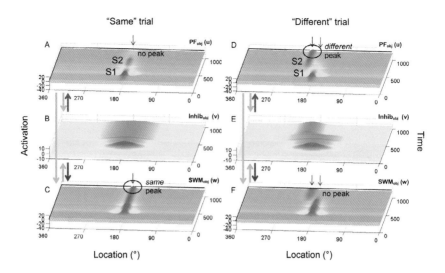

Figure 14.8 Position discrimination in the DFT. In *A–C*, two stimuli (S1 and S2) are presented at 180° in quick succession (*A*). S1 leads to a trough of inhibition (*B*) and a peak in spatial working memory (*C*). When S2 is presented in the same location, activation is maintained in spatial working memory (*C*), leading to a same peak, and suppressed in the perceptual field (*A*). In *D–F*, the stimuli are presented in different locations (*D*). Because S2 falls outside of the inhibited region in the perceptual field (*D*) created by the peak in spatial working memory (*F*), S2 builds a different peak in the perceptual field (*D*), which suppresses activation in spatial working memory (*F*). Axes and arrows are as in figure 14.4.

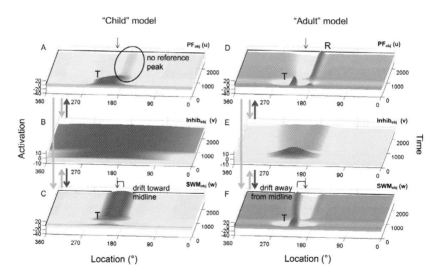

Figure 14.10 Developmental change in geometric bias in the DFT. When the target (T) is presented at 220° (*A*), the "child" model (*A–C*) forms a broad, self-sustaining peak in spatial working memory (*C*) due to broader and weaker neural interactions early in development. During the delay, the reference input does not create a sustained reference peak in the perceptual field (*A*). Consequently, the peak in spatial working memory is attracted toward midline (*C*) due to excitatory input (green arrow) from the perceptual field (*A*). By contrast the "adult" model drifts away from 180° (*D–F*) for comparison (see figure 14.6*A–C*). Axes and arrows are as in figure 14.4

delay (see circle in figure 14.4B).[3] This occurs because of the locally excitatory/laterally inhibitory interactions among neurons in the w and v layers. Specifically, neurons in the w field near the peak of activation excite one another, keeping activation around in the absence of input. At the same time, this local population of neurons excites associated neurons in the v field, which laterally inhibit neurons that code for different locations. This prevents activation from diffusing across the network. Note, however, that in the presence of noise, the location of the peak "drifts" during the delay (see movement of the circled peak in figure 14.4B): at the end of the delay in this simulation, the peak is centered at 223°. Consequently, the model would recall a location 3° to the right of the target. Thus, although the network remains stably in the "on" state, the positioning of the peak is only marginally stable (see also Compte et al., 2000).

The second simulation in figure 14.4D–F shows a bifurcation (i.e., dynamic transition) from the "on" to the "off" state. All the details of this simulation are identical to the one described above, but the behavior of the model is quite different. Now, rather than stably remembering the location during the 10 second delay, spontaneous fluctuations cause an initially self-sustaining peak to die out before the end of the trial (see the disappearance of the circled peak in figure 14.4E). This highlights that both "on" and "off" states are simultaneously available to the model; that is, the system is bistable.

14.2.2 Metric Memory Relative to Reference Frames and Geometric Categories

The concepts above describe a neurally plausible, bistable network for spatial working memory; however, what precisely does this model remember? The location the model actively represents must somehow be linked to a concrete location in the task space. We made this trivially easy by assigning a stable reference frame to the field, with the midline of the task space at 180° and the target at 220°. This is, of course, not realistic (although this is the approach taken by the majority of the spatial memory models proposed to date; see, e.g., J. Huttenlocher et al., 1991). What we need is a way to dynamically link spatial memories to a stable reference frame despite changes in the position of the observer (e.g., due to eye movements) or changes in the environment (e.g., due to movement of the reference frame). In this section, we first describe our approach to the dynamics of reference frame calibration and realignment. Then, we describe how we integrate our approach to spatial working memory with this real-time calibration system.

14.2.2.1 THE DYNAMICS OF REFERENCE FRAME CALIBRATION   To make the challenges of establishing a stable reference frame concrete, consider the representation of a location in space within two reference frames—an egocentric, retinotopic frame and an object-centered frame where 180° maps onto a perceived reference axis in the task space (e.g., the two dots shown in figure 14.1; see Simmering et al., 2006). How do we stably map the perception of the reference dots—which could land at any spot on the retina—onto 180° in the object frame?

We illustrate our approach to calibration in figure 14.5, which uses the top four layers in our theory: a single-layer egocentric perceptual field (PF_{ego}; figure 14.5A),[4] a system that transforms (e.g., rotates) an angular location in an egocentric frame into a location in an object-centered frame (shift; figure 14.5B), a single-layer object-centered perceptual field (PF_{obj}; figure 14.5C), and a long-term memory field associated with the object-centered

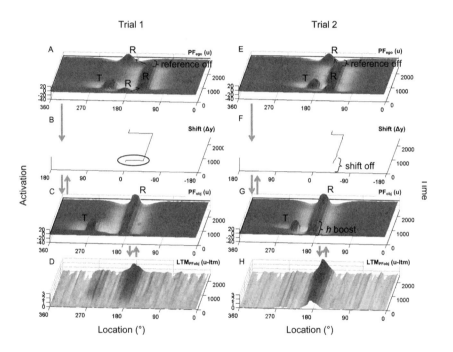

Figure 14.5 Reference frame calibration and realignment in the DFT. On the first trial (*A–D*), activation from the reference frame (R) is originally presented at 180° in the egocentric perceptual field (*A*). Across eye movements (indicated by arrows in *A*), the reference frame and target inputs (T; presented 40° from the reference) shift; this shift in the egocentric frame is corrected (*B*) to bring the reference frame input into 180° in the object-centered perceptual field (*C*). The continued activation of the object-centered reference frame leaves a trace in long-term memory (*D*). The second trial (*E–H*) begins with a resting level boost (*h*-boost in *G*), which creates a peak in the object-centered field (*G*) due to input from long-term memory (*H*). After a brief interval when the shift mechanism is off (*F*), reference input in the egocentric perceptual field (*E*) is realigned (*F*) with the reference from the previous trial. Axes and arrows are as in figure 14.4. See color insert.

perceptual field (LTM_{PFobj}; figure 14.5D). This simulation begins with perception of the midline reference frame in the task space at $180°$ in the egocentric frame (i.e., on the retina; see R at the front of figure 14.5A). Since this is the first trial in this task context, the initial mapping from the egocentric frame to the object-centered frame is arbitrary: the perception of the reference frame on the retina creates a pattern of activation in PF_{ego} that can pass directly into PF_{obj} with no "shift" required.

Once the egocentric and object-centered frames are in register, the system has to maintain this alignment even when the eyes move and the position of the reference frame on the retina shifts. For example, toward the start of the trial in figure 14.5A (at 500 msec), we shifted the position of the reference frame $-40°$ in the retinal frame (reflecting a $+40°$ eye movement; see arrow toward the front of figure 14.5A). Consequently, when activation is passed from PF_{ego} to PF_{obj}, everything must be "shifted" by $+40°$ so that the perception of the reference frame in the retinal field maps onto $180°$ in the object-centered field (for a neurally plausible approach to such transformations, see Sauser & Billard, 2005). How does the nervous system know the shift amount (Δy) that will keep activation in one frame aligned with activation in the other?

There are many relevant sources of information the nervous system could use to solve this problem provided that an initial alignment has been established (e.g., multisensory integration [see Bard, Fleury, Teasdale, Paillard, & Nougier, 1995] and efference copy signals [see Krommenhoek, van Opstal, Gielen, & van Gisbergen, 1993]). For simplicity, the simulations in figure 14.5 relied on a single, novel calibration mechanism. At each time step, the model computed the spatial correlation between the pattern of activation across the x-axis in PF_{ego} and the pattern of activation across the x-axis in PF_{obj} at *every possible shift value* (imagine taking the activation profile in PF_{ego} and shifting it to the left and right to find the best "match" with the profile in PF_{obj}). If the maximum correlation was above a criterion threshold, we updated the shift parameter, setting it to the shift amount associated with the maximum correlation. This allowed the model to dynamically adjust the mapping from PF_{ego} to PF_{obj}, compensating for any shift of the reference frame on the retina due to self motion.[5] For example, the initial eye movement in figure 14.5A caused a change in the shift value (see circle in figure 14.5B), such that the peak of activation in PF_{ego} at $140°$ was input correctly at $180°$ in PF_{obj} after the eye movement (see the single reference peak R at $180°$ in figure 14.5C).

But, of course, this is not quite yet the full picture because the system is not just tracking a reference frame—it is also perceiving targets, distractors, and so on. Thus, the system must be able to distinguish the reference signal from other inputs and update the shift parameter only when the reference is detected. One distinguishing feature of reference signals is that they remain stably visible in the task space (vs., e.g., "target" stimuli that are transiently visible or movable). To capitalize on this feature of reference frames and facilitate reference frame tracking, we gave PF_{obj} weakly self-sustaining dynamics: this field could hold on to the reference frame for short periods of time.

The simulation in figure 14.5 shows that this produces robust calibration. For instance, we turned a target on at 220° in the retinal frame at 1 second in this simulation (T in figure 14.5A). Because the reference frame is still visible and tracked by PF_{obj}, this event does not cause a realignment. Rather, the system brings the target input into PF_{obj} at the correct location in an object-centered frame—260° (T in figure 14.5C). Weakly self-sustaining dynamics in PF_{obj} can also help avoid spurious updating that might occur during, for instance, short-term occlusions of the frame. In figure 14.5A, we turned the reference signal off in PF_{ego} at 9 seconds. Despite this occlusion event, PF_{obj} holds on to the current frame (sustained peak in figure 14.5C). When the frame reappears at a new location (second arrow toward the back of figure 14.5A), the system updates the shift parameter (figure 14.5B) and realigns the reference frame.

The final piece of the puzzle is that the system needs some way to reinstantiate the same object-centered frame from trial to trial (or from situation to situation). Recall that we initially passed activation from the retinal frame into the object-centered frame at the start of trial 1. But this will not work on trial 2! Rather, we want to make sure that, wherever the system perceives midline on the retina at the start of trial 2, it correctly brings this input into PF_{obj} at 180°. To achieve this, we can give PF_{obj} a simple form of long-term memory (LTM_{PFobj} in figure 14.5D). Whenever there is above-threshold activation in PF_{obj}, this leaves a trace in LTM_{PFobj}. Reversely, activation traces in LTM_{PFobj} feed back as excitatory input into PF_{obj}. Importantly, LTM_{PFobj} has a longer time scale. Thus, activation traces grow slowly in this field and decay slowly in the presence of competing input. As shown in figure 14.5D, the dynamic interaction between PF_{obj} and LTM_{PFobj} on trial 1 results in a robust trace of the midline reference frame at 180°. Importantly, there is virtually no trace of the target location. This reflects the fact that the target input was transient while the reference input was visible in the task space for most of the trial. Thus, LTM_{PFobj} emergently performs an important function—it remembers reference frames.

Given this, how can the system use the information in LTM_{PFobj} on trial 2? The simulation in figure 14.5E–H shows our approach to this issue. At the start of trial 2, we turned the shift mechanism off for the first 500 msec (figure 14.5F). In addition, we boosted the resting level (h) of neurons in PF_{obj} (h boost in figure 14.5G). In the presence of input from LTM_{PFobj}, this boost causes an activation peak to form in PF_{obj} at the location of maximal input from LTM_{PFobj}, that is, at 180°. Next, we relowered the resting level and turned the shift mechanism back on. The system computed the correct shift amount needed to map the midline activation peak at 140° in the retinal field onto 180° in the object-centered field. Thus, the system effectively reacquired the old reference frame on trial 2 with a relatively brief (500 msec) and conceptually simple modulation of the calibration dynamics. From that point on, the simulation functions as before: the system correctly mapped perception of the target (T in figure 14.5E) to the correct location in the object-centered frame and survived another occlusion/eye movement sequence at the end of the trial (arrow toward the back of figure 14.5E). Note that, by the end of trial 2, the system is starting to construct a relatively strong long-term memory of the object-centered reference frame. This will make the realignment process even more robust on subsequent trials.

In summary, figure 14.5 highlights several key innovations in our theory: (1) the weakly self-sustaining dynamics of PF_{obj} can help maintain calibration despite, for instance, transient occlusions; (2) the stability of reference frames in the task space simplifies the challenges of calibration; (3) given a stable and reliable reference input, a simple form of long-term memory can suffice to build a robust memory of the reference frame across trials; (4) the DFT can use this type of long-term memory to reliably realign reference frames from trial to trial. Although our approach has several innovations, it is, of course, limited. For instance, we did not include processes that would determine if the person or the world moved (e.g., efference copy), nor did we include nonspatial features that will have to play an important role in the identification of reference frames. Nevertheless, the four layers of the DFT described in this section ground the model in a perceived frame of reference, moving beyond several other models of spatial memory (e.g., J. Huttenlocher et al., 1991).

14.2.2.2 SPATIAL WORKING MEMORY WITHIN A STABLE REFERENCE FRAME
Given that the DFT has a mechanism for dealing with the calibration and realignment of reference frames, we turn to the next central question: how does our model form a stable working memory of a location relative to a perceived reference frame? Conceptually, this requires the integration of a spatial working memory field (figure 14.4) with an object-centered perceptual field (figure 14.5). This integration is shown in figure 14.6, which shows three layers from our model: the excitatory layer of a perceptual field (PF_{obj}; figure 14.6A), the excitatory layer of a spatial working memory field (SWM_{obj}; figure 14.6C), and a shared layer of interneurons (Inhib$_{obj}$; figure 14.6B). The arrows in figure 14.6 show how these layers are coupled.

What does this particular type of integration achieve? First, consider the behavior of the perceptual field. As can be seen in figure 14.6A, PF_{obj} operates as before—at the start of the trial, it brings the midline input into 180° in an object-centered reference frame. Next, the target appears at 220° (T in figure 14.6A). This creates a peak of activation centered at this location. When the target disappears, a peak reforms in PF_{obj} at 180° as the system locks onto the stable reference cues in the task space. The effect of coupling PF_{obj} to SWM_{obj} is shown in figure 14.6C. At the start of the trial, SWM_{obj} receives relatively weak reference input from PF_{obj}. Next, the target is turned on, passing strong target-related input into the working memory field. This event moves the working memory field into a strongly

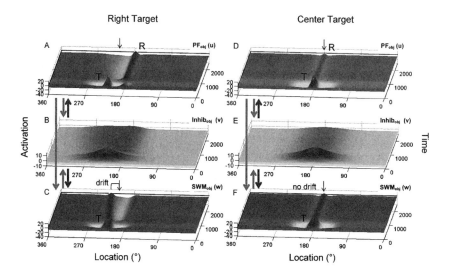

Figure 14.6   Spatial working memory within a stable reference frame. The perceptual field (*A*) maintains the reference frame (R) throughout the trial, leaving an inhibitory trace in (*B*). The target (T), presented at 220°, forms a self-sustaining peak in spatial working memory (*C*); this peak drifts away from 180° (see "drift" in *C*) over delay due to the inhibition associated with the reference frame. In contrast, when the target is prescntcd at 180° (*D–F*), activation from the reference frame in the perceptual field (*D*) aligns with the target peak in spatial working memory (*F*); this peak does not drift over delay (*F*). Rather the peak is stabilized by excitatory input (light gray arrow) from the perceptual field (*D*). Axes and arrows are as in figure 14.4. See color insert.

self-sustaining state. After the target disappears, the SWM_{obj} field maintains an active memory of the target location during the delay. Importantly, this occurs even though PF_{obj} has reacquired the reference frame. This highlights the useful bistability of SWM_{obj} described previously—because SWM_{obj} is in a stable attractor state, it can effectively hold on to the target, even while PF_{obj} deals with the dynamics of reference frame calibration. Thus, the three-layer system shown in figure 14.6 can achieve the dual goals of remembering the target item and staying calibrated with a perceived reference frame.

This dual ability has both costs and benefits for the cognitive system. One "cost" is readily apparent in figure 14.6C: the peak of activation in SWM_{obj} "drifts" away from 180° during the memory delay ("drift" toward the back of figure 14.6C). Thus, our model shows an emergent geometric category bias. This occurs because the peak of activation at midline in PF_{obj} passes activation to the $Inhib_{obj}$ layer at 180°. This creates greater inhibition on the 180° side of the target-related peak in SWM_{obj}, effectively repelling this peak away from the reference frame (for evidence of such effects, see

Spencer & Hund, 2002, 2003). Although this produces a systematic bias in memory, J. Huttenlocher and colleagues (J. Huttenlocher et al., 1991; J. Huttenlocher, Hedges, & Vevea, 2000) have pointed out such biases can have adaptive consequences. For instance, geometric bias minimizes the number of cross-category confusions, that is, cases where the target was shown to the left of midline but participants respond to the right. This bias also helps exaggerate the "leftness" or "rightness" of the target item, which could facilitate recall from long-term memory. Indeed, from a Bayesian perspective, geometric category boundaries can help create an optimal spatial memory system, trading off systematic bias for an overall reduction in variance (see J. Huttenlocher et al., 2000).

We agree that this is a viable interpretation, particularly in the context of our model that integrates SWM_{obj} with reference frame calibration: one could have a very accurate memory of an item in memory, but if this memory is not grounded in the world, effectively that "accurate" memory cannot be realized in an accurate response. Thus, although the reference calibration processes in our model lead to systematic bias, they can also lead to enhanced performance. This is captured in the simulation shown in figure 14.6D–F. Here, we presented a target aligned with midline (i.e., at 180°). During the memory delay, SWM_{obj} is stabilized because it is attracted toward/stabilized by the midline input from PF_{obj}. This is consistent with empirical results: children as young as 3 years as well as adults show lower variability for targets aligned with reference frames with no systematic bias (Schutte & Spencer, 2002; Spencer & Hund, 2002, 2003).

14.2.3 Integration of Short-Term and Long-Term Spatial Memories

The theory and model implementation we have sketched thus far offers a neurally plausible account of the real-time processes that construct and maintain a memory of a single target location within a particular, well-calibrated reference frame, as well as how these processes give rise to geometric category biases. The next step is to integrate these real-time processes with processes that live at the trial-to-trial time scale (and beyond). Our use of a long-term memory field (LTM_{PFobj}) to deal with reference frame realignment foreshadowed our approach to this issue.

Figure 14.7 shows a simulation of the bottom five layers in our model (see C–G in figure 14.2), though we show only four of these layers for ease of viewing: PF_{obj} (figure 14.7A), LTM_{PFobj} (figure 14.7B), SWM_{obj} (figure 14.7C), and a long-term memory field coupled to spatial working memory (LTM_{SWMobj}; figure 14.7D). We have already discussed the first three layers in this figure. The final layer—LTM_{SWMobj}—operates in a manner comparable to LTM_{PFobj}. Specifically, whenever there is above threshold activation present in SWM_{obj}, a trace is left at the associated locations in LTM_{SWMobj}. Conversely, these long-term memory traces feed back as excitatory inputs into SWM_{obj}.

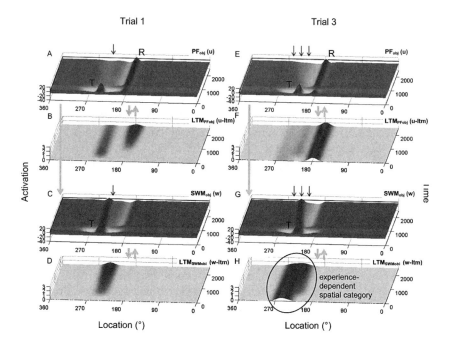

Figure 14.7   Integration of short-term and long-term spatial memories in the DFT. On the first trial (*A–D*), the perceptual field (*A*) maintains the reference frame (R) throughout the trial. Activation from both the target (T) and the reference leave traces in the associated long-term memory field (*B*). The target, presented at 240°, forms a self-sustaining peak in spatial working memory (*C*), which drifts away from midline over delay. The peak in spatial working memory leaves a trace of activation in the associated long-term memory field (*D*). By the third trial (*E–H*), the repeated activation from the reference frame in the perceptual field (*E*) has left a robust memory for the reference in long-term memory (*F*). The target, presented at 220°, still drifts away from midline in spatial working memory (*G*), but now long-term memory (*H*) shows traces of three target locations—an experience-dependent spatial category. Axes and arrows are as in figure 14.4. See color insert.

As illustrated in figure 14.7, the reciprocal interplay between SWM_{obj} (figure 14.7C) and LTM_{SWMobj} (figure 14.7D) leads to the emergent formation of experience-dependent spatial categories. The simulation in figure 14.7A–D shows the first trial in a spatial recall task. The target in this simulation was presented at 240°. During the course of a single trial, the model builds up a graded long-term memory of the target location (figure 14.7D) that has an impact on SWM_{obj}. For instance, we ran a simulation to the 240° target with the same model parameters, but without LTM_{SWMobj}. The model showed a stronger bias away from midline in this case (by 2°). Thus, the excitatory input from LTM_{SWMobj} into SWM_{obj} serves to stabilize against drift—even on a single trial.

But this is only the case when the distribution of activation in LTM-$_{SWMobj}$ is centered around the target location. If the model visits several close locations in a row and is then shown a target at a different (but not too distant) location, the working memory of the new location will be biased toward the previously responded-to targets. This is shown in figure 14.7E–H. Here, we simulated the model across two trials with close targets (240° and 260°; see arrows in figure 14.7E,G). Then we probed the model's response when an "inner" target (220°) was presented (figure 14.7E). The model showed a *larger* bias away from midline in this case relative to a simulation where LTM$_{SWMobj}$ was not present. Why?

At the start of this recall trial, the distribution of activation in LTM-$_{SWMobj}$ is centered at 255° (circle in figure 14.7H). Consequently, the working memory peak built by the target presentation is both repelled from midline *and* attracted toward 250°. Note, however, that by the end of this trial, the distribution of activation in LTM$_{SWMobj}$ has shifted closer to 220°. This shows the complex dynamics that underlie the formation of experience-dependent spatial categories. Although we have yet to probe these dynamics at this trial-to-trial level, the model effectively captures the buildup of long-term memory effects over blocks of trials, as well as the systematic shift in bias created by having participants move more frequently to an inner or outer target (Hund & Spencer, 2003; Spencer & Hund, 2002, 2003). Finally, we note that while LTM$_{SWMobj}$ is forming a representation of the target distribution, its counterpart—LTM$_{PFobj}$—is forming a robust memory of the reference frame (see figure 14.7F). This distribution of effort by the model emerges from the different dynamics of PF$_{obj}$ and SWM$_{obj}$, rather than some a priori knowledge about the difference between targets and reference frames.

14.2.4 Task Generality and Behavioral Flexibility

The preceding sections describe how the DFT accounts for several basic spatial cognitive abilities, but all of our simulation examples were grounded in a particular task—spatial recall. Can the DFT generalize to other spatial cognitive tasks and take a critical step toward task generality and behavioral flexibility?

We illustrate the flexibility of the DFT by showing how this theory generalizes to a new task—position discrimination (for a related example, see Spencer et al., 2006). Recall that in position discrimination tasks, two stimuli (S1 and S2) are presented in quick succession (e.g., 500 msec apart), and the participant judges whether the stimuli were in the "same" or "different" locations (see Simmering et al., 2006). To capture performance in this task, the DFT must generate a *same/different* decision. Such decisions can be achieved by increasing the resting level of neurons in PF$_{obj}$ and Inhib$_{obj}$ when the second stimulus is presented. In some cases, this will result in a peak in SWM$_{obj}$ (and no peak in PF$_{obj}$)—the basis for a "same" response. In other cases, this will result in a self-sustaining peak in PF$_{obj}$ (and no peak in SWM$_{obj}$)—the basis for a "different" response.

Figure 14.8 shows a simulation of a "same" (figure 14.8A–C) and "different" (figure 14.8D–F) response (note that we did not include a reference input in these simulations for simplicity). These simulations are identical except for the positioning of the stimuli: we presented two sequential stimuli at the same location in figure 14.8A–C (arrow toward the back of figure 14.8A,C), while we presented two sequential stimuli at slightly different locations in figure 14.8D–F (arrows in figure 14.8D,F). Note that the stimuli were "on" for 1 second each with a 1 second delay between (see Simmering & Spencer, 2006b). As shown in figure 14.8A–C, the presentation of the first stimulus (S1 in figure 14.8A) creates a peak of activation in SWM_{obj} that is sustained during the brief delay. When the second stimulus is presented at the same location (S2 in figure 14.8A), this input blends with the activation peak in SWM_{obj}, which in turn suppresses activation in PF_{obj} at the associated location (via $Inhib_{obj}$). Consequently, when the stimulus turns off, the SWM_{obj} peak remains and the model responds "same" (figure 14.8C).[6]

The same initial events occur in the simulation in figure 14.8D–F. Now, however, the second stimulus is presented to the left of the first (S2 in figure 14.8D). Importantly, this stimulus comes into PF_{obj} at a site that is

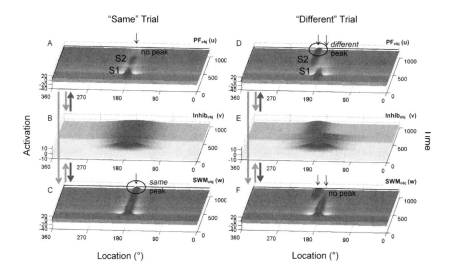

Figure 14.8   Position discrimination in the DFT. In A–C, two stimuli (S1 and S2) are presented at 180° in quick succession (A). S1 leads to a trough of inhibition (B) and a peak in spatial working memory (C). When S2 is presented in the same location, activation is maintained in spatial working memory (C), leading to a same peak, and suppressed in the perceptual field (A). In D–F, the stimuli are presented in different locations (D). Because S2 falls outside of the inhibited region in the perceptual field (D) created by the peak in spatial working memory (F), S2 builds a different peak in the perceptual field (D), which suppresses activation in spatial working memory (F). Axes and arrows are as in figure 14.4. See color insert.

just outside of the inhibitory range of the spatial working memory peak. This allows activation to grow in PF_{obj}. At the same time, the resting level boost in PF_{obj} and $Inhib_{obj}$ makes the perceptual field more strongly self-sustaining. Consequently, a peak forms in PF_{obj}, and this suppresses activation in SWM_{obj} (via $Inhib_{obj}$). At the end of the trial, there is an above-threshold peak in PF_{obj} (figure 14.8D) and a below-threshold peak in SWM_{obj} (figure 14.8F). Note that we can easily "update" spatial working memory by moving the resting levels in PF_{obj} and $Inhib_{obj}$ back to their initial state. When this occurs, a peak builds in SWM_{obj} at the site of S2.

The ability of the DFT to account for recall and discrimination performance within the same framework *and using the same parameters* is unique—we know of no other model of spatial cognition that captures this range of performance (for an example of behavioral flexibility within the domain of object category formation, see Love, Medin, & Gureckis, 2004). Importantly, our theory has also generated several novel behavioral predictions that have been successfully tested with both children and adults (Simmering & Spencer, 2006b; Simmering et al., 2006). And we are currently extending our theory to account for performance in other tasks, including multi-item change detection (Johnson, Spencer, & Schöner, 2006).

14.3 IN WHAT SENSE IS THE DFT NEURALLY PLAUSIBLE?

We began this chapter with two observations about the search for developmental mechanisms: (1) there is a growing trend to search for mechanisms of development in brain–behavior relations, and (2) as researchers explore the longer time scales of learning and development, it becomes difficult to offer a detailed, process-based account of real-time behavior. Thus, there is a need to develop theories of development grounded in a rich understanding of brain–behavior relations that offer both a detailed account of real-time behavior and an account of the longer time scales of learning and development. In this section, we position the DFT within the field of theoretical neuroscience and evaluate whether this theory is grounded in an understanding of brain–behavior relations. This sets the stage for our explorations of development in the subsequent sections.

Before discussing the ways in which the DFT is based on neural principles, we first place our theory within the broader field of theoretical neuroscience. A growing number of researchers have argued that we should take inspiration from the densely interconnected and dynamic nature of the brain to rethink cognition (e.g., Barsalou, 1999; Skarda & Freeman, 1987; Spencer & Schöner, 2003). A centerpiece of this approach is to embrace the use of complex, dynamic neural networks to capture brain–behavior relations. Although neural networks have architectures that can be depicted as separate systems, they are—at their core—complex, reentrant, densely interconnected systems that violate core assumptions of encapsulation and separability. We alluded to this in the overview of the

DFT by noting that PF_{obj} plays a role in virtually every phenomenon we have modeled.

One of the dominant approaches in theoretical neuroscience takes a biophysical approach to the study of brain–behavior relations: theoreticians attempt to build neurally realistic models of single neurons that capture key elements of neuronal firing rates, neurotransmitter action, and so on (Durstewitz, Seamans, & Sejnowski, 2000; Salinas, 2003). These neural models are then coupled together into populations, and populations are coupled together based on evidence of, for instance, cortical–cortical connections. Although the biophysical approach has led to new insights into brain function and neuronal dynamics, such models typically fail to capture many behavioral details. This is partly due to concrete limitations: such models are very complex, have immense computational demands, and are difficult to analyze (Haskell, Nykamp, & Tranchina, 2001). Thus, while this approach to rethinking cognition is very promising, biophysical models do well at the level of neurons but poorly at the level of behavior (Finkel, 2000).

We contend that the DFT overcomes this limitation with its emphasis on the functional organization of behavior while maintaining a strong commitment to neural principles. Dynamic fields were first proposed to account for neural activation in visual cortex (Amari, 1977; Amari & Arbib, 1977). Continuous dynamic fields provided a natural way to capture the neural dynamics of this cortical area given its topographic organization. The advent of population coding ideas extended this application to non-topographically organized cortical areas such as motor cortex (Bastian, Riehle, Erlhagen, & Schöner, 1998; Bastian, Schöner, & Riehle, 2003). Now, rather than ordering neurons in a field by their position on the cortical surface, one can order them based on the continuous, metric features that each neuron "codes" for—including space (for evidence of spatially tuned neural activity across a range of cortical areas, see di Pellegrino & Wise, 1993; Georgopoulos, Kettner, & Schwartz, 1988; Georgopoulos, Taira, & Lukashin, 1993; Wilson, Scalaidhe, & Goldman-Rakic, 1993). Critically, although neurons in many cortical areas are not topographically ordered, they still interact in a locally excitatory and laterally inhibitory manner (e.g., Georgopoulos et al., 1993).

This basic form of interaction leads to different types of self-sustaining dynamics. For instance, evidence suggests that patterns of activation in posterior parietal cortex are weakly self-sustaining, while patterns in prefrontal and premotor cortex are more strongly self-sustaining. As an example, patterns of activation in both parietal and prefrontal cortical areas are sustained during delays in spatial versions of delayed match-to-sample tasks; however, activation in posterior parietal cortex does not survive the presentation of new stimuli (Constantinidis & Steinmetz, 1996; Steinmetz & Constantinidis, 1995), while activation in prefrontal cortex does (di Pellegrino & Wise, 1993). We were informed by these data when we made PF_{obj} weakly self-sustaining and SWM_{obj} strongly self-sustaining.

But in our theory, we link these two fields together via a shared layer of interneurons. This seems to violate the distant cortical–cortical connections that link parietal and prefrontal cortex. Although this is the case in terms of the architecture of the model, we prefer the three-layered perceptual field–inhibitory field–spatial working memory structure because it more strongly mirrors the cytoarchitecture of visual cortex (Douglas & Martin, 1998), giving us an entry point into the dynamics that emerge from the layered structure of cortex.

In addition to these ties to real-time cortical dynamics, our approach to the modulation of resting levels in, for instance, $Inhib_{obj}$ and SWM_{obj} during a recall trial is neurally plausible. Such modulation of resting levels can be achieved, for instance, by global excitatory input from one cortical area to another. Finally, our approach to long-term memory is based on established neural principles: the long-term memory fields in the DFT capture a form of Hebbian learning (Schöner, 2006; Wilimzig & Schöner, 2006). Because this raises the issue of how we approach the integration of time scales, including the time scales of development, we save further discussion of these issues for section 14.6.

Connections between the DFT and neurophysiology provide important constraints for our theory. But they also raise the exciting possibility of testing our theory using neurophysiological techniques. Indeed, several recent studies have demonstrated that dynamic fields can be directly estimated using single-unit recording (Bastian et al., 1998, 2003; Erlhagen, Bastian, Jancke, Riehle, & Schöner, 1999; Jancke et al., 1999). The first step in these studies was to map the responses of neurons to basic stimuli and create a field by ordering the neurons based on their "preferred" stimulus. This was followed by a behavioral task that probed, for instance, several reaction-time predictions by a DFT of movement preparation (Bastian et al., 1998, 2003; Erlhagen & Schöner, 2002). Note that this same theory has also been tested using event-related potential (ERP) techniques (McDowell, Jeka, Schöner, & Hatfield, 2002). These studies all reported a robust relationship between predictions of dynamic field models and neural measures, suggesting that this particular marriage between theoretical and behavioral neuroscience could be extremely generative in the future.

14.4 THE DEVELOPMENT OF SPATIAL COGNITION

One issue central to *any* theory of spatial cognition is to explain the mechanisms that underlie developmental changes in the diverse phenomena described previously (see section 14.1). We have already alluded to some of these changes. First, there is an improvement in children's ability to actively and stably maintain spatial information in working memory beginning around 10 months (Thelen et al., 2001) and continuing throughout childhood. This results in a systematic reduction in errors over development in the spaceship task. Specifically, 3-year-olds typically made 10–20° errors to targets to the left and right of midline following delays of 5–10 seconds

(Schutte & Spencer, 2002). By contrast, 6- and 11-year-old children typically made 6–8° errors over delays (Spencer & Hund, 2003), whereas adults' errors generally ranged between 3° and 5° (Spencer & Hund, 2002; for related effects, see Hund & Plumert, 2002, 2003, 2005; Hund et al., 2002; Plumert & Hund, 2001).

Second, there is a qualitative shift in how younger versus older children remember locations near axes of symmetry in spatial memory tasks. Two- to 3-year-olds show biases *toward* symmetry axes, while 6- to 11-year-olds show biases *away from* the same axes (Hund & Spencer, 2003; Schutte & Spencer, 2002; Schutte et al., 2003; Spencer & Hund, 2003). Note that these age ranges differ slightly across tasks (see, e.g., J. Huttenlocher et al., 1994; Sandberg et al., 1996). According to the category adjustment model proposed by J. Huttenlocher et al. (1991), the shift in geometric biases reflects a change in how children categorize space: younger children form large geometric categories and are biased toward a spatial prototype at the center of the space (e.g., at midline), while older children subdivide space into smaller regions, showing biases away from a category boundary at midline (see J. Huttenlocher et al., 1991, 1994). As we alluded to above, this model does not offer an explanation for *how* this qualitative developmental shift occurs.

In addition to changes in geometric category biases, young children show developmental changes in experience-dependent category biases. Specifically, as spatial working memory becomes more precise, the long-term traces created by short-term memories also become more precise. Evidence for this comes from a sandbox version of the canonical Piagetian A-not-B task (Schutte et al., 2003; Spencer & Schutte, 2004; Spencer et al., 2001). In this task, a toy is hidden in a large rectangular sandbox and covered up so that there are no visible cues marking the hiding location. After a short delay, children are allowed to dig up the toy. If the toy is repeatedly hidden at an "A" location, and then hidden at a nearby "B" location, 2- to 6-year-old children will search for the toy at locations shifted systematically toward A, that is, they search near A and not B. Importantly, there is a systematic reduction in the spatial range across which such errors occur over development: 2- and 4-year-olds show biases toward an A location that is 6–9 inches away from B, while 6-year-olds only show biases toward an A location 2 inches away, and 11-year-olds show only a marginal bias toward A at this separation (Schutte et al., 2003).

Finally, there are improvements in behavioral flexibility over development (see, e.g., Hund & Plumert, 2005). In a recent study, for example, we examined children's and adults' ability to modulate performance across recall and recognition versions of a simple paper and pencil task (Spencer et al., 2006). The recall task was similar to the recall tasks described previously: participants were shown a dot inside a small rectangle, the dot was covered up, there was a short delay, and then people placed an "X" at the remembered location in a blank rectangular frame (see also J. Huttenlocher et al., 1994). The recognition task was identical through the delay interval; however, after the delay, participants were shown a set of colored dots—the "choice" set—inside a rectangular frame. Their task was to say the color of the dot that was in the same location as the original "target" dot. Children and adults showed comparable geometric biases across tasks as long as the choice set presented in the recognition task had a large number of items that spanned a relatively large spatial range. With a smaller number of items to choose from, children were strongly influenced by the local details of the choice set. Although this was maladaptive on some trials, it led to more accurate performance on others. In some cases, children selected a dot that was more accurate than their recall response because their memory had "drifted" beyond the range of possible choices. In other cases, children showed a bias against selecting the outermost choices in favor of a more accurate selection. This points toward developmental differences in how effectively children can "rise above" the local details of the situation, as well as the potentially adaptive and maladaptive consequences of this lack of behavioral flexibility.

14.5 THE DEVELOPMENT OF SPATIAL COGNITION, THE DFT, AND THE SPATIAL PRECISION HYPOTHESIS

We have made promising advances in understanding the development of spatial cognition using a relatively simple hypothesis—the *spatial precision hypothesis* (SPH). This hypothesis states that the spatial precision of neural interactions becomes more precise and more stable over development (Schutte et al., 2003; Spencer & Hund, 2003). This hypothesis is illustrated in figure 14.9 using the same interaction function shown in figure 14.3A. Each curve in this figure shows an example of an interaction function at some point in development, with early development shown with darker lines and later development with lighter lines. As the interaction functions move from early to later development, the spatial precision of locally excitatory interactions narrows and excitation increases. At the same time, laterally inhibitory interactions expand their spatial range and grow stronger. These changes result in relatively unstable self-sustaining interactions early in development that are sensitive to input across a broad spatial range, as well as stable self-sustaining peaks later in development that are sensitive only to input at narrow separations. This can explain the reduction in A-not-B-type effects in the sandbox task over development: with enhanced precision, A and B must be spatially close for the working memory associated with B to "feel" the effects of the long-term memory of A (for details, see Schutte et al., 2003). The enhanced stability of spatial working memory captured by the SPH also explains the reduction in constant and variable errors evident in a number of spatial recall tasks across a broad range of ages from 3 years to adulthood (Hund & Spencer, 2003; Plumert & Hund, 2001; Schutte & Spencer, 2002; Spencer & Hund, 2002, 2003).

Although the SPH captures a number of changes in performance across a range of ages, many of these developmental effects are quite

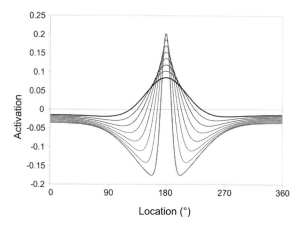

Figure 14.9 Illustration of the SPH. Early in development (black line) interaction is broad and primarily excitatory. Later in development (light gray line) excitation is narrower and stronger with stronger lateral inhibition. Intermediate lines show the hypothesized gradual nature of this change over development.

intuitive—spatial memory gets better over development! Does the SPH capture something less obvious? For instance, one of the more dramatic developmental changes in spatial cognition is the shift in geometric category biases: young children show biases toward symmetry axes, while older children show biases away from such axes (J. Huttenlocher et al., 1994; Schutte & Spencer, 2002; Spencer & Hund, 2003). Can we capture this *qualitative* developmental transition using the same hypothesis?

Figure 14.10 shows that the answer is yes. This figure shows the performance of a "child" (figure 14.10A–C) and "adult" (figure 14.10D–F) version of the DFT for a single trial in a spatial recall task, focusing on three layers of the model—PF_{obj}, $Inhib_{obj}$, and SWM_{obj}. Note that the simulation in figure 14.10D–F is identical to the simulation in figure 14.6A–C. We reproduced this simulation here for comparison. As shown in figure 14.10A–C, the "child" model forms a stable spatial working memory of the target at the start of the trial (T in figure 14.10C). Interestingly, the formation of this peak takes more time than with the adult model. During the delay, this peak drifts toward midline, rather than away from midline (see "drift" toward the back of figure 14.10C). Why does this occur? Because the peak in SWM_{obj} is much broader (reflecting the broad interactions specified by the SPH), this peak produces broad activation in $Inhib_{obj}$, which, combined with the relatively weak self-sustaining dynamics in the perceptual field, prevents a reference peak from building in PF_{obj} (at 180°; see circle in figure 14.10A). Consequently, SWM_{obj} receives some excitatory input around midline (due to the excitatory projection from PF_{obj} to SWM_{obj}), but no associated inhibitory "push" away from a reference peak at midline.

It is important to emphasize that the simulations in figure 14.10 capture a *qualitative* shift in geometric category biases in our task via a *quantitative* shift in model parameters. In particular, to shift from the "child" to "adult" parameters, we simply scaled the inputs and projections among the layers as specified by the SPH. This is consistent with other examples of nonlinear, dynamical systems that capture both quantitative and qualitative developmental change without positing new control processes. Rather, qualitative developmental changes can emerge via a reorganization of the system during the transition (e.g., Thelen & Smith, 1994; van der Maas & Molenaar, 1992; Van Geert, 1998). This stands in contrast to the dominant explanation of the developmental shift in geometric biases. According to the category adjustment model, this shift reflects a change in children's ability to subdivide space into smaller categories (J. Huttenlocher et al., 1994). Thus, an explicit new ability—spatial subdivision—is used to explain children's performance. Importantly, however, this model offers no account of how this new ability comes on-line.

Our model takes a critical step closer to explaining the developmental process at work in this case, offering a view of developmental continuity

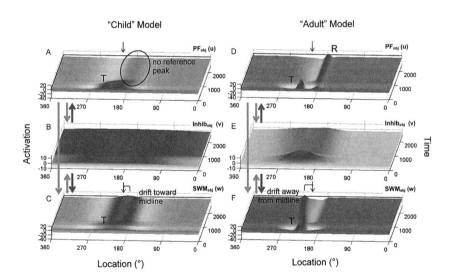

Figure 14.10 Developmental change in geometric bias in the DFT. When the target (T) is presented at 220° (*A*), the "child" model (*A–C*) forms a broad, self-sustaining peak in spatial working memory (*C*) due to broader and weaker neural interactions early in development. During the delay, the reference input does not create a sustained reference peak in the perceptual field (*A*). Consequently, the peak in spatial working memory is attracted toward midline (*C*) due to excitatory input (light gray arrow) from the perceptual field (*A*). By, contrast, the "adult" model (*D–F*) drifts away from 180° (*F*; for comparison see figure 14.6*A–C*). Axes and arrows are as in figure 14.4. See color insert.

even as qualitatively new behaviors emerge over time. This continuity has led to a set of novel predictions regarding how the transition in geometric effects unfolds over development. In particular, as excitation narrows and becomes stronger, the "child" model in figure 14.10 shows a narrowing of the attraction effect; that is, responses are biased toward midline only when targets are presented relatively close to this axis. Eventually, neural interactions in the perceptual field become strong enough to create a reference-related peak and repulsion emerges, but only at a few select locations to the left and right of midline. As interactions strengthen further, the repulsion effect increases and extends across a broad spatial range. All of these predictions were recently confirmed with 3- to 5-year-old children (see Schutte, 2004).

These data highlight that the SPH offers a detailed account of how real-time behavior changes over the time scale of development—one of the central goals we highlighted in the introduction to this chapter. Is the SPH also grounded in a rich understanding of brain–behavior relations? Put differently, is there neurophysiological evidence of this type of development in cortex around the ages probed in our studies (e.g., 3–6 years)? It is likely that the development of the prefrontal cortex (PFC) is related to the spatial recall tasks we discussed. Data from several studies demonstrate that the PFC plays a central role in spatial working memory (Awh et al., 1999; di Pellegrino & Wise, 1993; Kessels, Postma, Wijnalda, & de Haan, 2000; Nelson et al., 2000), and maturation of PFC is still occurring between 3 and 6 years of age. In fact, there is evidence that the development of the PFC continues into the postadolescent years (Gogtay et al., 2004; Rakic, 1995; Sowell, Thompson, Tessner, & Toga, 2001). Synaptic density in the PFC reaches its peak at about 2 years of age in humans (P. R. Huttenlocher, 1979) and then declines until it finally reaches adult levels at about 16 years of age (P. R. Huttenlocher, 1990). Myelination is also still occurring in the frontal lobe between 2 and 6 years of age (Sampaio & Truwit, 2001). Thus, there is dramatic brain development happening during the time period when we see dramatic changes in spatial cognition. At this point, however, there is no strong neurophysiological support for the type of changes captured by the SPH. That said, to the extent that the changes noted above (e.g., myelination and pruning) lead to more efficient neural processing, they are, at least at a qualitative level, consistent with the SPH.

To summarize, the SPH effectively captures a broad array of developmental changes in spatial cognition, including changes in A-not-B-type effects (Schutte et al., 2003), changes in the stability of spatial working memory (Schutte, 2004; Spencer & Schöner, 2003), developmental differences in spatial recall versus spatial recognition performance (Spencer et al., 2006), and the qualitative developmental shift in geometric category biases (Schutte, 2004). Thus, this relatively simple, intuitive hypothesis about how neural interactions change systematically over the longer time scale of development has been quite generative. This is no accident: in our view, the richly structured real-time and learning-time dynamics of the DFT require less from development because they have much to offer. Importantly, we contend that the relatively modest view of development captured by our theory brings an understanding of developmental mechanism within reach.

14.6 THE DFT, THEORETICAL NEUROSCIENCE, AND THE *HOW* OF DEVELOPMENT

The DFT offers both a rich view of brain–behavior relations and a detailed account of real-time behavior. In addition, this theory specifies a mechanism that leads to the formation of long-term memory across a trial-to-trial time scale. Finally, the SPH offers a relatively simple view of change at an even longer time scale that effectively captures a range of phenomena. This brings us back to the issue of developmental mechanism: does the SPH offer a developmental mechanism that explains key changes in spatial cognitive development? Have we successfully arrived at the *how* of development?

From one perspective, the answer is "no" because we have yet to "close the loop" on development (Simon, 1962). That is, we have yet to formalize how our model can *change itself* over the longer time scale of development to yield the changes specified by the SPH. One candidate process is Hebbian learning. Hebbian learning has been shown to produce the type of continuous, graded, metric changes captured by the SPH (e.g., Kohonen, 1982). Concretely, we could implement a Hebbian learning rule that would gradually modify the strength with which neurons in our model interact. We contend that this type of account is within reach.

Although we have not yet arrived at this developmental goal, we want to stress where we have come to date. The SPH specifies precisely what we need from a developmental mechanism—metric changes in the precision of neural interactions. And we have shown the developmental outcomes of this type of change—both quantitative and qualitative changes in performance in spatial cognitive tasks. Any account of developmental mechanism must achieve this level of precision. As we stated at the outset, this has been a challenge for theories of developmental change: as researchers explore the longer time scales of learning and development, it becomes difficult to offer a detailed, process-based account of real-time behavior.

We contend that our approach that builds from the shortest time scales to the longer time scale of development will ultimately arrive at both a detailed account of behavior-in-the-moment as well as specific developmental mechanisms. In this context, however, we acknowledge the utility of taking different approaches to the mechanism question. For instance, if a Hebbian account can effectively "close the loop" on development in our model, this would be an ideal marriage between our dynamic systems approach and previous work on Hebbian learning using connectionist models.

With this diversity in mind, we conclude by addressing the issue emphasized in our title: what does theoretical neuroscience have to offer the study of behavioral development? Our answer: constraints and clarity.

With regard to the former, the neural principles that underlie the DFT provide strong constraints on the real-time behaviors of our model, and these real-time dynamics constrain what is learned. Reversely, learning dynamics constrain the link between past and present, and the dynamics that live at both time scales provide strong constraints for what might develop. What we have discovered, however, is that these constraints—far from limiting—provide clarity on development: because of the rich dynamics at the shorter time scales, developmental change might be relatively simple.

This level of clarity is certainly tied to the formalization we have achieved within the dynamic field framework. Although formal models are often useful for clarifying and constraining concepts, we have a sense that this is particularly important when studying development given the tough challenge of thinking about dynamics over multiple time scales. As an example, when we started exploring the development of geometric biases, we had little sense that a gradual, quantitative change might underlie what has been described in the literature as a dramatic shift in how children "conceptualize" space. But because we started by asking questions about behavior-in-the-moment, we were drawn to the issue of what might be special about symmetry axes. This, in turn, led us to probe the coupling between perception and working memory and the utility of reference frames for spatial cognition. Once we had developed a framework that could integrate spatial memory with perceived reference frames, we explored whether the SPH might account for the developmental shift in geometric effects. To our excitement, the answer was positive: we arrived at a complex pattern of behavioral development using a relatively simple, neurally grounded hypothesis.

Looking to the future, this neural grounding might ultimately provide a bridge between our theoretical work and the emerging field of developmental cognitive neuroscience (Nelson & Luciana, 2001). To date, theoretical neuroscience is an underutilized approach in this field which has been dominated by the use of particular methods—ERPs, fMRI, and so on. Ultimately, one exciting direction would be to marry theoretical work with these new techniques. For instance, there is the potential to test DFT-derived hypotheses using ERPs (McDowell et al., 2002), and we noted ties between the SPH and results from studies using structural MRI to map developmental changes in PFC in the previous section (see, e.g., Gogtay et al., 2004). There are also ways to test predictions of the SPH using fMRI. For instance, we suspect there are key changes in posterior parietal cortex during the transition in geometric bias. Recall that evidence suggests parietal cortex has weakly self-sustaining dynamics (Constantinidis & Steinmetz, 1996; Steinmetz & Constantinidis, 1995) and is involved in reference frame calibration (Pouget et al., 2002). Thus, this cortical area is a good candidate for the functions subserved by our object-centered perceptual field. According to our account of the transition in geometric bias, this field undergoes dramatic changes over development with the emergence of a reference-related peak during the memory delay in recall tasks around

4 years, 4 months. It should be possible to detect such a transition in parietal areas using fMRI (for related ideas, see chapter 13).

In conclusion, the dynamic field theory we outline in the present chapter takes an important step toward achieving an elusive goal in developmental science: providing an account of developmental mechanism that retains strong ties to behavior in context. Although we are not yet at the *how* of development, our work on the DFT might specify a path for how to get there.

NOTES

1. This type of spatial category bias is related to work on the formation of object categories. Several researchers have shown that recall of metric object features can be biased based on the distribution of exemplars to which one is exposed (e.g., J. Huttenlocher et al., 2000). Thus, contrary to a recent report (J. Huttenlocher et al., 2004), spatial memory is sensitive to the distribution of exemplar locations in the task space.

2. Earlier versions of this theory are described in Schutte et al. (2003) and Spencer and Schöner (2003).

3. There is some controversy about when it is appropriate to refer to "working" memory versus, for instance, short-term memory (see, e.g., Miyake & Shah, 1999). According to Baddeley (1986), working memory is a specific form of memory that can be used in the service of other, typically complex tasks where memory is just one component. An overlooked aspect of memory necessitated by this definition is stability: the nervous system cannot "use" a memory in the service of some task if the memory is unstable. Since stability is at the core of the "on" state we describe in our theory, we have adopted the "working" memory terminology. Note that although our use of this term has important ties to Baddeley's original formulation, the DFT is not isomorphic with Baddeley's theory.

4. We used single-layer perceptual fields in these simulations for simplicity. Such fields show the same dynamic properties as the two-layered dynamic field shown in figure 14.3, but they are computationally easier to simulate. The cost is that our approach to reference frame calibration is less grounded in neural reality. This was warranted by the complexity of the calibration problem and our desire to focus on specific aspects of establishing a stable reference frame.

5. This calibration process can be integrated with other approaches (e.g., efference copy) within the dynamic field framework (for a demonstration of this in the domain of autonomous robotics, see Steinhage & Schöner, 1997, 1998).

6. We have implemented an explicit "same/different" response system using two bistable neurons that are dedicated to these labels (i.e., when the "same" node receives strong input, it goes into a self-sustaining state that represents the generation of this response). This allows us to generate an explicit response and to generate realistic reaction time curves as well.

ACKNOWLEDGMENTS   This research was funded by NIMH RO1 MH62480, NSF BCS 00-91757, and NSF HSD 0527698 awarded to J.P.S., as well as support from the Obermann Center for Advanced Studies at the University of Iowa awarded to J.P.S. and G.S. We thank the parents, children, and undergraduates who participated in this research, as well as the many undergraduate research assistants who helped with data collection. We also thank Jeff Johnson, John Lipinski, Sammy Perone, Larissa Samuelson, and Wendy Troob for their valuable contributions to the manuscript and the development of the dynamic field theory.

REFERENCES

Amari, S. (1977). Dynamics of pattern formation in lateral-inhibition type neural fields. *Biological Cybernetics, 27*, 77–87.
Amari, S. (1989). Dynamical stability of formation of cortical maps. In M. A. Arbib & S. Amari (Eds.), *Dynamic interactions in neural networks: Models and data* (pp. 15–34). New York: Springer.
Amari, S., & Arbib, M. A. (1977). Competition and cooperation in neural nets. In J. Metzler (Ed.), *Systems neuroscience* (pp. 119–165). New York: Academic Press.
Awh, E., Jonides, J., Smith, E. E., Buxton, R. B., Frank, L. R., Love, T., et al. (1999). Rehearsal in spatial working memory: Evidence from neuroimaging. *Psychological Science, 10*, 433–437.
Baddeley, A. D. (1986). *Working memory*. Oxford: Oxford University Press.
Bard, C., Fleury, M., Teasdale, N., Paillard, J., & Nougier, V. (1995). Contribution of proprioception for calibrating and updating the motor space. *Canadian Journal of Physiology & Pharmacology, 73*, 246–254.
Barnett, R., Maruff, P., Vance, A., Luk, E. S. L., Costin, J., Wood, C., et al. (2001). Abnormal executive function in attention deficit hyperactivity disorder: The effect of stimulant medication and age on spatial working memory. *Psychological Medicine, 31*, 1107–1115.
Barsalou, L. W. (1999). Perceptual symbol systems. *Behavioral & Brain Sciences, 22*, 577–660.
Bastian, A., Riehle, A., Erlhagen, W., & Schöner, G. (1998). Prior information preshapes the population representation of movement direction in motor cortex. *NeuroReport, 9*, 315–319.
Bastian, A., Schöner, G., & Riehle, A. (2003). Preshaping and continuous evolution of motor cortical representations during movement preparation. *European Journal of Neuroscience, 18*, 2047–2058.
Beh, H., Wenderoth, P., & Purcell, A. (1971). The angular function of a rod-and-frame illusion. *Perception & Psychophysics, 9*, 353–355.
Braun, M. (1994). *Differential equations and their applications* (4th ed.). New York: Springer Verlag.
Bridgeman, B. (1999). Separate visual representations for perception and for visually guided behavior. In G. Aschersleben, T. Bachmann, & J. Müsseler (Eds.), *Cognitive contributions to the perception of spatial and temporal events. Advances in psychology* (pp. 316–327). Amsterdam: Elsevier Science.
Bridgeman, B., Gemmer, A., Forsman, T., & Huemer, V. (2000). Processing spatial information in the sensorimotor branch of the visual system. *Vision Research, 40*, 3539–3552.
Brungart, D. S., Rabinowitz, W. M., & Durlach, N. I. (2000). Evaluation of response methods for the localization of nearby objects. *Perception & Psychophysics, 62*(1), 48–65.
Compte, A., Brunel, N., Goldman-Rakic, P. S., & Wang, X.-J. (2000). Synaptic mechanisms and network dynamics underlying spatial working memory in a cortical network model. *Cerebral Cortex, 10*, 910–923.

Constantinidis, C., & Steinmetz, M. A. (1996). Neuronal activity in posterior parietal area 7a during the delay periods of a spatial memory task. *Journal of Neurophysiology, 76*, 1352–1355.

DeLoache, J. S. (2004). Becoming symbol-minded. *Trends in Cognitive Sciences, 8*, 66–70.

Deneve, S., & Pouget, A. (2003). Basis functions for object-centered representations. *Neuron, 37*(2), 347–359.

di Pellegrino, G., & Wise, S. P. (1993). Visuospatial versus visuomotor activity in the premotor and prefrontal cortex of a primate. *Journal of Neuroscience, 13*(3), 1227–1243.

Douglas, R., & Martin, K. (1998). Neocortex. In G. M. Shepherd (Ed.), *The synaptic organization of the brain* (pp. 459–509). New York: Oxford University Press.

Durstewitz, D., Seamans, J. K., & Sejnowski, T. J. (2000). Neurocomputational models of working memory. *Nature Neuroscience Supplement, 3*, 1184–1191.

Engebretson, P. H., & Huttenlocher, J. (1996). Bias in spatial location due to categorization: Comment on Tversky and Schiano. *Journal of Experimental Psychology: General, 125*(1), 96–108.

Erlhagen, W., Bastian, A., Jancke, D., Riehle, A., & Schöner, G. (1999). The distribution of neuronal population activation (DPA) as a tool to study interaction and integration in cortical representations. *Journal of Neuroscience Methods, 94*, 53–66.

Erlhagen, W., & Schöner, G. (2002). Dynamic field theory of movement preparation. *Psychological Review, 109*, 545–572.

Finkel, L. H. (2000). Neuroengineering models of brain disease. *Annual Review of Biomedical Engineering, 2*, 577–606.

Fuster, J. M. (1995). *Memory in the cerebral cortex: An empirical approach to neural networks in the human and nonhuman primate.* Cambridge, MA: MIT Press.

Georgopoulos, A. P., Kettner, R. E., & Schwartz, A. B. (1988). Primate motor cortex and free arm movements to visual targets in three-dimensional space. II. Coding of the direction of movement by a neuronal population. *Journal of Neuroscience, 8*(8), 2928–2937.

Georgopoulos, A. P., Taira, M., & Lukashin, A. V. (1993). Cognitive neurophysiology of the motor cortex. *Science, 260*, 47–52.

Gilmore, R. O., & Johnson, M. H. (1997). Egocentric action in early infancy: Spatial frames of reference for saccades. *Psychological Science, 83*(3), 224–230.

Gogtay, N., Giedd, J. N., Lusk, L., Hayashi, K. M., Greenstein, D., Vaituzis, A. C., et al. (2004). Dynamic mapping of human cortical development during childhood through early adulthood. *Proceedings of the National Academy of Sciences of the United States of America, 101*, 8174–8179.

Graziano, M., Hu, X. T., & Gross, C. G. (1997). Coding the locations of objects in the dark. *Science, 277*, 239–241.

Haskell, E., Nykamp, D. Q., & Tranchina, D. (2001). Population density methods for large-scale modelling of neuronal networks with realistic synaptic kinetics: Cutting the dimension down to size. *Network: Computation in Neural Systems, 12*, 141–174.

Hund, A. M., & Plumert, J. M. (2002). Delay-induced bias in children's memory for location. *Child Development, 73*, 829–840.

Hund, A. M., & Plumert, J. M. (2003). Does information about what things are influence children's memory for where things are? *Developmental Psychology, 39*, 939–948.

Hund, A. M., & Plumert, J. M. (2005). The stability and flexibility of spatial categories. *Cognitive Psychology*, *50*(1), 1–44.

Hund, A. M., Plumert, J. M., & Benney, C. J. (2002). Experiencing nearby locations together in time: The role of spatiotemporal contiguity in children's memory for location. *Journal of Experimental Child Psychology*, *82*, 200–225.

Hund, A. M., & Spencer, J. P. (2003). Developmental changes in the relative weighting of geometric and experience-dependent location cues. *Journal of Cognition & Development*, *4*(1), 3–38.

Huttenlocher, J., Hedges, L. V., Corrigan, B., & Crawford, L. E. (2004). Spatial categories and the estimation of location. *Cognition*, *93*(2), 75–97.

Huttenlocher, J., Hedges, L. V., & Duncan, S. (1991). Categories and particulars: Prototype effects in estimating spatial location. *Psychological Review*, *98*, 352–376.

Huttenlocher, J., Hedges, L. V., & Vevea, J. L. (2000). Why do categories affect stimulus judgment? *Journal of Experimental Psychology: General*, *129*, 220–241.

Huttenlocher, J., Newcombe, N. S., & Sandberg, E. H. (1994). The coding of spatial location in young children. *Cognitive Psychology*, *27*, 115–147.

Huttenlocher, P. R. (1979). Synaptic density in human frontal cortex—developmental changes and effects of aging. *Brain Research*, *163*, 195–205.

Huttenlocher, P. R. (1990). Morphometric study of human cerebral cortex development. *Neuropsychologia*, *28*, 517–527.

Jancke, D., Erlhagen, W., Dinse, H. R., Akhavan, A. C., Giese, M., Steinhage, A., et al. (1999). Parametric population representation of retinal location: Neuronal interaction dynamics in cat primary visual cortex. *Journal of Neuroscience*, *19*, 9016–9028.

Johnson, J. S., Spencer, J. P., & Schöner, G. (2006). A dynamic neural field theory of multi-item visual working memory and change detection. In *Proceedings of the 28th Annual Conference of the Cognitive Science Society,* (pp. 399–404), Mahwah: Lawrence Erlbaum Associates, Inc.

Karatekin, C., & Asarnow, R. F. (1998). Working memory in childhood-onset schizophrenia and attention-deficit/hyperactivity disorder. *Psychiatry Research*, *80*, 165–176.

Kessels, R. P. C., Postma, A., Wijnalda, E. M., & de Haan, E. H. F. (2000). Frontal-lobe involvement in spatial memory: Evidence from PET, fMRI, and lesion studies. *Neuropsychology Review*, *10*, 101–113.

Kohonen, T. (1982). Self-organized formation of topologically correct feature maps. *Biological Cybernetics*, *43*, 59–69.

Krommenhoek, K. P., van Opstal, A. J., Gielen, C. C., & van Gisbergen, J. A. (1993). Remapping of neural activity in the motor colliculus: A neural network study. *Vision Research*, *33*, 1287–1298.

Landau, B. (2003). Axes and direction in spatial language and spatial cognition. In E. van der Zee & J. Slack (Eds.), *Representing direction in language and space* (pp. 18–38). Oxford: Oxford University Press.

Lawrence, A. D., Watkins, L. H. A., Sahakian, B. J., Hodges, J. R., & Robbins, T. W. (2000). Visual object and visuospatial cognition in Huntington's disease: Implications for information processing in coticostriatal circuits. *Brain*, *123*, 1349–1364.

Li, W., & Westheimer, G. (1997). Human discrimination of the implicit orientation of simple symmetrical patterns. *Vision Research*, *37*, 565–572.

Love, B. C., Medin, D. L., & Gureckis, T. M. (2004). SUSTAIN: A network model of category learning. *Psychological Review*, *111*, 309–332.

McClelland, J. L., & Jenkins, E. (1991). Nature, nurture, and connections: Implications of connectionist models for cognitive development. In K. Van-Lehn (Ed.), *Architectures for intelligence: The twenty-second Carnegie Mellon Symposium on Cognition* (pp. 41–73). Hillsdale, NJ: Lawrence Erlbaum.

McDowell, K., Jeka, J. J., Schöner, G., & Hatfield, B. D. (2002). Behavioral and electrocortical evidence of an interaction between probability and task metrics in movement preparation. *Experimental Brain Research, 144*, 303–313.

McIntyre, J., Stratta, F., & Lacquaniti, F. (1998). Short-term memory for reaching to visual targets: Psychophysical evidence for body-centered reference frames. *Journal of Neuroscience, 18*(20), 8423–8435.

Miller, E. K., Erickson, C. A., & Desimone, R. (1996). Neural mechanisms of visual working memory in prefrontal cortex of the macaque. *Journal of Neuroscience, 16*(16), 5154–5167.

Miyake, A., & Shah, P. (Eds.). (1999). *Models of working memory: Mechanisms of active maintenance and executive control*. Cambridge: Cambridge University Press.

Munakata, Y., & McClelland, J. L. (2003). Connectionist models of development. *Developmental Science, 6*, 413–429.

Nelson, C. A., & Luciana, M. (Eds.). (2001). *Handbook of developmental cognitive neuroscience*. Cambridge, MA: MIT Press.

Nelson, C. A., Monk, C. S., Lin, J., Carver, L. J., Thomas, K. M., & Truwit, C. L. (2000). Functional neuroanatomy of spatial working memory in children. *Developmental Psychology, 36*, 109–116.

Newcombe, N. S., & Huttenlocher, J. (2000). *Making space: The development of spatial representation and reasoning*. Cambridge, MA: MIT Press.

Plumert, J. M., & Hund, A. M. (2001). The development of location memory: What role do spatial prototypes play? *Child Development, 72*, 370–384.

Posner, M. I. (2001). Educating the human brain: A commentary. In J. L. McClelland & R. S. Siegler (Eds.), *Mechanisms of cognitive development: Behavioral and neural perspectives* (pp. 387–400). Mahwah, NJ: Lawrence Erlbaum.

Pouget, A., Deneve, S., & Duhamel, J. R. (2002). A computational perspective on the neural basis of multisensory spatial representations. *Nature Reviews Neuroscience, 3*(9), 741–747.

Quinn, P. C. (2000). Perceptual reference points for form and orientation in young infants: Anchors or magnets? *Perception & Psychophysics, 62*, 1625–1633.

Rakic, P. (1995). The development of the frontal lobe: A view from the rear of the brain. *Advances in Neurology, 66*, 1–8.

Rao, S. C., Rainer, G., & Miller, E. K. (1997). Integration of what and where in the primate prefrontal cortex. *Science, 276*, 821–824.

Rogers, T. T., & McClelland, J. L. (2004). *Semantic cognition: A parallel distributed processing approach*. Cambridge, MA: MIT Press.

Salinas, E. (2003). Background synaptic activity as a switch between dynamical states in a network. *Neural Computation, 15*(7), 1439–1475.

Sampaio, R. C., & Truwit, C. L. (2001). Myelination in the developing human brain. In C. A. Nelson & M. Luciana (Eds.), *Handbook of developmental cognitive neuroscience* (pp. 35–44). Cambridge, MA: MIT Press.

Sandberg, E. H., Huttenlocher, J., & Newcombe, N. S. (1996). The development of hierarchical representation of two-dimensional space. *Child Development, 67*, 721–739.

Sauser, E., & Billard, A. (2005). Three dimensional frames of reference transformations using recurrent populations of neurons. *Neurocomputing, 64*, 5–24.

Schiano, D. J., & Tversky, B. (1992). Structure and strategy in encoding simplified graphs. *Memory & Cognition, 20*(1), 12–20.

Schöner, G. (in press). Development as change of system dynamics: Stability, instability, and emergence. In J. P. Spencer, M. S. Thomas, & J. L. McClelland (Eds.), *Toward a new grand theory of development? Connectionism and dynamic systems theory re-considered*. New York: Oxford University Press.

Schutte, A. R. (2004). *A developmental transition in spatial working memory*. Unpublished doctoral dissertation. Iowa City, IA: University of Iowa.

Schutte, A. R., & Spencer, J. P. (2002). Generalizing the dynamic field theory of the A-not-B error beyond infancy: Three-year-olds' delay- and experience-dependent location memory biases. *Child Development, 73*, 377–404.

Schutte, A. R., Spencer, J. P., & Schöner, G. (2003). Testing the dynamic field theory: Working memory for locations becomes more spatially precise over development. *Child Development, 74*(5), 1393–1417.

Simmering, V. R., & Spencer, J. P. (2006a). *Carving up space at imaginary joints: Can people mentally impose spatial category boundaries?* Unpublished manuscript.

Simmering, V. R., & Spencer, J. P. (2006b). *Generality with specificity: The dynamic field theory generalizes across tasks and time scales*. Unpublished manuscript.

Simmering, V. R., Spencer, J. P., & Schöner, G. (2006). Reference-related inhibition produces enhanced position discrimination and fast repulsion near axes of symmetry. *Perception & Psychophysics, 63*, 1027–1046.

Simon, H. A. (1962). An information processing theory of intellectual development. In W. Kessen & C. Kuhlman (Eds.), *Thought in the young child* (pp. 150–161). Yellow Springs, OH: Antioch Press.

Skarda, C. A., & Freeman, W. J. (1987). How brains make chaos in order to make sense of the world. *Behavioral & Brain Sciences, 10*(2), 161–195.

Smith, L. B., Thelen, E., Titzer, R., & McLin, D. (1999). Knowing in the context of acting: The task dynamics of the A-not-B error. *Psychological Review, 106*, 235–260.

Smyrnis, N., Taira, M., Ashe, J., & Georgopoulos, A. P. (1992). Motor cortical activity in a memorized delay task. *Experimental Brain Research, 92*, 139–151.

Soechting, J. F., & Flanders, M. (1991). Arm movements in three dimensional space: Computation, theory, and observation. *Exercise Sports Science Review, 19*, 389–418.

Sowell, E. R., Thompson, P. M., Tessner, K. D., & Toga, A. W. (2001). Mapping continued brain growth and gray matter density reduction in dorsal frontal cortex: Inverse relationships during postadolescent brain maturation. *Journal of Neuroscience, 21*, 8819–8829.

Spencer, J. P., & Hund, A. M. (2002). Prototypes and particulars: Geometric and experience-dependent spatial categories. *Journal of Experimental Psychology: General, 131*, 16–37.

Spencer, J. P., & Hund, A. M. (2003). Developmental continuity in the processes that underlie spatial recall. *Cognitive Psychology, 47*(4), 432–480.

Spencer, J. P., & Schöner, G. (2003). Bridging the representational gap in the dynamical systems approach to development. *Developmental Science, 6*, 392–412.

Spencer, J. P., & Schutte, A. R. (2004). Unifying representations and responses: Perseverative biases arise from a single behavioral system. *Psychological Science, 15*(3), 187–193.

Spencer, J. P., Simmering, V. R., & Schutte, A. R. (2006). Toward a formal theory of flexible spatial behavior: Geometric category biases generalize across pointing and verbal response types. *Journal of Experimental Psychology: Human Perception & Performance, 32*, 473–490.

Spencer, J. P., Smith, L. B., & Thelen, E. (2001). Tests of a dynamic systems account of the A-not-B error: The influence of prior experience on the spatial memory abilities of 2-year-olds. *Child Development, 72*, 1327–1346.

Steinhage, A., & Schöner, G. (1997). Self-calibration based on invariant view recognition: Dynamic approach to navigation. *Robotics & Autonomous Systems, 20*, 133–156.

Steinhage, A., & Schöner, G. (1998). Dynamical systems for the behavioral organization of autonomous robot navigation. *Proceedings of SPIE, 3523*, 160–180.

Steinmetz, M. A., & Constantinidis, C. (1995). Neurophysiological evidence for a role of posterior parietal cortex in redirecting visual attention. *Cerebral Cortex, 5*, 448–456.

Stiles, J., Bates, E. A., Thal, D., Trauner, D. A., & Reilly, J. (1998). Linguistic and spatial cognitive development in children with pre- and perinatal focal brain injury: A ten-year overview from the San Diego Longitudinal Project. *Advances in Infacy Research, 12*, 131–164.

Thelen, E., Schöner, G., Scheier, C., & Smith, L. B. (2001). The dynamics of embodiment: A field theory of infant perseverative reaching. *Behavioral & Brain Sciences, 24*, 1–86.

Thelen, E., & Smith, L. B. (1994). *A dynamic systems approach to the development of cognition and action.* Cambridge, MA: MIT Press.

Tversky, B., & Schiano, D. J. (1989). Perceptual and conceptual factors in distortions in memory for graphs and maps. *Journal of Experimental Psychology: General, 118*(4), 387–398.

van der Maas, H. L. J., & Molenaar, P. C. M. (1992). Stagewise cognitive development: An application of catastrophe theory. *Psychological Review, 99*, 395–417.

Van Geert, P. (1998). A dynamic systems model of basic developmental mechanisms: Piaget, Vygotsky, and beyond. *Psychological Review, 105*, 634–677.

Wenderoth, P., & van der Zwan, R. (1991). Local and gloabal mechanisms of one-and two-dimensional orientation illusions. *Perception & Psychophysics, 50*, 321–332.

Werner, S., & Diedrichsen, J. (2002). The time course of spatial memory distortions. *Memory & Cognition, 30*(5), 718–730.

Wilimzig, C., & Schöner, G. (2006). *A dynamic field theory of categorical and continuous response generation.* Unpublished manuscript.

Wilson, F. A. W., Scalaidhe, S. P., & Goldman-Rakic, P. S. (1993). Dissociation of object and spatial processing domains in primate prefrontal cortex. *Science, 260*, 1955–1958.

15

COMMENTARY: SPECIFICITY, MECHANISMS, AND TIMING IN THE STUDY OF SPATIAL COGNITION

Courtney Stevens & Edward Awh

The chapters in part III examine spatial cognition using a diverse set of methodologies ranging from behavioral and neuroimaging techniques to cognitive modeling based on theoretical neuroscience. What unites the chapters is a focus on characterizing changes in spatial cognition, whether they occur as a function of trial-to-trial learning in adults (chapter 14), aberrant sensory or language experience (chapter 12), or the microdeletion of chromosomal material in a genetic disorder (chapter 13). Amidst this diversity of methodologies and populations, or perhaps because of it, the chapters provide rich insight into fundamental questions about spatial cognition.

In this commentary, we focus on three issues broadly relevant to spatial cognition that surfaced as emergent themes in these chapters, which we will refer to as the "what, how, and when" of changes in spatial cognition. The first theme characterizes what changes in spatial cognition occur in special populations. These data emphasize the relative domain specificity of spatial cognition as well as distinctions between component processes within spatial cognition. The second theme explores how both typical and atypical changes in spatial cognition are realized at the level of neural mechanisms. The third theme examines the time periods when changes in spatial cognition occur, including whether sensitive periods constrain the mechanisms

362

available to mediate these changes. In exploring each of these three themes, the overarching goal of this commentary is to highlight the role of integration across both adult and developmental studies, as well as multiple methodologies, in clarifying the what, how, and when of changes in spatial cognition.

15.1 ASKING WHAT: DOMAIN SPECIFICITY WITHIN SPATIAL COGNITION

An enduring question in the study of cognition is the degree to which different systems show relative independence, or domain specificity, relative to other cognitive processes. Although few would argue for complete independence of cognitive processes, studies of special populations suggest that spatial cognition can show relative dissociation from other cognitive domains (e.g., language). Perhaps more striking, though, are the relative dissociations that emerge within tasks considered part of spatial cognition. Both chapters 12 and 13 indicate that spatial cognition does not function as a single set of abilities that are uniformly depressed, spared, or enhanced in special populations. Instead, profiles of plasticity are uneven across domains and tasks.

In chapter 13 on selective spatial breakdown in Williams syndrome (WS), Landau and Hoffman document the uneven profile of cognitive abilities in individuals with WS. Nearly two decades ago, Bellugi, Sabo, and Vaid (1988), also in an edited volume on spatial cognition, first described surprising performance discrepancies across domains in three adolescents with WS. These three children showed severe impairments in drawing, construction, and spatial transformation tasks amidst relatively spared language and facial processing skills. Using data from larger samples of both children and adults with WS, Landau and Hoffman review research examining whether failure on the visuospatial tasks can be localized to more precise cognitive processes. Landau and Hoffman demonstrate that the spatial deficit in WS cannot be reduced to a problem in perception, either in individual objects or in perceptual grouping. Like their typically developing peers, children and adults with WS are able to recognize objects from both canonical and atypical views and are susceptible to visual illusions. However, deficits emerge in WS when tracking multiple moving objects, as well as during visually guided action or when coordinating reference frames between an image and test figure. These findings suggest that aspects of spatial cognition can show differential degrees of impairment.

Chapter 12 by Mitchell describes selective enhancements in spatial cognition following sensory deprivation and further supports the idea of specificity within spatial cognition. For example, deaf signers are faster than hearing signers and nonsigners at detecting peripheral motion and show larger effects of attention on sensorineural processing for peripheral, but not central, visual stimuli. Congenitally blind adults also show an advantage in discriminating small differences in auditory spatial stimuli and in the spatial tuning of auditory attention. However, these differences are not uniform across auditory space—behavioral and event-related potential (ERP) indices of attentional tuning reveal advantages in the blind when attending to peripheral, but not central, auditory space. Similarly, minimal audible angle measures are improved in the azimuth, but not vertical, direction. Taken together, these data suggest remarkable specificity in the aspects of spatial cognition showing plasticity following sensory deprivation.

If, as suggested by the studies of WS, deaf, and blind populations, certain aspects of spatial cognition are selectively modifiable, what is it that unites these processes? Landau and Hoffman suggest in chapter 13 that aspects of spatial cognition showing deficits in WS may be linked to the dorsal stream and, more specifically, parietal areas. More direct support for the possibility that parietally mediated tasks are impaired in WS is found in neuroimaging work, in which individuals with WS show hypoactivation in parietal areas when performing spatial tasks (Meyer-Lindenberg et al., 2004). A selective deficit in parietally mediated functions is consistent with adult neuroimaging data indicating that many tasks that are relatively spared in WS (e.g., face processing and object recognition) rely primarily on ventral visual areas. In contrast, those aspects of visuospatial cognition showing deficits rely primarily on more dorsal or parietal cortical areas. Thus, the adult neuropsychological literature suggests a common neural substrate for many of the aspects of spatial cognition showing vulnerability in WS.

However, as noted by Landau and Hoffman, the differences are not this simple. Individuals with WS show patterns of selective sparing for different aspects of motion-related processing, typically considered a dorsal pathway task. Likewise, other research shows WS deficits in aspects of face processing (Karmiloff-Smith, 1997), which is typically associated with ventral cortical areas. As noted by Landau and Hoffman, one aspect of motion processing showing deficits in WS, extracting two-dimensional structure from motion, involves segregating a signal from a noisy background and could be considered, then, a problem of segmentation or selective attention. In fact, selective attention deficits are implicated in many developmental disorders, including autism (Bird, Catmur, Silani, Frith, & Frith, 2006), schizophrenia (Carter, Mintun, Nichols, & Cohen, 1997), specific language impairment (Stevens, Sanders, & Neville, 2006), and dyslexia (Sperling, Lu, Manis, & Seidenberg, 2005). These data raise the possibility that differences in selective attention may underlie at least some cognitive differences observed in special populations. To our knowledge, selective attention has not been directly assessed in WS. Exploring how differences in selective attention mediate some of the changes observed in spatial cognition represents an exciting direction for future research.

Both chapters 12 and 13 note that the aspects of spatial cognition showing plasticity have longer developmental time courses. These chapters suggest that aspects of spatial cognition with protracted time courses of development may be more susceptible to change in atypical populations. This hypothesis may be compatible with the dorsal/parietal hypothesis raised previously. Indeed, there is considerable, though not unequivocal, evidence indicating that the dorsal pathway matures more slowly than the ventral pathway (Coch, Skendzel, Grossi, & Neville, 2005; Hollants-Gilhuijs, Ruijter, & Spekreijse, 1998a, 1998b; Mitchell & Neville, 2004). Interestingly, recent research suggests that the time course of development for configural face processing, which shows deficits in WS (Karmiloff-Smith, 1997), is more protracted than that of featural face processing (Mondloch, Le Grand, & Maurer, 2002). Furthermore, recent developmental neuroimaging work suggests that during facial processing, children, in addition to showing more diffuse face-specific processing in fusiform areas than adults, also recruit additional middle temporal regions not seen in adults. The additional middle temporal activations are hypothesized to reflect the role of working memory in performing this task for children. These data underscore the importance of combining adult and developmental research using multiple methodologies. Children may recruit additional systems or neural areas early in development that provide scaffolding for the emergence of a particular skill. These same supplementary systems can be silent once mature, adultlike levels of performance are reached, belying the reliance of apparently specialized processing on other more generalized systems during development (see also chapter 3).

The specificity of changes in dorsal or later maturing systems is typically confounded by differences in task difficulty. That is, tasks that rely on later maturing systems are typically more difficult than tasks that are mastered earlier in development. As such, it is possible that group differences emerge only on those tasks where most participants are not performing at or near ceiling levels. Modifiability might be more generalized, but there is room to see group differences only on more difficult tasks. To address this possibility, Stevens and Neville (2006) recently tested two special populations using both a peripheral motion detection (putative dorsal/parietal) task and a central visual field detection (putative ventral pathway) task. Unlike most previous studies, the ventral pathway task in this study measured contrast sensitivity thresholds, and no individual approached ceiling performance on the task. They predicted that whereas deaf adults would show enhancements on the motion detection task, dyslexic adults would show deficits on the same task. No group differences were predicted on the central visual contrast sensitivity task. These predictions were upheld, providing direct evidence for the two sides of plasticity: a system that is vulnerable to deficit under certain conditions might, under different conditions, be modifiable and show enhancement. Importantly, even though no participant approached ceiling performance in the central visual field task, no group differences emerged. In a similar vein, two recent studies have provided evidence for selective dorsal pathway modifiability in special populations using dorsal and ventral pathway tasks with identical task structure (Armstrong, Neville, Hillyard, & Mitchell, 2002; Sperling, Lu, Manis, & Seidenberg, 2003). These findings suggest that selective modifiability of dorsal/parietal or later maturing systems is not merely an artifact of task difficulty and may reflect a meaningful distinction in characterizing what aspects of spatial cognition are most open to change.

15.2 ASKING HOW: THE MECHANISMS OF CHANGE IN SPATIAL COGNITION

Although chapters 12 and 13 primarily focus on changes in spatial cognition that occur in special populations, it is also apparent that many aspects of spatial cognition change over the course of typical development. Indeed, in chapter 13 Landau and Hoffman argue that characterizing such typical developmental trajectories is critical in assessing whether deficits in special populations represent deviance or delay. Given that spatial cognition undergoes changes throughout life, a remaining question, then, is how these changes, both typical and atypical, come about.

During atypical development, one major mechanism of change, described by Mitchell in chapter 12, involves functional reorganization. In the case of profound sensory deprivation, Mitchell argues that functional reallocation of cortical areas occurs. For example, an individual born deaf might co-opt cortical areas typically devoted to audition for visual processing. Neuroimaging data provide evidence for this possibility. When attending to peripheral visual space, deaf signers show a more anterior distribution of the N1 ERP waveform, suggesting possible recruitment of auditory cortical areas (Neville & Lawson, 1987). There is also evidence to suggest hypertrophy of the remaining modalities. For example, functional MRI data indicate that deaf individuals show a larger spatial extent of activation in middle temporal regions when monitoring motion in the peripheral, but not central, visual fields. When attending to peripheral motion, deaf individuals also show greater recruitment of the posterior superior temporal sulcus, a polymodal brain area (Bavelier et al., 2001). Similar differences are observed in electrophysiological indices of peripheral attention in blind adults. Here, the spatial distribution of the N1 is more posterior in the blind, suggesting possible recruitment of visual cortical areas (Röder et al., 1999). More recently, positron emission tomography has revealed that congenitally blind individuals who show enhanced performance on an auditory localization task also recruit occipital (visual) regions during this task. Further, these differences are not observed in blind individuals who do not show enhanced performance on the task, suggesting that the occipital activity plays a true functional role in auditory processing (Gougoux, Zatorre, Lassonde, Voss, & Lepore, 2005).

In the case of deaf individuals, cortical reorganization appears to be attributable to sensory deprivation, as opposed to experience learning a manual-spatial language. Separating the effects of deafness and altered language experience has been possible by including groups of hearing native signers (i.e., hearing children born to deaf parents who are raised learning sign language as a first language). Studies of hearing native signers have revealed that functional reorganization is characteristic of only the deaf signers, suggesting that deafness, rather than signing, causes these changes. An interesting question is whether deafness leads to such changes by virtue of the unused cortical real estate that can be taken over or co-opted, the functional demands of missing one modality, or a combination of these factors.

Taken together, the data on sensory deprivation suggest that a number of neural mechanisms may underlie the behavioral changes observed, including the co-opting of cortex typically devoted to the absent modality, compensatory hypertrophy of remaining modalities, and a redistribution of specialization in polymodal regions. As a final note, it is worth pointing out that many of the changes observed in neuroimaging studies, including enhanced N1 ERP components and expansion of middle temporal activations, are typically associated with attentional modulation. This provides further support for the idea that attention may play a critical role in mediating the changes observed in spatial cognition.

A second major mechanism of changes in spatial cognition, described in both chapters 12 and 14, is increased precision of spatial representations. For example, in chapter 12 Mitchell describes more precise tuning of peripheral spatial attention in congenitally blind adults. In this study, blind adults were better able to narrow the focus of spatial attention to select a peripheral speaker located at 90°, while ignoring sounds coming from nearby, distracting speakers.

Increased spatial precision is characteristic of typical development, as well. In chapter 14, Spencer, Simmering, Schutte, and Schöner review the evidence for developmental changes in spatial precision, and they provide a framework within theoretical neuroscience that can explain changes in the precision of spatial memory that occur over two distinct time scales. The model, based on dynamic field theory, accounts for both real-time changes in adults' spatial precision resulting from trial-to-trial learning, as well as the changes that occur over the longer time scale of children's normal development. Their neurobiologically plausible model captures the activity of large populations of neurons—including interactions with short- and long-term memory systems, random "noise," and inhibitory connections—to explore how memory biases and changes in spatial precision emerge. The model's ability to account for quantitative and qualitative shifts in children's spatial memory performance suggests strong links between research on spatial cognition in children and adults. Interestingly, although their particular model was developed to account for performance in a spatial recall task, the model could also explain performance in a different, position discrimination task. This suggests that a set of general mechanisms, if well specified based on a specific problem space, may generalize and explain performance in other, related tasks.

In the study of the mechanisms of change in spatial cognition, we see a special role for analysis at many levels. Whereas behavioral studies help to characterize what types of changes are occurring, neuroscience perspectives have helped to elucidate the neural substrates and mechanisms underlying those changes. In contrast, theoretical neuroscience and cognitive modeling have the potential to use specific principles, based on basic research in neuroscience, to develop models that can account for performance in a specific domain and generate novel predictions for behavioral and neuroimaging research, as well as elucidate certain general characteristics of related tasks or systems. However, it remains unclear whether the changes that occur in spatial cognition are limited to particular time windows, or sensitive periods, in development. This is the focus of the next section, where neuroimaging data play a pivotal role in distinguishing behavioral phenocopies, or examples of similar levels of behavioral performance arising from fundamentally different neural mechanisms.

15.3 ASKING WHEN: THE TEMPORAL DYNAMICS OF CHANGES IN SPATIAL COGNITION

When examining the temporal dynamics of changes in spatial cognition, an important question is whether there is a difference between the mechanisms of change available early versus later in life. As with most enduring dichotomies, the answer would seem to be a little bit of both.

In chapter 14, Spencer and colleagues address this question by developing a cognitive model, described above, that explains both real-time changes in a spatial recall task, as well as the changes that occur over the longer timescale of normal development. This model suggests that similar mechanisms might underlie changes in the precision of spatial memory observed both in adults across the time period of minutes and in children across the time period of years. Thus, a clean model of adult performance that includes trial-to-trial local updating of working memory can, through the modification of parameters (as opposed to the addition of new modules or processes), account for both quantitative and qualitative shifts in spatial cognition during development. It will be interesting to see this approach applied to other tasks within spatial cognition, as well as to other cognitive domains.

Another way of framing the question of timing is to ask whether particular changes are limited to a certain time window (i.e., "sensitive period") or can occur throughout life. Two examples from the literature on cross-modal plasticity bear on this question. First, as discussed by Mitchell in chapter 12, mental rotation times are faster in both deaf and hearing native signers than in hearing nonsigners. This suggests that changes in mental rotation abilities arise as a consequence of learning a manual-spatial language. Interestingly, similar changes are also observed in late learners of American Sign Language, suggesting that mental rotation abilities remain plastic into adulthood. However, it should be noted that because this work was behavioral, it is unclear whether these two groups of signers (early vs. late learners) use the same underlying mechanisms to achieve similarly enhanced behavioral performance.

A second example illustrates how performance and mechanism can dissociate. Mitchell reports that congenitally blind adults show improved spatial tuning of attention to the periphery, but not center, of auditory space when compared to blindfolded sighted adults. A recent study by Fieger, Röder, Teder-Sälejärvi, Hillyard, and Neville (2006) tested adults blinded later in life using the same auditory attention task. Although the late-blind group showed the same behavioral enhancement in peripheral spatial tuning, they did not show a steeper gradient of N1 attention effects evidenced in the early-blind individuals. How, then, did the late-blind group achieve improved performance? Did behavioral performance dissociate from neural mechanisms? The authors examined a different ERP component, the P3 response to target stimuli, and found that the late-blind adults showed steeper attentional gradients than did blindfolded sighted adults on this later, P3 component. This study suggests that the mechanisms underlying changes in spatial cognition may indeed differ depending upon the time at which the changes occur. As we hope the preceding discussion has made clear, understanding the temporal dynamics of changes in a system cannot be achieved without combining traditionally developmental and adult studies. Such study also requires combining many different levels of analysis, with neuroimaging data providing an important window into whether different neural mechanisms underlie behavior that, on the surface, is similar or even identical.

15.4 SUMMARY AND CONCLUSIONS

Studying the changes that take place in spatial cognition, whether they occur in adults, children, or special populations, provides important insights into fundamental questions about the nature of spatial cognition. The chapters reviewed here suggest that spatial cognition encompasses a number of distinct abilities that are differentially modifiable in special populations. In this sense, spatial cognition shows a degree of domain specificity, as do different processes considered a part of spatial cognition. While macro groupings (e.g., of dorsal vs. ventral pathway processing) may capture some of these differences, it is clear that many nuances remain to be explained. For example, distinctions might emerge on the basis of systems or processes with longer time courses of development or among tasks that engage certain processes (e.g., selective attention) to a greater or lesser degree.

While much has been learned about the changes that occur in spatial cognition, in particular in special populations, much less is known about the mechanisms underlying these changes. An increased specialization of the human brain suggests one possible means of plasticity following sensory deprivation. The available evidence indicates that unused cortical space is co-opted by the remaining modalities, that hypertrophy occurs in remaining modalities, and that a redistribution of specialization occurs in polymodal brain regions. In both typical and atypical development of spatial cognition, increased spatial precision appears to be one mechanism of change that can be described using models informed by theoretical neuroscience. Neuropsychological studies, which integrate behavioral and brain studies, will be critical in continuing to explore the neural mechanisms of changes in spatial cognition.

Finally, it is clear that the temporal dynamics of changes in spatial cognition may at times be explained using a common set of neural mechanisms at different points in development, but at other times may reflect different mechanisms of change available at different points in time. The largest benefit of neuroimaging may be in distinguishing "behavioral phenocopies," where individuals may show similar behavioral performance but rely on different underlying neural mechanisms.

The three chapters in part III each provide a unique vantage point for examining the changes that occur in spatial cognition. We believe that it is through the integration of such diverse lines of inquiry—including studies of typical and atypical populations at different ages and stages of development and using a wide range of different methodologies—that we will come closer to understanding the what, how, and when of changes in spatial cognition.

REFERENCES

Armstrong, B. A., Neville, H. J., Hillyard, S. A., & Mitchell, T. V. (2002). Auditory deprivation affects processing of motion, but not color. *Cognitive Brain Research*, *14*, 422–434.

Bavelier, D., Brozinsky, C., Tomann, A., Mitchell, T., Neville, H., & Liu, G. (2001). Impact of early deafness and early exposure to sign language on the cerebral organization for motion processing. *Journal of Neuroscience*, *21*, 8931–8942.

Bellugi, U., Sabo, H., & Vaid, J. (1988). Spatial deficits in children with Williams syndrome. In J. Stiles-David, M. Kritchevsky, & U. Bellugi (Eds.), *Spatial cognition: Brain bases and development* (pp. 273–298). Hillsdale, NJ: Lawrence Erlbaum.

Bird, G., Catmur, C., Silani, G., Frith, C., & Frith, U. (2006). Attention does not modulate neural responses to social stimuli in autism spectrum disorders. *NeuroImage, 31,* 1614–1624.

Carter, C., Mintun, M., Nichols, T., & Cohen, J. (1997). Anterior cingulate gyrus dysfunction and selective attention deficits in schizophrenia: [^{15}O]H$_2$O PET study during single-trial Stroop task performance. *American Journal of Psychiatry, 154,* 1670–1675.

Coch, D., Skendzel, W., Grossi, G., & Neville, H. (2005). Motion and color processing in school-age children and adults: An ERP study. *Developmental Science*, *8,* 372–386.

Fieger, A., Röder, B., Teder-Sälejärvi, W., Hillyard, S., & Neville, H. J. (2006). Auditory spatial tuning in late-onset blindness in humans. *Journal of Cognitive Neuroscience, 18,* 149–157.

Gougoux, F., Zatorre, R. J., Lassonde, M., Voss, P., & Lepore, F. (2005). A functional neuroimaging study of sound localization: Visual cortex activity predicts performance in early-blind individuals. *Public Library of Science: Biology, 3,* 324–333.

Hollants-Gilhuijs, M. A. M., Ruijter, J. M., & Spekreijse, H. (1998a). Visual half-field development in children: Detection of colour-contrast-defined forms. *Vision Research, 38*, 645–649.

Hollants-Gilhuijs, M. A. M., Ruijter, J. M., & Spekreijse, H. (1998b). Visual half-field development in children: Detection of motion-defined forms. *Vision Research, 38*, 651–657.

Karmiloff-Smith, A. (1997). Crucial differences between developmental cognitive neuroscience and adult neuropsychology. *Developmental Neuropsychology, 13*, 513–524.

Mitchell, T., & Neville, H. (2004). Asynchronies in the development of electro-physiological responses to motion and color. *Journal of Cognitive Neuroscience, 16*, 1363–1374.

Meyer-Lindenberg, A., Kohn, P., Mervis, C.B., Kippenhan, J.S., Olsen, R.K., Morris, C.A., & Berman KF. (2004). Neural basis of genetically determined visuospatial construction deficit in Williams syndrome. *Neuron, 43*: 623–631.

Mondloch, C. J., Le Grand, R., & Maurer, D. (2002). Configuring face processing develops more slowly than featural face processing. *Perception, 31*, 553–566.

Neville, H. J., & Lawson, D. (1987). Attention to central and peripheral visual space in a movement detection task: An event-related potential and behavioral study. II. Congenitally deaf adults. *Brain Research, 405*, 253–267.

Passarotti, A., Paul, B., Bussiere, J., Buxton, R., Wong, E., & Stiles, J. (2003). The development of face and location processing: An fMRI study. *Developmental Science, 6*, 100–117.

Röder, B., Teder-Salejarvi, W., Sterr, A., Rosler, F., Hillyard, S. A., & Neville, H. J. (1999). Improved auditory spatial tuning in blind humans. *Nature, 400*, 162–166.

Sperling, A. J., Lu, Z., Manis, F. R., & Seidenberg, M. S. (2003). Selective magnocellular deficits in dyslexia: A "phantom contour" study. *Neuropsychologia, 41*, 1422–1429.

Sperling, A. J., Lu, Z., Manis, F. R., & Seidenberg, M. S. (2005). Deficits in perceptual noise exclusion in developmental dyslexia. *Nature Neuroscience, 8*, 862–863.

Stevens, C., & Neville, H. (2006). Neuroplasticity as a double-edged sword: Deaf enhancements and dyslexic deficits in motion processing. *Journal of Cognitive Neuroscience, 18*, 701–714.

Stevens, C., Sanders, L., & Neville, H. (2006). Neurophysiological evidence for selective auditory attention deficits in children with specific language impairment. *Brain Research, 1111*, 143–152.

IV

CONCLUSIONS

16

WHAT MAKES THINKING ABOUT DEVELOPMENT SO HARD?

JOHN P. SPENCER & JODIE M. PLUMERT

The charge we gave to the authors of this volume was a seemingly straightforward one. We asked them to address two issues in their chapters: (1) what changes in spatial cognition occur over development, and (2) how these changes come about. With respect to the "what" question, we asked the authors to describe the developmental changes they had uncovered in their research on a particular topic. With respect to the "how" question, we asked them to speculate on the developmental processes or mechanisms that might lead to these changes. We suggested that authors might describe ongoing work designed to examine how developmental change comes about or discuss the kinds of research needed to address the processes underlying developmental change. We told them that we were interested in accounts of developmental process at different levels of analysis (e.g., neural or behavioral) and that we fully expected these accounts to come in various forms (e.g., functional descriptions, verbal/conceptual theories, or computational models).

As we read the authors' first drafts, we were struck by the fact that responses to the "what" question were rich and provocative, but most responses to the "how" question were brief or nonexistent. (We admit that even we found addressing the "how" question the most difficult part of writing our chapters.) With some encouragement from us, the authors ultimately provided their views on the processes—both general and specific—underlying developmental change. Although we were very pleased with the substantive discussion of the "how" question in this volume, it is clear that there are fundamental gaps between our understanding of "what" and "how" in our field (and, we contend, in developmental science more generally).

A central goal for the future is to do a better job of integrating approaches to these two questions. Toward that end, in the sections below we sketch our thoughts about why it is so difficult to investigate both "what" and "how" in spatial cognitive development. We then discuss the progress our field has made thus far in addressing each question in turn. This sets the stage for consideration of next steps. We conclude with our hopeful forecast for the future: from our vantage point, the field of spatial cognitive development offers an exciting case study for thinking about the processes that underlie developmental change in general, and, we contend, our field is on the verge of truly substantive progress that can integrate the "what" and "how" of development.

16.1 WHY IS "HOW" SO HARD?

One of the most striking aspects of this volume is its vast coverage of spatial cognition. The chapters presented here cover a lot of ground, in terms of both the spatial problems that the authors tackled and the basic processes at work as children and adults solve these problems. This leads us to one concrete reason why thinking about how developmental change occurs is difficult—the sheer complexity of spatial cognition!

16.1.1 Complex Spatial Problems

To illustrate one aspect of the complexity of spatial cognition, consider the myriad of spatial problems discussed in the core chapters of this volume:

Finding/replacing previously seen objects (chapters 1, 2, 3, 13, 14). Finding missing objects or replacing previously seen objects are common everyday spatial problems. Examples include tasks such as relocating your coffee cup after turning away for a moment or replacing the entire contents of a room in their correct locations after a remodeling project.

Attending to key features of the world and ignoring distractors (chapters 6, 7, 12). Moving adaptively through the world involves avoiding objects directly in one's path while monitoring events in the periphery. This problem becomes especially apparent in the case of deaf or blind individuals who cannot rely on multiple modalities (e.g., vision and audition) to carry out these two tasks simultaneously.

Staying oriented while moving through space and reorienting when needed (chapters 3, 4, 12, 14). Spatial orientation is a central challenge for wayfinding, be it through a relatively small-scale environment such as moving from room to room in a house or through a large-scale environment such as navigating across a college campus. In both cases, the challenges of maintaining spatial orientation are dramatically revealed when people are disorientated (i.e., lost!).

Figuring out how to get from point A to point B (chapters 4, 9, 10, 12). It is not enough to know where one is in space; it is also critical to know where one is going. This requires survey-like knowledge of locations to plan how to move from one place to another. In some cases, such knowledge is built up based on direct experience, while in other cases, people can infer routes they have never directly taken.

Communicating about locations/spatial relations (chapters 6, 7, 8, 10, 12). Describing where something is and how to get someplace are common, everyday spatial problems. Although we typically use spatial language to communicate about location, we also use a host of other "embodied" cues: the direction of looking, pointing gestures, and so on. Indeed, these two central aspects of communication are beautifully interwoven in American Sign Language.

Creating/interpreting spatial media (chapters 9, 10, 13). Another way to facilitate communication in space is to use spatial media: maps, graphs, and so on. Such depictions are challenging both to read and to create. This is evident in the performance of special populations such as people with Williams syndrome in drawing/copying tasks.

16.1.2 Complex Processes

Each of the spatial problems listed above involves a host of processes that "live" at different levels of abstraction (e.g., from perceptual to conceptual) and at different time scales (e.g., from second to second and from trial to trial). This makes thinking about space quite challenging. To make this concrete, consider the following list of core processes that underlie the spatial problems listed above. Note that these processes are not linked in a one-to-one manner with the individual problems per se. Rather, different problems tap into different collections of processes.

Perceptual processes involved in detecting spatial structure in the world (chapters 1, 2, 3, 6, 14). To make use of geometric features such as boundaries, angles, and shapes, perceptual processes must detect and integrate relevant structure in the world. In some cases, this involves the extraction of novel relations such as axes of symmetry. In other cases, the perceptual system must integrate information across saccades to form configurations of relations. Further processes may be necessary that help separate relevant and irrelevant structure in the context of specific problems.

Processes of selective attention (chapters 6, 7, 12). Selective attention is needed to deal with the competing demands of behaving in a complex spatial world. For example, selectively attending to objects and events in central space is necessary to avoid collisions, but, at the same time, one must devote some resources to monitoring information in the periphery in case one needs to respond quickly to a peripheral object or event. Likewise, young children must learn to selectively attend to the spatial features that are relevant to the way their language encodes spatial relations.

Reference frame (re)alignment and spatial orientation processes (chapters 3, 4, 14). Processes for coordinating frames of reference are needed so people can keep track of where they are in the world and where objects are relative to one another. The need to coordinate egocentric and allocentric reference frames becomes especially obvious after disorientation. To find a previously seen location after disorientation, children and adults must bring into alignment their current egocentric heading with a remembered egocentric or allocentric representation of the location. Even when movement produces no disorientation, processes are required for maintaining and reestablishing alignment of egocentric and allocentric reference frames.

Perception–action processes involved in perceiving/generating optic flow and other motion cues (chapter 4, 13). As people move through the world, this self-motion generates a complex visual pattern relative to the observer referred to as optic flow. Optic flow plays a prominent role in navigation and wayfinding because it links perception and action. In fact, experimental manipulations that change the correlation between how fast one moves and the resulting optic flow lead to systematic changes in the representation of distance.

Memory processes involved in maintaining spatial information over both short and long time scales (chapters 1, 2, 14). Many spatial problems require the maintenance of information in memory, whether from one saccade to the next or from one viewpoint to another. Metric or "fine-grained" memories of locations appear to be maintained by self-sustaining patterns of neural activation. Such memories can be integrated with both perceptual cues (e.g., reference frames) and long-term memory (e.g., categorical information) to create systematic distortions in what people remember.

Perceptual and memory processes that "chunk" spatial information into categories (chapters 1, 2, 6, 10, 14). Forming spatial categories involves processes that "chunk" together locations based on cues such as visible boundaries that divide locations into groups, experience with visiting nearby locations together in time, or even semantic/thematic relations among objects occupying nearby locations.

Memory processes and mental operations involved in integrating information over space and time (chapters 4, 9, 10). Children and adults often experience the world in piecemeal: they move from one viewpoint to another as they turn the corner, they listen to sequentially organized directions for finding things, and they see parts of maps presented on different pages of a book. In order to form survey representations based on these experiences, processes are needed to integrate information over space and time. One process that may be important here is creating a spatial framework within which to fit pieces of spatial information.

Linguistic/nonlinguistic processes that segment, identify, and give words meaning (chapters 7, 8). A central issue in spatial cognition is how linguistic and nonlinguistic processes come together during communicative interchanges involving space. For instance, naturalistic observations show that mothers who consistently separate objects in space while labeling them have children who learn the labels for those objects more quickly. Thus, guiding young children's attention to a location in space can serve as an important cue for attaching a label to an object. Moreover, children excel at pulling out statistical regularities in social exchanges to identify the meanings of words. That is, children are quite good at extracting the meanings of words (e.g., "in" or "into") by detecting the repeated pairing of specific phrases (e.g., "It's going in the cup") with certain functional relationships (e.g., someone pouring water into a cup).

Considered together the sheer number of spatial problems and processes tackled in this volume underscores the complexity of spatial cognition (and this is without even considering the problem of development!). This complexity is also evident in that multiple processes are usually involved in solving a single problem and solutions to seemingly very different problems often tap into the same process. For example, even the "simple" problem of reaching for a coffee cup after you have turned away for a few seconds involves actively maintaining information in working memory, calibrating frames of reference, and integrating perceptual and motor processes. But, of course, many of these same challenges present themselves when trying to explain to someone else where the coffee cup is.

16.2 "WHAT" DEVELOPS? GENERAL TRENDS IN SPATIAL COGNITIVE DEVELOPMENT

This brief survey of the everyday spatial problems confronting children (and adults) and the processes involved in solving these problems clearly illustrates the complexity of spatial cognition. However, we contend that the field as a whole has made good progress in identifying and understanding these basic problems and processes. This includes work on real-time processes that have been a central focus in the cognitive and neuroscience fields. Although further work on these basic processes and additional integration across subfields is critical, we suggest that a better understanding of the developmental processes that give rise to mature spatial behavior is essential to move the field forward. Quite simply, understanding how a system was put together makes understanding how the system operates much easier.

So what have we learned about the development of spatial cognition to date? First, we have identified several key differences between age groups and between special populations and normal individuals in the processing of spatial information. We review a few selected examples below before turning to the issue of what these age-related differences reveal about the mechanisms of developmental change.

Precision of metric coding (chapters 1, 2, 9, 10, 12, 13, 14). One age-related difference that features prominently in several chapters is the precision with which older and younger children reproduce locations or localize targets. Younger children are consistently less precise than older children and adults in moving to targets, searching for objects, and replacing objects in their correct locations. There are also differences between normal individuals and people with Williams syndrome or deaf/blind individuals in their ability to reproduce locations or localize targets. Interestingly, individuals with Williams syndrome typically exhibit deficits relative to normals, whereas deaf and blind individuals sometimes exhibit enhancements relative to normals. These age and population differences observed in so many studies of spatial development indicate that there are major changes over development in how metric information is coded and maintained.

Forming and using spatial categories (chapters 1, 2, 6, 14). Another age-related difference that appeared in several of the chapters was the emerging ability of younger and older infants and children to form and use spatial categories. For example, there are several situations in which older, but not younger, infants are able to form spatial categories of above/below, left/right, and between. Other work shows that younger children exhibit biases consistent with treating a long, narrow space as a single region, whereas older children and adults exhibit biases consistent with treating the same space as two halves. In addition, age differences in the tendency to place objects from the same group or region closer together than they really are appear to be partially dependent on the strength of the spatial categories formed by younger and older children and adults. Together, these findings indicate that the nature of spatial categories as well as the ease with which younger and older children form spatial categories undergoes substantial change over development. Such changes have functional consequences for behavior. They also signal important changes in the processes involved with detecting structure in the world and integrating spatial information in memory.

Attending to, remembering, and transforming spatial relations (chapters 6, 7, 9, 10, 13). A third age-related difference highlighted in this volume was the ease with which younger and older infants and children attend to and remember spatial relations. As noted above, older infants attend to more complex spatial relations than do younger infants. There are also interesting age differences in younger and older children's responsiveness to spatial relations that either do or do not capture features that are important for the representation of spatial relations in their native language. Likewise, age differences exist in children's ability to learn spatial relations presented in maps or through verbal descriptions. Moreover, there are some significant individual differences even among adults in the ability to detect spatial relational correspondences between the world and a map. Finally, there are significant deficits in processing spatial relational information in individuals with Williams syndrome as evidenced by poor performance on spatial reconstruction tasks such as copying figures and block design. These age differences and individual differences suggest that the processes underlying the detection of spatial relations and the formation of configural representations undergo substantial change over development.

16.3 FROM "WHAT" TO "HOW": TASK DEPENDENCIES REVEAL INSIGHTS ABOUT PROCESS

Although there is strong empirical support for the general age-related changes described above, the literature is complicated by the simple fact that "it all depends." In particular, many studies have shown that the details of the age-related trends above can be pushed around via task-specific manipulations. Rather than viewing these task effects as a nuisance, we view task effects as an important signature of the underlying processes at work. More specifically, task manipulations can provide insight into both the real-time processes at work as children and adults perform these tasks as well as into the developmental processes that constrain how far one can accelerate/decelerate developmental change (i.e., the "boundary conditions"). For instance, if introducing a particular perturbation or support in a task influences the performance of younger, but not older children, one might ask what the underlying processes are that might be affected by this manipulation and how these processes change over this age range. This then leads to further manipulations designed to probe the hypothesized changes in greater detail. In this sense, these task manipulations provide a bridge from "what" toward "how".

A good example of this comes from work described by Newcombe and Ratliff (chapter 3) on integrating geometric and landmark information to locate hidden objects following disorientation. A central claim in this literature is that developmental changes in orientation abilities emerge when children become able to integrate room shape and distinctive landmarks through language. Specifically, once children learn the terms for left and right, they can use linguistic coding to penetrate a "geometric module," thereby integrating room shape and landmark information (e.g., "it's in the corner with the long wall to my left and the bookcase in front of me"). Newcombe and her colleagues clearly refute this idea by showing that even 4-year-olds (who do not know the terms for left and right) can succeed in integrating room shape and landmark information if the room is larger. Newcombe uses these and other kinds of task manipulations to argue for a new theory of spatial coding—the adaptive combination approach. Whether this new theory will ultimately account for the phenomena of interest is still an open question. Nevertheless, this program of research provides a nice illustration of how we gain insight into developmental change through observing how children of different ages respond to systematic task manipulations.

A second example of using task manipulations to better understand developmental change comes from work by Plumert and her colleagues on categorical bias in children's memory for location (chapter 2). This work starts with the idea that thinking emerges out of the interaction of the organism and the environment. Thus, thinking (like perceiving and acting) is a dynamic process in which changes in the organism or the environment (or both) alter the nature of the interaction, resulting in changes in cognition and behavior. They illustrate these ideas by showing clear variations both in how the same age group responds to different task structure and in how different age groups respond to the same task structure. This work turns over simplistic explanations of change by showing that neither the cognitive system nor environmental structure has causal priority in explaining spatial thinking. An important implication of this view is that cognition is not something that sits in the head of the organism. Rather, it is an emergent product of a system that includes both the organism and the environment. Thus, development needs to be characterized as changes in organism–environment interactions rather than as changes exclusively in the head of the organism.

A third example comes from work by Spencer and colleagues described in chapter 14. These researchers have examined how children and adults integrate perceived frames of reference, short-term working memory for metric locations, and long-term memory in simple spatial recall tasks. The processes that achieve this integration have been formalized in a neural network model—the dynamic field theory (DFT). A unique feature of the DFT is that it has been used to explain performance in multiple tasks. This provides a powerful context within which to probe processes of development. In particular, if one has a good handle on the processes at work as the situation is varied within a specific task *and* as people move from task to task, it is possible to identify those things that are common across situations/tasks. By then examining how these commonalties change across age groups, one can piece together a detailed picture of what underlies developmental change. In the case of spatial recall and recognition tasks, Spencer and colleagues have proposed a single developmental hypothesis—the spatial precision hypothesis—that effectively integrates a host of empirical data. This provides a bridge for moving from "what" to "how" because it focuses the latter question. Rather than explaining a host of detailed, task-specific, and age-related changes, the theoretical task is to explain the mechanisms that give rise to a single, integrated developmental change. Although Spencer and colleagues have yet to formalize these mechanisms, they outline several exciting possibilities, including ties to work on Hebbian learning in connectionist networks.

16.4 "HOW" DEVELOPMENT HAPPENS: CANDIDATE MECHANISMS OF CHANGE

In the sections above, we identified several age-related differences in how children solve spatial problems and task manipulations that affect these solutions. A critical issue that remains is understanding the mechanisms that underlie developmental change. This involves integrating what we know about the basic processes involved in solving spatial problems with what we know about age-related changes in how children solve these problems to identify the mechanisms/processes of change at work. We turn now to considering some of the candidate developmental processes discussed in this volume.

Mechanisms that accumulate traces of contextually grounded experience (chapters 2, 4, 8, 9, 10, 14). Many of the authors in this volume discussed the role of accumulated, step-by-step, task-specific experience in shaping the spatial mind. This included experience with spatial media such as maps, specific experiences moving through space from one place to another, experience remembering where objects are typically located in the local surrounds, and experience learning about objects and object labels in a scaffolded, social context. Underlying all of these examples are processes that leave traces of task- and context-specific experiences that can be reaccessed and built upon at a later time. We note that these mechanisms are not usually specified in our field (for an exception, see chapter 14), although there are many known processes of learning that can produce change via step-by-step experience.

Extraction of correlations in the physical or social environment (chapters 4, 7, 8). Several chapters either implicitly or explicitly pointed to the extraction of correlations as a candidate mechanism of change. For example, the detection of perception–action correlations was proposed as the primary mechanism whereby perception, action, and representation become linked. Likewise, a possible mechanism underlying the formation of spatial semantic categories involves picking up on the statistical regularities in the environment that are highlighted by the caregiver's actions and speech. As with the case of step-by-step experience discussed above, few of the chapters in this volume invoked specific statistical learning mechanisms. One exception was the use of Edelman's ideas of neural selection in chapter 8 by Smith, Maouene, and Hidaka. Interestingly, as in the discussion of perception–action correlations in chapter 4 by Rieser and Pick, embodiment played a strong role in Smith et al.'s account of early word learning because the body has a profound influence on structuring the correlations that children perceive and remember.

Processes of adaptation (chapters 1, 2, 3). Several chapters discussed evidence that the "weighting" children place on different sources of spatial information changes over development. According to the adaptive combination approach, these changes in weighting result from noticing the correlation between using a particular cue and success solving particular spatial problems (e.g., finding a hidden object). Thus, everyday experiences (that are dependent on the type of organism and the cues present in the environment) result in systematic changes in weighting over time. What are the characteristics of the mechanisms that underlie changes in "weights"? One possibility is that the process is Bayesian; that is, people update their estimates of earlier learned conditional probabilities (i.e., priors) based on posterior probabilities (i.e., outcomes).

Tuning of neural interactions involved in spatial perception/cognition (chapters 12, 14). Two of the chapters discussed tuning of neural interactions as a candidate mechanism of change. For example, a major mechanism involved in increased sensitivity to visual and auditory information in the periphery in the deaf and blind is the tuning of neurons in visual and auditory cortex via sensory experience, as well as the co-opting of cortex that normally sub-serves the absent sensory modality. Chapter 12 by Mitchell nicely empha-sizes the bidirectional nature of neural tuning and sensory experience. Specifically, she proposes that the functional pressures of blindness or deaf-ness lead to increased attention to the periphery. In turn, the experiences generated by increased attention to the periphery tune (i.e., sharpen) neural interactions, allowing for further increases in sensitivity to information in the periphery. The tuning of neural interactions is the primary mechanism underlying the developmental changes described in chapter 14, as well. Here, Spencer and colleagues highlight how such tuning might arise via Hebbian learning over the longer time scales of development. This sets up the exciting possibility that the tuning mechanisms that operate on the short-term might also lead to long-term change.

Neural specialization and genetic expression/constraints (chapters 12, 13). In addition to the tuning of neural interactions, processes that drive neural specialization and influence gene expression can have a powerful influence on developmental change. This is most clearly illustrated in chapter 13 by Landau and Hoffman, detailing the candidate mechanisms that lead to "ar-rested" development in Williams syndrome. For instance, the absence of specific genes might yield abnormal pruning or formation of neural con-nections in parietal cortex, a region of the brain that specializes in reference frame calibration and sensorimotor transformations. One source of evi-dence for this hypothesis is hypoactivation of parietal areas normally active during spatial construction tasks.

16.5 WHERE NEXT? KEY CHALLENGES ON THE HORIZON

Although our field has made a great deal of progress in understanding spa-tial development over the last several decades, what are future challenges that must be tackled to more effectively move from the current focus on "what" to a more central focus on "how"? First, to more effectively tackle processes of developmental change, we need to do a better job of bridging different time scales. One thing we noticed about the chapters (including our own) in this volume is that those chapters that focused more on longer time scales had relatively little to say about the real-time processes underly-ing behavior. Conversely, chapters that focused on the real-time processes had relatively little to say about long-term change.

Clearly, to make real progress in understanding behavioral develop-ment, we need to link up real-time processes with changes over longer time scales. To do this, we need more studies that track behavioral, cognitive, or neural change over an experimental session or across longer periods of time, perhaps using microgenetic methods. We also need more theoretical models of how short-term change can realistically lead to long-term change (e.g., links between short-term processes involved in learning and, for in-stance, processes of neural tuning over longer time scales).

A related issue is bridging the gap between domain-general and domain-specific developmental change. As we focus more intently on the processes that produce change over longer time scales, we must deal with the fact that development in one skill is often connected with the development of other skills. This raises questions of whether change is isolated to one domain or generalizes across domains. In the present volume, this was evident in the tendency for chapters to present either a very broad view of developmental change that was only loosely related to specific changes in tasks/situations or a very specific model of performance in specific tasks/situations that was not linked to more general views of developmental change.

To move beyond these limitations, we must address whether general developmental processes exist that are separate from domain-specific processes. This requires advances on both theoretical and empirical fronts. With regard to the latter, it is important for future work to deconstruct some of the tasks used in spatial cognitive development, that is, to better understand the link between the spatial problems and processes we describe above. We also need to balance controlled studies in the laboratory with studies in the real world. It is unfortunate that these are often pitted in opposition, because an understanding of domain-specific and domain-general developmental change certainly requires the perspective offered by both empirical approaches.

Finally, we think the time is ripe in our field to begin to put these themes together and begin testing specific hypotheses derived from the candidate developmental mechanisms we reviewed. A key tool on this front is to introduce experimental manipulations designed to affect these mechanisms of change and track the effects over time. This approach has been used recently in the word learning domain. For instance, Smith, Samuelson, and their colleagues have taught children different types of vocabularies and produced precocious word learning biases (for a discussion of this and related work, see chapter 8).

Although there are clearly substantive (and in some cases, daunting) challenges facing our field, we believe that the field of spatial cognitive development holds promise for moving forward our understanding of development *in general*. This is due both to advances in our understanding of spatial cognition in the past several decades and to several unique characteristics associated with studying the spatial mind. First, critical aspects of the environment or the task can be easily manipulated (at least in small-scale spaces). Such manipulations of the task or environment are important for determining how behavior emerges in the moment and over time. Virtual environment technology may hold the promise of doing the same thing for large-scale spaces in the future. Second, because the behaviors of interest often involve physical movement, there is the potential to precisely track changes in these behaviors over time (at least in the short term). Observing real-time change is critical for understanding processes of change. Third, as the chapters illustrate, the foundation already exists for exciting integration across areas of spatial functioning and levels of description. Such integration has the potential to provide even deeper insights into the emerging spatial mind. Last but not least, the tasks we use to study spatial development are appealing to research participants from infancy to adulthood. This is advantageous for two reasons. First, we have unique access to early development because young children love these tasks. And second, we can often use the same or very similar tasks across a wide range of ages, making direct comparisons of performance across ages possible. These comparisons can be very useful for pinpointing which aspects of thinking are undergoing change.

Let us end by saying that our experiences with reading these chapters have enriched and broadened our own thinking. Although our synopsis only scratches the surface of the ideas presented in this volume, we hope that others will find it useful for thinking about development and for stimulating further research. We look forward to hearing about progress in the field in the coming decades!

AUTHOR INDEX

SUBJECT INDEX